RESEARCH METHODS

The Concise Knowledge Base

RESEARCH
METHODS

The Concise Knowledge Base

William M. K. Trochim
Cornell University

ATOMIC**dog**PUBLISHING

Cincinnati, Ohio
www.atomicdog.com

When ordering this title, use ISBN 1-59260-146-4.

To order only the online version (Online Study Guide Edition), of this title, use ISBN 1-59260-147-2.

ISBN 1-59260-145-6

Library of Congress Control Number: 2004108632

Printed in the United States of America by Atomic Dog Publishing, 1148 Main Street, Third Floor, Cincinnati, OH 45202-7236.

10 9 8 7 6 5 4 3 2 1

**For
Mary and Nora,
who continue to astonish me
with their resilience, patience, and love.**

Brief Contents

Contents

Preface

Less is more.
—*Mies van der Rohe*

So, why did I set out to write a more concise textbook in research methods than my previous book *The Research Methods Knowledge Base?* For one thing, I am concerned about the increased bloat of contemporary textbooks. I haven't studied it myself, but my hypothesis would be that the average weight of student backpacks has been increasing at an alarming rate. While that may be great news for chiropractors, I doubt that textbook weight is correlated with student learning.

I also had in mind the rising cost of textbooks and the possibility that a more concise text might be able to be priced less expensively.

I also believe that when professors select research methods texts for their course, they already bring a career's worth of examples that are well tailored to their disciplines. They are looking for the core material in research methods around which they can teach their discipline-specific knowledge.

One other factor I considered is the level of detail desired in a research methods text. Research methods introductory courses, especially at the undergraduate level, are always challenging endeavors. Often, such courses are required, and students delay taking them because of unfounded fears that the material will be too boring or challenging. (All right, maybe they aren't unfounded fears.) Being faced with a text that weighs about as much as a dictionary doesn't help get students off on the right foot. And I would wager that within months of completing such a course, most students probably forget much of the specific content covered in their texts.

But perhaps most of all, I set out to write a more concise text because I think the great modern architect Mies van der Rohe may have had it right—"less is more" if done well. That's what I set out to do.

You can approach the study of research methods in many different ways. Here, I'm going to give you two metaphors to use for thinking about how you might work your way through the material in this book.

The Road to Research

Remember when you were a little kid, piling into the family car and setting off on a trip? It might have been to Grandma's house, or it might have been a cross-country vacation, but there was the thrill of the journey to come, the unexpected, perhaps even something exciting. Or maybe you didn't do the family car thing. Perhaps, it was setting off on the subway for the museum on a Saturday afternoon. Or getting on a plane to fly off to new places. Never traveled when you were a kid? Okay, this metaphor won't work—skip down to the next section and I'll try again. But if you did any traveling, you know how exciting and mysterious setting out can be. Research is a lot like setting out on a new trip. No, really. You're going to have fun. Honest.

Well, I thought it might be useful to visualize the research endeavor sequentially, like taking a trip, like moving down a road—the Road to Research. Figure 1 shows the contents of this text in a way that pictures the research process as a practical sequence of events, a trip down the road (truthfully, I think the actual trip down the research road is a little more exciting than Figure 1 suggests!). You might visualize a research project as a journey where you pass certain landmarks along your way. Think of it like a trip through Middle Earth with your friends, where you are constantly avoiding dangers, defying death, and trying to get the ring into the fiery volcano. Okay, perhaps it's not that exciting. But research is like a journey in that it typically involves a set of steps. Every research project needs to start with a clear problem formulation. As you develop your project, you will find critical junctions where you will make choices about how to proceed, where you will

FIGURE 1
The Research Road Map

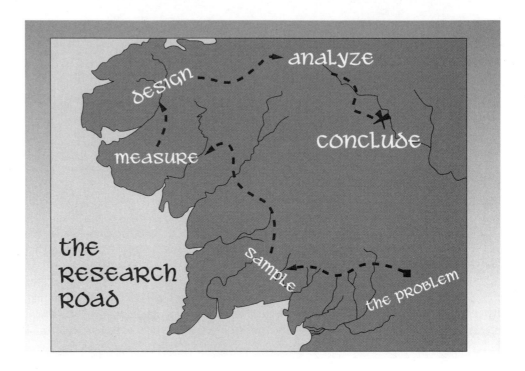

consider issues of sampling, measurement, design, and analysis, as well as the theories of validity behind each step. In the end, you will need to think about the whole picture and write up your findings. You might even find yourself backtracking from time to time and reassessing your previous decisions. This is a two-way road; planning and reflection are critical and interdependent. Think of the asphalt of the road as the foundation of research philosophy and practice. Without consideration of the basics in research, you'll find yourself bogged down in the mud! And if you really want to go nuts, you might think of your teacher as the kids in the back seat, constantly needling you with, "Are we there yet?"

The Yin and the Yang of Research

For this second metaphor of the research process, imagine that you're a Buddhist. (Don't know what a Buddhist is? Then go to the previous metaphor and try that instead.) To the Buddhist, everything in the universe is connected to everything else. To the Buddhist researcher (actually, I don't know any Buddhist researchers personally, so I'm guessing a bit here), all parts of the research process are interconnected. The Buddhist view of research might be something like that shown in Figure 2. The left side of the figure refers to the theory of research. The right side of the figure refers to the practice of research. The yin-yang figure in the center shows you that theory and practice are always interconnected. For every area of practice on the right, there is a way to think about it theoretically on the left.

The four arrow links on the left describe the four types of validity in research. The idea of validity provides a unifying theory for understanding the criteria for good research. The four arrow links on the right point to the research practice areas that correspond with each validity type. For instance, external validity is related to the theory of how to generalize research results. Its corresponding practice area is sampling methodology, which is concerned with how to draw representative samples so that generalizations are possible.

The figure as a whole illustrates the yin and yang of research—the inherent complementarities of theory and practice—that I try to convey throughout this book. If you can

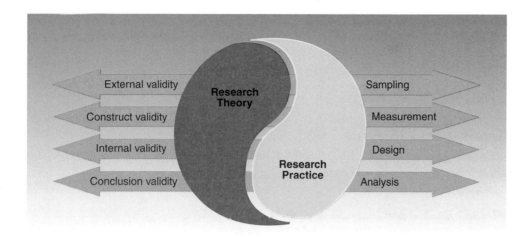

come to an understanding of this deeper relationship, you will be a better researcher, one who is able to create research processes, rather than simply use them.

Okay, it's time for you to sit cross-legged and meditate on the yin and yang of it all as we start down the road to research. . . .

Acknowledgments

This work, as is true for all significant efforts in life, is a collaborative achievement. It is also one that has evolved in unexpected ways since the publication of the original website on which it is based. I want to thank especially the students and friends who assisted and supported me in various ways over the years.

For this latest edition, I want to especially thank Jim Donnelly for his incredibly enthusiastic and invariably cheerful support. Whenever I speak with him, I come away re-charged and enthused about this work—must be the psychologist in him. I also want to acknowledge the many graduate teaching assistants who helped me make the transition to a web-based course and contributed their efforts and insights to this work and the teaching of research methods. I especially thank Dominic Cirillo, who labored tirelessly over several years on the original web-based and printed versions of *The Research Methods Knowledge Base* and without whom I simply would not have survived. Finally, I would like to acknowledge Ted Whitley for his thoughtful authoring of test bank questions.

It never ceases to amaze me that the *Knowledge Base* has evolved from a simple website for my students to a real text in both electronic and hard-copy versions. That simply would not have happened without all of my friends and colleagues at Atomic Dog Publishing, who supplied the enthusiasm and vision and, yes, okay, I'll admit it, the PRODDING—the endless, badgering, NAGGING… (okay, okay, calm down)—to move this effort to the next step. Actually, as the role model for the irresponsible and hopelessly late author, I hereby confess that they had their work cut out for them and that no jury in the land would hold them accountable for the drastic measures I forced them to take to squeeze this text out of me. At the top of my list is Ed Laube, the best editor-in-chief I could ever hope for, and certainly far better than I ever deserved. Thanks for your patience, your enthusiasm, and your encouragement. Bet you never thought you'd live to see this day. And I want to thank my developmental editor, Christine Abshire, and project coordinator, Mary Monner. You must have wondered what you had done earlier in life to deserve such a fate. I must say, I've gotten so accustomed to your regular phone calls and emails to prod me along that I actually think I'll have to hire someone to contact me on a regular basis to make up for the social loss I'll experience. This book simply would not have happened without the kindness, gentle manners, and continuous support from the three of you. You deserve the credit for that; I'll take the blame for the rest. And my thanks to the many people at Atomic Dog who do all of the incredible things that need to get done to make a book like this a reality. You're the best publisher an author could have—and you can quote me on that!

And, of course, I want to thank all of the students, both undergraduate and graduate, who participated in my courses over the years and used the *Knowledge Base* in its various incarnations. You have been both my challenge and inspiration.

Online and in Print

Research Methods: The Concise Knowledge Base is available online as well as in print. The Online Study Guide Edition demonstrates how the interactive media components of the text enhance presentation and understanding. For example,

- Animated illustrations help to clarify concepts.
- Clickable glossary terms provide immediate definitions of key concepts.
- Highlighting capabilities allow students to emphasize main ideas. Students can also add personal notes in the margin.
- The search function allows students to quickly locate discussions of specific topics throughout the text.

Students may choose to use just the Online Study Guide Edition, or both the online and print versions together. This gives them the flexibility to choose which combination of resources works best for them. To assist those who use the online and print versions together, the primary heads and subheads in each chapter are numbered the same. For example, the first primary head in Chapter 1 is labeled 1-1, the second primary head in this chapter is labeled 1-2, and so on. The subheads build from the designation of their corresponding primary head: 1-1a, 1-1b, etc. This numbering system is designed to make moving between the Online Study Guide Edition and the print book as seamless as possible.

Finally, an icon like that shown in the margin on the left appears next to a number of figures in the print version of the text. The icon indicates that this figure in the Online Study Guide Edition is interactive in a way that applies, illustrates, or reinforces the concept.

Supplements

- A *workbook* provides students with practical exercises tied to the content in *Research Methods: The Concise Knowledge Base*.
- A *test bank*, comprised of over 700 questions in ExamView ® Pro, enables instructors to create printed tests using either a Windows or Macintosh computer. Instructors can enter their own questions and customize the appearance of the tests they create.
- An *instructor's manual* includes learning objectives, lecture guides, and other resources for each chapter.
- *PowerPoint ® presentations* are available for classroom use of text materials.

About the Author

DR. WILLIAM TROCHIM is professor, Department of Policy Analysis and Management at Cornell University, and is a faculty member in the graduate fields of education, human development, and community and rural development at Cornell. His Ph.D. is from the Department of Psychology at Northwestern University in the area of methodology and evaluation research.

Dr. Trochim's research is broadly in the area of applied social research methodology, with an emphasis on program planning and evaluation methods. Among experimentalists, he is known for his work in quasi-experimental alternatives to randomized experimental designs, especially the regression discontinuity and regression point displacement designs. In terms of research theory, he has extended the theory of validity through his articulation and investigation of the idea of pattern matching. In multivariate and applied contexts, he is recognized for the development of a multivariate form of structured conceptual mapping, a general method for mapping the ideas of a group of people on any topic of interest that integrates traditional group processes (e.g., brainstorming, Delphi, focus groups, nominal group technique) with multivariate statistical methods (e.g., multidimensional scaling, hierarchical cluster analysis).

Dr. Trochim has written several books, and his articles have appeared in *American Journal of Evaluation, New Directions for Program Evaluation, Evaluation and Program Planning, Evaluation Review, Journal of Clinical Epidemiology, Consulting and Clinical Psychology, Controlled Clinical Trials, Performance Improvement,* and *Medical Decision Making,* among others. He has been an active member of the American Evaluation Association, serving multiple terms on its Board. He is also the developer of the Concept System® software and methodology, and co-owner of the company Concept Systems Incorporated that provides the software, training, and consulting services to support the method.

He does all these things for the loves of his life—his spouse Mary and his daughter Nora.

FOUNDATIONS

1 Foundations

1

Foundations

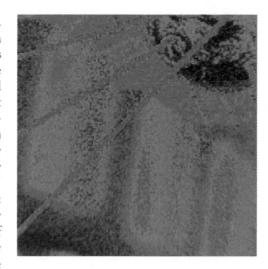

You have to begin somewhere. Unfortunately, you can only be in one place at a time and, even less fortunately for you, you happen to be right here right now, so you may as well consider this a place to begin, and what better place to begin than an introduction? Here's where I cover all the stuff you think you already know, and probably should already know, but most likely don't know as well as you think you do.

This chapter begins with the basic language of research, the introductory vocabulary you need to read the rest of the text. With the basic terminology under your belt, I'll show you some of the underlying philosophical issues that drive the research endeavor. Social research always occurs in a social context. It is a human endeavor. I'll point out some of the critical ethical issues that affect the researcher, research participants, and the research effort generally. For instance, you'll consider how much risk your research participants can be placed under and how you must ensure their privacy. Finally, in the section on conceptualization, I answer such questions as where do research problems come from and how do I develop a research question?

That ought to be enough to get you started. At least, it ought to be enough to get you thoroughly confused. But don't worry, there's stuff that's far more confusing than this yet to come.

1-1 THE LANGUAGE OF RESEARCH

Learning about research is a lot like learning about anything else. To start, you need to learn the jargon people use, the big controversies they fight over, and the different factions that define the major players. Research blends an enormous range of skills and activities. Learning about research is a lot like learning a new language. You need to develop a specialized vocabulary of terms that describe the different types of research, the methods used, and the issues and problems that arise. You need to learn how to use those words correctly in a sentence. You need to understand the local idioms of this language. Just as in any language, if you aren't aware of the subtle way words are used, you run the risk of embarrassing yourself. To begin, we'll introduce some basic ideas like the types of studies you can perform, the role of time in research, and the different types of relationships you can estimate. Then we define some basic terms like *variable, hypothesis, data,* and *unit of analysis*.

1-1a Research Vocabulary

Just to get you warmed up to the idea that learning about research is in many ways like learning a new language, I want to introduce you to four terms that I think help describe some of the key aspects of contemporary social research. This list is not exhaustive. It's really just the first four terms that came into my mind when I was thinking about research language. Think of these as a "word of the day" for the next four days. You might even try to work one term into your conversation each day (go ahead, I dare you) to become more at ease with this language.

I present the first two terms—*theoretical* and *empirical*—together because they are often contrasted with each other. Social research is **theoretical,** meaning that much of it is concerned with developing, exploring, or testing the theories or ideas that social

theoretical Pertaining to theory. Social research is theoretical, meaning that much of it is concerned with developing, exploring, or testing the theories or ideas that social researchers have about how the world operates.

empirical Based on direct observations and measurements of reality.

probabilistic Based on probabilities.

causal Pertaining to a cause-effect relationship.

researchers have about how the world operates. It is also **empirical,** meaning that it is based on observations and measurements of reality—on what you perceive of the world around you. You can even think of most research as a blending of these two terms—a comparison of theories about how the world operates with observations of its operation.

In the old days, many scientists thought that one major purpose of science was to measure what was "really there," and some believed that we could develop measuring instruments that were accurate. Alas, experience has shown that even the most accurate of our instruments and measurement procedures inevitably have some inaccuracy in them. Whether measuring the movement of subatomic particles or the height or weight of a person, there is some error in all measurement. Thus, the third big word that describes much contemporary social research is **probabilistic,** or based on probabilities. The inferences made in social research have probabilities associated with them; they are seldom meant to be considered as covering laws that pertain to all cases. Part of the reason statistics has become so dominant in social research is that it enables the estimation of the probabilities for the situations being studied.

The last term I want to introduce is *causal.* You have to be careful with this term. Note that it is spelled *causal* not *casual.* You'll really be embarrassed if you write about the "casual hypothesis" in your study! The term **causal** has to do with the idea of cause and effect (Cook & Campbell, 1979; Shadish, Cook, & Campbell, 2002). A lot of social researchers are interested (at some point) in looking at cause-effect relationships. For instance, we might want to know whether a new program causes improved outcomes or performance. Now, don't get me wrong. There are lots of studies that don't look at cause-and-effect relationships. Some studies simply observe; for instance, a survey might be used to describe the percent of people holding a particular opinion. Many studies explore relationships—for example, studies often attempt to determine whether there is a relationship between gender and salary. Probably the vast majority of applied social research consists of these descriptive and correlational studies. So, why am I talking about causal studies? Because for most social sciences, it is important to go beyond just passively observing the world or looking at relationships. You might like to be able to change the world, to improve it and help address some of its major problems. If you want to change the world (especially if you want to do this in an organized, scientific way), you are automatically interested in causal relationships—ones that tell how causes (for example, programs and treatments) affect the outcomes of interest.

1-1b Types of Studies

Research projects usually can be classified into one of three basic forms:

1. *Descriptive* studies are designed primarily to document what is going on or what exists. Public opinion polls that seek to describe the proportion of people who hold various opinions are primarily descriptive in nature. For instance, if you want to know what percent of the population would vote for a Democrat or a Republican in the next presidential election, you are simply interested in describing something.

2. *Relational* studies look at the relationships between two or more variables. A public opinion poll that compares the proportion of males and females that say they would vote for a Democratic or a Republican candidate in the next presidential election is essentially studying the relationship between gender and voting preference.

3. *Causal* studies are designed to determine whether one or more variables (for example, a program or treatment variable) cause or affect one or more outcome variables. If you performed a public opinion poll to try to determine whether a recent political advertising campaign changed voter preferences, you would essentially be studying whether the campaign (cause) changed the proportion of voters who would vote Democratic or Republican (effect).

The three study types can be viewed as cumulative. That is, a relational study generally assumes that you can first describe (by measuring or observing) each of the variables you are trying to relate. A causal study generally assumes that you can describe both the cause and effect variables and that you can show that they are related to each other.

1-1c Time in Research

Time is an important element of any research design, and here I want to introduce one of the most fundamental distinctions in research design nomenclature: cross-sectional versus longitudinal studies. A **cross-sectional** study is one that takes place at a single point in time. In effect, you are taking a slice or cross-section of whatever it is you're observing or measuring. A **longitudinal** study is one that takes place over time. In a longitudinal study, you measure your research participants on at least two separate occasions or at least two points in time. When you measure at different time points, we often say that you are measuring multiple waves of measurement. Just as with the repeated motion of the waves in the ocean or of waving with your hand, multiple waves of measurement refers to taking measurements on a variable several times.

A further distinction is made between two types of longitudinal designs: repeated measures and time series. There is no universally agreed-upon rule for distinguishing between these two terms, but in general, if you have two or a few waves of measurement, you are using a **repeated measures** design. If you have many waves of measurement over time, you have a **time series** (Box & Jenkins, 1976). How many is many? Usually, you wouldn't use the term *time series* unless you had at least 20 waves of measurement. With fewer waves than that, you would usually call it a *repeated measures* design.

> **cross-sectional** A study that takes place at a single point in time.

> **longitudinal** A study that takes place over time.

> **repeated measures** Two or more waves of measurement over time.

> **time series** Many waves of measurement over time.

1-1d Variables

You won't be able to do much in research unless you know how to talk about variables. A **variable** is any entity that can take on different values (Marriott, 1990). Okay, so what does that mean? Anything that can vary can be considered a variable. For instance, *age* can be considered a variable because age can take different values for different people or for the same person at different times. Similarly, *country* can be considered a variable because a person's country can be assigned a value.

Variables aren't always quantitative or numerical. The variable *gender* consists of two text values: *male* and *female*. If it is useful, quantitative values can be assigned instead of (or in place of) the text values, but it's not necessary to assign numbers for something to be a variable. It's also important to realize that variables aren't the only things measured in the traditional sense. For instance, in much social research and in program evaluation, the treatment or program (that is, the "cause") is considered to be a variable. An educational program can have varying amounts of time on task, classroom settings, student-teacher ratios, and so on. Therefore, even the program can be considered a variable, which can be made up of a number of subvariables.

An **attribute** is a specific value on a variable. For instance, the variable *sex* or *gender* has two attributes (male and female), or the variable *agreement* might be defined as having five attributes:

1 = strongly disagree

2 = disagree

3 = neutral

4 = agree

5 = strongly agree

Another important distinction having to do with the term *variable* is the distinction between an independent and dependent variable (Marriott, 1990). This distinction is particularly relevant when you are investigating cause-effect relationships. It took me the longest time to learn this distinction. (Of course, I'm someone who gets confused about the signs for arrivals and departures at airports—do I go to arrivals because I'm arriving at the airport, or does the person I'm picking up go to arrivals because he or she is arriving on the plane?) I originally thought that an independent variable was one that would be free to vary or respond to some program or treatment, and that a dependent variable must be one that *depends* on my efforts (that is, it's the *treatment*). However, this is entirely backward! In fact, the **independent variable** *is what you (or nature) manipulates*—a treatment or program or cause. The **dependent variable** *is what you presume to be affected*

> **variable** Any entity that can take on different values. For instance, age can be considered a variable because age can take on different values for different people at different times.

> **attribute** A specific value of a variable. For instance, the variable *sex* or *gender* has two attributes: male and female.

> **independent variable** The variable that you manipulate. For instance, a program or treatment is typically an independent variable.

> **dependent variable** The variable affected by the independent variable; for example, the outcome.

by the independent variable—your effects or outcomes. For example, if you are studying the effects of a new educational program on student achievement, the program is the independent variable and your measures of achievement are the dependent ones. Or if you are looking at the effects of a new surgical treatment for cancer on rates of mortality for that cancer, the independent variable would be the surgical treatment and the dependent variable would be the mortality rates. The independent variable is what you (or nature) do, and the dependent variable is what results from that.

Finally, the attributes of a variable should be both exhaustive and mutually exclusive. Each variable's attributes should be **exhaustive,** meaning that they should include all possible answerable responses. For instance, if the variable is *religion* and the only options are *Protestant, Jewish,* and *Muslim,* there are quite a few religions I can think of that haven't been included. The list does not exhaust all possibilities. On the other hand, if you exhaust all the possibilities with some variables—religion being one of them—you would simply have too many responses. The way to deal with this is to list the most common attributes and then use a general category like *Other* to account for all remaining ones. In addition to being exhaustive, the attributes of a variable should be **mutually exclusive,** meaning that no respondent should be able to have two attributes simultaneously. Although this might seem obvious, it is often rather tricky in practice. For instance, you might be tempted to represent the variable *Educational Status* by asking the respondent to check one of the following response attributes: *High School Degree, Some College, Two-Year College Degree, Four-Year College Degree,* and *Graduate Degree.* However, these attributes are not mutually exclusive—a person who has a two-year or four-year college degree also could correctly check *Some College!* In fact, if someone went to college, got a two-year degree and then got a four-year degree, he or she could check all three. The problem here is that you ask the respondent to provide a single response to a set of attributes that are not mutually exclusive. But don't researchers often use questions on surveys that ask the respondent to check all that apply and then list a series of categories? Yes, but technically speaking, each of the categories in a question like that is its own variable and is treated dichotomously as either checked or unchecked—as attributes that *are* mutually exclusive.

1-1e Types of Relationships

A **relationship** refers to the correspondence between two variables (see Section 1-1d, "Variables"). When you talk about types of relationships, you can mean that in at least two ways: the *nature* of the relationship or the *pattern* of it.

The Nature of a Relationship We start by making a distinction between two types of relationships: a correlational relationship and a causal relationship. A correlational relationship simply says that two things perform in a synchronized manner. For instance, economists often talk of a correlation between inflation and unemployment. When inflation is high, unemployment also tends to be high. When inflation is low, unemployment also tends to be low. The two variables are correlated, but knowing that two variables are correlated does not tell whether one *causes* the other. For instance, there is a correlation between the number of roads built in Europe and the number of children born in the United States. Does that mean that if fewer children are desired in the United States, there should be a cessation of road building in Europe? Or does it mean that if there aren't enough roads in Europe, U.S. citizens should be encouraged to have more babies? Of course not. (At least, I hope not.) Although there is a relationship between the number of roads built and the number of babies, it's not likely that the relationship is a causal one. A **causal relationship** is a synchronized relationship between two variables just as a correlational relationship is, but in a causal relationship, we say that one variable *causes* the other to occur.

This leads to consideration of what is often termed the **third-variable problem.** In the previous example, it may be that a third variable is causing both the building of roads and the birth rate, and causing the correlation that is observed. For instance, perhaps the

exhaustive The property of a variable that occurs when you include all possible answerable responses.

mutually exclusive The property of a variable that ensures that the respondent is not able to assign two attributes simultaneously. For example, gender is a variable with mutually exclusive options if it is impossible for the respondents to simultaneously claim to be both male and female.

relationship Refers to the correspondence between two variables.

causal relationship A cause-effect relationship. For example, when you evaluate whether your treatment or program causes an outcome to occur, you are examining a causal relationship.

third-variable problem An unobserved variable that accounts for a correlation between two variables.

general world economy is responsible for both. When the economy is good, more roads are built in Europe, and more children are born in the United States. The key lesson here is that you have to be careful when you interpret correlations. If you observe a correlation between the number of hours students use the computer to study and their grade point averages (with high computer users getting higher grades), you *cannot* assume that the relationship is causal—that computer use improves grades. In this case, the third variable might be socioeconomic status—richer students, who have greater resources at their disposal, tend to both use computers and make better grades. Resources drive both use and grades; computer use doesn't cause the change in the grade point averages.

Patterns of Relationships   Several terms describe the major different types of patterns one might find in a relationship. First, there is the case of *no relationship* at all where, if you know the values on one variable, you don't know anything about the values on the other. For instance, I suspect that there is no relationship between the length of the lifeline on your hand and your grade point average. If I know your GPA, I don't have any idea how long your lifeline is. Figure 1-1a shows the case where there is no relationship.

Then, there is the **positive relationship.** In a positive relationship, high values on one variable are associated with high values on the other, and low values on one are associated with low values on the other. Figure 1-1b shows an idealized positive relationship between years of education and the salary one might expect to be making.

On the other hand, a **negative relationship** implies that high values on one variable are associated with low values on the other. This is also sometimes termed an *inverse* relationship. Figure 1-1c shows an idealized negative relationship between a measure of self-esteem and a measure of paranoia in psychiatric patients.

positive relationship
A relationship between variables in which high values for one variable are associated with high values on another variable, and low values are associated with low values.

negative relationship
A relationship between variables in which high values for one variable are associated with low values on another variable.

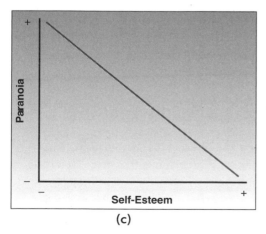

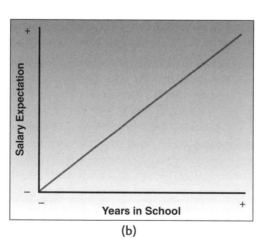

(a)   (b)

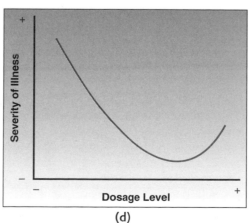

(c)   (d)

FIGURE 1-1
Four Types of Possible Relationships

(a) No relationship. *(b)* A positive relationship. *(c)* A negative relationship. *(d)* A curvilinear relationship.

These are the simplest patterns of relationships that might typically be estimated in research. However, the pattern of a relationship can be more complex than this. For instance, Figure 1-1*d* (see page 7) shows a relationship that changes over the range of both variables, a curvilinear relationship. In this example, the horizontal axis represents dosage of a drug for an illness, and the vertical axis represents a severity of illness measure. As the dosage rises, the severity of illness goes down. But at some point, the patient begins to experience negative side effects associated with too high a dosage, and the severity of illness begins to increase again.

1-1f Hypotheses

An **hypothesis** is a specific statement of prediction. It describes in concrete (rather than theoretical) terms what you expect to happen in your study. Not all studies have hypotheses. Sometimes, a study is designed to be exploratory (see Section 1-2b, "Deduction and Induction," later in this chapter). There is no formal hypothesis, and perhaps the purpose of the study is to explore some area more thoroughly to develop some specific hypothesis or prediction that can be tested in future research. A single study may have one or many hypotheses.

Actually, whenever I talk about an hypothesis, I am really thinking simultaneously about *two* hypotheses. Let's say that you predict that there will be a relationship between two variables in your study. The way to set up the hypothesis test is to formulate two hypothesis statements: one that describes your prediction and one that describes all the other possible outcomes with respect to the hypothesized relationship. Your prediction might be that variable A and variable B will be related. (You don't care whether it's a positive or negative relationship.) Then the only other possible outcome would be that variable A and variable B are *not* related. Usually, the hypothesis that you support (your prediction) is called the **alternative hypothesis,** and the hypothesis that describes the remaining possible outcomes is termed the **null hypothesis.** Sometimes, a notation like H_A or H_1 is used to represent the alternative hypothesis or your prediction, and H_O or H_0 to represent the **null case.** You have to be careful here, though. In some studies, your prediction might well be that there will be no difference or change. In this case, you are essentially trying to find support for the null hypothesis, and you are opposed to the alternative (Marriott, 1990).

If your prediction specifies a direction, the null hypothesis automatically includes both the no-difference prediction *and* the prediction that would be opposite in direction to yours. This is called a **one-tailed hypothesis.** For instance, let's imagine that you are investigating the effects of a new employee-training program and that you believe one of the outcomes will be that there will be *less* employee absenteeism. Your two hypotheses might be stated something like this:

The null hypothesis for this study is

H_O: As a result of the XYZ company employee-training program, there will either be no significant difference in employee absenteeism or there will be a significant *increase*,

which is tested against the alternative hypothesis:

H_A: As a result of the XYZ company employee-training program, there will be a significant *decrease* in employee absenteeism.

In Figure 1-2, this situation is illustrated graphically. The alternative hypothesis—your prediction that the program will decrease absenteeism—is shown there. The null must account for the other two possible conditions: no difference, or an increase in absenteeism. The figure shows a hypothetical distribution of absenteeism differences. That is, a value of zero means that there has been no difference in absenteeism observed, a positive value means that absenteeism has increased, and a negative value means it has decreased. The term *one-tailed* refers to the tail of the distribution on the outcome variable.

hypothesis A specific statement of prediction.

alternative hypothesis A specific statement of prediction that usually states what you expect will happen in your study.

null hypothesis The hypothesis that describes the possible outcomes other than the alternative hypothesis. Usually, the null hypothesis predicts there will be no effect of a program or treatment you are studying.

null case A situation in which the treatment has no effect.

one-tailed hypothesis A hypothesis that specifies a direction; for example, when your hypothesis predicts that your program will increase the outcome.

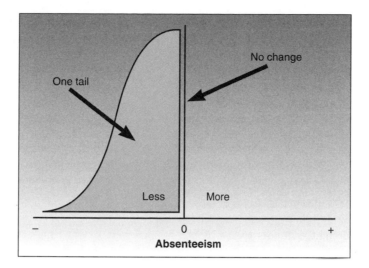

When your prediction does not specify a direction, you have a **two-tailed hypothesis.** For instance, let's assume you are studying a new drug treatment for depression. The drug has gone through some initial animal trials, but it has not yet been tested on humans. You believe (based on theory and the previous research) that the drug will have an effect, but you are not confident enough to hypothesize a direction and say the drug will reduce depression. (After all, you've seen more than enough promising drug treatments come along that eventually were shown to have severe side effects that actually worsened symptoms.) In this case, you might state the two hypotheses like this:

two-tailed hypothesis
A hypothesis that does not specify a direction. For example, if your hypothesis is that your program or intervention will have an effect on an outcome, but you are unwilling to specify whether that effect will be positive or negative, you are using a two-tailed hypothesis.

The null hypothesis for this study is:

> H_O: As a result of 300mg/day of the ABC drug, there will be no significant difference in depression,

which is tested against the alternative hypothesis:

> H_A: As a result of 300mg/day of the ABC drug, there will be a significant difference in depression.

Figure 1-3 illustrates this two-tailed prediction for this case. Again, notice that the term *two-tailed* refers to the tails of the distribution for your outcome variable.

The important thing to remember about stating hypotheses is that you formulate your prediction (directional or not), and then you formulate a second hypothesis that is

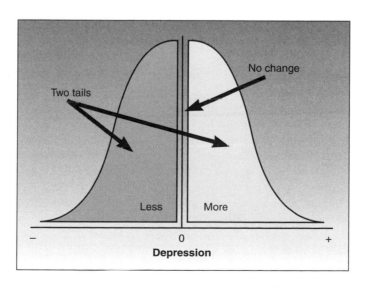

mutually exclusive of the first and incorporates all possible alternative outcomes for that case. When your study analysis is completed, the idea is that you will have to choose between the two hypotheses. If your prediction is correct, you would (usually) reject the null hypothesis and accept the alternative. If your original prediction was not supported in the data, you will accept the null hypothesis and reject the alternative. The logic of hypothesis testing (Marriott, 1990) is based on these two basic principles:

- Two mutually exclusive hypothesis statements that, together, exhaust all possible outcomes need to be developed.
- The hypotheses must be tested so that one is necessarily accepted and the other rejected.

Okay, I know it's a convoluted, awkward, and formalistic way to ask research questions, but it encompasses a long tradition in science and statistics called the **hypothetico-deductive model** (Nagel, 1979; Popper, 1959). Sometimes, things are just done because they're traditions. Anyway, if all of this hypothesis testing were easy enough that anybody could understand it, how do you think statisticians and methodologists would stay employed?

1-1g Types of Data

Data will be discussed in lots of places in this text, but here I just want to make a fundamental distinction between two types of data: qualitative and quantitative. Typically, data is called **quantitative data** if it is in numerical form and **qualitative data** if it is not. Note that qualitative data could be much more than just words or text. Photographs, videos, sound recordings, and so on, can be considered qualitative data.

Personally, although I find the distinction between qualitative and quantitative data to have some utility, I think most people draw too hard a distinction, and that can lead to all sorts of confusion. In some areas of social research, the qualitative-quantitative distinction has led to protracted arguments with the proponents of each arguing the superiority of their kind of data over the other. The quantitative types argue that their data is hard, rigorous, credible, and scientific. The qualitative proponents counter that their data is sensitive, nuanced, detailed, and contextual.

For many of us in social research, this kind of polarized debate has become less than productive. Additionally, it obscures the fact that qualitative and quantitative data are intimately related to each other. *All quantitative data is based upon qualitative judgments, and all qualitative data can be summarized and manipulated numerically.* For instance, think about a common quantitative measure in social research—a self-esteem scale. The researchers who developed such instruments had to make countless judgments in constructing them: how to define self-esteem, how to distinguish it from other related concepts, how to word potential scale items, how to make sure the items would be understandable to the intended respondents, what kinds of contexts they could be used in, what kinds of cultural and language constraints might be present, and so on. Researchers who decide to use such a scale in their studies have to make another set of judgments: how well the scale measures the intended concept, how reliable or consistent it is, how appropriate it is for the research context and intended respondents, and so on. Believe it or not, even the respondents make many judgments when filling out such a scale: what various terms and phrases mean, why the researcher is giving this scale to them, how much energy and effort they want to expend to complete it, and so on. Even the consumers and readers of the research make judgments about the self-esteem measure and its appropriateness in that research context. What may look like a simple, straightforward, cut-and-dried quantitative measure is actually based on lots of qualitative judgments made by many different people.

On the other hand, all qualitative information can be easily converted into quantitative, and many times, doing so would add considerable value to your research. The sim-

hypothetico-deductive model
A model in which two mutually exclusive hypotheses that together exhaust all possible outcomes are tested, such that if one hypothesis is accepted, the second must therefore be rejected.

quantitative data Data that appears in numerical form.

qualitative data Data in which the variables are not in a numerical form, but are in the form of text, photographs, sound bytes, and so on.

plest way to do this is to divide the qualitative information into categories and number them! I know that sounds trivial, but even simply assigning a number to each category can enable you to organize and process qualitative information more efficiently. Perhaps a more typical example of converting qualitative data into quantitative is when we do a simple content coding. For example, imagine that you have a written survey and as the last question, you ask the respondent to provide any additional written comments they might wish to make. What do you do with such data? A straightforward approach would be to read through all of the comments from all respondents and, as you're doing so, develop a list of categories into which they can be classified. Once you have a simple classification or "coding" scheme, you can go back through the statements and assign the best code to each specific comment. If you use a computer to analyze these comments, you might summarize the results by counting the number of comments in each category. Or, you might use percentages to describe what percent of all comments each category constitutes. This is a simple example of coding qualitative data so that it can be summarized quantitatively. There are more sophisticated approaches for analyzing qualitative data quantitatively (see, for example, Section 6-2b, "Content Analysis," in Chapter 6), but the essential point should be clear: Qualitative and quantitative data are intimately related, and we often move from one form to another in the course of a research project.

1-1h The Unit of Analysis

One of the most important ideas in a research project is the **unit of analysis.** The unit of analysis is whatever entity you are analyzing in your study. For instance, any of the following could be a unit of analysis in a study:

- Individuals
- Groups
- Artifacts (books, photos, newspapers)
- Geographical units (town, census tract, state)
- Social interactions (dyadic relations, divorces, arrests)

For instance, if you conduct a survey where you ask individuals to tell you their opinions about something, and you combine their responses to get some idea of what the "typical" individual thinks, your unit of analysis is the individual. On the other hand, if you collect data about crime rates in major cities in the country, your unit of analysis would be the city. Why is it called the unit of analysis and not something else (like, the unit of sampling)? Because *it is the analysis you do in your study that determines what the unit is.* For instance, if you are comparing the children in two classrooms on achievement test scores, the unit is the individual child because you have a score for each child. On the other hand, if you are comparing the two classes on noise levels, your unit of analysis is the group—in this case, the classroom—because you will measure noise for the class as a whole, not separately for each individual student.

For different analyses in the same study, you may have different units of analysis. If you decide to base an analysis on student scores, the individual is the unit. However, you might decide to compare average achievement test performance for the classroom with the classroom climate score. In this case, the data that goes into the analysis is the average itself, not the individuals' scores. Even though you have data at the student level, if the analysis is based on group averages, then the group is the unit of that analysis. In many areas of social research, these hierarchies of analysis units have become particularly important and have spawned a whole area of statistical analysis sometimes referred to as **hierarchical modeling.** In education, for instance, where a researcher might want to compare classroom climate data with individual student level achievement data, hierarchical modeling allows you to include data at these two different levels within the same analysis without averaging the individual student data first.

unit of analysis The entity that you are analyzing in your analysis; for example, individuals, groups, or social interactions.

hierarchical modeling The incorporation of multiple units of analysis at different levels of a hierarchy within a single analytic model. For instance, in an educational study, you might want to compare student performance with teacher expectations. To examine this relationship would require averaging student performance for each class because each teacher has multiple students and you are collecting data at both the teacher and student level.

1-2 THE RATIONALE OF RESEARCH

You probably think of research as something abstract and complicated. It can be, but you'll see (I hope) that if you understand the basic logic or rationale that underlies research, it's not nearly as complicated as it may seem at first glance.

A research project has a well-known structure: a beginning, middle, and end. I introduce the basic *phases* of a research project in Section 1-2a, "Structure of Research." Here, I also introduce some important distinctions in research: the different types of questions you can ask in a research project, and the major components or parts of a research project.

Before the modern idea of research emerged, there was a term for what philosophers used to call research: logical reasoning. So, it should come as no surprise that some of the basic distinctions in logic have carried over into contemporary research. In Section 1-2b, "Deduction and Induction," later in this chapter, I discuss how two major logical systems—the inductive and deductive methods of reasoning—are related to modern research.

When we're doing research, we want to minimize major potential problems. Sometimes, the problem is that we just aren't thinking logically. An error in logic is often called a *fallacy*, and there are a number of fallacies that tend to come up repeatedly in conducting research. In Section 1-2c, "Two Research Fallacies," I present two of the most common of these.

Finally, I describe what we mean by the term *validity* in research. How do we know whether the answers we get from research are sensible and accurate? How valid are the results of your research? What factors contribute to making a study more or less valid, stronger or weaker? The theory of validity is central to the rationale for research.

1-2a Structure of Research

Most research projects share the same general structure. You might think of this structure as following the shape of an hourglass, as shown in Figure 1-4. The research process usually starts with a broad area of interest, the initial problem that the researcher wishes to study. For instance, the researcher could want to investigate how to use computers to improve the performance of students in mathematics, but this initial interest is far too broad to study in any single research project. (It might not even be addressable in a lifetime of research.) The researcher has to narrow the question down to one that can reasonably be studied in a research project. This might involve formulating a hypothesis or a focus question. For instance, the researcher might hypothesize that a particular method of computer instruction in math will improve the ability of elementary school students in a specific district. At the narrowest point of the research hourglass, the researcher is engaged in direct measurement or observation of the question of interest. This is the point at which the "rubber hits the road," and the researcher is most directly involved in interacting with the environment within which the research is being conducted.

Once the basic data is collected, the researcher begins trying to understand it, usually by analyzing it in a variety of ways. Even for a single hypothesis, there are a number of analyses a researcher might typically conduct. At this point, the researcher begins to formulate some initial conclusions about what happened as a result of the computerized math program. Finally, the researcher often will attempt to address the original broad question of interest by generalizing from the results of this specific study to other related situations. For instance, on the basis of strong results indicating that the math program had a positive effect on student performance, the researcher might conclude that other school districts similar to the one in the study might expect similar results.

Notice that both ends of the hourglass represent the realm of ideas and the research questions that guide the project. The hourglass center is the most concrete or specific part of the process. The parts in between show how we translate the research questions into procedures for measurement (top part of the hourglass) and how we translate the data we observe into conclusions and new or revised questions (bottom part).

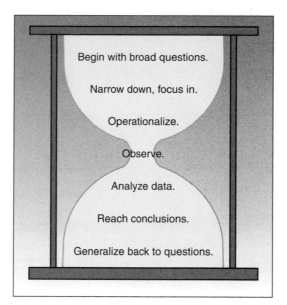

FIGURE 1-4
The Hourglass Metaphor for the Research Process

Components of a Study   What are the basic components or parts of a research study? Here, I'll describe the basic components involved in a causal study. Remember that earlier in the chapter (see Section 1-1b, "Types of Studies"), you learned that causal studies build on descriptive and relational questions, therefore, many of the components of causal studies will also be found in descriptive and relational studies.

Most social research originates from some general *research problem*. You might, for instance, be interested in which programs enable the unemployed to get jobs. Usually, the problem is broad enough that you could not hope to address it adequately in a single research study. Consequently, the problem is typically narrowed down to a more specific **research question** that can be addressed. The research question is often stated in the context of some theory that has been advanced to address the problem. For instance, you might have a theory that ongoing support services are needed to assure that the newly employed remain employed. The research question is the central issue being addressed in the study and is often phrased in the language of theory. A research question might be:

> Is a program of supported employment more effective (than no program at all) at keeping newly employed persons on the job?

The problem with such a question is that it is still too general to be studied directly. Consequently, in much research, an even more specific statement, called an hypothesis, is developed that describes in *operational* terms exactly what you think will happen in the study (see Section 1-1f, "Hypotheses," earlier in this chapter). For instance, the hypothesis for your employment study might be something like the following:

> The Metropolitan Supported Employment Program will significantly increase rates of employment after six months for persons who are newly employed (after being out of work for at least one year), compared with persons who receive no comparable program.

Notice that this hypothesis is specific enough that a reader can understand quite well what the study is trying to assess.

In causal studies, there are at least two major variables of interest: the cause and the effect. Usually, the cause is some type of event, program, or treatment (the cause is also sometimes called the *independent variable*, as I mentioned in Section 1-1d, "Variables"). A distinction is made between causes that the researcher can control (such as a program) versus causes that occur naturally or outside the researcher's influence (such as a change

research question   The central issue being addressed in the study, which is typically phrased in the language of theory.

in interest rates, or the occurrence of an earthquake). The effect (or dependent variable) is the outcome that you wish to study.

For both the cause and effect, a distinction is made between the idea of the cause or effect (the *construct*) and how they are actually manifested in reality. For instance, when you think about what a program of support services for the newly employed might be, you are thinking of the construct. On the other hand, the real world is not always what you think it is. In research, a distinction is made between your view of an entity (the construct) and the entity as it exists (the *operationalization*). Ideally, the two should agree, but in most situations, the reality falls short of your ideal.

Social research is always conducted in a social context. Researchers ask people questions, observe families interacting, or measure the opinions of people in a city. The units that participate in the project are important components of any research project. Units are directly related to sampling. Note that there is a distinction between units (the participants in your study) and the units of analysis (as described in Section 1-1h, "The Unit of Analysis") in any particular analysis. In most projects, it's not possible to involve everyone it might be desirable to involve. For instance, in studying a program of support services for the newly employed, you can't possibly include in your study everyone in the world, or even in the country, who is newly employed. Instead, you have to try to obtain a representative sample of such people. When sampling, a distinction is made between the theoretical population of interest and the final sample that is actually included in the study. Usually, the term *units* refers to the people who are sampled and from whom information is gathered, but for some projects, the units are organizations, groups, or geographical entities like cities or towns. Sometimes, the sampling strategy is multilevel; a number of cities are selected, and within them, families are sampled. Sampling will be discussed in greater detail in Chapter 2.

In causal studies, the interest is in the effects of some cause on one or more *outcomes*. The outcomes are directly related to the research problem; usually, the greatest interest is in outcomes that are most reflective of the problem. In the hypothetical supported-employment study, you would probably be most interested in measures of employment—is the person currently employed, or what is his or her rate of absenteeism?

Finally, in a causal study, the effects of the cause of interest (for example, the program) are usually compared to other conditions (for example, another program or no program at all). Thus, a key component in a causal study concerns how you decide which units (people) receive the program and which are placed in an alternative condition. This issue is directly related to the *research design* that you use in the study. One of the central themes in research design is determining how people wind up in or are placed in various programs or treatments that you are comparing. Different types of research designs will be explored in Chapters 7 through 10.

These, then, are the major components in a causal study:

- The research problem
- The research question
- The program (cause)
- The units
- The outcomes (effect)
- The design

1-2b Deduction and Induction

In logic, a distinction is often made between two broad methods of reasoning known as the deductive and inductive approaches (Beveridge, 1950; Hempel, 1966).

deductive Top-down reasoning that works from the more general to the more specific.

Deductive reasoning works from the more general to the more specific (see Figure 1-5). Sometimes, this is informally called a *top-down approach*. You might begin with

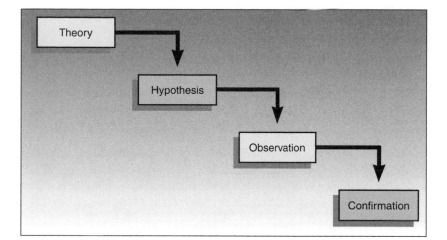

thinking up a *theory* about your topic of interest. You then narrow that down into more specific *hypotheses* that you can test. You narrow down even further when you collect *observations* to address the hypotheses. This ultimately leads you to be able to test the hypotheses with specific data—a *confirmation* (or not) of your original theories.

Inductive reasoning works the other way, moving from specific observations to broader generalizations and theories (see Figure 1-6). Informally, this is sometimes called a *bottom-up approach*. (Please note that it's *bottom* up and not *bottoms* up, which is the kind of thing the bartender says to customers when he's trying to close for the night!) In inductive reasoning, you begin with specific observations and measures, begin detecting patterns and regularities, formulate some tentative hypotheses that you can explore, and finally end up developing some general conclusions or theories.

These two methods of reasoning have a different feel to them when you're conducting research. Inductive reasoning, by its nature, is more open-ended and exploratory, especially at the beginning. Deductive reasoning is narrower in nature and is concerned with testing or confirming hypotheses. Even though a particular study may look like it's purely deductive (for example, an experiment designed to test the hypothesized effects of some treatment on some outcome), most social research involves both inductive and deductive reasoning processes at some time in the project. In fact, it doesn't take a rocket scientist to see that you could assemble the two graphs from Figures 1-5 and 1-6 into a single circular one that continually cycles from theories down to observations and back up again to theories. Even in the most constrained experiment, the researchers might observe patterns in the data that lead them to develop new theories.

inductive Bottom-up reasoning that begins with specific observations and measures and ends up as general conclusion or theory.

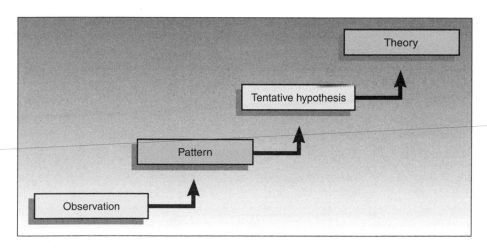

1-2c Two Research Fallacies

A *fallacy* is an error in reasoning, usually based on mistaken assumptions. Researchers are familiar with all the ways they could go wrong and the fallacies they are susceptible to. To give you an example of what fallacies are and why they are important, I discuss two of the most common ones.

ecological fallacy Faulty reasoning that results from making conclusions about individuals based only on analyses of group data.

The **ecological fallacy** occurs when you make conclusions about individuals based only on analyses of group data (Robinson, 1950). For instance, assume that you measured the math scores of a particular classroom and found that they had the highest average score in the district. Later (probably at the mall), you run into one of the kids from that class and you think to yourself, "She must be a math whiz." Aha! Fallacy! Just because she comes from the class with the highest *average* doesn't mean that she is automatically a high-scorer in math. She could be the lowest math scorer in a class that otherwise consists of math geniuses.

exception fallacy A faulty conclusion reached as a result of basing a conclusion on exceptional or unique cases.

An **exception fallacy** is sort of the reverse of the ecological fallacy. It occurs when you reach a group conclusion on the basis of exceptional cases. This kind of fallacious reasoning is at the core of a lot of sexism and racism. The stereotype is of the guy who sees a woman make a driving error and concludes that women are terrible drivers. Wrong! Fallacy!

Both of these fallacies point to some of the traps that exist in research and in everyday reasoning. They also point out how important it is to do research. It is important to determine empirically how individuals perform, rather than simply rely on group averages. Similarly, it is important to look at whether it is legitimate to conclude that certain behaviors in individuals generalize appropriately to groups.

1-3 VALIDITY OF RESEARCH

Quality is one of the most important issues in research. **Validity** is a term that we use to discuss the quality of various conclusions you might reach based on a research project (Campbell, 1988; Shadish et al., 2002). Here's where I have to give you the pitch about validity. When I mention validity, most students roll their eyes, curl up into a fetal position, or go to sleep. They think validity is just something abstract and philosophical (and I guess it is at some level). But I think if you can understand *validity*—the principles that are used to judge the quality of research—you'll be able to do much more than just complete a research project. You'll be able to be a virtuoso at research because you'll have an understanding of *why* you need to do certain things to ensure quality. You won't just be plugging in standard procedures you learned in school—sampling method X, measurement tool Y—you'll be able to help create the next generation of research technology.

validity The best available approximation of the truth of a given proposition, inference, or conclusion.

Validity is technically defined as "the best available approximation to the truth of a given proposition, inference, or conclusion" (Cook & Campbell, 1979). What does this mean? The first thing to ask is: "validity of *what?*" When people think about validity in research, they typically think in terms of research components. You might say that a measure is a valid one, or that a valid sample was drawn, or that the design had strong validity, but all of those statements are technically incorrect. Measures, samples, and designs don't *have* validity—only propositions can be said to be valid. Technically, you should say that a measure leads to valid conclusions or that a sample enables valid inferences, and so on. Validity is relevant to a proposition, inference, or conclusion.

Researchers make lots of different inferences or conclusions while conducting research. Many of these are related to the process of doing research and are not the major questions or hypotheses of the study. Nevertheless, like the bricks that go into building a wall, these intermediate processes and methodological propositions provide the foundation for the substantive conclusions that they wish to address. For instance, virtually all social research involves measurement or observation, and no matter what researchers measure or observe, they are concerned with whether they are measuring what they intend to measure or with how their observations are influenced by the circumstances in which they are made. They reach conclusions about the quality of their measures—

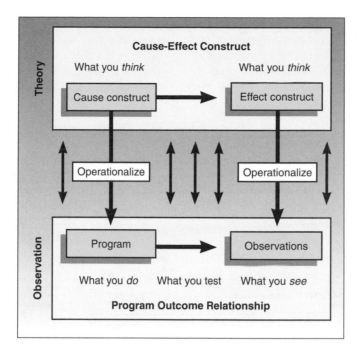

FIGURE 1-7
The Major Realms and Components of Research

conclusions that will play an important role in addressing the broader substantive issues of their study. When researchers talk about the validity of research, they are often referring to the many conclusions they reach about the quality of different parts of their research methodology.

Validity is typically subdivided into four types (Cook & Campbell, 1979; Shadish et al., 2002). Each type addresses a specific methodological question. To understand the types of validity, you have to know something about how researchers investigate a research question. I will use a causal study as an example because only causal questions involve all four validity types.

Figure 1-7 shows that two realms are involved in research. The first, on the top, is the land of theory. It is what goes on inside your head. It is where you keep your theories about how the world operates. The second, on the bottom, is the land of observations. It is the real world into which you translate your ideas: your programs, treatments, measures, and observations. When you conduct research, you are continually moving back and forth between these two realms, between what you think about the world and what is going on in it. When you are investigating a cause-effect relationship, you have a theory (implicit or otherwise) of what the cause is (the **cause construct**). For instance, if you are testing a new educational program, you have an idea of what it would look like ideally. Similarly, on the effect side, you have an idea of what you are ideally trying to affect and measure (the **effect construct**). But each of these—the cause and the effect—have to be translated into real things, into a program or treatment and a measure or observational method. The term *operationalization* (Bridgman, 1927) is used to describe the act of translating a construct into its manifestation. In effect, you take your idea and describe it as a series of operations or procedures. Now, instead of it only being an idea in your mind, it becomes a public entity that others can look at and examine for themselves. It is one thing, for instance, for you to say that you would like to measure self-esteem (a construct). But when you show a 10-item paper-and-pencil self-esteem measure that you developed for that purpose, others can look at it and understand more clearly what you mean by the term *self-esteem*.

Now, back to explaining the four validity types. They build on one another, with two of them (conclusion and internal) referring to the land of observation on the bottom of Figure 1-7, one of them (construct) emphasizing the linkages between the bottom and the top, and the last (external) being primarily concerned about the range of the theory on the top.

cause construct Your abstract idea or theory of what the cause is in a cause-effect relationship you are investigating.

effect construct Your abstract idea or theory of what the outcome is in a cause-effect relationship you are investigating.

Imagine that you want to examine whether use of a World Wide Web virtual classroom improves student understanding of course material. Assume that you took these two constructs, the *cause construct* (the website) and the *effect construct* (understanding), and *operationalized* them, turned them into realities by constructing the website and a measure of knowledge of the course material. Here are the four validity types and the question each addresses:

- *Conclusion validity*—In this study, is there a relationship between the two variables? In this example, this question might be worded: In this study, is there a relationship between the website and knowledge of course material? There are several conclusions or inferences you might draw to answer such a question. You could, for example, conclude that there is a relationship. You might conclude that there is a positive relationship. You might infer that there is no relationship. When you assess the validity of each of these conclusions or inferences, you are addressing conclusion validity. Conclusion validity will be discussed in more detail in Section 11-1, "Conclusion Validity," in Chapter 11.

- *Internal validity*—Assuming that there is a relationship in this study, is the relationship a causal one? Just because you find that use of the website and knowledge are correlated, you can't necessarily assume that website use causes the knowledge. Both could, for example, be caused by the same factor. For instance, it may be that wealthier students, who have greater resources, would be more likely to have access to a website and would excel on objective tests. When you want to make a claim that your program or treatment caused the outcomes in your study, and not something else, you are assessing the validity of a causal assertion and addressing internal validity. Internal validity will be discussed in more detail in Section 7-1, "Internal Validity," in Chapter 7.

- *Construct validity*—Assuming that there is a causal relationship in this study, can you claim that the program reflected well your construct of the program and that your measure reflected well your idea of the construct of the measure? In simpler terms, did you implement the program you intended to implement, and did you measure the outcome you wanted to measure? In yet other terms, did you operationalize well the ideas of the cause and the effect? Is the website what you intended it would be? Does it look like and work the way you imagined it would? Does it have the content you thought it should? When your research is over, you would like to be able to conclude that you did a credible job of operationalizing your constructs—that you can provide evidence for the construct validity of such a conclusion. Construct validity will be discussed in more detail in Section 3-1, "Construct Validity," in Chapter 3.

- *External validity*—Assuming that there is a causal relationship in this study between the constructs of the cause and the effect, can you generalize this effect to other persons, places, or times? Would a virtual classroom work with different target groups at different times, on different subject matters? You are likely to make some claims that your research findings have implications for other groups and individuals in other settings and at other times. When you do, you need to address the external validity of these claims. External validity will be discussed in more detail in Section 2-1, "External Validity," in Chapter 2.

Notice how the question that each validity type addresses presupposes an affirmative answer to the previous one. This is what I mean when I say that the validity types build on one another. Figure 1-8 shows the idea of the cumulativeness of validity as a staircase, along with the key question for each validity type.

For any inference or conclusion, there are always possible **threats to validity.** Here's the logic. You reach a conclusion about some aspect of your study. There are lots of reasons why you might be wrong in reaching this conclusion. These are the threats to the validity of your conclusion. Some are more reasonable or plausible, others more far-

threats to validity Reasons your conclusion or inference might be wrong.

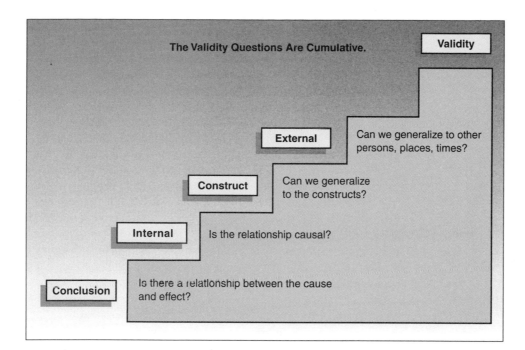

FIGURE 1-8
The Validity Staircase, Showing the Major Question for Each Type of Validity

fetched. You essentially want to rule out the plausible threats to validity or "alternative explanations," thereby leaving your explanation as the most reasonable one remaining.

For instance, imagine a study examining whether there is a relationship between the amount of training in a specific technology and subsequent rates of use of that technology. Because the interest is in a relationship, it is considered an issue of *conclusion validity*. Assume that the study is completed and no significant correlation between amount of training and adoption rates is found. On this basis, it is *concluded* that there is no relationship between the two. How could this conclusion be wrong—that is, what are the threats to conclusion validity? For one, it's possible that there isn't sufficient statistical power to detect a relationship even if it exists. Perhaps the sample size is too small or the measure of amount of training is unreliable. Or maybe assumptions of the correlational test are violated given the variables used. Perhaps there were random irrelevancies in the study setting or random heterogeneity in the respondents that increased the variability in the data and made it harder to see the relationship of interest. The inference that there is no relationship will be stronger—have greater conclusion validity—if you can show that these alternative explanations are not credible. The distributions might be examined to see whether they conform with assumptions of the statistical test, or analyses might be conducted to determine whether there is sufficient statistical power. The concept of statistical power will be explained more thoroughly in the section "Statistical Power" in Section 11-1a in Chapter 11.

The theory of validity and the many lists of specific threats provide a useful scheme for assessing the quality of research conclusions. The theory is general in scope and applicability, well-articulated in its philosophical suppositions, and virtually impossible to explain adequately in a few minutes. As a framework for judging the quality of evaluations, it is indispensable and well worth understanding.

1-4 ETHICS IN RESEARCH

This is a time of profound change in the understanding of the ethics of applied social research. From the time immediately after World War II until the early 1990s, there was a gradually developing consensus about the key ethical principles that should underlie research. Two marker events stand out (among many others) as symbolic of this consensus. The Nuremberg war crimes trial following World War II brought to public view the ways German scientists had used captive human subjects as subjects in often gruesome experiments (Annas & Grodin, 1995). In the 1950s and 1960s, the Tuskegee syphilis study (Jones, 1993) involved the withholding of known effective treatment for syphilis from African-American participants who were infected. Events like these forced the reexamination of ethical standards and the gradual development of a consensus that potential human subjects needed to be protected from being used as guinea pigs in scientific research.

By the 1990s, the dynamics of the situation changed. Cancer patients and persons with AIDS fought publicly with the medical research establishment about the length of time needed to get approval for and complete research into potential cures for fatal diseases. In many cases, it is the ethical assumptions of the previous 30 years that drive this go-slow mentality. According to previous thinking, it is better to risk denying treatment for awhile until there is enough confidence in a treatment, than risk harming innocent people (as in the Nuremberg and Tuskegee events). Recently, however, people threatened with fatal illness have been saying to the research establishment that they *want* to be test subjects, even under experimental conditions of considerable risk. Several vocal and articulate patient groups who wanted to be experimented on came up against an ethical review system designed to protect them from being the subjects of experiments!

Although the last few years in the ethics of research have been tumultuous ones, a new consensus is beginning to evolve that involves the stakeholder groups most affected by a problem participating more actively in the formulation of guidelines for research. Although it's not entirely clear, at present, what the new consensus will be, it is almost certain that it will not fall at either extreme: protecting against human experimentation at all costs versus allowing anyone who is willing to be the subject of an experiment.

1-4a The Language of Ethics

As in every other aspect of research, the area of ethics has its own vocabulary (Resnik, 1998; Sales & Folkman, 2000). In this section, I present some of the most important language regarding ethics in research.

The principle of **voluntary participation** requires that people not be coerced into participating in research. This is especially relevant where researchers had previously relied on captive audiences for their subjects—prisons, universities, and places like that. Closely related to the notion of voluntary participation is the requirement of **informed consent.** Essentially, this means that prospective research participants must be fully informed about the procedures and risks involved in research and must give their consent to participate. Ethical standards also require that researchers not put participants in a situation where they might be at *risk of harm* as a result of their participation. Harm can be defined as both physical and psychological. Two standards are applied to help protect the privacy of research participants. Almost all research guarantees the participants **confidentiality;** they are assured that identifying information will not be made available to anyone who is not directly involved in the study. The stricter standard is the principle of **anonymity,** which essentially means that the participant will remain anonymous throughout the study, even to the researchers themselves. Clearly, the anonymity standard is a stronger guarantee of privacy, but it is sometimes difficult to accomplish, especially in situations where participants have to be measured at multiple time points (for example in a pre-post study). Increasingly, researchers have had to deal with the ethical issue of a person's **right to service.** Good research practice often requires the use of a no-treatment control group—a group of participants who do *not* get the treatment or program that is being studied. But when that treatment or program may have beneficial effects, persons assigned to the no-treatment control may feel their rights to equal access to services are being curtailed.

Even when clear ethical standards and principles exist, at times the need to do accurate research runs up against the rights of potential participants. No set of standards can possibly anticipate every ethical circumstance. Furthermore, there needs to be a proce-

voluntary participation For ethical reasons, researchers must ensure that study participants are taking part in a study voluntarily and are not coerced.

informed consent A policy of informing study participants about the procedures and risks involved in research that ensures that all participants must give their consent to participate.

confidentiality An assurance made to study participants that identifying information about them acquired through the study will not be released to anyone outside of the study.

anonymity The assurance that no one, including the researchers, will be able to link data to a specific individual.

right to service The ethical issue involved when participants do not receive a service that they would be eligible for if they were not in your study. For example, members of a control group might not receive a drug because they are in a study.

dure that assures that researchers will consider all relevant ethical issues in formulating research plans. To address such needs, most institutions and organizations have formulated an **institutional review board (IRB),** a panel of persons who review research proposals with respect to ethical implications and decide whether additional actions need to be taken to assure the safety and rights of participants. By reviewing proposals for research, IRBs also help protect the organization and the researcher against potential legal implications of neglecting to address important ethical issues of participants.

institutional review board (IRB)
A panel of people who review research proposals with respect to ethical implications and decide whether additional actions need to be taken to assure the safety and rights of participants.

1-5 CONCEPTUALIZING

"Well begun is half done" —Aristotle, quoting an old proverb

One of the most difficult aspects of research—and one of the least discussed—is how to develop the idea for the research project in the first place. In training students, most faculty members simply assume that if students read enough of the research in an area of interest, they will somehow magically be able to produce sensible ideas for further research. Now, that may be true. And heaven knows that's the way researchers have been doing this higher education thing for some time now, but we probably could do a better job of helping our students learn *how* to formulate good research problems. One thing we can do (and some texts at least cover this at a surface level) is to give students a better idea of how professional researchers typically generate research ideas (Leong & Pfaltzgraff, 1996). Some of this is introduced in the discussion of problem formulation that follows.

1-5a Where Research Topics Come From

So, how do researchers come up with the idea for a research project? Probably one of the most common sources of research ideas is the experience of *practical problems in the field*. Many researchers are directly engaged in social, health, or human service program implementation and come up with their ideas based on what they see happening around them. Others aren't directly involved in service contexts, but work with (or survey) people to learn what needs to be better understood. Many of the ideas would strike the outsider as silly or worse. For instance, in health services areas, there is great interest in the problem of back injuries among nursing staff. It's not necessarily the thing that comes first to mind when you think about the health care field, but if you reflect on it for a minute longer, it should be obvious that nurses and nursing staff do an awful lot of lifting while performing their jobs. They lift and push heavy equipment, and they lift and push heavy patients! If 5 or 10 out of every hundred nursing staff were to strain their backs on average over the period of one year, the costs would be enormous, and that's pretty much what's happening. Even minor injuries can result in increased absenteeism. Major ones can result in lost jobs and expensive medical bills. The nursing industry figures this problem costs tens of millions of dollars annually in increased health care. Additionally, the health care industry has developed a number of approaches, many of them educational, to try to reduce the scope and cost of the problem. So, even though it might seem silly at first, many of these practical problems that arise in practice can lead to extensive research efforts.

Another source for research ideas is the *literature in your specific field*. Certainly, many researchers get ideas for research by reading the literature and thinking of ways to extend or refine previous research. Another type of literature that acts as a source of good research ideas is the **requests for proposals (RFPs)** that are published by government agencies and some companies. These RFPs describe some problem that the agency would like researchers to address; they are virtually handing the researcher an idea. Typically, the RFP describes the problem that needs addressing, the contexts in which it operates, the approach they would like you to take to investigate the problem, and the amount they would be willing to pay for such research. Clearly, there's nothing like potential research funding to get researchers to focus on a particular research topic.

Finally, let's not forget the fact that many researchers simply *think up their research* topic on their own (Adams, 1980). Of course, no one lives in a vacuum, so you would

requests for proposals (RFPs)
RFPs, published by government agencies and some companies, describe some problem that the agency would like researchers to address. Typically, the RFP describes the problem that needs addressing, the contexts in which it operates, the approach the agency would like you to take to investigate the problem, and the amount the agency would be willing to pay for such research.

expect that the ideas you come up with on your own are influenced by your background, culture, education, and experiences.

1-5b Feasibility

Soon after you get an idea for a study, reality begins to kick in and you begin to think about whether the study is feasible at all. Several major considerations come into play. Many of these involve making *trade-offs between rigor and practicality*. Performing a scientific study may force you to do things you wouldn't do normally. You might want to ask everyone who used an agency in the past year to fill in your evaluation survey, only to find that there were thousands of people and it would be prohibitively expensive. Or you might want to conduct an in-depth interview on your subject of interest, only to learn that the typical participant in your study won't willingly take the hour that your interview requires. If you had unlimited resources and unbridled control over the circumstances, you would always be able to do the best quality research. But those ideal circumstances seldom exist, and researchers are almost always forced to look for the best trade-offs they can find to get the rigor they desire.

When you are determining the project's feasibility, you almost always need to bear in mind several practical considerations. First, you have to think about *how long the research will take* to accomplish. Second, you have to question whether any important *ethical constraints* require consideration. Third, you must determine whether you can acquire the *cooperation* needed to take the project to its successful conclusion. And finally, you must determine the degree to which the costs will be manageable. Failure to consider any of these factors can mean disaster later.

1-5c The Literature Review

One of the most important early steps in a research project is the conducting of the literature review. This is also one of the most humbling experiences you're likely to have. Why? Because you're likely to find out that just about any worthwhile idea you will have has been thought of before, at least to some degree. I frequently have students who come to me complaining that they couldn't find anything in the literature that was related to their topic. And virtually every time they have said that, I was able to show them that was only true because they only looked for articles that were *exactly* the same as their research topic. A literature review is designed to identify related research, to set the current research project within a conceptual and theoretical context. When looked at that way, almost no topic is so new or unique that you can't locate relevant and informative related research.

Here are some tips about conducting the literature review. First, *concentrate your efforts on the scientific literature*. Try to determine what the most credible research journals are in your topical area and start with those. Put the greatest emphasis on research journals that use a blind or juried review system. In a blind or juried review, authors submit potential articles to a journal editor who solicits several reviewers who agree to give a critical review of the paper. The paper is sent to these reviewers with no identification of the author so that there will be no personal bias (either for or against the author). Based on the reviewers' recommendations, the editor can accept the article, reject it, or recommend that the author revise and resubmit it. Articles in journals with blind review processes are likely to have a fairly high level of credibility. Second, *do the review early* in the research process. You are likely to learn a lot in the literature review that will help you determine what the necessary trade-offs are. After all, previous researchers also had to face trade-off decisions.

What should you look for in the literature review? First, you might be able to find a study that is quite similar to the one you are thinking of doing. Since all credible research studies have to review the literature themselves, you can check their literature review to get a quick start on your own. Second, prior research will help ensure that you include all of the major relevant constructs in your study. You may find that other similar studies routinely look at an outcome that you might not have included. Your study would not be judged credible if it ignored a major construct. Third, the literature review will help you to find and select appropriate measurement instruments. You will readily see what measurement instruments researchers used themselves in contexts similar to yours. Finally, the literature review will help you to anticipate common problems in your research context. You can use the prior experiences of others to avoid common traps and pitfalls.

SUMMARY

We've covered a lot of territory in this initial chapter, grouped roughly into four broad areas. First, we considered the language of research and enhanced your vocabulary by introducing key terms like *variable, attribute, causal relationship, hypothesis,* and *unit of analysis*. We next considered the rationale or logic of research and discussed how research is structured, the major components of a research project, deductive and inductive reasoning, several major research

fallacies, and the critical topic of validity in research. This was followed by a discussion of ethics in research that introduced issues like informed consent and anonymity. Finally, we briefly considered how research is thought up or conceptualized. It certainly is a formidable agenda. But it provides you with the basic foundation for the material that's coming in subsequent chapters.

SUGGESTED WEBSITES

Note: These websites were functional when we went to press. Please access the Online Study Guide Edition for the most up-to-date URLs.

The National Library of Medicine PubMed Tutorial
http://www.nlm.nih.gov/bsd/pubmed_tutorial/m1001.html
This web-based learning program will show you how to search PubMed®, the National Library of Medicine's (NLM™) journal literature search system.

The National Institutes of Health Human Participant Protections Education for Research Teams
http://cme.cancer.gov/clinicaltrials/learning/humanparticipant-protections.asp
This site will allow you to take the online course, complete the self-test, and then provide the documentation required by your local institutional review board to conduct research.

KEY TERMS

alternative hypothesis (p. 8)
anonymity (p. 20)
attribute (p. 5)
causal (p. 4)
causal relationship (p. 6)
cause construct (p. 17)
confidentiality (p. 20)
cross-sectional (p. 5)
deductive (p. 14)
dependent variable (p. 5)
ecological fallacy (p. 16)
effect construct (p. 17)
empirical (p. 4)
exception fallacy (p. 16)
exhaustive (p. 6)
hierarchical modeling (p. 11)

hypothesis (p. 8)
hypothetico-deductive model (p. 10)
independent variable (p. 5)
inductive (p. 15)
informed consent (p. 20)
institutional review board (IRB) (p. 21)
longitudinal (p. 5)
mutually exclusive (p. 6)
negative relationship (p. 7)
null case (p. 8)
null hypothesis (p. 8)
one-tailed hypothesis (p. 8)
positive relationship (p. 7)
probabilistic (p. 4)
qualitative data (p. 10)
quantitative data (p. 10)

relationship (p. 6)
repeated measures (p. 5)
requests for proposals (RFPs) (p. 21)
research question (p. 13)
right to service (p. 20)
theoretical (p. 3)
third-variable problem (p. 6)
threats to validity (p. 18)
time series (p. 5)
two-tailed hypothesis (p. 9)
unit of analysis (p. 11)
validity (p. 16)
variable (p. 5)
voluntary participation (p. 20)

REVIEW QUESTIONS

Note: You can find the correct answers to these questions by taking the quiz and then submitting your answers in the Online Study Guide Edition. The program will automatically score your submission. If you miss a question, the program will provide the correct answer, a rationale for the answer, and the section number in the chapter where the topic is discussed.

1. When researchers claim that their research is "empirical," they are stating that it is
   a. concerned with developing, exploring, or testing theories.
   b. based on observations and measurements of reality.
   c. concerned with rules that pertain to general cases.
   d. concerned with rules that pertain to individual cases.

2. When conducting a survey that examines peoples' opinions about whether the electoral college should continue to be used to select the president of the United States, what type of research is involved?
   a. descriptive
   b. ecological
   c. relational
   d. causal

3. Stella Chess and Alexander Thomas have studied temperament for over thirty years, following the same individuals from infancy through adulthood. This is an example of what type of time study?
   a. cross-sectional study
   b. longitudinal study
   c. multiple measures study
   d. cross-causal study

4. Researchers investigating the effects of aging on cognition have found that, as we get older, our short-term memory deteriorates. This is an example of what kind of pattern of relationship if we are measuring age and the effectiveness of short-term memory?
   a. a curvilinear relationship
   b. a positive relationship
   c. a negative correlation
   d. no relationship

5. In an experiment, which variable measures the outcome?
   a. quantitative variable
   b. qualitative variable
   c. independent variable
   d. dependent variable

6. If we were conducting an experiment to test a hypothesis that people with religious backgrounds engage in more altruistic behavior than people with nonreligious histories, what would the null hypothesis be?
   a. People with religious backgrounds engage in no more or less altruistic behavior than people with nonreligious histories.
   b. People with religious backgrounds are more altruistic than people with nonreligious backgrounds.
   c. People with nonreligious backgrounds are more altruistic than people with religious backgrounds.
   d. There would be no null hypothesis for this experiment.

7. If the data is expressed numerically, it is considered
   a. qualitative.
   b. quantitative.
   c. independent.
   d. causal.

8. In a research journal, you read an article about final exam performance of self-described "morning" people versus "night" people who take an 8 A.M. class. In this study, the unit of analysis is
   a. the class as a whole.
   b. the "morning group" versus the "night group."
   c. individual students in the class.
   d. impossible to quantify accurately.

9. As a whole, Asian Americans tend to perform better on math tests than Caucasian Americans. What kind of research fallacy would be reflected in the assumption that Lang Lee, an Asian American, would be a better-than-average math student?
   a. economical fallacy
   b. exceptional fallacy
   c. exception fallacy
   d. ecological fallacy

10. Since research projects generally share the same structure, one resembling an hourglass, the narrowest point of focus, occurs when the researcher is engaged in
    a. narrowing down the question.
    b. operationalizing the question.
    c. direct observations or measurements.
    d. drawing conclusions.

11. In a causal study, the treatment or program variable would be accurately called the
    a. independent variable.
    b. exhaustive variable.
    c. dependent variable.
    d. mutually exclusive variable.

12. If two variables are correlated, it does not mean that one causes the other.
    a. True
    b. False

13. A TV news report of a car accident notes that the driver of the car that caused the accident was a "senior citizen." A viewer of this report who says, "Those old fogies are a menace—they shouldn't let old people drive," is probably making a questionable conclusion based on the exception fallacy.
    a. True
    b. False

14. In designing the ethical considerations of a study, it is best to guarantee that participants' responses will be both anonymous and confidential.
    a. True
    b. False

15. The ethical principle of informed consent means that researchers must get a form signed by their participants.
    a. True
    b. False

part 2

SAMPLING

2 Sampling

2

Sampling

Chapter Outline

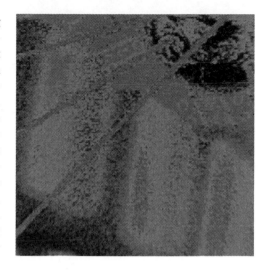

Sampling is the process of selecting units (such as people and organizations) from a population of interest so that, by studying the sample, you can fairly generalize your results to the population from which the units were chosen. In this chapter, I begin by covering some of the key terms in sampling, like *population* and *sampling frame*. Then, because some types of sampling rely on quantitative models, I'll talk about some of the statistical terms used in sampling. Finally, I'll discuss the major distinction between probability and nonprobability sampling methods and work through the major types in each.

2-1 EXTERNAL VALIDITY

It may seem odd to begin a chapter about sampling by discussing external validity. So, I want to take a minute to explain how these topics are linked. In research, our sample consists of the people who actually participate in our study. But when we conduct research, we are often interested in reaching conclusions not just about our sample in the time and place where we conducted our study. We're also often interested in making some conclusions that are broader than that, in concluding what might happen with other people at other times and in other places than just our sample. When we try to reach conclusions that extend beyond the sample in our study, we say that we are generalizing. So, why is external validity so important to the issue of sampling? Because external validity is centrally related to the idea of generalizing. Recall from Section 1-3, "Validity of Research," in Chapter 1, that validity of any type refers to the approximate truth of propositions, inferences, or conclusions. External validity refers to the approximate truth of conclusions that involve generalizations. Put in everyday terms, **external validity** is the degree to which the conclusions in your study would hold for other persons in other places and at other times (Cook & Campbell, 1979; Shadish, Cook, & Campbell, 2002).

Science uses two major approaches to gather evidence to support generalizations. I'll call the first approach the **sampling model.** In the sampling model, you start by identifying the population you would like to generalize to (see Figure 2-1). Then, you draw a representative sample from that population and conduct your research with the sample. Finally, because the sample is representative of the population, you can automatically generalize your results back to the population. This approach has several problems. First, at the time of your study, you might not know what part of the population you will ultimately want to generalize to. Second, you may not be able to draw a fair or representative sample easily. Third, it's impossible to sample across all times that you might like to generalize to, such as next year.

The second approach is called the **proximal similarity model** (Campbell, 1986) (see Figure 2-2). Proximal means nearby and similarity means . . . well, it means similarity. In the proximal similarity approach, you begin by thinking about different contexts you might want to generalize to, and which are more similar to your study and which are less so. For instance, you might imagine several settings, some having people who are more similar to the people in your sample, others having people who are less similar. This process also holds for times and places. Now picture this in terms of gradations of closeness to your study. Some combinations of people, places, and times are "closer" to those in your study, while others are more "distant" or less similar. The technical term for this

external validity The degree to which the conclusions in your study would hold for other persons in other places and at other times.

sampling model A model for generalizing in which you identify your population, draw a fair sample, conduct your research, and finally, generalize your results to other population groups.

proximal similarity model A model for generalizing from your study to another context based upon the degree to which the other context is similar to your study context.

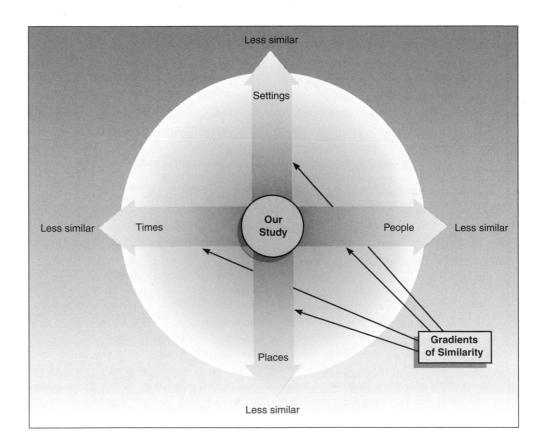

FIGURE 2-1
The Sampling Model for External Validity

The researcher draws a sample for a study from a defined population to generalize the results to the population.

gradient of similarity The dimension along which your study context can be related to other potential contexts to which you might wish to generalize. Contexts that are closer to yours along the gradient of similarity of place, time, people, and so on can be generalized to with more confidence than ones that are further away.

idea is the **gradient of similarity.** There are some groups, for instance, that are more similar to your sample and would be closer along this gradient. Others would be less similar and further away along this imaginary gradient. For example, imagine that the sample in your study consisted of females between the ages of 18 and 22 in a small midwestern college town. Who would likely be more similar to your sample—a group of females age 18–22 from another midwestern college town or a group of females age 18–22 from Paris? Most likely, you would argue that the group from another small midwestern college town is "closer" to your sample than the one from Paris. That is, you would be saying they are closer along a gradient of similarity. So, how do you use the idea of the gradient of similarity from the proximal similarity framework to generalize? Simple. You generalize with

FIGURE 2-2
The Proximal Similarity Model for External Validity

greater confidence the results of your study to other persons, places, or times that are more like (that is, more proximally similar to) your study. Notice that here, you never generalize with certainty; such generalizations are always a question of more or less similar, always a question of degree.

Which approach is right? Which is better? There's no simple way to answer these questions. The sampling model is the more traditional and widely accepted of the two. If you are able to draw the sample well (a real challenge in many situations) and if you don't have too many subjects who don't respond (nonresponse is a growing problem in social research), then the sampling model makes sense. But the proximal similarity approach applies in any study as a guideline for thinking about external validity and generalizability. Even in situations where you aren't able to sample well from a population or when you have many subjects who don't respond or who drop out, you can *always* ask yourself what groups, places, and times are more or less similar to those in your study.

2-1a Threats to External Validity

A **threat to external validity** is an explanation of how you might be wrong in making a generalization. For instance, imagine that you conclude that the results of your study (which was done in a specific place, with certain types of people, and at a specific time) can be generalized to another context (for instance, another place, with slightly different people, at a slightly later time). In such a case, three major threats to external validity exist because there are three ways you could be wrong: people, places, and times. Your critics could, for example, argue that the results of your study were due to the unusual type of people who were in the study, or, they could claim that your results were obtained only because of the unusual place in which you performed the study. (Perhaps you did your educational study in a college town with lots of high-achieving, educationally oriented kids.) They might suggest that you did your study at a peculiar time. For instance, if you did your smoking-cessation study the week after the surgeon general issued the well-publicized results of the latest smoking and cancer studies, you might get different results than if you had done it the week before.

> **threat to external validity** Any factor that can lead you to make an incorrect generalization from the results of your study to other persons, places, times, or settings.

2-1b Improving External Validity

How can you improve external validity? One way, based on the sampling model, suggests that you do a good job of drawing a sample from a population. From the perspective of the sampling model, you should use random selection, if possible, rather than a nonrandom procedure. Additionally, once selected, you should try to assure that the respondents participate in your study and that you keep your dropout rates low. A second approach would be to use the theory of proximal similarity more effectively. How? You could do a better job of describing the ways your context differs from others by providing data about the degree of similarity between various groups of people, places, and even times. Perhaps the best approach to criticisms of generalizations is simply to show critics that they're wrong—do your study in a variety of places, with different people, and at different times. That is, your external validity (ability to generalize) will be stronger the more you replicate your study in different contexts.

2-2 SAMPLING TERMINOLOGY

As with anything else in life, you have to learn the language of an area if you're going to ever hope to use it. Here, I want to introduce several different terms for the major groups that are involved in a sampling process and the role that each group plays in the logic of sampling. There are numerous specialized introductory (Kalton, 1983; Williams, 1978) and advanced (Kish, 1995; Sudman, 1976) texts that address sampling in greater detail.

The major question that motivates sampling in the first place is: "Whom do you want to generalize to?" (Or should it be: "To whom do you want to generalize?") In most social research, you are interested in more than just the people directly participating in your study. You would like to be able to talk in general terms and not be confined to only the people in your study. There may be times you won't be concerned about generalizing. Maybe you're just evaluating a program in a local agency and don't care whether the

FIGURE 2-3
The Different Groups in the Sampling Model

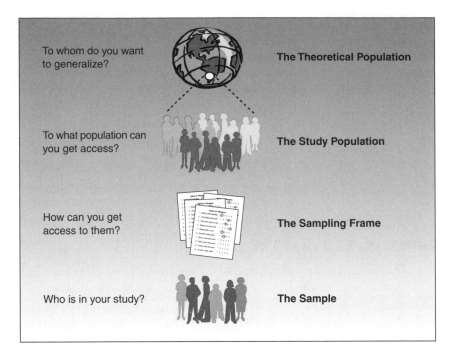

program would work with other people in other places and at other times. In that case, sampling and generalizing might not be of interest. In other cases, you would really like to be able to generalize almost universally. When psychologists do research, they are often interested in developing theories that would hold for all humans, but in most applied social research, researchers are interested in generalizing to specific groups.

The group you wish to generalize to is called the **population** in your study (see Figure 2-3). This is the group you would like to sample from because this is the group you are interested in generalizing to. Let's imagine that you want to generalize to urban homeless males between the ages of 30 and 50 in the United States. If that is the population of interest, you are likely to have a hard time developing a reasonable sampling plan. You are probably not going to find an accurate listing of this population, and even if you did, you would almost certainly not be able to mount a national sample across hundreds of urban areas. So, you probably should make a distinction between the population you would like to generalize to and the population that is accessible to you. We'll call the former the *theoretical population* and the latter the *accessible population*. In this example, the accessible population might be homeless males between the ages of 30 and 50 in six selected urban areas across the United States.

After you identify the theoretical and accessible populations, you have to do one more thing before you can actually draw a sample: Get a list of the members of the accessible population. (Or, you have to spell out in detail the procedures you will follow to contact them to assure representativeness.) The listing of the accessible population from which you'll draw your sample is called the **sampling frame.** If you were doing a phone survey and selecting names from the telephone book, the phone book would be your sampling frame. That wouldn't be a great way to sample because significant subportions of the population either don't have a phone or have moved in or out of the area since the last phone book was printed. Notice that in this case, you might identify the area code and all 3-digit prefixes within that area code and draw a sample simply by randomly dialing numbers (cleverly known as *random-digit-dialing*). In this case, the sampling frame is not a list *per se*, but is rather a procedure that you follow as the actual basis for sampling. Finally, you actually draw your sample, using one of the many sampling procedures described later in this chapter. The **sample** is the group of people you select to be in your study. **Sampling** is the process of drawing the sample. Notice that I didn't say that the sample was the group of people who are actually *in* your study. You may not be able to contact or recruit all of the people you actually sample, or some could drop out over the course of the study. The group that actually completes your study is a subsample of the

population The group you want to generalize to and the group you sample from in a study.

sampling frame The list from which you draw your sample. In some cases, there is no list; you draw your sample based upon an explicit rule. For instance, when doing quota sampling of passersby at the local mall, you do not have a list *per se*, and the sampling frame consists of both the population of people who pass by within the time frame of your study and the rule(s) you use to decide whom to select.

sample The actual units you select to participate in your study.

sampling The process of drawing a subset of objects from a population so that results with the subset may be generalized to the population.

sample; it doesn't include nonrespondents or dropouts. (The problem of nonresponse and its effects on a study will be addressed in Chapter 7, "Design," when discussing mortality threats to internal validity.)

People often confuse the idea of **random selection** with the idea of random assignment. You should make sure that you understand the distinction between random selection and random assignment described in Chapter 8, "Experimental Design."

At this point, you should appreciate that sampling is a challenging multistep process and that you can go wrong in many places. In fact, as you move from each step to the next in identifying a sample, there is the possibility of introducing systematic error or *bias*. For instance, even if you are able to identify perfectly the population of interest, you may not have access to all of it. Even if you do, you may not have a complete and accurate sampling frame from which to select. Even if you do, you may not draw the sample correctly or accurately. And even if you do, your participants may not all come and they may not all stay. Depressed yet? Sampling is a difficult business indeed. At times like this, I'm reminded of what one of my professors, Donald Campbell, used to say (I'll paraphrase here): "Cousins to the amoeba, it's amazing that we know anything at all!"

random selection Process or procedure that assures that the different units in your population are selected by chance.

2-3 STATISTICAL TERMS IN SAMPLING

Let's begin by defining some simple terms that are relevant here. First, let's look at the results of sampling efforts. When you sample, the units that you sample—usually people—supply you with one or more responses. In this sense, a **response** is a specific measurement value that a sampling unit supplies. In Figure 2-4, the person responding to a survey instrument gives a response of "4." When you summarize the numerical responses from a group of people, you use a **statistic** (Marriott, 1990). There are a wide variety of statistics you can use: mean, median, mode, and so on. In this example, the mean or average for the sample is 3.72, but the reason you sample is to get an estimate for the population from which you sampled. If you could, you would probably prefer to measure the entire population. If you measure the entire population and calculate a value like a mean or average, this is not referred to as a statistic; it is a **population parameter.**

response A specific measurement value that a sampling unit supplies.

statistic A specific value that is estimated from data.

population parameter The mean or average you would obtain if you were able to sample the entire population.

2-3a The Sampling Distribution

So, how do you get from sample statistic to an estimate of the population parameter? A crucial midway concept you need to understand is the **sampling distribution** (Marriott, 1990). To understand it, you have to be able and willing to do a thought experiment.

sampling distribution The theoretical distribution of an infinite number of samples of the population of interest in your study.

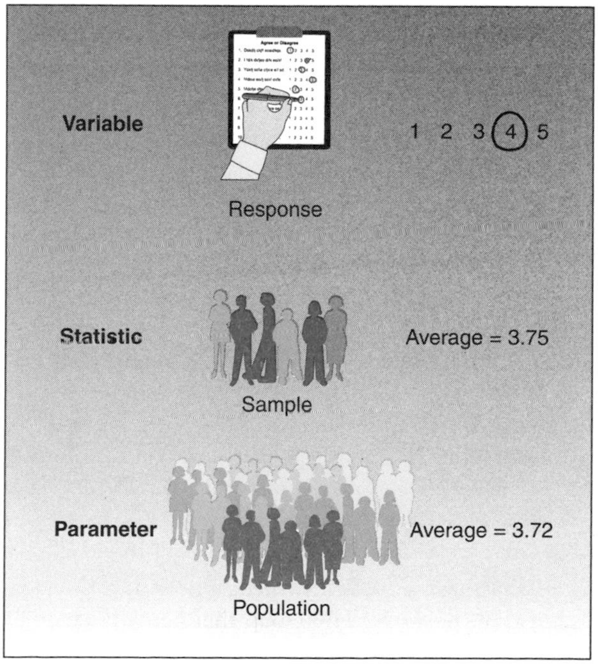

FIGURE 2-4
Statistical Terms in Sampling

Variable

Response

Statistic

Average = 3.75

Sample

Parameter

Average = 3.72

Population

FIGURE 2-5
The Sampling Distribution

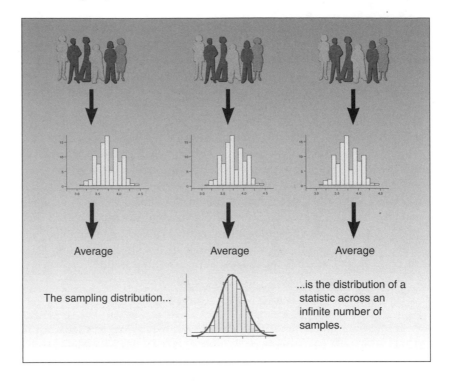

Imagine that instead of just taking a single sample like you do in a typical study, you took three independent samples of the same population. Furthermore, imagine that for each of your three samples, you collected a single response and computed a single statistic—say, the mean of the response for each sample. This is depicted in the top part of Figure 2-5. Even though all three samples came from the same population, you wouldn't expect to get the exact same statistic from each. They would differ slightly due to the random luck of the draw or to the natural fluctuations of drawing a sample. However, you would expect all three samples to yield a similar statistical estimate because they were drawn from the same population.

Now, for the leap of imagination! Imagine that you took an *infinite* number of samples from the same population and computed the average for each one. If you plotted the averages on a histogram or bar graph, you should find that most of them converge on the same central value and that you get fewer and fewer samples that have averages farther up or down from that central value. In other words, the bar graph would be well described by the bell-curve shape that is an indication of a normal distribution in statistics. This is depicted in the bottom part of Figure 2-5. The distribution of an infinite number of samples of the same size as the sample in your study is known as the *sampling distribution*.

You don't ever actually construct a sampling distribution. Why not? You're not paying attention! Because to construct one, you would have to take an *infinite* number of samples and at least the last time I checked, on this planet infinite is not a number we know how to reach. So, why do researchers even talk about a sampling distribution? Now that's a good question! Because you need to realize that your sample is just one of a potentially infinite number of samples that you could have taken. When you keep the sampling distribution in mind, you realize that while the statistic from your sample is probably near the center of the sampling distribution (because most of the samples would be there), you could have gotten one of the extreme samples just by chance. If you take the average of the sampling distribution—the average of the averages of an infinite number of samples— you would be much closer to the true population average—the parameter of interest.

So, the average of the sampling distribution is essentially equivalent to the parameter. But what is the **standard deviation** of the sampling distribution? (Okay, don't remember what a standard deviation is? This is discussed in detail in Section 11-3, "Descriptive Statistics," in Chapter 11.) The standard deviation of the sampling distribution tells us something about how different samples would be distributed. In statistics, it is referred to

standard deviation The spread or variability of the scores around their average in a *single sample*. The standard deviation, often abbreviated SD, is mathematically the square root of the variance. The standard deviation and variance both measure dispersion, but because the standard deviation is measured in the same units as the original measure and the variance is measured in squared units, the standard deviation is usually more directly interpretable and meaningful.

as the **standard error** (so you can keep it separate in your minds from standard deviations). Getting confused? Go get a cup of coffee and come back in 10 minutes. . . . Okay, let's try once more. . . . A standard deviation is the spread of the scores around the average in a *single sample*. The standard error is the spread of the averages around the average of averages in a *sampling distribution*. Got it?

2-3b Sampling Error

In sampling, the standard error is called **sampling error.** Sampling error gives you some idea of the precision of your statistical estimate. A low sampling error means that you had relatively less variability or range in the sampling distribution. High sampling error means that you had relatively greater variability. But here I go again; you never actually see the sampling distribution! So, how do you calculate sampling error? You base your calculation *on the standard deviation of your sample*: the greater the sample's standard deviation, the greater the standard error (and the sampling error). The standard error is also related to the sample size: the greater your sample size, the *smaller* the standard error. Why? Because the greater the sample size, the closer your sample is to the actual population itself. If you take a sample that consists of the entire population, you actually have no sampling error because you don't have a sample; you have the entire population. In that case, the mean you estimate *is* the parameter.

2-3c The 65, 95, 99 Percent Rule

You've probably heard this one before, but it's so important that it's always worth repeating. There is a general rule that applies whenever you have a normal or bell-shaped distribution. Start with the average—the center of the distribution. If you go up and down (that is, left and right) from the center one standard unit, you will include approximately 65 percent of the cases in the distribution (65 percent of the area under the curve). If you go up and down two standard units, you will include approximately 95 percent of the cases. If you go plus or minus three standard units, you will include 99 percent of the cases.

Notice that I didn't specify in the previous few sentences whether I was talking about standard *deviation* units or standard *error* units. That's because the same rule holds for both types of distributions (the raw data and sampling distributions). For instance, in Figure 2-6, the mean of the distribution is 3.75 and the standard unit is .25. (If this were a distribution of raw data, we would be talking in standard-deviation units. If it were a sampling distribution, we'd be talking in standard-error units.) If you go up and down one

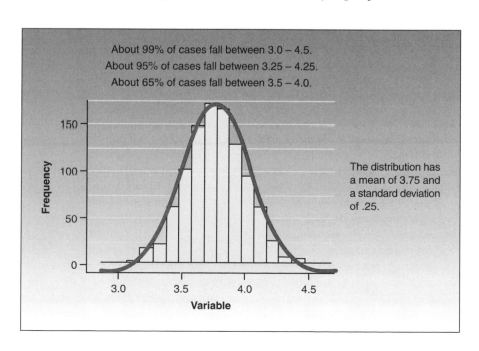

About 99% of cases fall between 3.0 – 4.5.
About 95% of cases fall between 3.25 – 4.25.
About 65% of cases fall between 3.5 – 4.0.

The distribution has a mean of 3.75 and a standard deviation of .25.

FIGURE 2-6
The 65, 95, 99 Percent Rule

standard unit from the mean, you would be going up and down .25 from the mean of 3.75. Within this range—3.5 to 4.0—you would expect to see approximately 65 percent of the cases. I leave it to you to figure out the other ranges. What does this all mean, you ask? If you are dealing with raw data and you know the mean and standard deviation of a sample, you can *predict* the intervals within which 65, 95, and 99 percent of your cases would be expected to fall. We call these intervals the—guess what—65, 95, and 99 percent confidence intervals.

Now, here's where everything should come together in one great Aha! experience if you've been following along. If you have a *sampling distribution*, you should be able to predict the 65, 95, and 99 percent confidence intervals for where the population parameter should be, and isn't that why you sampled in the first place? So that you could predict where the population is on that variable? There's only one hitch. You don't actually have the sampling distribution. (I know this is the third time I've said this.) However, you do have the distribution for the sample itself, and from that distribution, you can estimate the standard error (the sampling error) because it is based on the standard deviation and you have that. Of course, you don't actually know the *population parameter* value; you're trying to find that out, but you can use your best estimate for that—the sample statistic. Now, if you have the mean of the sampling distribution (or set it to the mean from your sample) and you have an estimate of the standard error, which you calculate from your sample, you have the two key ingredients that you need for your sampling distribution to estimate confidence intervals for the population parameter.

Perhaps an example will help. Let's assume you did a study and drew a single sample from the population. Furthermore, let's assume that the average for the sample was 3.75 and the standard deviation was .25. This is the raw data distribution depicted in Figure 2-7. What would the sampling distribution be in this case? Well, you don't actually construct it (because you would need to take an infinite number of samples), but you *can* estimate it. For starters, you must assume that the mean of the sampling distribution is the mean of the sample, which is 3.75. Then, you calculate the standard error. To do this, use the standard deviation for your sample and the sample size (in this case, N = 100), which gives you a standard error of .025 (just trust me on this). Now you have everything you need to estimate a confidence interval for the population parameter. You would estimate that the probability is 65 percent, that the true parameter value falls between 3.725 and 3.775 (3.75 plus and minus .025), that the 95 percent confidence interval is 3.700 to 3.800, and that you can say with 99 percent confidence that the population value is between 3.675 and 3.825. Using your sample, you have just estimated the average for your

FIGURE 2-7
Estimating the Population Using a Sampling Distribution

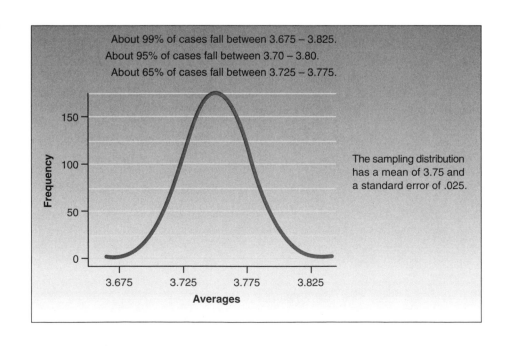

population (that is, the mean of the sample, which is 3.75), and you have given odds that the actual population mean falls within certain ranges.

2-4 PROBABILITY SAMPLING

A **probability sampling** (Henry, 1990) method is any method of sampling that utilizes some form of random selection. To have a random selection method, you must set up some process or procedure that assures that the different units in your population have equal probabilities of being chosen. Humans have long practiced various forms of random selection, such as picking a name out of a hat, or choosing the short straw. These days, we tend to use computers as the mechanism for generating random numbers as the basis for random selection.

probability sampling Method of sampling that utilizes some form of random selection.

2-4a Some Definitions

Before I can explain the various probability methods, I have to define the following basic terms:

- N is the number of cases in the sampling frame.
- n is the number of cases in the sample.
- NCn is the number of combinations (subsets) of n from N.
- $f = n/N$ is the sampling fraction.

That's it. Now that you understand those terms, I can define the different probability sampling methods.

2-4b Simple Random Sampling

The simplest form of random sampling is called **simple random sampling.** Pretty tricky, huh? Here's the quick description of simple random sampling:

- *Objective*—To select n units out of N such that each NCn has an equal chance of being selected.

- *Procedure*—Use a table of random numbers, a computer random-number generator, or a mechanical device to select the sample.

simple random sampling A method of sampling that involves drawing a sample from a population so that every possible sample has an equal probability of being selected.

Let's see if I can make this somewhat general description a little more real. How do you select a simple random sample? Let's assume that you are doing some research with a small service agency to assess clients' views of quality of service over the past year. First, you have to get the *sampling frame* organized. To accomplish this, you go through agency records to identify every client over the past 12 months. If you're lucky, the agency has accurate computerized records and can quickly produce such a list (see Figure 2-8). Then, you have to draw the *sample* and decide on the number of clients you would like to have in the final sample. For the sake of the example, let's say you want to select 100 clients to survey and that there were 1,000 clients over the past 12 months. Then, the sampling fraction is $f = n/N = 100/1000 = .10$ or 10 percent. To draw the sample, you have several options. You could print the list of 1,000 clients, tear them into separate strips, put the strips in a hat, mix them up, close your eyes, and pull out the first 100. This mechanical procedure would be tedious, and the quality of the sample would depend on how thoroughly you mixed up the paper strips and how randomly you reached into the hat. Perhaps a better procedure would be to use the kind of ball machine that is popular with many of the state lotteries. You would need three sets of balls numbered 0 to 9, one set for each of the digits from 000 to 999. (If you select 000, you call that 1,000.) Number the list of names from 1 to 1,000 and then use the ball machine to select the three digits that select each person. The obvious disadvantage here is that you need to get the ball machines. (Where do they make those things, anyway? Is there a ball machine industry?)

Neither of these mechanical procedures is typically feasible and, with the development of inexpensive computers, there is a much easier way. Here's a simple procedure

FIGURE 2-8
Simple Random Sampling

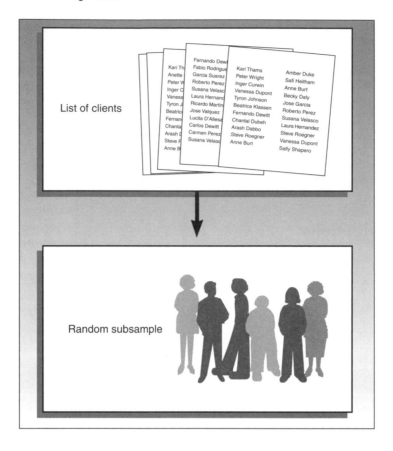

that's especially useful if you have the names of the clients already on the computer. Many computer programs can generate a series of random numbers. Let's assume you copy and paste the list of client names into a column in an Excel spreadsheet. Then, in the column right next to it, paste next to each name the function =RAND(), which is Excel's way of putting a random number between 0 and 1 in the cells. Then, sort both columns—the list of names and the random number—by the column with the random numbers. This rearranges the name list in random order from the lowest to the highest random number. Then, all you have to do is take the first hundred names in this sorted list. Pretty simple. You could probably accomplish the whole thing in under a minute.

Simple random sampling is easy to accomplish and explain to others. Because simple random sampling is a fair way to select a sample, it is reasonable to generalize the results from the sample back to the population. Simple random sampling is not the most statistically efficient method of sampling and you may—just because of the luck of the draw—not get a good representation of subgroups in a population. To deal with these issues, you have to turn to other sampling methods.

2-4c Stratified Random Sampling

stratified random sampling
A method of sampling that involves dividing your population into homogeneous subgroups and then taking a simple random sample in each subgroup.

Stratified random sampling, also sometimes called *proportional* or *quota* random sampling, involves dividing your population into homogeneous subgroups and then taking a simple random sample in each subgroup. A homogeneous subgroup is a group in which all of the members are relatively similar. The following restates this in more formal terms:

Objective: Divide the population into nonoverlapping groups (*strata*) $N1$, $N2$, $N3$, . . . Ni, such that $N1 + N2 + N3 + . . . + Ni = N$. Then do a simple random sample of $f = n/N$ in each strata.

You might prefer stratified sampling to simple random sampling for several reasons. First, it assures that you will be able to represent not only the overall population, but also key subgroups of the population, especially small minority groups. If you want to be able to talk about subgroups, this may be the only way to ensure effectively that you'll be able

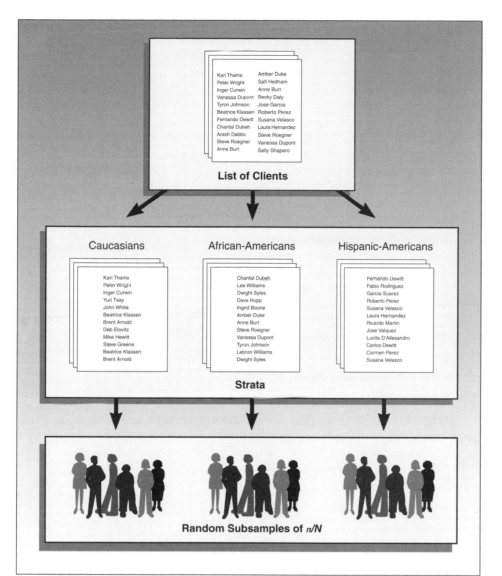

FIGURE 2-9
Stratified Random Sampling

to do so. If the subgroup is extremely small, you can use different sampling fractions (*f*) within the different strata to randomly oversample the small group. (Although you'll then have to weight the within-group estimates using the sampling fraction whenever you want overall population estimates. What does this mean? In a weighted analysis, you typically multiply the estimate by the weight—in this case, the sampling fraction.) When you use the same sampling fraction within strata, you are conducting *proportionate* stratified random sampling. Using different sampling fractions in the strata is called *disproportionate* stratified random sampling. Second, stratified random sampling has more statistical precision than simple random sampling if the strata or groups are homogeneous. If they are, you should expect the variability within groups to be lower than the variability for the population as a whole. Stratified sampling capitalizes on that fact.

For example, let's say that the population of clients for your agency can be divided as shown in Figure 2-9 into three groups: Caucasian, African-American, and Hispanic-American. Furthermore, let's assume that both the African-Americans and Hispanic-Americans are relatively small minorities of the clientele (10 percent and 5 percent, respectively). If you just did a simple random sample of $n = 100$ with a sampling fraction of 10 percent, you would expect by chance alone to get 10 and 5 persons from each of the two smaller groups. And, by chance, you could get even fewer than that! If you stratify, you can do better. First, you would determine how many people you want to have in each group. Let's say you still want to take a sample of 100 from the population of 1,000 clients over the past year, but suppose you think that to say anything about subgroups, you will need at least 25 cases in each group. So, you sample 50 Caucasians, 25 African-Americans, and 25 Hispanic-Americans. You know that 10 percent of the population, or 100 clients, are African-American. If you randomly sample 25 of these, you have a within-stratum sampling fraction of 25/100 = 25%. Similarly, you know that 5 percent, or 50 clients, are Hispanic-American. So, your within-stratum sampling fraction will be 25/50 = 50%. Finally, by subtraction you know there are 850 Caucasian clients. Your within-stratum sampling fraction for them is 50/850 = about 5.88%. Because the groups are more homogeneous within group than across the population as a whole, you can expect greater statistical precision (less variance), and, because you stratified, you know you will have enough cases from each group to make meaningful subgroup inferences.

2-4d Systematic Random Sampling

systematic random sampling
A sampling method in which you determine randomly where you want to start selecting in the sampling frame and then follow a rule to select every xth element in the sampling frame list (where the ordering of the list is assumed to be random).

Systematic random sampling is a sampling method where you determine randomly where you want to start selecting in the *sampling frame* and then follow a rule to select every xth element in the sampling frame list (where the ordering of the list is assumed to be random). To achieve a systematic random sample, follow these steps:

1. Number the units in the population from 1 to N.
2. Decide on the n (sample size) that you want or need.
3. Calculate K = N/n = the interval size.
4. Randomly select an integer between 1 and K.
5. Take every Kth unit.

All of this will be much clearer with an example. Let's assume, as shown in Figure 2-10, that you have a population that only has N = 100 people in it and that you want to take a sample of n = 20. To use systematic sampling, the population must be listed in

FIGURE 2-10
Systematic Random Sampling

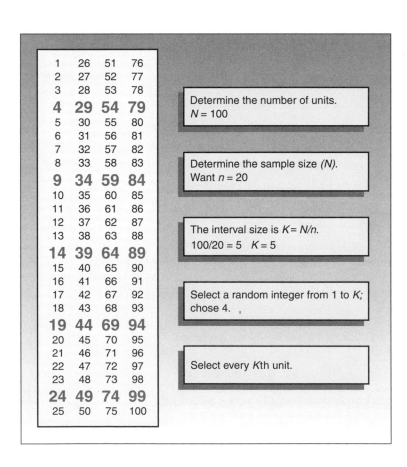

a random order. The sampling fraction would be f = 20/100 = 20%. In this case, the interval size, K, is equal to N/n = 100/20 = 5. Now, select a random integer from 1 to 5. In this example, imagine that you chose 4. Now, to select the sample, start with the 4th unit in the list and take every Kth unit (every 5th, because K = 5). You would be sampling units 4, 9, 14, 19, and so on to 100, and you would wind up with 20 units in your sample.

For this to work, it is essential that the units in the population be randomly ordered, at least with respect to the characteristics you are measuring. Why would you ever want to use systematic random sampling? For one thing, it is fairly easy to do. You only have to select a single random number to start things off. It may also be more precise than simple random sampling. Finally, in some situations, there is simply no easier way to do random sampling. For instance, I once had to do a study that involved sampling from all the books in a library. Once selected, I would have to go to the shelf, locate the book, and record when it last circulated. I knew that I had a fairly good sampling frame in the form of the shelf list (which is a card catalog where the entries are arranged in the order they occur on the shelf). To do a simple random sample, I could have estimated the total number of books and generated random numbers to draw the sample, but how would I find book #74,329 easily if that is the number I selected? I couldn't very well count the cards until I came to 74,329! Stratifying wouldn't solve that problem either. For instance, I could have stratified by card catalog drawer and drawn a simple random sample within each drawer. But I'd still be stuck counting cards. Instead, I did a systematic random sample. I estimated the number of books in the entire collection. Let's imagine it was 100,000. I decided that I wanted to take a sample of 1,000 for a sampling fraction of 1,000/100,000 = 1%. To get the sampling interval K, I divided N/n = 100,000/1,000 = 100. Then I selected a random integer between 1 and 100. Let's say I got 57. Next, I did a little side study to determine how thick a thousand cards are in the card catalog (taking into account the varying ages of the cards). Let's say that, on average, I found that two cards that were separated by 100 cards were about .75 inches apart in the catalog drawer. That information gave me everything I needed to draw the sample. I counted to the 57th by hand and recorded the book information. Then, I took a compass. (Remember those from your high-school math class? They're the funny little metal instruments with a sharp pin on one end and a pencil on the other that you used to draw circles in geometry class.) Then I set the compass at .75 inches, stuck the pin end in at the 57th card, and pointed with the pencil end to the next card (approximately 100 books away). In this way, I approximated selecting the 157th, 257th, 357th, and so on. I was able to accomplish the entire selection procedure in very little time using this systematic random sampling approach. I'd probably still be there counting cards if I'd tried another random sampling method. (Okay, so I have no life. I was compensated nicely, I don't mind saying, for coming up with this scheme.)

2-4e Cluster (Area) Random Sampling

The problem with random sampling methods when you have to sample a population that's spread across a wide geographic region is that you will have to cover a lot of ground geographically to get to each of the units you sampled. Imagine taking a simple random sample of all the residents of New York State to conduct personal interviews. By the luck of the draw, you will wind up with respondents who come from all over the state. Your interviewers are going to have a lot of traveling to do. It is precisely to address this problem that **cluster** or **area random sampling** was invented.

In cluster sampling, you follow these steps:

1. Divide population into clusters (usually along geographic boundaries).

2. Randomly sample clusters.

3. Measure *all* units within sampled clusters.

For instance, Figure 2-11 shows a map of the counties in New York State. Let's say that you have to do a survey of town governments that requires you to go to the towns

cluster or **area random sampling**
A sampling method that involves dividing the population into groups called *clusters*, randomly selecting clusters, and then sampling each element in the selected clusters. This method is useful when sampling a population that is spread across a wide geographic area.

FIGURE 2-11

A County-Level Map of New York State Illustrating Cluster (Area) Random Sampling

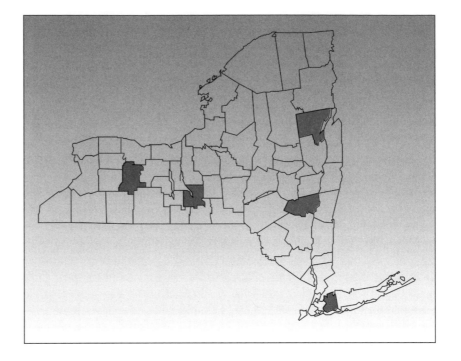

personally to interview key town officials. If you do a simple random sample of towns statewide, your sample is likely to come from all over the state and you will have to be prepared to cover the entire state geographically. Instead, you can do a cluster sampling of counties, let's say five counties in this example (shaded in the figure). Once these are selected, you go to *every* town government in the five county areas. Clearly, this strategy will help you economize on mileage. Instead of having to travel all over the state, you can concentrate exclusively within the counties you selected. Cluster or area sampling is useful in situations like this and is done primarily for efficiency of administration.

2-4f Multistage Sampling

The four methods covered so far—simple, stratified, systematic, and cluster—are the simplest random sampling strategies. In most real applied social research, you would use sampling methods that are considerably more complex than these simple variations. The most important principle here is that you can combine these simple methods in a variety of useful ways to help you address your sampling needs in the most efficient and effective manner possible. Combining sampling methods is called **multistage sampling.**

For example, consider the idea of sampling New York State residents for face-to-face interviews. Clearly, you would want to do some type of cluster random sampling as the first stage of the process. You might sample townships or census tracts throughout the state. In cluster sampling, you would then measure everyone in the clusters you selected. Even if you are sampling census tracts, you may not be able to measure *everyone* who is in the census tract. So, you might set up a systematic random sampling process within the clusters. In this case, you would have a two-stage sampling process with stratified samples within cluster samples. Alternatively, consider the problem of sampling students in grade schools. You might begin with a national sample of school districts stratified by economics and educational level. Within selected districts, you might do a simple random sample of schools; within schools, you might do a simple random sample of classes or grades; and within classes, you might even do a simple random sample of students. In this case, you have three or four stages in the sampling process, and you use both stratified and simple random sampling. By combining different sampling methods, you can achieve a rich variety of probabilistic sampling methods to fit a wide range of social research contexts.

multistage sampling The combining of several sampling techniques to create a more efficient or effective sample than the use of any one sampling type can achieve on its own.

2-5 NONPROBABILITY SAMPLING

The difference between nonprobability and probability sampling is that **nonprobability sampling** (Henry, 1990) does not involve random selection and probability sampling does. Does that mean that nonprobability samples aren't representative of the population? Not necessarily, but it does mean nonprobability samples cannot depend upon the rationale of probability theory. At least with a probabilistic sample, you know the odds or probability that you have represented the population well. You can estimate confidence intervals for the statistic. With nonprobability samples, you may or may not represent the population well, and it will often be hard for you to know how well you've done so. In general, researchers prefer probabilistic or random sampling methods to nonprobabilistic ones and consider them to be more accurate and rigorous. However, in some circumstances in applied social research, it is not feasible, practical, or theoretically sensible to use random sampling. In the following paragraphs, I will present a variety of nonprobabilistic sampling alternatives to the probabilistic methods described earlier.

Nonprobability sampling methods are divided into two broad types: *accidental* or *purposive*. Most sampling methods are purposive in nature because the sampling problem is usually approached with a specific plan in mind. The most important distinctions among nonprobability sampling methods are between the different types of purposive sampling approaches.

nonprobability sampling
Sampling that does not involve random selection.

2-5a Accidental, Haphazard, or Convenience Sampling

One of the most common methods of sampling goes under the various titles listed here: accidental, haphazard, or convenience. I would include in this category the traditional man-on-the-street (of course, now it's probably the person-on-the-street) interviews conducted frequently by television news programs to get a quick (although nonrepresentative) reading of public opinion. I would also argue that the typical use of college students in much psychological research is primarily a matter of convenience. (You don't really believe that psychologists use college students because they think they're representative of the population at large, do you?) In clinical practice, you might use clients available to you as your sample. In many research contexts, you sample by asking for volunteers. Clearly, the problem with all these types of samples is that you have no evidence that they are representative of the populations you're interested in generalizing to, and in many cases, you would suspect that they are not.

2-5b Purposive Sampling

In purposive sampling (Henry, 1990), you sample with a *purpose* in mind. Usually you would be seeking one or more specific predefined groups. For instance, have you ever run into people in a mall or on the street carrying clipboards and stopping various people and asking to interview them? Most likely, they are conducting a purposive sample (and most likely they are engaged in market research). They might be looking for Caucasian females between 30 and 40 years old. They size up the people passing by and stop people who look to be in that category and ask whether they will participate. One of the first things they're likely to do is verify that the respondent does in fact meet the criteria for being in the sample. Purposive sampling can be useful in situations where you need to reach a targeted sample quickly and where sampling for proportionality is not the primary concern. With a purposive sample, you are likely to get the opinions of your target population, but you are also likely to over-represent subgroups in your population that are more readily accessible.

All of the methods that follow can be considered subcategories of purposive sampling methods. You might sample for specific groups or types of people as in modal instance, expert, or quota sampling. You might sample for diversity, as in heterogeneity sampling, or you might capitalize on informal social networks to identify specific respondents who are hard to locate otherwise, as in snowball sampling. In all of these methods, you know what you want—you are sampling with a purpose.

Modal Instance Sampling

In statistics, the *mode* is the most frequently occurring value in a distribution. In sampling, when you use **modal instance sampling,** you are sampling the most frequent case, or the typical case. Many informal public opinion polls, for instance, interview a typical voter. For instance, you see this approach used all the time on evening news programs. The newscaster goes out and interviews a "typical" voter to get an idea of what voters are thinking about. Or they interview a few people from a "typical" town (an example of modal sampling towns rather than individuals). This sampling approach has a number of problems: First, how do you know what the typical or modal case is? You could say that the modal voter is a person of average age, educational level, and income in the population, but it's not clear that using the averages of these is the fairest (consider the skewed distribution of income, for instance). Additionally, how do you know that those three variables—age, education, income—are the ones most relevant for classifying the typical voter? What if religion or ethnicity is an important determinant of voting decisions? Clearly, modal instance sampling is only sensible for informal sampling contexts.

Expert Sampling

Expert sampling involves the assembling of a sample of persons with known or demonstrable experience and expertise in some area. A common example of this type of sample is a panel of experts. There are actually two reasons you might do expert sampling. First, it is the best way to elicit the views of persons who have specific expertise. Here, it's clear why we consider expert sampling a subtype of purposive sampling. When someone says they used expert sampling in a study, all they are saying is that the specific purpose for their sampling was to identify experts. The other reason you might use expert sampling is to provide evidence for the *validity* of another sampling approach you've chosen. For instance, let's say you do modal instance sampling and are concerned that the criteria you used for defining the modal instance is subject to criticism. You might assemble an expert panel consisting of persons with acknowledged experience and insight into that field or topic and ask them to examine your modal definitions and comment on their appropriateness and validity. The advantage of doing this is that you aren't out on your own trying to defend your decisions; you have some acknowledged experts to back you. The disadvantage is that even the experts can be, and often are, wrong.

Quota Sampling

In **quota sampling,** you select people nonrandomly according to some fixed quota. The two types of quota sampling are proportional and nonproportional. In **proportional quota sampling,** you want to represent the major characteristics of the population by sampling a proportional amount of each. For instance, if you know the population has 40 percent women and 60 percent men, and that you want a total sample size of 100, you should continue sampling until you get those percentages and then stop. So, if you already have the 40 women for your sample, but not the 60 men, you would continue to sample men but even if legitimate women respondents come along, you would not sample them because you have already met your quota. The problem here (as in much purposive sampling) is that you have to decide the specific characteristics on which you will base the quota. Will it be by gender, age, education, race, or religion, etc.?

Nonproportional quota sampling is less restrictive. In this method, you specify the minimum number of sampled units you want in each category. Here, you're not concerned with having numbers that match the proportions in the population. Instead, you simply want to have enough to assure that you will be able to talk about even small groups in the population. This method is similar to stratified random sampling in that it is typically used to assure that smaller groups are adequately represented in your sample.

Heterogeneity Sampling

You sample for heterogeneity when you want to include all opinions or views, and you aren't concerned about representing these views proportionately. Another term for this is sampling for *diversity*. In many brainstorming or nominal group processes, you would use some form of heterogeneity sampling because your primary interest is in getting a broad spectrum of ideas, not identifying the average or modal instance ones. In effect, what you would like to be sampling is not people, but ideas. You imagine that there is a universe of all possible ideas relevant to some topic and that you want to sample this population, not the population of people who have the ideas. Clearly, to get all of the ideas, and especially the unusual ones, you have to include a broad and diverse range of participants. **Heterogeneity sampling** is, in this sense, almost the opposite of modal instance sampling.

heterogeneity sampling Sampling for diversity or variety.

Snowball Sampling
In **snowball sampling,** you begin by identifying people who meet the criteria for inclusion in your study. You then ask them to recommend others they know who also meet the criteria. In recent years, there have been some exciting developments in snowball sampling approaches. A method called respondent-driven sampling (RDS), although essentially a form of snowball sampling, has been shown to yield results comparable to probability sampling (Heckathorn, 1997). Snowball sampling is especially useful when you are trying to reach populations that are inaccessible or hard to find. For instance, if you are studying the homeless, you are not likely to be able to find good lists of homeless people within a specific geographical area. However, if you go to that area and identify one or two, you may find that they know who the other homeless people in their vicinity are and how you can find them.

snowball sampling A sampling method in which you sample participants based upon referral from prior participants.

SUMMARY

So, that's the basics of sampling methods. Quite a few options, aren't there? How about a table to summarize the choices and give you some idea of when they might be appropriate? Table 2-1 shows each sampling method, when it might best be used, and the major advantages and disadvantages of each.

Sampling is a critical component in virtually all social research. Although I've presented a wide variety of sampling methods in this chapter, it's important that you keep them in perspective. The key is not which sampling method you use. The key is *external validity*—how valid the inferences from your sample are. You can have the best sampling method in the world and it won't guarantee that your gen-

eralizations are valid (although it does help!). Alternatively, you can use a relatively weak nonprobability sampling method and find that it is perfectly useful for your context. Ultimately whether your generalizations from your study to other persons, places, or times are valid is a judgment. Your critics, readers, friends, supporters, funders, and so on, will judge the quality of your generalizations, and they may not even agree with each other in their judgment. What might be convincing to one person or group may fail with another. Your job as a social researcher is to create a sampling strategy that is appropriate to the context and will assure that your generalizations are as convincing as possible to as many audiences as is feasible.

SUGGESTED WEBSITES

Note: These websites were functional when we went to press. Please access the Online Study Guide Edition for the most up-to-date URLs.

The National Opinion Research Center
http://www.norc.uchicago.edu/
Located at the University of Chicago, this research center conducts both national and smaller scale survey research projects. Perusing the site will show you many excellent examples of the kind of research that can be done using surveys and the ways that sampling strategies are developed.

Web Interface for Statistics Education
http://wise.cgu.edu/
Dale Berger is a professor at Claremont Graduate University in California. His statistics education website offers a wealth of resources, including tutorials on sampling that will help further your understanding of the material in this chapter. The site also has many other interesting and helpful tutorials, as well as links relevant to other topics in the text.

TABLE 2-1   **Summary of Sampling Methods**

Sampling Method	Use	Advantages	Disadvantages
Simple random sampling	Anytime	Simple to implement; easy to explain to nontechnical audiences	Requires a sample list (sampling frame) from which to select
Stratified random sampling	When concerned about underrepresenting smaller subgroups	Allows you to oversample minority groups to assure enough for subgroup analyses	Requires a sample list (sampling frame) from which to select
Systematic random sampling	When you want to sample every Kth element in an ordered set	Don't have to count through all of the elements in the list to find the ones randomly selected	If the order of elements is nonrandom, could be systematic bias
Cluster (area) random sampling	When organizing geographically makes sense	More efficient than other methods when sampling across a geographically dispersed area	Usually not used alone; coupled with other methods in a multistage approach
Multistage random sampling	Anytime	Combines sophistication with efficiency	Can be complex and difficult to explain to nontechnical audiences
Accidental, haphazard, or convenience nonprobability sampling	Anytime	Very easy to do; almost like not sampling at all	Very weak external validity; likely to be biased
Modal instance purposive nonprobability sampling	When you only want to measure a typical respondent	Easily understood by nontechnical audiences	Results only limited to the modal case; little external validity
Expert purposive nonprobability sampling	As an adjunct to other sampling strategies	Experts' opinions support research conclusions	Likely to be biased; limited external validity
Quota purposive nonprobability sampling	When you want to represent subgroups	Allows for oversampling smaller subgroups	Likely to be more biased than stratified random sampling; often depends on who comes along when
Heterogeneity purposive nonprobability sampling	When you want to sample for diversity or variety	Easy to implement and explain; useful when you're interested in sampling for variety rather than representativeness	Won't represent population views proportionately
Snowball purposive nonprobability sampling	With hard-to-reach populations	Can be used when there is no sampling frame	Low external validity when used in its traditional form; can have high external validity in its newer respondent-driven sampling (RDS) variation

KEY TERMS

area random sampling (p. 39)
cluster random sampling (p. 39)
expert sampling (p. 42)
external validity (p. 27)
gradient of similarity (p. 28)
heterogeneity sampling (p. 43)
modal instance sampling (p. 42)
multistage sampling (p. 40)
nonprobability sampling (p. 41)
nonproportional quota sampling (p. 42)
population (p. 30)

population parameter (p. 31)
probability sampling (p. 35)
proportional quota sampling (p. 42)
proximal similarity model (p. 27)
quota sampling (p. 42)
random selection (p. 31)
response (p. 31)
sample (p. 30)
sampling (p. 30)
sampling distribution (p. 31)
sampling error (p. 33)

sampling frame (p. 30)
sampling model (p. 27)
simple random sampling (p. 35)
snowball sampling (p. 43)
standard deviation (p. 32)
standard error (p. 33)
statistic (p. 31)
stratified random sampling (p. 36)
systematic random sampling (p. 38)
threat to external validity (p. 29)

REVIEW QUESTIONS

Note: You can find the correct answers to these questions by taking the quiz and then submitting your answers in the Online Study Guide Edition. The program will automatically score your submission. If you miss a question, the program will provide the correct answer, a rationale for the answer, and the section number in the chapter where the topic is discussed.

1. One way to generalize the results in a study to other persons, places, and times is to develop an idea of the degree to which the other contexts are similar to the study context. What is the phrase that describes this theoretical similarity framework?
   a. relationship of similarity
   b. setting of similarity
   c. gradient of similarity
   d. threats to similarity

2. What is the sampling term used to describe the population that a researcher has access to—the sample from which he or she will draw a sample?
   a. the theoretical population
   b. the accessible population
   c. the drawn population
   d. the studied population

3. If we looked at the average college entrance exam score for all first-year college students in the United States, we would be recording what is referred to as a
   a. statistic of that population.
   b. response of that population.
   c. sample distribution of that population.
   d. parameter of that population.

4. A standard error is
   a. the spread of scores around the average of a single sample.
   b. the spread of scores around the average of averages in a sampling distribution.
   c. the spread of scores around the standard deviation of a single sample.
   d. the spread of scores around the standard deviation in a sampling distribution.

5. Which of the following statements about sampling error is most accurate?
   a. The smaller the size of a sample in a research project, the smaller the standard error.
   b. The larger the size of a sample in a research project, the smaller the standard error.
   c. The standard error is completely independent of the size of a sample.
   d. The standard error is synonymous with a sampling error.

6. Picking a name out of a hat is a simple form of
   a. random selection.
   b. stratified selection.
   c. systematic selection.
   d. cluster selection.

7. Three hundred adolescents sign up for a research project that only one hundred can complete. If each adolescent has a 33.3 percent chance of being selected for the project, then the sample is considered a
   a. simple random sampling.
   b. stratified random sampling.
   c. systematic random sampling.
   d. cluster random sampling.

8. If one thousand college sophomores sign up for a research project designed to assess gender and ethnic differences in dating, what must researchers do to ensure that they have a proportionate stratified random sample?
   a. Divide the groups into subgroups according to gender; then randomly draw a sample of equal males and females from the pool.
   b. Divide the groups into subgroups according to ethnic identity and gender; then randomly draw a sample population that would include an equal number of members from each subgroup.
   c. Divide the groups into homogenous subgroups according to ethnic identity and gender; then randomly draw a sample population with the same percentage in each subgroup.
   d. Divide the groups into heterogeneous subgroups according to ethnic identity and gender; then randomly draw a sample population that would reflect the percentage of subgroup membership reflected in the general population.

9. Which sampling process begins with the selection of a single random number and assumes that the characteristics being measured are randomly distributed in the population?
   a. simple random sampling
   b. stratified random sampling
   c. systematic random sampling
   d. cluster random sampling

10. What is the sampling technique that is best used when there is a large geographical area to cover?
   a. simple random sampling
   b. stratified random sampling
   c. systematic random sampling
   d. cluster (area) random sampling

11. The normal distribution is often referred to as the "bell curve" because it provides the "ring of truth."
   a. True
   b. False

12. Surveys reported in the media almost always mention that the numbers presented are accurate within a few percentage points. The statistic used to determine the accuracy of such results is called the standard error.
   a. True
   b. False

13. A study based on a nonprobability sampling method can never be considered representative of the population.
   a. True
   b. False

14. A researcher was trying to study a hard-to-research population (for example, homeless adolescents, migrant workers, cocaine dealers, etc.). The researcher decided to try sampling by tapping the social network of the local population, beginning with the first person she could find and then asking that person to help identify others, who would then be asked to further identify possible participants. This researcher is using a sampling technique known as "avalanche sampling" because pretty soon she could expect to have a very large number of participants.
   a. True
   b. False

15. The main advantage of multistage sampling is that it combines sophistication with efficiency, while the main disadvantage is that it can be complex and difficult to explain to nontechnical audiences.
   a. True
   b. False

MEASUREMENT

3

The Theory of Measurement

Chapter Outline

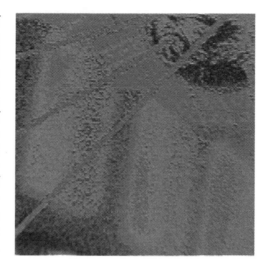

easurement is the process of observing and recording the observations that are collected as part of a research effort. In this chapter, I focus on how we think about and assess quality of measurement. In the section on construct validity, I present the theory of what constitutes a good measure. In the section on reliability of measurement, I consider the consistency or dependability of measurement, including the idea of true score theory and several ways to estimate reliability. In the section on levels of measurement, I describe the four major levels of measurement: nominal, ordinal, interval, and ratio.

3-1 CONSTRUCT VALIDITY

Construct validity refers to the degree to which inferences can legitimately be made from the **operationalizations** in your study to the theoretical constructs on which those operationalizations are based (Cook & Campbell, 1979; Cronbach & Meehl, 1955; Shadish, Cook, & Campbell, 2002). Whoa! Can you believe that the term *operationalization* has eight syllables? That's a mouthful. What does it mean? The key is in the root term "operation." In everyday language, an operation is a specific procedure, the steps you follow to accomplish something. In research, you "operationalize" a concept you want to measure when you describe exactly *how* you'll measure it. An operationalization is your translation of the idea or construct into something real and concrete. Let's say you have an idea for a treatment or program you would like to create. The operationalization is the program or treatment itself, as it exists after you create it. Construct validity is the degree to which the actual (operationalized) program accurately reflects the ideal (the program as you conceptualize or envision it). Imagine that you want to measure the construct of self-esteem. You have an idea of what self-esteem means. Perhaps you construct a 10-item paper-and-pencil instrument to measure that self-esteem concept. The instrument is the operationalization; it's the translation of the idea of self-esteem into something concrete. The construct validity question here would be how well the 10-item instrument (the operationalization) reflects the idea you had of self-esteem. I'll cover this in more detail later in this chapter, but I didn't want to start the chapter by confusing you with an 8-syllable word.

Like external validity (see the discussion in Chapter 2, "Sampling"), construct validity is related to generalizing. However, where external validity involves generalizing from your study context to other people, places, or times, construct validity involves generalizing from your program or measures to the *concept or idea* of your program or measures. You might think of construct validity as a labeling issue. When you implement a program that you call a Head Start program, is your label an accurate one? When you measure what you call self-esteem is that what you are really measuring?

I would like to address two major issues here. The first is the more straightforward one. I'll discuss several ways of thinking about the idea of construct validity, and several metaphors that might provide you with a sense of how profound and rich this idea is. Then, I'll discuss the major construct validity threats, the kinds of arguments your critics are likely to raise when you make a claim that your program or measure is valid.

In this text, as in most research methods texts, construct validity is presented in the section on measurement; it is typically presented as one of many different types of validity (for example, face validity, predictive validity, or concurrent validity) that you might

construct validity The degree to which inferences can legitimately be made from the operationalizations in your study to the theoretical constructs on which those operationalizations are based.

operationalization The act of translating a construct into its manifestation—for example, translating the idea of your treatment or program into the actual program, or translating the idea of what you want to measure into the real measure. The result is also referred to as an *operationalization*; that is, you might describe your actual program as an *operationalized program*.

want to be sure your measures have. I don't see it that way at all. I see construct validity as the overarching quality of measurement with all of the other measurement validity labels falling beneath it. And construct validity is not limited only to measurement. As I've already suggested, it is as relevant to the independent variable—the program or treatment—as it is to the dependent variable. So, I'll try to make some sense of the various measurement validity types in this chapter and try to move you to think instead of the validity of *any* operationalization as falling within the general category of construct validity, with a variety of subcategories and subtypes.

3-1a Measurement Validity Types

There's an awful lot of confusion in the methodological literature that stems from the wide variety of labels used to describe the validity of measures. I want to make two cases here. First, it's dumb to limit our scope only to the validity of measures. I really want to talk about the validity of any operationalization. That is, any time you translate a concept or construct into a functioning and operating reality (the *operationalization*), you need to be concerned about how well you performed the translation. This issue is as relevant when talking about treatments or programs as it is when talking about measures. In fact, come to think of it, you could also think of sampling in this way. The population of interest in your study is the construct, and the sample is your operationalization. If you think of it this way, you are essentially talking about the construct validity of the sampling, and construct validity merges with the idea of external validity as discussed in Chapter 2, "Sampling." The construct validity question, "How well does my sample represent the idea of the population?" merges with the *external validity* question, "How well can I generalize from my sample to the population?" Second, I want to use the term *construct validity* to refer to the general case of translating any construct into an operationalization. Let's use all of the other validity terms to reflect different ways you can demonstrate different aspects of construct validity.

With all that in mind, here's a list of the validity types that are typically mentioned in texts and research papers when talking about the quality of measurement and how I would organize and categorize them:

Construct Validity

- Translation validity
  - Face validity
  - Content validity
- Criterion-related validity
  - Predictive validity
  - Concurrent validity
  - Convergent validity
  - Discriminant validity

I have to warn you here that I made this list up. I'd never heard of translation validity before, but I needed a good name to summarize what both face and content validity are getting at, and that one seemed sensible. (See how easy it is to be a methodologist?) All of the other labels are commonly known, but the way I've organized them is different than I've seen elsewhere.

Let's see if I can make some sense out of this list. First, as mentioned previously, I would like to use the term *construct validity* to be the overarching category. Construct validity is the approximate truth of the conclusion that your operationalization accurately reflects its construct. All of the other validity types essentially address some aspect of this general issue (which is why I've subsumed them under the general category of construct validity). Second, I make a distinction between two broad types of construct validity: translation validity and criterion-related validity. That's because I think these correspond to the two major ways you can assure/assess the validity of an operationalization.

In **translation validity,** you focus on whether the operationalization is a good translation of the construct. This approach is definitional in nature; it assumes you have a good, detailed definition of the construct and that you can check the operationalization against it. In **criterion-related validity,** you examine whether the operationalization behaves the way it should according to some criteria based on your understanding of the construct. This type of validity is a more relational approach to construct validity. It assumes that your operationalization should function in predictable ways in relation to other operationalizations based upon your theory of the construct. (If all this seems a bit dense, hang in there until you've gone through the following discussion and then come back and reread this paragraph.) Let's go through the specific validity types.

translation validity A type of construct validity related to how well you translated the idea of your measure into its operationalization.

criterion-related validity The validation of a measure based on its relationship to another independent measure as predicted by your theory of how the measures should behave.

Translation Validity

In essence, both of the translation validity types (face and content validity) attempt to assess the degree to which you accurately *translated* your construct into the operationalization. Let's look at the two types of translation validity.

Face Validity

In **face validity,** you look at the operationalization and see whether on its face it seems like a good translation of the construct. In other words, does the way you are measuring the construct appear to measure what you want it to? This is probably the weakest way to try to demonstrate construct validity. For instance, you might look at a measure of math ability, read through the questions, and decide it seems like this is a good measure of math ability (the label math ability seems appropriate for this measure). Or you might observe a teenage pregnancy-prevention program and conclude that it is indeed a teenage pregnancy-prevention program. Of course, if this were all you did to assess face validity, it would clearly be weak evidence because it is essentially a subjective judgment call. (Note that just because it is weak evidence doesn't mean that it is wrong. You need to rely on your subjective judgment throughout the research process. It's just that this form of judgment won't be especially convincing to others.) You can improve the quality of a face-validity assessment considerably by making it more systematic. For instance, if you were trying to assess the face validity of a math-ability measure, it would be more convincing if you sent the test to a carefully selected sample of experts on math-ability testing and they all reported back with the judgment that your measure appears to be a good measure of math ability.

face validity A type of validity that assures that "on its face" the operationalization seems like a good translation of the construct.

Content Validity

In **content validity,** you essentially check the operationalization against the relevant content domain for the construct. The content domain is like a comprehensive checklist of the traits of your construct. This approach assumes that you have a good detailed description of the content domain, something that's not always true. Let's look at an example where it is true. You might lay out all of the characteristics of a teenage pregnancy-prevention program. You would probably include in this domain specification the definition of the target group, a description of whether the program is preventive in nature (as opposed to treatment-oriented), and the content that should be included, such as basic information on pregnancy, the use of abstinence, birth control methods, and so on. Then, armed with these characteristics, you create a type of checklist when examining your program. Only programs that have these characteristics can legitimately be defined as teenage pregnancy-prevention programs. This all sounds fairly straightforward, and for many operationalizations, it may be. However, for other constructs (such as self-esteem or intelligence), it will not be easy to decide which characteristics constitute the content domain.

content validity A check of the operationalization against the relevant content domain for the construct.

Criterion-Related Validity

In criterion-related validity, you check the performance of your operationalization against some criterion. How is this different from translation validity? In translation validity, the question is, how well did you translate the idea of the construct into its manifestation? No other measure comes into play. In criterion-related validity, you usually make a prediction about how the operationalization will *perform on some other measure* based on your theory of the construct. The differences among the criterion-related validity types are in the criteria they use as the standard for judgment.

For example, think again about measuring self-esteem. For content validity, you would try to describe all the things that self-esteem is in your mind and translate that into a measure. You might say that self-esteem involves how good you feel about yourself, that it includes things like your self-confidence and the degree to which you think positively about yourself. You could translate these notions into specific questions, a translation validity approach. On the other hand, you might reasonably expect that people with high self-esteem, as you interpret it, would tend to act in certain ways. You might expect that you could distinguish them from people with low self-esteem. For instance, you might argue that high self-esteem people will volunteer for a task that requires self-confidence (such as speaking in public). Notice that in this case, you validate your self-esteem measure by demonstrating that it is correlated with some other independent indicator (raising hands to volunteer) that you theoretically expect high self-esteem people to exhibit. This is the essential idea of criterion-related validity: validating a measure based on its relationship to another independent measure.

predictive validity A type of construct validity based on the idea that your measure is able to predict what it theoretically should be able to predict.

Predictive Validity In **predictive validity,** you assess the operationalization's ability to predict something it should theoretically be able to predict. For instance, you might theorize that a measure of math ability should be able to predict how well a person will do in an engineering-based profession. You could give your measure to experienced engineers and see whether there is a high correlation between scores on the measure and their salaries as engineers. A high correlation would provide evidence for predictive validity; it would show that your measure can correctly predict something that you theoretically think it should be able to predict.

concurrent validity An operationalization's ability to distinguish between groups that it should theoretically be able to distinguish between.

Concurrent Validity In **concurrent validity,** you assess the operationalization's ability to distinguish between groups that it should theoretically be able to distinguish between. For example, if you come up with a way of assessing depression, your measure should be able to distinguish between people who are diagnosed as depressed and those diagnosed paranoid schizophrenic. If you want to assess the concurrent validity of a new measure of empowerment, you might give the measure to both migrant farm workers and to the farm owners, theorizing that your measure should show that the farm owners are higher in empowerment. As in any discriminating test, the results are more powerful if you are able to show that you can discriminate between two similar groups than if you can show that you can discriminate between two groups that are very different.

convergent validity The degree to which the operationalization is similar to (converges on) other operationalizations to which it should be theoretically similar.

Convergent Validity In **convergent validity,** you examine the degree to which the operationalization is similar to (converges on) other operationalizations to which it theoretically should be similar. For instance, to show the convergent validity of a Head Start program, you might gather evidence that shows that the program is similar to other Head Start programs. To show the convergent validity of a test of arithmetic skills, you might correlate the scores on your test with scores on other tests that purport to measure basic math ability, where high correlations would be evidence of convergent validity.

discriminant validity The degree to which concepts that should not be related theoretically are, in fact, not interrelated in reality.

Discriminant Validity In **discriminant validity,** you examine the degree to which the operationalization is not similar to (diverges from) other operationalizations that it theoretically should not be similar to. For instance, to show the discriminant validity of a Head Start program, you might gather evidence that shows that the program is not similar to other early childhood programs that don't label themselves as Head Start programs. To show the discriminant validity of a test of arithmetic skills, you might correlate the scores on your test with scores on tests of verbal ability, where low correlations would be evidence of discriminant validity.

3-1b Idea of Construct Validity

Construct validity refers to the degree to which inferences can legitimately be made from the operationalizations in your study to the theoretical constructs on which those operationalizations were based. (I know I've said this before, but it never hurts to repeat some-

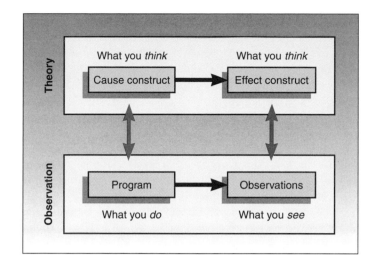

thing, especially when it sounds complicated.) I find that it helps me when thinking about construct validity to make a distinction between two broad territories that I call the *land of theory* and the *land of observation,* as illustrated in Figure 3-1. The land of theory is what goes on inside your mind, and your attempt to explain or articulate this to others. It is all of the ideas, theories, hunches, and hypotheses you have about the world. In the land of theory, you think of the program or treatment as it should be. In the land of theory, you have the idea or construct of the outcomes or measures you are trying to affect. The land of observation, on the other hand, consists of what you actually see or measure happening in the world around you and the public manifestations of that world. In the land of observation, you find your actual program or treatment, and your actual measures or observational procedures. If you have construct validity, then you have constructed the land of observation based on your ideas in the land of theory. You developed the program to reflect the kind of program you had in mind. You created the measures to get at what you wanted to get at.

Construct validity is an assessment of how well your actual programs or measures reflect your ideas or theories—how well the bottom of Figure 3-1 reflects the top. Why is this important? Because when you think about the world or talk about it with others (land of theory), you are using words that represent concepts. If you tell parents that a special type of math tutoring will help their child do better in math, you are communicating at the level of concepts or constructs. You aren't describing in operational detail the specific things that the tutor will do with their child. You aren't describing the specific questions that will be on the math test on which their child will excel. You are talking in general terms, using constructs. If you based your recommendation on research that showed that the special type of tutoring improved children's math scores, you would want to be sure that the type of tutoring you are referring to is the same as what that study implemented and that the type of outcome you're saying should occur was the type the study measured. Otherwise, you would be mislabeling or misrepresenting the research. In this sense, construct validity can be viewed as a *truth in labeling* issue.

3-1c Convergent and Discriminant Validity

Convergent and discriminant validity are both considered subcategories or subtypes of construct validity (Campbell & Fiske, 1959). The important thing to recognize is that they work together; if you can demonstrate that you have evidence for both convergent and discriminant validity, you have by definition demonstrated that you have evidence for construct validity. However, neither one alone is sufficient for establishing construct validity.

I find it easiest to think about convergent and discriminant validity as two interlocking propositions. In simple words, I would describe what they are doing as follows:

- Measures of constructs that theoretically *should* be related to each other are, in fact, observed to be related to each other (that is, you should be able to show a correspondence or *convergence* between similar constructs).

- Measures of constructs that theoretically should *not* be related to each other are, in fact, observed not to be related to each other (that is, you should be able to *discriminate* between dissimilar constructs).

To estimate the degree to which any two measures are related to each other you would typically use the correlation coefficient discussed in Chapter 11, "Analysis." That is, you look at the patterns of intercorrelations among the measures. Correlations between theoretically similar measures should be "high," whereas correlations between theoretically dissimilar measures should be "low."

The main problem that I have with this convergent-discriminant idea has to do with my use of the quotations around the terms *high* and *low* in the previous sentence. The problem is simple: How high do correlations need to be to provide evidence for convergence, and how low do they need to be to provide evidence for discrimination? The answer is that nobody knows! In general, convergent correlations should be as high as possible, and discriminant ones should be as low as possible, but there is no hard and fast rule. Well, let's not let that stop us. One thing you can assume to be true is that the convergent correlations should always be higher than the discriminant ones. At least that helps a bit.

Before we get too deep into the idea of convergence and discrimination, let's take a look at each one by using a simple example.

Convergent Validity   To establish convergent validity, you need to show that measures that should be related are in reality related. In Figure 3-2, you see four measures (each is an item on a scale) that supposedly reflect the construct of self-esteem. For instance, Item 1 might be the statement, "I feel good about myself," rated using a 1-to-5 scale. You theorize that all four items reflect the idea of self-esteem (which is why I labeled the top part of the figure "Theory"). On the bottom part of the figure ("Observation"), you see the intercorrelations of the four scale items. This might be based on giv-

FIGURE 3-2
Convergent Validity Correlations

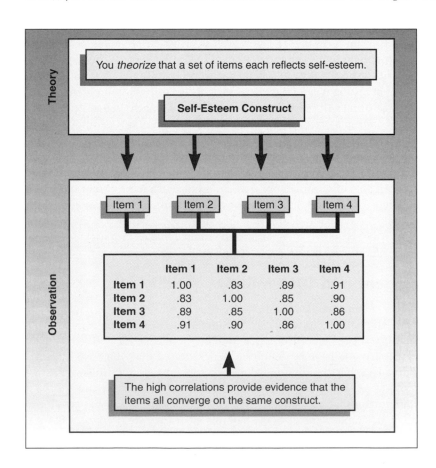

You *theorize* that a set of items each reflects self-esteem.

Self-Esteem Construct

	Item 1	Item 2	Item 3	Item 4
Item 1	1.00	.83	.89	.91
Item 2	.83	1.00	.85	.90
Item 3	.89	.85	1.00	.86
Item 4	.91	.90	.86	1.00

The high correlations provide evidence that the items all converge on the same construct.

ing your scale out to a sample of respondents. You should readily see that the item intercorrelations for all item pairings are extremely high. (Remember that correlations range from −1.00 to +1.00.) The correlations provide support for your theory that all four items are related to the same construct.

Notice, however, that whereas the high intercorrelations demonstrate that the four items are probably related to the same construct, that doesn't automatically mean that the construct is self-esteem. Maybe there's some other construct to which all four items are related (see "Putting It All Together" in Section 3-1c).

However, at least, you can assume from the pattern of correlations that the four items are converging on the same thing, whatever it might be called.

Discriminant Validity   To establish discriminant validity, you need to show that measures that should not be related are in reality not related. In Figure 3-3, you again see four measures (each is an item on a scale). Here, however, two of the items are thought to reflect the construct of self-esteem, whereas the other two are thought to reflect a different construct called locus of control. The top part of the figure shows the theoretically expected relationships among the four items. If you have discriminant validity, the relationship between measures from different constructs should be low. (Again, nobody knows how low they should be, but I'll deal with that later.) There are four correlations between measures that reflect different constructs, and these are shown on the bottom of the figure ("Observation"). You should see immediately that these four cross-construct correlations are low (near zero) and certainly much lower than the convergent correlations in Figure 3-2.

Just because there is evidence that the two sets of two measures seem to be related to different constructs (because their intercorrelations are so low) doesn't mean that the constructs they're related to are self-esteem and locus of control. However, the correlations do provide evidence that the two sets of measures are discriminated from each other.

Putting It All Together   Okay, so where does this leave us? I've shown how to provide evidence for convergent and discriminant validity separately, but as I said at the outset, to argue for construct validity, you really need to be able to show that both of these

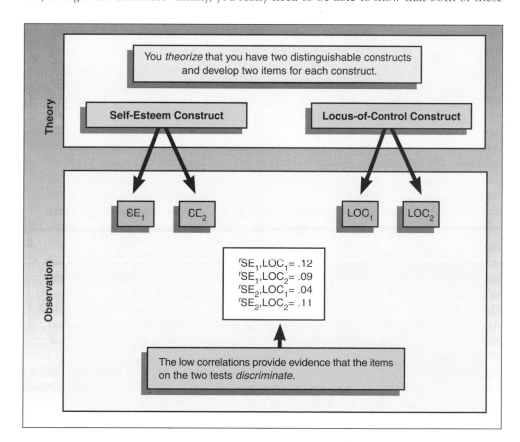

FIGURE 3-3
Discriminant Validity Correlations

FIGURE 3-4
Convergent and Discriminant Validity Correlations in a Single Table or Correlation Matrix

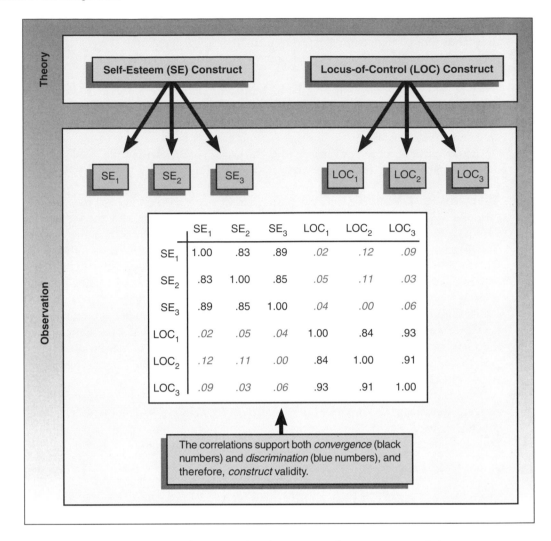

	SE$_1$	SE$_2$	SE$_3$	LOC$_1$	LOC$_2$	LOC$_3$
SE$_1$	1.00	.83	.89	*.02*	*.12*	*.09*
SE$_2$	.83	1.00	.85	*.05*	*.11*	*.03*
SE$_3$	.89	.85	1.00	*.04*	*.00*	*.06*
LOC$_1$	*.02*	*.05*	*.04*	1.00	.84	.93
LOC$_2$	*.12*	*.11*	*.00*	.84	1.00	.91
LOC$_3$	*.09*	*.03*	*.06*	.93	.91	1.00

The correlations support both *convergence* (black numbers) and *discrimination* (blue numbers), and therefore, *construct* validity.

types of validity are supported. Given the discussions of convergent and discriminant validity, you should be able to see that you could put both principles together into a single analysis to examine both at the same time. This is illustrated in Figure 3-4.

Figure 3-4 shows six measures: three that are theoretically related to the construct of self-esteem and three that are thought to be related to locus of control. The top part of the figure shows this theoretical arrangement. The bottom of the figure shows what a correlation matrix based on a pilot sample might show. To understand this table, first you need to be able to identify the convergent correlations and the discriminant ones. The two sets or blocks of convergent coefficients appear in regular type: one 3 × 3 block for the self-esteem intercorrelations in the upper left of the table, and one 3 × 3 block for the locus-of-control correlations in the lower right. Additionally, two 3 × 3 blocks of discriminant coefficients appear in italics, although if you're really sharp you'll recognize that they are the same values in mirror image. (Do you know why? You might want to read up on correlations in Chapter 11, "Analysis.")

How do you make sense of the correlations' patterns? There are no firm rules for how high or low the correlations need to be to provide evidence for either type of validity, but that the convergent correlations should always be higher than the discriminant ones. Take a good look at the table and you will see that in this example the convergent correlations are always higher than the discriminant ones. I would conclude from this that the correlation matrix provides evidence for both convergent and discriminant validity, all in one table!

It's true the pattern supports discriminant and convergent validity, but does it show that the three self-esteem measures actually measure self-esteem or that the three locus-of-control measures actually measure locus of control? Of course not. That would be much too easy.

So, what good is this analysis? It does show that, as you predicted, the three self-esteem measures seem to reflect the same construct (whatever that might be). The three locus-of-control measures also seem to reflect the same construct (again, whatever that is), and the two sets of measures seem to reflect two different constructs (whatever they are). That's not bad for one simple analysis.

Okay, so how do you get to the really interesting question? How do you show that your measures are actually measuring self-esteem or locus of control? I hate to disappoint you, but there is no simple answer to that. (I bet you knew that was coming.) You can do several things to address this question. First, you can use other ways to address construct validity to help provide further evidence that you're measuring what you say you're measuring. For instance, you might use a face validity or content validity approach to demonstrate that the measures reflect the constructs you say they are. (See Section 3-1a, "Measurement Validity Types," earlier in this chapter for more information.)

One of the most powerful approaches is to include even more constructs and measures. The more complex your theoretical model (if you find confirmation of the correct pattern in the correlations), the more evidence you are providing that you know what you're talking about (theoretically speaking). Of course, it's also harder to get all the correlations to give you the exact right pattern as you add more measures. In many studies, you simply don't have the luxury of adding more and more measures because it's too costly or demanding. Despite the impracticality, if you can afford to do it, adding more constructs and measures enhances your ability to assess construct validity.

3-1d Threats to Construct Validity

Before I launch into a discussion of the most common threats to construct validity, take a moment to recall what a threat to validity is. In a research study, you are likely to reach a conclusion that your program was a good operationalization of what you wanted and that your measures reflected what you wanted them to reflect. Would you be correct? How will you be criticized if you make these types of claims? How might you strengthen your claims? The kinds of questions and issues your critics will raise are what I mean by **threats to construct validity.**

The authoritative list of threats to construct validity (Cook & Campbell, 1979) that I follow tends to be a bit academic in its language. Although I love their discussion, I do find some of their terminology a bit cumbersome. Much of what I'll do here is try to translate their terms into words that are more understandable to us normal human beings. Here, then, are the major threats to construct validity (drum roll, please):

Inadequate Preoperational Explication of Constructs   Okay, this is a fairly daunting phrase, but don't panic. Breathe in. Breathe out. Let's decipher this phrase one part at a time. It isn't nearly as complicated as it sounds. You know what *inadequate* means, don't you? (If you don't, I'd say you're pretty inadequate!) Here, *preoperational* is what you were thinking about before you developed your measures or treatments. *Explication* is just a fancy word for explanation. Put it all together and what this phrase means is that you didn't do a good enough job defining what you meant by the construct before you tried to translate it into a measure or program. In other words, you weren't thinking carefully. How is this a threat? Imagine that your program consisted of a new type of approach to rehabilitation. A critic comes along and claims that, in fact, your program is neither *new* nor a true *rehabilitation* program. You are being accused of doing a poor job of thinking through your constructs. Here are some possible solutions:

- Think through your concepts better.
- Use structured methods (for example, concept mapping) to articulate your concepts.
- Get experts to critique your operationalizations.

Mono-Operation Bias   **Mono-operation bias** occurs when you use only one version of the treatment or program in your study. Note that it is only relevant to the independent variable, cause, program, or treatment in your study. It does not pertain to

threat to construct validity Any factor that causes you to make an incorrect conclusion about whether your operationalized variables (for example, your program or outcome) reflect well the construct they are intended to represent.

mono-operation bias A threat to construct validity that occurs when you rely on only a single implementation of your independent variable, cause, program, or treatment in your study.

measures or outcomes (see the "Mono-Method Bias" in Section 3-1d). If you only use a single version of a program in a single place at a single point in time, you may not be capturing the full breadth of the concept of the program. Every operationalization is a flawed imperfect reflection of the construct on which it is based. If you conclude that your program reflects the construct of the program, your critics are likely to argue that the results of your study reflect only the peculiar version of the program that you implemented, and not the full breadth of the construct you had in mind. Solution: Try to implement multiple versions of your program.

Mono-Method Bias   Mono-method bias occurs when you only use one measure of a construct. Note that it is only relevant to your measures or observations, not to your programs or causes. Otherwise, it's essentially the same issue as mono-operation bias. With only a single version of a self-esteem measure, you can't provide much evidence that you're really measuring self-esteem. Your critics will suggest that you aren't measuring self-esteem, that you're only measuring part of it, for instance. Solution: Try to implement multiple measures of key constructs and try to demonstrate (perhaps through a pilot or side study) that the measures you use behave as you theoretically expect them to behave.

> **mono-method bias** A threat to construct validity that occurs because you use only a single method of measurement.

Interaction of Different Treatments   You give a new program designed to encourage high-risk teenage girls to go to school and not become pregnant. The results of your study show that the girls in your treatment group have higher school attendance and lower pregnancy rates. You're feeling pretty good about your program until your critics point out that the targeted at-risk treatment group in your study is also likely to be involved simultaneously in several other programs designed to have similar effects. Can you really claim that the program effect is a consequence of your program? The real program that the girls received may actually be the *combination* of the separate programs in which they participated. What can you do about this threat? One approach is to try to isolate the effects of your program from the effects of any other treatments. You could do this by creating a research design that uses a control group (This is discussed in detail in Chapter 7, "Design.") In this case, you could randomly assign some high-risk girls to receive your program and some to a no-program control group. Even if girls in both groups receive some other treatment or program, the only systematic difference between the groups is your program. If you observe differences between them on outcome measures, the differences must be due to the program. By using a control group that makes your program the only thing that differentiates the two groups, you control for the potential confusion or "confounding" of multiple treatments.

Interaction of Testing and Treatment   Does testing or measurement itself make the groups more sensitive or receptive to the treatment? If it does, the testing is essentially a part of the treatment; it's inseparable from the effect of the treatment. This is a labeling issue (and, hence, a concern of construct validity) because you want to use the label *program* to refer to the program alone, but in fact, it also includes the testing. As in the previous threat, one way to control for this is through research design. If you are worried that a pretest makes your program participants more sensitive or receptive to the treatment, randomly assign your program participants into two groups, where one group gets the treatment and the other doesn't. If there are differences on outcomes between these groups, you have evidence that there is an effect of the testing. If not, the testing doesn't matter. In fact, there is a research design known as the *Solomon Four-Group Design* that was created explicitly to control for this.

Restricted Generalizability across Constructs   This is what I like to refer to as the *unintended consequences* threat to construct validity. You do a study and conclude that Treatment X is effective. In fact, Treatment X is effective, but only on the outcome you measured. What you failed to anticipate is that the treatment may have drastic negative consequences or side effects on other outcomes. When you say that Treatment X is effective, you have defined *effective* in regards to only the outcomes you measured. But, in fact, significant unintended consequences might affect constructs you did not measure and cannot generalize to. This threat should remind you that you have to be careful about whether your observed effects (Treatment X is effective) would generalize to other potential outcomes. How can you deal with this threat? The critical issue here is to try to anticipate the unintended and measure a broad range of potential relevant outcomes.

Confounding Constructs and Levels of Constructs Imagine a study to test the effect of a new drug treatment for cancer. A fixed dose of drug X is given to a randomly assigned treatment group and a placebo to the other group. No treatment effects are detected. But perhaps the observed result is only true for a certain dosage level. Slight increases or decreases of the dosage of drug X may radically change the results. In this context, it is not fair for you to label the treatment as "drug X" because you only looked at a narrow range of dose of the drug. Like the other construct validity threats, this threat is essentially a labeling issue; your label is not a good description for what you implemented. What can you do about it? If you find a treatment effect at a specific dosage, be sure to conduct subsequent studies that explore the range of effective doses. Note that, although I use the term *dose* here, you shouldn't limit the idea to medical studies. If you find an educational program effective at a particular dose—say one hour of tutoring a week—conduct subsequent studies to see if dose responses change as you increase or decrease from there. Similarly, if you don't find an effect with an initial dose, don't automatically give up. It may be that at a higher dose the desired outcome will occur.

The Social Threats to Construct Validity The remaining major threats to construct validity can be distinguished from the ones I discussed so far because they are all related to the social and human nature of research.

Hypothesis Guessing Most people don't just participate passively in a research project. They guess at what the real purpose of the study is. Therefore, they are likely to base their behavior on what they guess, not just on your treatment. In an educational study conducted in a classroom, students might guess that the key dependent variable has to do with class participation levels. If they increase their participation not because of your program but because they think that's what you're studying, you cannot label the outcome as an effect of the program. It is this labeling issue that makes this a construct validity threat. This is a difficult threat to eliminate. In some studies, researchers try to hide the real purpose of the study, but this may be unethical, depending on the circumstances. In some instances, they eliminate the need for participants to guess by telling them the real purpose (although who's to say that participants will believe them). If this is a potentially serious threat, you may think about trying to control for it explicitly through your research design. For instance, you might have multiple program groups and give each one slightly different explanations about the nature of the study, even though they all get exactly the same treatment or program. If they perform differently, it may be evidence that they were guessing differently and that this was influencing the results.

Evaluation Apprehension Many people are anxious about being evaluated. Some are even phobic about testing and measurement situations. If their apprehension (and not your program conditions) makes them perform poorly, you certainly can't label that as a treatment effect. Another form of evaluation apprehension concerns the human tendency to want to look good or look smart, and so on. If, in their desire to look good, participants perform better (and not as a result of your program), you would be wrong to label this as a treatment effect. In both cases, the apprehension becomes confounded with the treatment itself, and you have to be careful about how you label the outcomes. Researchers take a variety of steps to reduce apprehension. In any testing or measurement situation, it is probably a good idea to give participants some time to get comfortable and adjusted to their surroundings. You might ask a few warm-up questions, knowing that you are not going to use the answers and trying to encourage the participant to get comfortable responding. In many research projects, people misunderstand what you are measuring. If it is appropriate, you may want to tell them that there are no right or wrong answers and that they aren't being judged or evaluated based on what they say or do.

Experimenter Expectancies   These days, where we engage in lots of nonlaboratory applied social research, we generally don't use the term *experimenter* to describe the person in charge of the research. So, let's relabel this threat *researcher expectancies* (Rosenthal, 1966). The researcher can bias the results of a study in countless ways, both consciously or subconsciously. Sometimes, the researcher can communicate what the desired outcome for a study might be (and the participants' desire to look good leads them to react that way). For instance, the researcher might look pleased when participants give a desired answer. If researcher feedback causes the response, it would be wrong to label the response a treatment effect. As in many of the previous threats, probably the most effective way to address this threat is to control for it through your research design. For instance, if resources allow, you can have multiple experimenters who differ in their characteristics. Or you can address the threat through measurement; you can measure expectations prior to the study and use the information in that analysis to attempt to adjust for expectations.

3-2 RELIABILITY

reliability The degree to which a measure is consistent or dependable; the degree to which it would give you the same result over and over again, assuming the underlying phenomenon is not changing.

Reliability is part of the quality of measurement. In its everyday sense, reliability is the consistency or repeatability of your measures. Before I can define reliability precisely, I have to lay the groundwork. First, you have to learn about the foundation of reliability, the true score theory of measurement. Along with that, you need to understand the different types of measurement error because errors in measures play a key role in degrading reliability. With this foundation, you can then consider the basic theory of reliability, including a precise definition of reliability. There you will find out that you cannot calculate reliability—you can only estimate it. Because of this, there are a variety of different types of reliability and multiple ways to estimate reliability for each type. In the end, it's important to integrate the idea of reliability with the other major criteria for the quality of measurement—validity—and develop an understanding of the relationships between reliability and validity in measurement.

3-2a True Score Theory

true score theory A theory that maintains that every measurement is an additive composite of two components: the true ability of the respondent and random error.

True score theory is a theory about measurement (Lord & Novick, 1968). Like all theories, you need to recognize that it is not proven; it is postulated as a model of how the world operates. Like many powerful models, true score theory is a simple one. Essentially, **true score theory** maintains that every measurement is the sum of two components: true ability (or the true level) of the respondent on that measure and random error. This is illustrated in Figure 3-5. You observe the measurement: a score on a test, the total for a self-esteem instrument, or the scale value for a person's weight. You don't observe what's on the right side of the equation. In true score theory, you assume that there are only the two components to the right side of the equal sign in the equation.

Why is true score theory important? For one thing, it is a simple yet powerful model for measurement. It is a reminder that most measurement has an error component. Second, true score theory is the foundation of reliability theory. A measure that has no ran-

FIGURE 3-5
The Basic Equation of True Score Theory

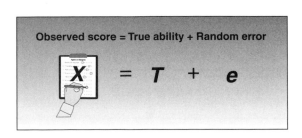

Observed score = True ability + Random error

$$X = T + e$$

dom error (is all true score) is perfectly reliable; a measure that has no true score (is nothing but random error) has zero reliability. Third, true score theory can be used in computer simulations as the basis for generating observed scores with certain known properties.

You should know that the true score model is not the only measurement model available. Measurement theorists continue to come up with more and more complex models that they think represent reality even better. However, these models are complicated enough that they lie outside the boundaries of this book. In any event, true score theory should give you an idea of why measurement models are important at all and how they can be used as the basis for defining key research ideas.

3-2b Measurement Error

True score theory is a good simple model for measurement, but it may not always be an accurate reflection of reality. In particular, it assumes that any observation is composed of the true value plus some random error value, but is that reasonable? What if all error is not random? Isn't it possible that some errors are systematic, that they hold across most or all of the members of a group? One way to deal with this notion is to revise the simple true score model by dividing the error component into two subcomponents: random error and systematic error. Figure 3-6 shows these two components of measurement error, what the difference between them is, and how they affect research.

What Is Random Error?   Random error is caused by any factors that randomly affect measurement of the variable across the sample. For instance, people's moods can inflate or deflate their performance on any occasion. In a particular testing, some children may be in a good mood, and others may be depressed. If mood affects the children's performance on the measure, it might artificially inflate the observed scores for some children and artificially deflate them for others. The important thing about random error is that it does not have any consistent effects across the entire sample. Instead, it pushes observed scores up or down randomly. This means that if you could see all the random errors in a distribution, they would have to sum to 0. There would be as many negative errors as positive ones. (Of course you can't see the random errors because all you see is the observed score X.) The important property of random error is that it adds variability to the data but does not affect average performance for the group (see Figure 3-7). Because of this, random error is sometimes considered *noise*.

What Is Systematic Error?   Systematic error is caused by any factors that systematically affect measurement of the variable across the sample. For instance, if there is

$$X = T + e$$
$$X = T + e_r + e_s$$

FIGURE 3-6

Random and Systematic Errors in Measurement

FIGURE 3-7

Random Error

Random error adds variability to a distribution but does not affect central tendency (the average).

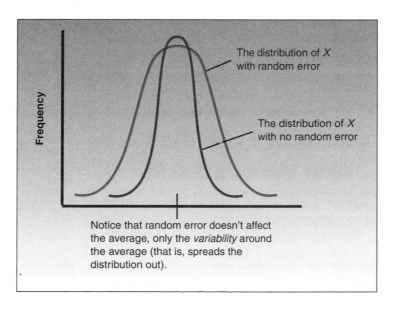

The distribution of X with random error

The distribution of X with no random error

Frequency

Notice that random error doesn't affect the average, only the *variability* around the average (that is, spreads the distribution out).

FIGURE 3-8
Systematic Error

Systematic error affects the
central tendency of a distribution.

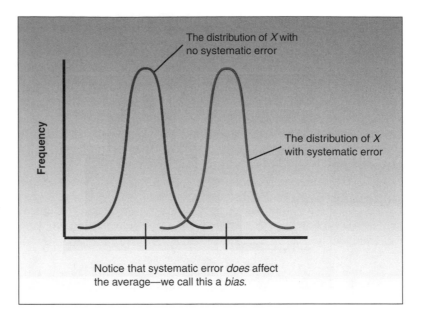

The distribution of *X* with
no systematic error

Frequency

The distribution of *X*
with systematic error

Notice that systematic error *does* affect
the average—we call this a *bias*.

loud traffic going by just outside of a classroom where students are taking a test, this noise is likely to affect all of the children's scores—in this case, systematically lowering them. Unlike random error, systematic errors tend to be either positive or negative consistently; because of this, systematic error is sometimes considered to be *bias* in measurement (see Figure 3-8).

Reducing Measurement Error   So, how can you reduce measurement errors, random or systematic? One thing you can do is to pilot-test your instruments to get feedback from your respondents regarding how easy or hard the measure was and how the testing environment affected their performance. Second, if you are gathering measures using people to collect the data (as interviewers or observers), you should make sure you train them thoroughly so that they aren't inadvertently introducing error. Third, when you collect the data for your study, you should double-check the data thoroughly. All data entry for computer analysis should be double-entered and verified. Ideally, you enter the data twice, the second time having the computer check that you are typing the exact same data you typed the first time. Fourth, you can use statistical procedures to adjust for measurement error. These range from rather simple formulas you can apply directly to your data to complex procedures for modeling the error and its effects. Finally, one of the best things you can do to deal with measurement errors, especially systematic errors, is to use multiple measures of the same construct. Especially if the different measures don't share the same systematic errors, you will be able to *triangulate* across the multiple measures and get a more accurate sense of what's happening.

3-2c Theory of Reliability

What is *reliability*? We hear the term used a lot in research contexts, but what does it really mean? If you think about how we use the word *reliable* in everyday language, you might get a hint. For instance, we often speak about a machine as reliable: "I have a reliable car." Or newspeople talk about a "usually reliable source." In both cases, the word *reliable* usually means dependable or trustworthy. In research, the term *reliable* also means dependable in a general sense, but that's not a precise enough definition. What does it mean to have a dependable measure or observation in a research context? The reason dependable is not a good enough description is that it can be confused too easily with the idea of a valid measure (see Section 3-1, "Construct Validity," earlier in this chapter). Certainly, when researchers speak of a dependable measure, we mean one that is both reliable and valid. So, we have to be a little more precise when we try to define reliability.

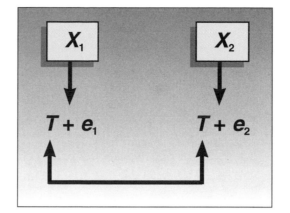

FIGURE 3-9
Reliability and True Score Theory

In research, the term *reliability* means repeatability or consistency. A measure is considered reliable if it would give you the same result over and over again (assuming that what you are measuring isn't changing).

Let's explore in more detail what it means to say that a measure is repeatable or consistent. I'll begin by defining a measure that I'll arbitrarily label X. It might be a person's score on a math achievement test or a measure of severity of illness. It is the value (numerical or otherwise) that you observe in your study. Now, to see how repeatable or consistent an observation is, you can measure it twice. You use subscripts to indicate the first and second observation of the same measure, as shown in Figure 3-9. If you assume that what you're measuring doesn't change between the time of the first and second observation, you can begin to understand how you get at reliability. Although you observe a single score for what you're measuring, you usually think of that score as consisting of two parts: the true score or actual level for the person on that measure, and the error in measuring it (Lord & Novick, 1968) (see Section 3-2a, "True Score Theory," earlier in this chapter).

It's important to keep in mind that you observe the X score; you never actually see the true (T) or error (e) scores. For instance, a student may get a score of 85 on a math achievement test. That's the score you observe, an X of 85. However, the reality might be that the student is actually better at math than that score indicates. Let's say the student's true math ability is 89 ($T = 89$). That means that the error for that student is −4. What does this mean? Well, while the student's true math ability may be 89, he or she may have had a bad day, may not have had breakfast, may have had an argument with someone, or may have been distracted while taking the test. Factors like these can contribute to errors in measurement that make students' observed abilities appear lower than their true or actual abilities.

Okay, back to reliability. Let's make a simple assumption to make the discussion more straightforward. Assume that you are repeatedly measuring some characteristic that is not changing over the period you are measuring it. For example, perhaps you are measuring heights of adults over a several day period, or intelligence in the same children within the same week. It's not likely that these characteristics would really change considerably in that time. If your measure is reliable, you should pretty much get the same result each time you measure it. Why would the results be essentially the same in these circumstances? If you look at Figure 3-9, you should see that the only thing that the two observations have in common is their true scores, T. How do you know that? Because the error scores (e_1 and e_2) have different subscripts, indicating that they are different values. (You are likely to have different errors on different occasions.) However, the true score symbol (T) is the same for both observations. What does this mean? The two observed scores, X_1 and X_2, are related only to the degree that the observations share a true score. You should remember that the error score is assumed to be random (see Section 3-2a, "True Score Theory," earlier in this chapter). Sometimes, errors will lead you to perform better on a test than your true ability (you had a good day guessing!), while other times, they will lead you to score worse. The true score—your true ability on that measure—would be the

FIGURE 3-10
**Reliability Expressed
as a Simple Ratio**

$$\frac{\text{true level on the measure}}{\text{the measure}}$$

FIGURE 3-11
**The Reliability Ratio
Expressed in Terms
of Variances**

$$\frac{\text{the variance of the true score}}{\text{the variance of the measure}}$$

same on both observations (assuming, of course, that your true ability didn't change between the two measurement occasions).

With this in mind, I can now define reliability more precisely. Reliability is a ratio or fraction. In layperson terms, you might define this ratio as shown in Figure 3-10.

You might think of reliability as the proportion of truth in your measure. Now, it makes no sense to speak of the reliability of a measure for an individual; reliability is a characteristic of a measure that's taken across individuals. So, to get closer to a more formal definition, I'll restate the definition of reliability in terms of a set of observations. The easiest way to do this is to speak of the variance of the scores. The variance is a measure of the spread or distribution of a set of scores (see Chapter 11, "Analysis"). So, I can now state the definition as shown in Figure 3-11.

I might put this into slightly more technical terms by using the abbreviated name for the variance and our variable names (see Figure 3-12).

$$\frac{var(T)}{var(X)}$$

We're getting to the critical part now. If you look at the equation in Figure 3-12, you should recognize that you can easily determine or calculate the bottom part of the reliability ratio; it's just the variance of the set of observed scores. (You remember how to calculate the variance, don't you? It's the sum of the squared deviations of the scores from their mean, divided by the number of scores. If you're still not sure, see Chapter 11, "Analysis.") So, how do you calculate the variance of the true scores? You can't see the true scores. (You only see X!) Therefore, if you can't calculate the variance of the true scores, you can't compute the ratio, which means *you can't compute reliability!* Everybody got that? Here's the bottom line:

You can't compute reliability because you can't calculate the variance of the true scores!

Great. So, where does that leave you? If you can't compute reliability, perhaps the best you can do is to estimate it. Maybe you can get an estimate of the variability of the true scores. How do you do that? Remember your two observations, X_1 and X_2? You assume (using true score theory) that these two observations would be related to each other to the degree that they share true scores. So, let's calculate the correlation between X_1 and X_2. Figure 3-13 shows a simple formula for the correlation.

$$\frac{\text{covariance } (X_1, X_2)}{sd(X_1) * sd(X_2)}$$

In Figure 3-13, the *sd* stands for the *standard deviation* (which is the square root of the variance). If you look carefully at this equation, you can see that the covariance, which simply measures the shared variance between measures, must be an indicator of the variability of the true scores because the true scores in X_1 and X_2 are the only things the two observations share! So, the top part is essentially an estimate of $var(T)$ in this context. Additionally, since the bottom part of the equation multiplies the standard deviation of one observation with the standard deviation of the same measure at another time, you would expect that these two values would be the same (it is the same measure we're taking) and that this is essentially the same thing as squaring the standard deviation for either observation. However, the square of the standard deviation is the same thing as the variance of the measure. So, the bottom part of the equation becomes the variance of the measure (or $var(X)$). If you read this paragraph carefully, you should see that the correlation between two observations of the same measure *is* an estimate of reliability. Got that? I've just shown that a simple and straightforward way to estimate the reliability of a measure is to compute the correlation of two administrations of the measure!

It's time to reach some conclusions. You know from this discussion that you cannot calculate reliability because you cannot measure the true score component of an observation. You also know that you can estimate the true score component as the covariance between two observations of the same measure. With that in mind, you can estimate the reliability as the correlation between two observations of the same measure. It turns out that there are several ways to estimate this reliability correlation. These are discussed in Section 3-2d, "Types of Reliability," later in this chapter.

There's only one other issue I want to address here. What is the range of a reliability estimate? What is the largest or smallest value a reliability can be? To figure this out, let's go back to the equation given earlier (see Figure 3-14).

Remember, because $X = T + e$, you can substitute it in the bottom of the ratio as shown in Figure 3-15.

With this slight change, you can easily determine the range of a reliability estimate. If a measure is *perfectly* reliable, there is no error in measurement; everything you observe is true score. Therefore, for a perfectly reliable measure, $var(e)$ is zero and the equation would reduce to the equation shown in Figure 3-16.

Therefore, reliability = 1. Now, if you have a perfectly unreliable measure, there is no true score; the measure is entirely error. In this case, the equation would reduce to the equation shown in Figure 3-17.

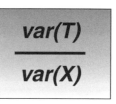

FIGURE 3-14
The Reliability Ratio Expressed in Terms of Variances in Abbreviated Form

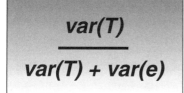

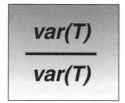

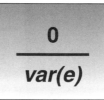

FIGURE 3-15
The Reliability Ratio Expressed in Terms of Variances with the Variance of the Observed Score Subdivided According to True Score Theory

FIGURE 3-16
Perfect Reliability

When there is no error in measurement, you have perfect reliability, and the reliability estimate is 1.0.

FIGURE 3-17
No Reliability

When there is only error in measurement, you have no reliability, and the reliability estimate is 0.

Therefore, the reliability = 0. From this you know that reliability will always range between 0 and 1.

The value of a reliability estimate tells you the proportion of variability in the measure attributable to the true score. A reliability of .5 means that about half of the variance of the observed score is attributable to truth and half is attributable to error. A reliability of .8 means the variability is about 80 percent true ability and 20 percent error, and so on.

3-2d Types of Reliability

You learned in Section 3-2c, "Theory of Reliability," earlier in this chapter that it's not possible to calculate reliability exactly. Instead, you have to estimate reliability, and this is always an imperfect endeavor. Here, I want to introduce the major reliability estimators and talk about their strengths and weaknesses.

There are four general classes of reliability estimates, each of which estimates reliability in a different way:

- *Inter-rater or inter-observer reliability*—Used to assess the degree to which different raters/observers give consistent estimates of the same phenomenon.

- *Test-retest reliability*—Used to assess the consistency of a measure from one time to another.

- *Parallel-forms reliability*—Used to assess the consistency of the results of two tests constructed in the same way from the same content domain.

- *Internal consistency reliability*—Used to assess the consistency of results across items within a test.

I'll discuss each of these in turn.

Inter-Rater or Inter-Observer Reliability
Whenever you use humans as a part of your measurement procedure, you have to worry about whether the results you get are reliable or consistent. People are notorious for their inconsistency. We are easily distractible. We get tired of doing repetitive tasks. We daydream. We misinterpret.

So, how do you determine whether two observers are being consistent in their observations? You probably should establish inter-rater reliability outside of the context of the measurement in your study. After all, if you use data from your study to establish reliability, and you find that reliability is low, you're kind of stuck. Probably it's best to do this as a side study or pilot study. If your study continues for a long time, you may want to reestablish inter-rater reliability from time to time to ensure that your raters aren't changing.

Here are two of the many ways to actually estimate inter-rater reliability. First, if your measurement consists of categories—the raters are checking off which category each observation falls in—you can calculate the percent of agreement between the raters. For instance, let's say you had 100 observations that were being rated by two raters. For each observation, the rater could check one of three categories. Imagine that on 86 of the 100 observations the raters checked the same category. In this case, the percent of agreement would be 86 percent. Okay, it's a crude measure, but it does give an idea of how much agreement exists, and it works no matter how many categories are used for each observation.

A second way to estimate inter-rater reliability is appropriate when the measure is a continuous, rather than categorical one. In such a case, all you need to do is calculate the correlation between the ratings of the two observers. For instance, they might be rating the overall level of activity in a classroom on a 1-to-7 scale. The correlation between the ratings of two raters would give you an estimate of the reliability or consistency between the raters (see Figure 3-18).

You might think of this type of reliability as calibrating the observers. There are other things you could do to encourage reliability between observers, even if you don't estimate it. For instance, I used to work in a psychiatric unit where every morning a nurse had to do a 10-item rating of each patient on the unit. Of course, we couldn't count on

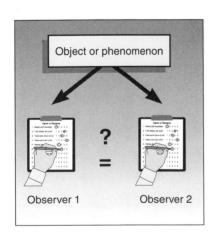

FIGURE 3-18
Inter-Rater or Inter-Observer Reliability

the same nurse being present every day, so we had to find a way to ensure that all the nurses would give comparable ratings. The way we did it was to hold weekly calibration meetings where we would have all of the nurses' ratings for several patients and discuss why they chose the specific values they did. If there were disagreements, the nurses would discuss them and attempt to come up with rules for deciding when they would give a 3 or a 4 for a rating on a specific item. Although this was not an estimate of reliability, it probably went a long way toward improving the reliability between raters.

Test-Retest Reliability   You estimate test-retest reliability when you administer the same test to the same (or a similar) sample on two different occasions (see Figure 3-19). This approach assumes that there is no substantial change in the construct being measured between the two occasions. The amount of time allowed between measures is critical. You know that if you measure the same thing twice, the correlation between the two observations will depend, in part, on how much time elapses between the two measurement occasions. The shorter the time gap, the higher the correlation; the longer the time gap, the lower the correlation because the two observations are related over time; the closer in time you get, the more similar the factors that contribute to error. Since this correlation is the test-retest estimate of reliability, you can obtain considerably different estimates depending on the time interval.

Parallel-Forms Reliability   In parallel-forms reliability, you first have to create two parallel forms. One way to accomplish this is to start with a relatively large set of questions that address the same construct and then randomly divide the questions into two sets. You administer both instruments to the same sample of people (see Figure 3-20). The correlation between the two parallel forms is the estimate of reliability. One major problem with this approach is that you have to be able to generate lots of items that reflect the same construct, which is often no easy feat. Furthermore, this approach makes the assumption that the randomly divided halves are parallel or equivalent. Even by chance, this will sometimes not be the case. The parallel-forms approach is similar to the split-half reliability described in Section 3-2d, "Types of Reliability." The major difference is that parallel forms are constructed so that the two forms can be used independently of each other and considered equivalent measures. For instance, you might be concerned about a testing threat to internal validity (see Chapter 7, "Design"). If you use Form A for the pretest and Form B for the posttest, you minimize that problem. It would

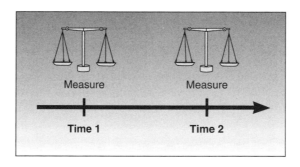

FIGURE 3-19
Test-Retest Reliability

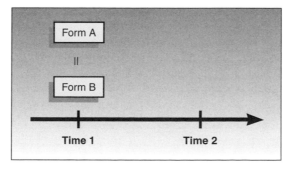

FIGURE 3-20
Parallel-Forms Reliability

even be better if you randomly assign individuals to receive Form A or B on the pretest and then switch them on the posttest. With split-half reliability, you have an instrument to use as a single-measurement instrument and only develop randomly split halves for purposes of estimating reliability.

Internal Consistency Reliability   In internal consistency reliability estimation, you use a single measurement instrument administered to a group of people on one occasion to estimate reliability. In effect, you judge the reliability of the instrument by estimating how well the items on the instrument that reflect the same construct yield similar results. You are looking at how consistent the results are for different items for the same construct within the measure. There are a wide variety of internal-consistency measures you can use.

Average Inter-Item Correlation   The average inter-item correlation uses all of the items on your instrument that are designed to measure the same construct. You first compute the correlation between each pair of items, as illustrated in Figure 3-21. For example, if you have six items, you will have 15 different item pairings (15 correlations). The average inter-item correlation is simply the average or mean of all these correlations. In the example, you find an average inter-item correlation of .90 with the individual correlations ranging from .84 to .95.

Average Item-Total Correlation   This approach also uses the inter-item correlations. In addition, you compute a total score for the six items and treat that in the analysis like an additional variable. Figure 3-22 shows the six item-to-total correlations at the bottom of the correlation matrix. They range from .82 to .88 in this sample analysis, with the average of these at .85.

Split-Half Reliability   In split-half reliability, you randomly divide into two sets all items that measure the same construct. You administer the entire instrument to a sample and calculate the total score for each randomly divided half of the measure. The split-half reliability estimate, as shown Figure 3-23, is simply the correlation between these two total scores. In the example, it is .87.

Cronbach's Alpha (α)   Imagine that you compute one split-half reliability and then randomly divide the items into another set of split halves and recompute, and keep doing this until you have computed all possible split-half estimates of reliability.

FIGURE 3-21
The Average Inter-Item Correlation

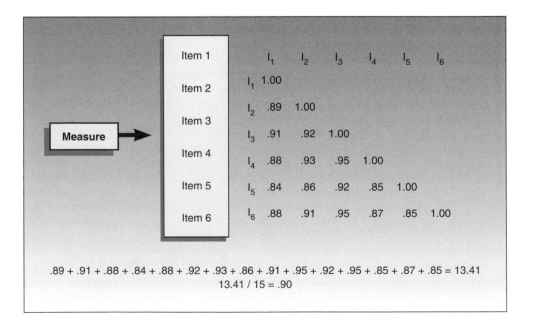

$$.89 + .91 + .88 + .84 + .88 + .92 + .93 + .86 + .91 + .95 + .92 + .95 + .85 + .87 + .85 = 13.41$$
$$13.41 / 15 = .90$$

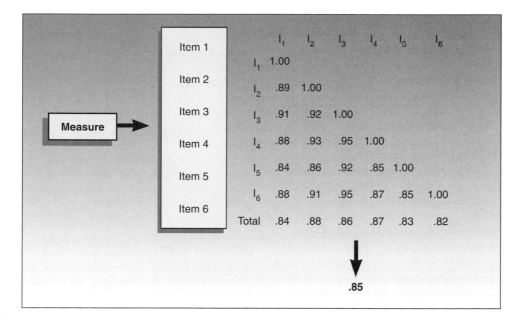

FIGURE 3-22
Average Item-Total Correlation

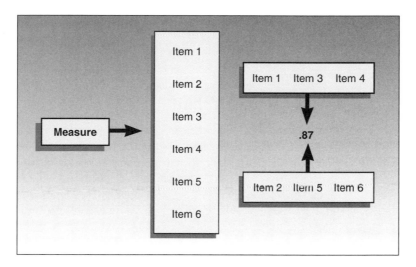

FIGURE 3-23
Split-Half Reliability

Cronbach's alpha (Miller, 1995) is mathematically equivalent to the average of all possible split-half estimates. Thankfully, that's not how we typically compute it. Some clever mathematician (Cronbach, no doubt!) figured out a way to get the mathematical equivalent a lot more quickly. One way is with the simple formula shown in Figure 3-24. This formula only requires that you have the average inter-item correlation and the number of items. The example shown in Figure 3-24 shows that if you had six items and an average inter-item correlation of .85, Cronbach's alpha would equal .97.

> **Cronbach's alpha** One specific method of estimating the reliability of a measure. Although not calculated in this manner, Cronbach's alpha can be thought of as analogous to the average of all possible split-half correlations.

Comparison of Reliability Estimators   Each of the reliability estimators has certain advantages and disadvantages. Inter-rater reliability is one of the best ways to estimate reliability when your measure is an observation. However, it requires multiple raters or observers. As an alternative, you could look at the correlation of ratings of the same single observer repeated on two different occasions. For example, let's say you collected videotapes of child-mother interactions and had a rater code the videos for how often the mother smiled at the child. To establish inter-rater reliability, you could take a sample of videos and have two raters code them independently. You might use the inter-rater approach especially if you were interested in using a team of raters and you wanted to establish that they yielded consistent results. If you get a suitably high inter-rater reliability, you could then justify allowing them to work independently on coding different videos. (When you only have a single rater and cannot easily train others, you might alternatively use a test-retest approach by having this person rate the same sample of

$$\text{Alpha} = \frac{K * \bar{r}}{1 + (K-1) * \bar{r}}$$

where:
K = Number of items on measure
$\bar{r}$ = Average inter-item correlation

Example:

If $K = 6$ and $\bar{r} = .85$:

$$\text{Alpha} = \frac{6 * .85}{1 + (6-1) * .85}$$

$$= \frac{5.1}{1 + 4.25}$$

$$= .97$$

FIGURE 3-24
Formula for and Example of Cronbach's Alpha Estimate of Reliability

videos on two occasions and computing the correlation). On the other hand, in some studies it is reasonable to do both to help establish the reliability of the raters or observers.

Use the parallel-forms estimator only in situations where you intend to use the two forms as alternate measures of the same thing. Both the parallel forms and all of the internal consistency estimators have one major constraint: You should have lots of items designed to measure the same construct. This is relatively easy to achieve in certain contexts like achievement testing. (It's easy, for instance, to construct many similar addition problems for a math test.) However, for more complex or subjective constructs, this can be a real challenge. Cronbach's alpha tends to be the most frequently used estimate of internal consistency.

The test-retest estimator is especially feasible in most experimental and quasi-experimental designs that use a no-treatment control group. In these designs, you always have a control group that is measured on two occasions (pretest and posttest). The main problem with this approach is that you don't have any information about reliability until you collect the posttest and, if the reliability estimate is low, it's too late to fix the pretest. However, even in this case, you may be able to identify a subset of items that are reliable and use only those.

Each of the reliability estimators gives a different value for reliability. In general, the test-retest and inter-rater reliability estimates will be lower in value than the parallel-forms and internal-consistency estimates because they involve measuring at different times or with different raters. Since reliability estimates are often used in statistical analyses of quasi-experimental designs (see Section 9-1, "The Nonequivalent Groups Design," in Chapter 9), the fact that different estimates can differ considerably makes the analysis even more complex.

3-2e Reliability and Validity

We often think of reliability and validity as separate ideas, but in fact, they're related to each other. One of my favorite metaphors for the relationship between reliability and validity is that of a target. Think of the center of the target as the concept you are trying to measure. Imagine that for each person you are measuring, you are taking a shot at the target. If you measure the concept perfectly for a person, you are hitting the center of the target. If you don't, you are missing the center. The more you are off for that person, the further you are from the center (see Figure 3-25).

Figure 3-25 shows four possible situations. In the first one, you are hitting the target consistently, but you are missing the center of the target. That is, you are consistently and systematically measuring the wrong value for all respondents. This measure is reliable but not valid. (It's consistent but wrong.) The second shows hits that are randomly spread across the target. You seldom hit the center of the target, but on average, you are getting the right answer for the group (but not very well for individuals). In this case, you get a valid group average, but you are inconsistent. Here, you can clearly see that reliability is directly related to the variability of your measure. The third scenario shows a case where

FIGURE 3-25
The Shooting-Target Metaphor for Reliability and Validity of Measurement

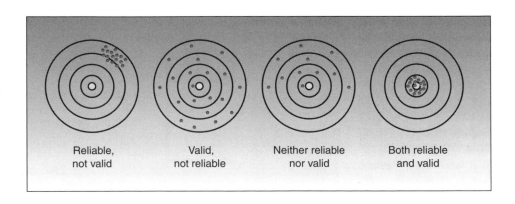

| Reliable, not valid | Valid, not reliable | Neither reliable nor valid | Both reliable and valid |

your hits are spread across the target and you are consistently missing the center. Your measure in this case is neither reliable nor valid. Finally, the figure shows the Robin Hood scenario; you consistently hit the center of the target. Your measure is both reliable and valid. (I bet you never thought of Robin Hood in those terms before.)

3-3 LEVELS OF MEASUREMENT

The level of measurement refers to the relationship among the values that are assigned to the attributes for a variable. What does that mean? Begin with the idea of the variable, for example, party affiliation (see Figure 3-26). That variable has a number of attributes. Let's assume that in this particular election context, the only relevant attributes are Republican, Democrat, and Independent. For purposes of analyzing the results of this variable, we arbitrarily assign the values 1, 2, and 3 to the three attributes. The *level of measurement* describes the relationship among these three values. In this case, the numbers function as shorter placeholders for the lengthier text terms. Higher values don't mean more of something, and lower numbers don't signify less. The value of 2 doesn't mean that Democrats are twice something than Republicans. Assigning a 1 for Republicans doesn't mean they are in first place or have the highest priority. In this case, the level of measurement can be described as nominal.

3-3a Why Is Level of Measurement Important?

First, knowing the level of measurement helps you decide how to interpret the data from that variable. When you know that a measure is nominal (like the one just described), you know that the numerical values are short codes for the longer names. Second, knowing the level of measurement helps you decide what statistical analysis is appropriate on the values that were assigned. If you know that a measure is nominal, then you would automatically know that you don't average the data values (except in certain circumstances like the use of "dummy" variables, described in Chapter 12, "Analysis for Research Design"). Why? Because it makes no sense to add "names" and then divide them by the number of names, which is how an average is calculated (see Chapter 12). And it also means that all statistical analyses that depend on the average or use it as part of their calculation (for example, the t-test as described in Chapter 12) would also not be appropriate.

There are four levels of measurement that are most commonly discussed (Stevens, 1946) (see Figure 3-27):

- *Nominal*—In nominal measurement, the numerical values simply name the attribute uniquely. No ordering of the cases is implied. For example, jersey numbers in basketball are measures at the nominal level. A player with number 30 is not more of anything than a player with number 15 and is certainly not twice whatever number 15 is.

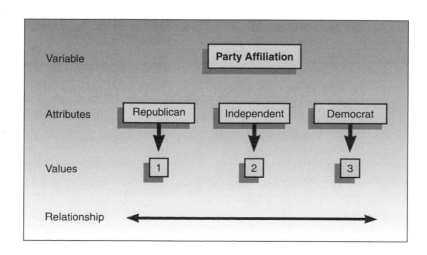

FIGURE 3-26
Level of Measurement

The level of measurement describes the relationship among the values associated with the attributes of a variable.

FIGURE 3-27
**The Hierarchy of
Measurement Levels**

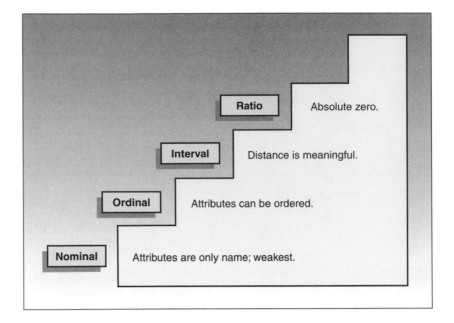

FIGURE 3-27
**The Hierarchy of
Measurement Levels**

- *Ordinal*—In ordinal measurement, the attributes can be rank-ordered. Here, distances between attributes do not have any meaning. For example, on a survey, you might code educational attainment as 0 = less than high school, 1 = some high school, 2 = high school degree, 3 = some college, 4 = college degree, 5 = post college. In this measure, higher numbers mean *more* education. Is distance from 0 to 1 the same as 3 to 4? Of course not. The interval between values is not interpretable in an ordinal measure.

- *Interval*—In interval measurement, the distance between attributes *does* have meaning. For example, when we measure temperature (in Fahrenheit), the distance from 30 to 40 is the same as the distance from 70 to 80. The interval between values is interpretable. Because of this, it makes sense to compute an average of an interval variable, where it doesn't make sense to do so for ordinal scales. So, it makes sense to discuss the average temperature. Note, however, that in interval measurement, ratios don't make any sense; 80 degrees is not twice as hot as 40 degrees (although the attribute value is twice as large).

- *Ratio*—In ratio measurement, there is always a meaningful absolute zero. This means that you can construct a meaningful fraction (or ratio) with a ratio variable. Weight is a ratio variable. We can say that a 100-pound bag weighs twice as much as a 50-pound one. In applied social research, most count variables are ratio—for example, the number of clients in the past six months. Why? Because you can have zero clients and because it is meaningful to say, "We had twice as many clients in the past six months as we did in the previous six months."

It's important to recognize that there is a hierarchy implied in the level of measurement idea. At lower levels of measurement, assumptions tend to be less restrictive and data analyses tend to be less sensitive. At each level up the hierarchy, the current level includes all of the qualities of the one below it and adds something new. In general, it is desirable to have a higher level of measurement (such as interval or ratio) rather than a lower one (such as nominal or ordinal).

SUMMARY

This chapter laid the foundation for the idea of measurement. Three broad topics were considered. First, *construct validity* refers to the degree to which you are measuring what you intended to measure. Construct validity is divided into translation validity (the degree to which you translated the construct well) and criterion-related validity (the degree to which your measure relates to or predicts other criteria as theoretically predicted). Second, *reliability* refers to the consistency or dependability of your measurement. Reliability is based upon *true score theory*, which holds that any observation can be divided into two values—a true score and error component. Reliability is defined as the ratio of the true score variance to the observed variance in a measure. There are a variety of methods for estimating reliability. Third, the level of a measure describes the relationship implicit among that measure's values and determines the type of statistical manipulations that are sensible. With these three ideas—construct validity, reliability, and level of measurement—as a foundation, you can now move on to some of the more practical and useful aspects of measurement in the next few chapters.

SUGGESTED WEBSITES

Note: These websites were functional when we went to press. Please access the Online Study Guide Edition for the most up-to-date URLs.

The Buros Center for Testing
http://www.unl.edu/buros/
Publishers of the *Mental Measurements Yearbooks*, the Buros Center (at the University of Nebraska) has an extensive program of test reviews, which are available online for a fee and provided as a database by some college and university libraries.

Testing and Assessment
http://www.apa.org/science/faq-findtests.html
This website, sponsored by the American Psychological Association, includes FAQs and links that will guide you to practical information on testing, test publishers, access to tests, and so on.

KEY TERMS

concurrent validity (p. 52)
construct validity (p. 49)
content validity (p. 51)
convergent validity (p. 52)
criterion-related validity (p. 51)
Cronbach's alpha (p. 69)

discriminant validity (p. 52)
face validity (p. 51)
mono-method bias (p. 58)
mono-operation bias (p. 57)
operationalization (p. 49)
predictive validity (p. 52)

reliability (p. 60)
threats to construct validity (p. 57)
translation validity (p. 51)
true score theory (p. 60)

REVIEW QUESTIONS

Note: You can find the correct answers to these questions by taking the quiz and then submitting your answers in the Online Study Guide Edition. The program will automatically score your submission. If you miss a question, the program will provide the correct answer, a rationale for the answer, and the section number in the chapter where the topic is discussed.

1. Which of the following is the broadest category of validity?
   a. content validity
   b. construct validity
   c. criterion-related validity
   d. translation validity

2. Claiming that a general psychology chapter test was unfair, a student argued that the test was heavily weighted with material related to four key concepts, rather than the possible twelve presented by the textbook author. This student was making an argument based on his awareness of what kind of validity?
   a. content validity
   b. construct validity
   c. criterion-related validity
   d. translation validity

3. What type of validity is assessed if an "integrity scale" is given to a group of prisoners and contrasted with the performance of a group of Rotary Club members?
   a. content validity
   b. face validity
   c. criterion-related validity
   d. translation validity

4. A newly created graduate performance prediction exam is given to a set of students. All are admitted to graduate school, and their performance is tracked. After five years, scores of the group who successfully completed the program are compared with scores of students who failed to graduate. This would be an example of what type of validity?
   a. face validity
   b. concurrent validity
   c. convergent validity
   d. translation validity

5. Cronbach's coefficient alpha is an internal consistency estimate of scale reliability that is mathematically equivalent to
   a. the average item-total correlation.
   b. all possible parallel forms reliability estimates.
   c. all possible split-half estimates of reliability.
   d. none of the above.

6. In the best of all worlds, we want convergent correlation coefficients to be as ___ as possible and discriminant correlation coefficients to be as ___ as possible.
   a. high, low
   b. high, high
   c. low, high
   d. low, low

7. What type of threat to construct validity exists if a single set of measures is used to assess a program and these measures are inappropriate?
   a. mono-construct bias
   b. mono-operation bias
   c. mono-method bias
   d. monolithic bias

8. What type of threat to construct validity exists when a researcher consciously or unconsciously communicates the desired response in her or his approach?
   a. hypothesis guessing
   b. evaluation apprehension
   c. experimenter expectancy
   d. all of the above

9. Construct validity can be divided into two subtypes of validity:
   a. concurrent validity and face validity.
   b. predictive validity and criterion-related validity.
   c. face validity and translation validity.
   d. translation validity and criterion-related validity.

10. Like _____ validity, construct validity is related to generalizing.
   a. external
   b. discriminant
   c. convergent
   d. content

11. Reliance on tried-and-true methods like self-report poses no particular issues in terms of threats to validity.
   a. True
   b. False

12. Inadequate preoperational explication of constructs is most likely to occur when a researcher hastily charges into a program of measurement of a new construct without critically thinking about the construct.
   a. True
   b. False

13. The overarching category of validity (the one that supercedes and connects the others) is construct validity.
   a. True
   b. False

14. The strongest way to demonstrate *construct* validity is through *face* validity.
   a. True
   b. False

15. Examining whether test performance is correlated with job performance in a particular field is a form of predictive validity.
   a. True
   b. False

4

Survey Research

Chapter Outline

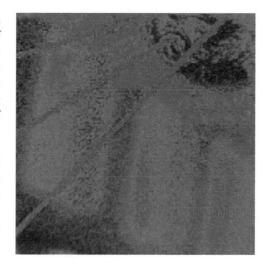

urvey research (Fowler, 2001) is one of the most important areas of measurement in applied social research. In this chapter, I'll begin at the most specific level: how to construct the questions for a survey. I'll discuss a number of issues, including the different types of questions, decisions about question content, decisions about question wording, decisions about response format, and question placement and sequence in your instrument. I'll turn next to some of the special issues involved when there is an interviewer collecting the responses. I'll then move to a broader view and examine the different types of surveys that are possible. These are roughly divided into two general categories: questionnaires and interviews. Next, I'll explain how you select the survey method that's best for your situation. Finally, I'll consider some of the advantages and disadvantages of each type of survey method.

4-1 CONSTRUCTING THE SURVEY

Constructing a survey instrument is an art in itself. You must make numerous small decisions—about content, wording, format, and placement—that can have important consequences for your entire study. Although there's no one perfect way to accomplish this job, I do have advice to offer that might increase your chances of developing a better final product.

There are three primary issues involved in writing a question:

- Determining the question content, scope, and purpose
- Choosing the response format that you use for collecting information from the respondent
- Figuring out how to word the question to get at the issue of interest

After you have your questions written, there is also the issue of how best to place them in your survey.

You'll see that although many aspects of survey construction are just common sense, if you are not careful, you can make critical errors that have dramatic effects on your results.

4-1a Types of Questions

Survey questions can be divided into two broad types: *structured* and *unstructured*. From an instrument design point of view, the structured questions pose the greater difficulties (see Section 4-1c, "Response Format," later in this chapter). From a content perspective, it may actually be more difficult to write good unstructured questions. Here, I'll discuss the variety of structured questions you can consider for your survey. (I discuss unstructured questioning more in Section 4-2, "Interviews," later in this chapter.)

Dichotomous Response Formats When a question has two possible responses, it has a **dichotomous response format.** Surveys often use dichotomous questions that ask for a Yes/No, True/False, or Agree/Disagree response (see Figure 4-1). There are a variety of ways to lay these questions out on a questionnaire.

dichotomous response format
A question with two possible responses.

Do you believe that the death penalty is ever justified?

_____ Yes

_____ No

Please enter your gender:

☐ Male   ☐ Female

FIGURE 4-1
Dichotomous Response Formats for a Survey Question

Occupational Class
1 = Truck driver
2 = Lawyer
3 = etc.

FIGURE 4-2

A Nominal-Level Response Format for a Survey Question

Rank the desserts in order of personal preference, from your most favorite (1) to your least favorite (4).

_____ Ice cream

_____ Cookies

_____ Cake

_____ Candy

FIGURE 4-3

An Ordinal-Level Response Format for a Survey Question

nominal response format
A response format that has a number beside each choice where the number has no meaning except as a placeholder for that response.

ordinal response format
A response format in which respondents are asked to rank the possible answers in order of preference.

interval-level response format
A response measured on an interval level, where the size of the interval between potential response values is meaningful. Most 1-to-5 rating responses can be considered interval level.

Likert response format
An interval-level response format that uses a 5-point integer scale. For instance, a 1-to-5 rating would be considered a Likert response format.

Questions Based on Level of Measurement   We can also classify questions in terms of the level of measurement used in the question's response format. (The idea of level of measurement is covered in Chapter 3, "The Theory of Measurement.") For instance, you might measure occupation using a nominal response format as in Figure 4-2. In a **nominal response format,** the number next to each response has no meaning except as a placeholder for that response; the choices in the example are a 2 for a lawyer and a 1 for a truck driver. From the numbering system used, you can't infer that a lawyer is twice something that a truck driver is. The primary reason you might number responses in this manner is to speed data entry. The person entering the data from this survey would only need to enter a short number rather than a longer category name like "truck driver."

When you ask respondents to rank order their preferences, you are using an **ordinal response format.** For example, in Figure 4-3, the respondent is asked to rate dessert preferences.

In this example, you want the respondent to put a 1, 2, 3, or 4 next to the dessert, where 1 is the respondent's first choice. Note that this could get confusing. The respondents might check their favorite dessert instead of entering a number, or assign higher numbers to desserts they prefer more instead of understanding that you want rank ordering where a higher number means a lower rank. Notice in the example that I stated the prompt (question) explicitly, so the respondent knows I want a number from 1 to 4.

You can also construct survey questions using an **interval-level response format.** One of the most common of these types is the traditional 1-to-5 rating (or 1-to-7, or 1-to-9, and so on). This is sometimes referred to as a Likert scale. However, as you will see in Chapter 5, "Scales and Indexes," a Likert scale is much more than this response format alone, so it's probably better to call the 1-to-5 rating a **Likert response format.** In Figure 4-4, you see how you might ask an opinion question using a 1-to-5 bipolar scale. (It's called *bipolar* because there is a neutral point, and the two ends of the scale are at opposite positions of the opinion.)

An interval response format is used with an approach called the **semantic differential,** as shown in Figure 4-5. Here, an item is assessed by the respondent on a set of bipolar adjective pairs (in this example, a 5-point rating *response scale* is used).

Finally, another type of interval response format occurs when you use a cumulative or Guttman scale to collect responses. Here, the respondents check each item with which they agree. The items themselves are constructed so that they are cumulative; if you agree with one item, you probably agree with all of the ones above it in the list (see Figure 4-6). Each item also has a scale score that is not shown with the item. A respondent's score is the highest scale score of an item with which he or she agreed.

Filter or Contingency Questions   Sometimes, you have to ask the respondents one question to determine whether they are qualified or experienced enough to answer a subsequent one. This requires using a **filter** or **contingency question.** For instance, you may want to ask one question if the respondent has ever smoked marijuana and a different question if he or she has not. In this case, you would have to construct a filter question to determine first whether the respondent has ever smoked marijuana (see Figure 4-7).

Filter questions can be complex. Sometimes, you have to have multiple filter questions to direct your respondents to the correct subsequent questions. You should keep the following conventions in mind when using filters:

- *Try to avoid having more than three levels (two jumps) for any question.* Too many jumps will confuse respondents and may discourage them from continuing with the survey.
- *If there are only two levels, use graphics to jump (for example an arrow and box).* The example in Figure 4-7 shows how you can make effective use of an arrow and box to help direct the respondent to the correct subsequent question.
- *If possible, jump to a new page.* If you can't fit the response to a filter on a single page, it's probably best to be able to say something like, *If YES, please turn to page 4,* rather

The death penalty is justifiable under some circumstances.

1	2	3	4	5
Strongly disagree	Disagree	Neutral	Agree	Strongly agree

FIGURE 4-4
An Interval-Level Response Format for a Survey Question

Please state your opinions on national health insurance on the scale below.

	Very much	Somewhat	Neither	Somewhat	Very much	
Interesting	☐	☐	☐	☐	☐	Boring
Simple	☐	☐	☐	☐	☐	Complex
Uncaring	☐	☐	☐	☐	☐	Caring
Useful	☐	☐	☐	☐	☐	Useless

FIGURE 4-5
A Semantic Differential Response Format for a Survey Question

Please check each item with which you agree.

____ Are you willing to permit immigrants to live in your country?

____ Are you willing to permit immigrants to live in your community?

____ Are you willing to permit immigrants to live in your neighborhood?

____ Would you be willing to have an immigrant live next door to you?

____ Would you let your child marry an immigrant?

FIGURE 4-6
A Cumulative Response Format for a Survey Question

Have you ever smoked marijuana?
☐ Yes
☐ No

If yes, about how many times have you smoked marijuana?
☐ Once
☐ 2 to 5 times
☐ 6 to 10 times
☐ 11 to 20 times
☐ More than 20 times

FIGURE 4-7
A Filter or Contingency Question

semantic differential (see p. 78)
A scaling method in which an
object is assessed by the
respondent on a set of bipolar
adjective pairs.

filter or **contingency question**
(see p. 78) A question you ask the
respondents to determine whether
they are qualified or experienced
enough to answer a subsequent
one.

than *If YES, please go to Question 38*, because the respondent will generally have an easier time finding a page than a specific question.

4-1b Question Content

For each question in your survey, you should ask yourself how well it addresses the content you are trying to get at. The following sections cover some content-related questions you can ask about your survey questions.

Is the Question Necessary and Useful?   Examine each question to determine whether you need to ask it at all and whether you need to ask it at the level of detail you currently have, as in the following examples:

• Do you need the age of each child or just the number of children under 16?
• Do you need to ask income or can you estimate?

Are Several Questions Needed?   Sometimes, we develop a question in which we try to ask about too many things at once, as in the following examples:

• What are your feelings toward African-Americans and Hispanic-Americans?
• What do you think of proposed changes in benefits and hours?

It's hard—often impossible—for respondents to answer such questions because they have conflicting opinions. They may feel very differently about African-Americans and Hispanic-Americans, or about changes in benefits versus changes in hours. You can often spot these kinds of problem questions by looking for the conjunction *and* in your question. We refer to this classic question-writing problem as the *double-barreled question*. You should think about splitting each of the questions into two separate ones.

Another reason you might need more than one question is that the question you ask does not cover all possibilities. For instance, if you ask about earnings, the respondent might not mention all income (such as dividends or gifts). If you ask respondents if they're in favor of public TV, they might not understand that you're asking about their general opinion. They may not be in favor of public TV for themselves (they never watch it), but might favor it for their children (who watch *Sesame Street* regularly). You might be better off asking two questions: one about their own viewing and one about the viewing habits of other members of their households.

Sometimes, you need to ask additional questions because your question does not provide you with enough context to interpret the answer. For instance, if you ask about attitudes toward Catholics, can you interpret this without finding out about your respondents' attitudes toward religion in general or other religious groups?

At times, you need to ask additional questions because your question does not determine the intensity of the respondent's attitude or belief. For example, if respondents say they support public TV, you probably should also ask whether they ever watch it or if they would be willing to have their tax dollars spent on it. It's one thing for respondents to tell you they support something, but the intensity of that response is greater if they are willing to back their sentiment of support with their behavior.

Do Respondents Have the Needed Information?   Look at each question in your survey to see whether the respondent is likely to have the necessary information to be able to answer the question. For example, let's say you want to ask the following question:

Do you think Dean Rusk acted correctly during the Bay of Pigs crisis?

The respondents won't be able to answer this question if they have no idea who Dean Rusk was or what the Bay of Pigs crisis was. In surveys of television viewing, you cannot expect the respondent to answer questions about shows they have never watched. You should ask a filter question first (such as, Have you ever watched the show *ER?*) before asking for opinions about it.

Does the Question Need to Be More Specific?

Sometimes, researchers ask their questions too generally and the information they obtain is difficult to interpret. For example, let's say you want to find out the respondent's opinions about a specific book. You could ask the following question:

How well did you like the book?

and offer some scale ranging from "Not at All" to "Extremely Well," but what would the response mean? What does it mean to say you liked a book extremely well? Instead, you might ask questions designed to be more specific:

Did you recommend the book to others?

or

Did you look for other books by that author?

Is the Question Sufficiently General?

You can err in the other direction as well by being too specific. For instance, if you ask people to list the television programs they liked best in the past week, you could get a different answer than if you asked them which show they've enjoyed most over the past year. Perhaps a show they don't usually like had a great episode in the past week, or their favorite show was preempted by another program.

Is the Question Biased or Loaded?

One danger in question writing is that your own biases and blind spots may affect the wording (see Section 4-1d, "Question Wording," later in this chapter). For instance, you might generally be in favor of tax cuts. If you ask the following question:

What do you see as the benefits of a tax cut?

you're only asking about one side of the issue. You might get a different picture of the respondents' positions if you also asked about the disadvantages of tax cuts. The same thing could occur if you are in favor of public welfare and you ask

What do you see as the disadvantages of eliminating welfare?

without also asking about the potential benefits.

Will the Respondent Answer Truthfully?

For each question on your survey, ask yourself whether respondents will have any difficulty answering the question truthfully. If there is some reason why they may not, consider rewording the question. For instance, some people are sensitive about answering questions about their exact age or income. In this case, you might give them **response brackets** to choose from (such as between 30 and 40 years old, or between $50,000 and $100,000 annual income). Sometimes, even bracketed responses won't be enough. Some people do not like to share how much money they give to charitable causes. (They may be afraid of opening themselves up to even more solicitations.) No matter how you word the question, they would not be likely to tell you their contribution rate. Sometimes, you can work around such problems by posing the question in terms of a *hypothetical projective respondent* (a little bit like a projective test). For example, they might respond if you ask how much money "people you know" typically give in a year to charitable causes. Finally, you can sometimes dispense with asking a question at all if you can obtain the answer unobtrusively. (This is covered in Chapter 6, "Qualitative and Unobtrusive Measures.") If you are interested in finding out which magazines the respondents read, you might instead tell them you are collecting magazines for a recycling drive and ask if they have any old ones to donate. Of course, you have to consider the ethical implications of such deception!

response brackets A question response type that includes groups of answers, such as between 30 and 40 years old, or between $50,000 and $100,000 annual income.

4-1c Response Format

response format The format you use to collect the answer from the respondent.

The **response format** is how you collect the answer from the respondent. Some people use the term *response scale,* but you will see in Chapter 5, "Scales and Indexes," that the term *scales* has a very specific meaning that we shouldn't confuse with the way you collect the data. Let's start with a simple distinction between what I call *structured response formats* and *unstructured response formats.*

structured response formats A response format that is determined prior to administration.

Structured Response Formats
Structured response formats help the respondent to respond more easily and help the researcher accumulate and summarize responses more efficiently, but they can also constrain the respondent and limit the researcher's ability to understand what the respondent really means. There are many different structured response formats, each with their own strengths and weaknesses. We'll review the major ones here.

Fill-in-the-Blank One of the simplest response formats is a blank line that can be used to collect data for a number of different response types. For instance, asking your name as shown in Figure 4-8 is one of the simplest fill-in-the-blank formats.

Name: _____

FIGURE 4-8
A Common Fill-in-the-Blank Question

Blanks are also used for checking responses in dichotomous questions, as illustrated in Figure 4-9.

Here, the respondent would probably put a check mark or an X next to the response. This is also an example of a *dichotomous* response because it only has two possible values. Other common dichotomous responses are True/False and Yes/No. Another common use of a fill-in-the-blank response format is in a preference ranking, as described earlier in Figure 4-3, where respondents entered their rank preferences for four desserts into the blank line in front of each category. Notice that, in this case, you expect the respondent to place a number on every blank, whereas in the previous example, you expect the respondent to choose only one.

And there's always the classic fill-in-the-blank test item (see Figure 4-10).

Please enter your gender:

_____ Male

_____ Female

FIGURE 4-9
Using Blanks for Checking a Response

Check the Answer The respondent places a check next to the response(s). The simplest form would be the example given previously in Figure 4-9, which asks the respondents to indicate their gender. Sometimes, you supply a box that the person can fill in with an X, which is sort of a variation on the check mark. Figure 4-11 shows a check-box format.

Notice that in this example, it is possible to check more than one response. By convention, you usually use the check-mark format when you want to allow the respondent to select multiple items.

One of President Lincoln's most famous speeches, the _____ Address, only lasted a few minutes when delivered.

FIGURE 4-10
A Fill-in-the-Blank Test Item

This type of question is sometimes referred to as a **multioption variable.** You have to be careful when you analyze data from a multioption variable. Because the respondent can select any of the options, you have to treat this type of variable in your analysis as though each option is a separate variable. For instance, for each option you would normally enter into a computer either a 0 if the respondent did not check it or a 1 if the respondent did check it. For the previous example, if the respondent had only a printer and CD-ROM drive, you would enter the sequence 1, 1, 0, 0, 0 in five separate variables. There is an important reason why you should code this variable as either 0 or 1 when you enter the data. If you do, and you want to determine what percent of your sample has a printer, all you have to do is compute the average of the 0's and 1's for the printer variable. For instance, if you have 10 respondents and only 3 have a printer, the average would be 3/10 = .30 or 30%, which is the percent who checked that item.

multioption variable A question format in which the respondent can pick multiple variables from a list.

The previous example is also a good example of a checklist item. When you use a checklist, you want to be sure that you ask the following questions:

- Are all of the alternatives covered?
- Is the list of reasonable length (not too long)?

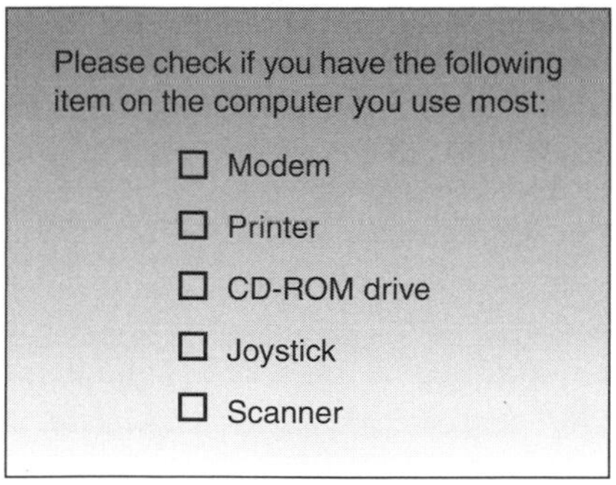

Please check if you have the following
item on the computer you use most:

☐ Modem
☐ Printer
☐ CD-ROM drive
☐ Joystick
☐ Scanner

FIGURE 4-11
The Check-Box Format

The check-box format is useful
when you want respondents
to select more than one item.

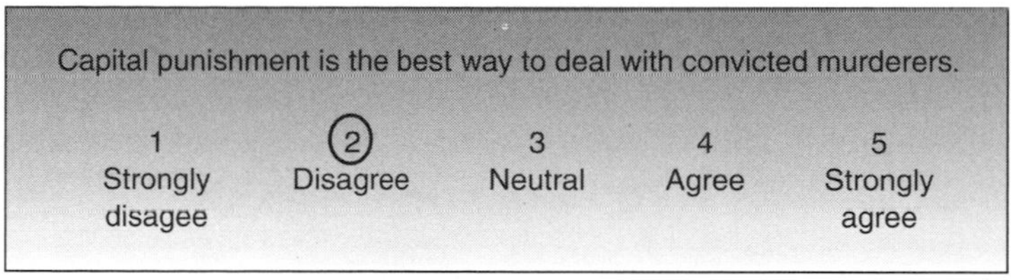

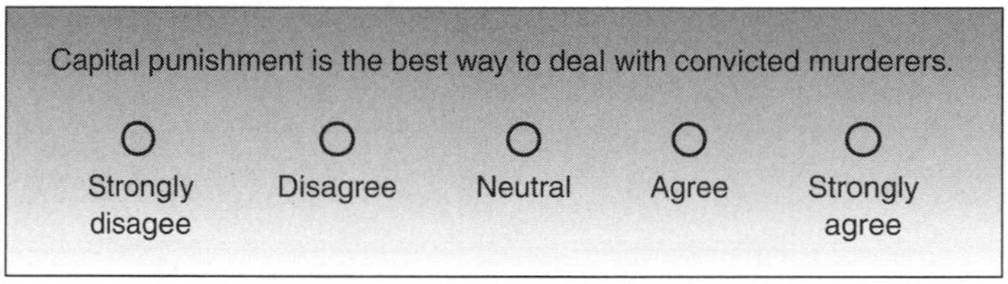

Capital punishment is the best way to deal with convicted murderers.

| 1 | ② | 3 | 4 | 5 |
| Strongly disagee | Disagree | Neutral | Agree | Strongly agree |

FIGURE 4-12 (top)
A Circle-the-Answer Response Format

Capital punishment is the best way to deal with convicted murderers.

| ○ | ○ | ○ | ○ | ○ |
| Strongly disagee | Disagree | Neutral | Agree | Strongly agree |

FIGURE 4-13 (bottom)
An Option Button Response Format on the Web

* Is the wording impartial?
* Is the form of the response easy, uniform?

Sometimes, you may not be sure that you have covered all of the possible responses in a checklist. If that is the case, you should probably allow the respondent to write in any other options that apply.

Circle the Answer Sometimes, respondents are asked to circle an item to indicate their response. Usually, you are asking them to circle a number. For instance, you might have the example shown in Figure 4-12.

If respondents are answering questions on a computer, it's not feasible to have them circle a response. In this case, you would most likely use an option button, as shown in Figure 4-13. With an option button, only one option at a time can be checked. The rule of thumb is that you ask people to circle an item or click a button when you only want them to be able to select one of the options. In contrast to the multioption variable, this type of item is referred to as a **single-option variable;** even though the respondents have multiple choices, they can only select one of them. You would analyze this as a single variable that can take the integer values from 1 to 5.

Unstructured Response Formats A wide variety of structured response formats exist; however, there are relatively few unstructured ones. What is an **unstructured response format?** Generally, it is written text. If the respondent (or interviewer) writes down text as the response, you have an unstructured response format. These can vary from short comment boxes to the transcript of an interview.

In almost every short questionnaire, there's usually one or more short text field questions. One of the most frequent is shown in Figure 4-14.

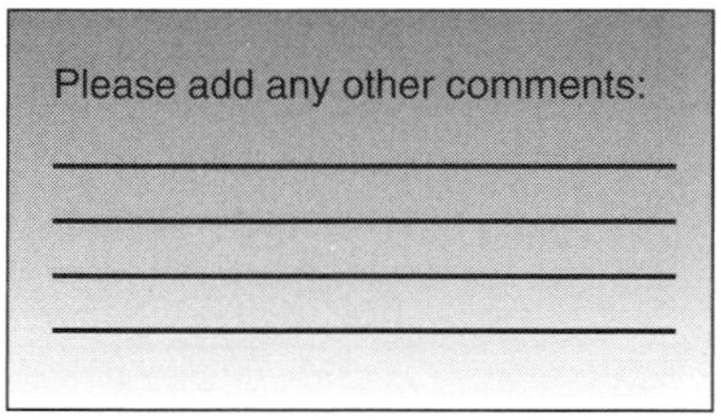

Actually, there's really not much more to text-based response formats of this type than writing the prompt and allowing enough space for a reasonable response.

Transcripts are an entirely different matter. In those cases, the transcriber has to decide whether to transcribe every word or only record major ideas, thoughts, quotes, and so on. In detailed transcriptions, you may also need to distinguish different speakers (such

single-option variable A question response list from which the respondent can check only one response.

unstructured response formats A response format that is not predetermined and where the response is determined by the respondent. An open-ended question is a type of unstructured response format.

Please add any other comments:
_____
_____
_____
_____

FIGURE 4-14
The Unstructured Response Format

The most common unstructured response format allows the respondent to add comments.

as the interviewer and respondent) and have a standard convention for indicating comments about what's going on in the interview, including nonconversational events that take place and thoughts of the interviewer.

4-1d Question Wording

One of the major difficulties in writing good survey questions is getting the wording right. Even slight wording differences can confuse the respondent or lead to incorrect interpretations of the question. Here, I outline some questions you can ask about how you worded each of your survey questions.

Can the Question Be Misunderstood?   The survey author always has to be on the lookout for questions that could be misunderstood or confusing. For instance, if you ask a person for his or her nationality, it might not be clear what you want. (Do you want someone from Indonesia to say *Indonesian, Asian,* or *Pacific Islander?*) Or, if you ask for marital status, do you want people to say simply that they are either married or not married? Or do you want more detail (like divorced, widow/widower, and so on)?

Some terms are too vague to be useful. For instance, if you ask a question about the mass media, what do you mean? The newspapers? Radio? Television?

Here's one of my favorites. Let's say you want to know the following:

What kind of headache remedy do you use?

Do you want to know what brand name medicine respondents take? Do you want to know about home remedies? Are you asking whether they prefer a pill, capsule, or caplet?

What Assumptions Does the Question Make?   Sometimes, you don't stop to consider how a question will appear from the respondent's point of view. You don't think about the assumptions behind the questions. For instance, if you ask what social class someone's in, you assume that they know what social class is and that they think of themselves as being in one. In this case, you may need to use a filter question first to determine whether either of these assumptions is true.

Is the Time Frame Specified?   Whenever you use the words *will, could, might,* or *may* in a question, you might suspect that the question asks a time-related question. Be sure that, if it does, you have specified the time frame precisely. For instance, you might ask:

Do you think Congress will cut taxes?

or something like

Do you think Congress could successfully resist tax cuts?

Neither of these questions specifies a time frame. You can specify a time frame for the first question, such as:

Do you think Congress will cut taxes during its current session?

How Personal Is the Wording?   By changing just a few words, a question can go from being relatively impersonal to probing into private perspectives. Consider the following three questions, each of which asks about the respondent's satisfaction with working conditions:

- Are working conditions satisfactory or not satisfactory in the plant where you work?
- Do you feel that working conditions are satisfactory or not satisfactory in the plant where you work?
- Are you personally satisfied with working conditions in the plant where you work?

The first question is stated from a fairly detached, objective viewpoint. The second asks how you feel. The last asks whether you are personally satisfied. Be sure the questions in your survey are at an appropriate level for your context, and be sure that level is consistent across questions in your survey.

Is the Wording Too Direct?   At times, asking a question too directly may be threatening or disturbing for respondents. For instance, consider a study in which you want to discuss battlefield experiences with former soldiers who experienced trauma. Examine the following three question options:

- How did you feel about being in the war?
- How well did the equipment hold up in the field?
- How well were new recruits trained?

The first question may be too direct. For this population, it may elicit powerful negative emotions based on individual recollections. The second question is a less direct one. It asks about equipment in the field, but for this population, it may also lead the discussion toward more difficult issues to discuss directly. The last question is probably the least direct and least threatening. Bashing the new recruits is standard protocol in almost any social context. The question is likely to get the respondent talking and recounting anecdotes, without eliciting much stress. Of course, all of this may simply be begging the question. If you are doing a study where the respondents might experience high levels of stress because of the questions you ask, you should reconsider the ethics of doing the study.

Other Wording Issues   The nuances of language guarantee that the task of the question writer is endlessly complex. Without trying to generate an exhaustive list, here are a few other guidelines to keep in mind:

- Questions should not contain difficult or unclear terminology.
- Questions should make each alternative clear.
- Question wording should not be objectionable.
- Question wording should not be loaded or slanted. That is, they should not steer the respondent to a particular response (Otherwise, why ask them the question?).

4-1e Question Placement

One of the most difficult tasks facing the survey designer involves the ordering of questions. Which topics should be introduced early in the survey, and which later? If you leave your most important questions until the end, you may find that your respondents are too tired to give them the kind of attention you would like. If you introduce them too early, they may not yet be ready to address the topic, especially if it is a difficult or disturbing one. There are no easy answers to these problems; you have to use your judgment. When you think about question placement, consider the following potential issues:

- The answer may be influenced by prior questions.
- The question may come too early or too late to arouse interest.
- The question may not receive sufficient attention because of the questions around it.

The Opening Questions   Just as in other aspects of life, first impressions are important in survey work. The first few questions you ask will determine the tone for the survey and can help put your respondent at ease. With that in mind, the opening few questions should, in general, be easy to answer. You might start with some simple descriptive questions that will get the respondent rolling. You should never begin your survey with sensitive or threatening questions.

Sensitive Questions   In much of your social research, you will have to ask respondents about difficult or uncomfortable subjects. Before asking such questions, you should attempt to develop some trust or rapport with the respondent. Often, preceding the sensitive questions with some easier warm-up ones will help, but you have to make sure that the sensitive material does not come up abruptly or appear unconnected to the rest of the survey. It is often helpful to have a transition sentence between sections of your instrument to give the respondent some idea of the kinds of questions that are coming. For instance, you might lead into a section on personal material with the following transition: "In this next section of the survey, we'd like to ask you about your personal relationships. Remember, we do not want you to answer any questions if you are uncomfortable doing so."

Guidelines for Question Sequencing   The survey-design business has lots of conventions or rules of thumb. You can use the following suggestions when reviewing your instrument:

- Start with easy, nonthreatening questions.
- Put more difficult, threatening questions near the end.
- Never start a mail survey with an open-ended question.
- For historical demographics, follow chronological order.
- Ask about one topic at a time.
- When switching topics, use a transition.
- Reduce response set (the tendency of the respondent to just keep checking the same response).
- For filter or contingency questions, make a flowchart.

4-1f The Golden Rule

You are imposing in the life of your respondents. You are asking for their time, their attention, their trust, and often, for their personal information. Therefore, you should always keep in mind the golden rule of survey research (and, I hope, for the rest of your life as well!):

Do unto your respondents as you would have them do unto you!

To put this in more practical terms, you should keep the following in mind:

- Thank the respondent at the beginning for allowing you to conduct your study.
- Keep your survey as short as possible—only include what is absolutely necessary.
- Be sensitive to the needs of the respondent.
- Be alert for any sign that the respondent is uncomfortable.
- Thank the respondent at the end for participating.
- Assure the respondent that you will send a copy of the final results—and make sure you do.

4-2 INTERVIEWS

Interviews (McCracken, 1988) are among the most challenging and rewarding forms of measurement. They require a personal sensitivity and adaptability as well as the ability to stay within the bounds of the designed protocol. Here, I describe the preparation you typically need to do for an interview study and the process of conducting the interview itself. Keep in mind that the distinction between an interview and a questionnaire is not always clear-cut. Interviewers typically use a type of questionnaire instrument as the script for conducting the interview. It often has both structured and unstructured questions on it. This type of interview questionnaire would also have instructions for the interviewer that are not seen by the respondent and may include space for the interviewer to record any observations about the progress and process of the interview. These features would not be present in a mailed questionnaire.

4-2a The Role of the Interviewer

The interviewer is really the jack-of-all-trades in survey research. The interviewer's role is complex and multifaceted. It includes the following tasks:

- *Locate and enlist cooperation of respondents.* The interviewer has to find the respondent. In door-to-door surveys, this means being able to locate specific addresses. Often, the interviewer has to work at the least desirable times (like immediately after dinner or on weekends) because that's when respondents are most readily available.

- *Motivate respondents to do a good job.* If the interviewer does not take the work seriously, why would the respondent? The interviewer has to be motivated and has to be able to communicate that motivation to the respondent. Often, this means that the interviewer has to be convinced of the importance of the research.

- *Clarify any confusion/concerns.* Interviewers have to be able to think on their feet. Respondents may raise objections or concerns that were not anticipated. The interviewer has to be able to respond candidly and informatively.

- *Observe quality of responses.* Whether the interview is personal or over the phone, the interviewer is in the best position to judge the quality of the information that is being recorded. Even a verbatim transcript will not adequately convey how seriously the respondent took the task, or any gestures or body language that was observed.

- *Conduct a good interview.* Last, and certainly not least, the interviewer has to conduct a good interview! Every interview has a life of its own. Some respondents are motivated and attentive; others are distracted or disinterested. The interviewer also has good or bad days. Assuring a consistently high-quality interview is a challenge that requires constant effort.

4-2b Training the Interviewers

One of the most important aspects of any interview study is the training of the interviewers themselves. In many ways, the interviewers are your measures, and the quality of the results is totally in their hands. Even in small studies involving only a single researcher-interviewer, it is important to organize in detail and rehearse the interviewing process before beginning the formal study.

Here are some of the major topics that you should consider during interviewer training:

- *Describe the entire study.* Interviewers need to know more than simply how to conduct the interview itself. They should learn about the background for the study, previous work that has been done, and why the study is important.

- *State who is the sponsor of research.* Interviewers need to know whom they are working for. They—and their respondents—have a right to know not only what agency or company is conducting the research, but also who is paying for the research.

- *Teach enough about survey research.* Although you seldom have the time to teach a full course on survey-research methods, the interviewers need to know enough that they respect the survey method and are motivated. Sometimes, it may not be apparent why a question or set of questions was asked in a particular way. The interviewers will need to understand the rationale behind the way you constructed the instrument.

- *Explain the sampling logic and process.* Naive interviewers may not understand why *sampling* is so important. They may wonder why you go through the difficulty of selecting the sample so carefully. You will have to explain that sampling is the basis for the conclusions that will be reached and for the degree to which your study will be useful.

- *Explain interviewer bias.* Interviewers need to know the many ways they can inadvertently bias the results. They also need to understand why it is important that they not bias the study. This is especially a problem when you are investigating political or moral issues on which people have strongly held convictions. Although the interviewers may think they are doing good for society by slanting results in favor of what they believe, they need to recognize that doing so could jeopardize the entire study in the eyes of others.

- *Walk through the interview.* When you first introduce the interview, it's a good idea to walk through the entire protocol so the interviewers can get an idea of the various parts or phases and how they interrelate.

- *Explain respondent selection procedures, including the following:*

     Reading maps: It's astonishing how many adults don't know how to follow directions on a map. In personal interviews, interviewers may need to locate respondents spread over a wide geographic area. They often have to navigate by night (respondents tend to be most available in evening hours) in neighborhoods they're not familiar with. Teaching basic map-reading skills and confirming that the interviewers can follow maps is essential.

     Identifying households: In many studies, it is impossible in advance to say whether every sample household meets the sampling requirements for the study. In your study, you may want to interview only people who live in single-family homes. It may be impossible to distinguish townhouses and apartment buildings in your *sampling frame*. The interviewer must know how to identify the appropriate target household.

     Identifying respondents: Just as with households, many studies require respondents who meet specific criteria. For instance, your study may require that you speak with a male head-of-household between the ages of 30 and 40 who has children under 18 living in the same household. It may be impossible to obtain statistics in advance to target such respondents. The interviewer may have to ask a series of filtering questions before determining whether the respondent meets the sampling needs.

- *Rehearse the interview.* You should probably have several rehearsal sessions with the interview team. You might even videotape rehearsal interviews to discuss how the trainees responded in difficult situations. The interviewers should be familiar with the entire interview before ever facing a respondent.

- *Explain supervision.* In most interview studies, the interviewers will work under the direction of a supervisor. In some contexts, such as university research, the supervisors may be faculty advisors; in others, such as a business context, they may be the boss. To assure the quality of the responses, the supervisor may have to observe a subsample of interviews, listen in on phone interviews, or conduct follow-up assessments of interviews with the respondents. This practice can be threatening to the interviewers. You need to develop an atmosphere in which everyone on the research team—interviewers and supervisors—feels like they're working together toward a common end.

- *Explain scheduling.* The interviewers have to understand the demands being made on their schedules and why these are important to the study. In some studies, it will be imperative to conduct the entire set of interviews within a certain time period. In most studies, it's important to have the interviewers available when it's convenient for the respondents, not necessarily the interviewer.

4-2c The Interviewer's Kit

It's important that interviewers have all of the materials they need to do a professional job. Usually, you will want to assemble an interviewer kit that can be easily carried and that includes all of the important materials, such as following:

- A professional-looking 3-ring notebook (this might even have the logo of the company or organization conducting the interviews)
- Maps

- Sufficient copies of the survey instrument
- Official identification (preferably a picture ID)
- A cover letter from the principal investigator or sponsor
- A phone number the respondent can call to verify the interviewer's authenticity

4-2d Conducting the Interview

Once all the preparation is complete, the interviewers, with their kits in hand, are ready to proceed. It's finally time to do an actual interview. Each interview is unique, like a small work of art (and sometimes the art may not be very good). Each interview has its own ebb and flow—its own pace. To the outsider, an interview looks like a fairly standard, simple, ordinary event, but to the interviewer, it can be filled with special nuances and interpretations that aren't often immediately apparent. Every interview includes some common components. There's the opening, where the interviewer gains entry and establishes the rapport and tone for what follows. There's the middle game, the heart of the process, which consists of the protocol of questions and the improvisations of the probe. Finally, there's the endgame, the wrap-up, during which the interviewer and respondent establish a sense of closure. Whether it's a two-minute phone interview or a personal interview that spans hours, the interview is a bit of theater, a mini-drama that involves real lives in real time.

Opening Remarks   In many ways, the interviewer has the same initial problem that a salesperson has. The interviewers have to get the respondents' attention initially for a long enough period that they can sell them on the idea of participating in the study. Many of the remarks here assume an interview that is being conducted at a respondent's residence, but the similarities to other interview contexts should be straightforward.

- *Gaining entry*—The first thing the interviewer must do is gain entry. Several factors can enhance the prospects. Probably the most important factor is initial appearance. The interviewer needs to dress professionally and in a manner that will be comfortable to the respondent. In some contexts, a business suit and briefcase may be appropriate; in others, it may intimidate. The way the interviewers appear initially to the respondent has to communicate some simple messages—that they're trustworthy, honest, and nonthreatening. Cultivating a manner of professional confidence, the sense that the respondent has nothing to worry about because the interviewers know what they're doing, is a difficult skill to teach interviewers and an indispensable skill for achieving initial entry.

- *Doorstep technique*—If the interviewer is standing on the doorstep and someone has opened the door, even if only halfway, the interviewer needs to smile and briefly state why he or she is there. Have your interviewers suggest what they would like the respondent to do. Not ask. Suggest. Instead of saying, "May I come in to do an interview?" have them try a more imperative approach like, "I'd like to take a few minutes of your time to interview you for a very important study."

- *Introduction*—If interviewers get this far without having doors slammed in their faces, chances are they will be able to get an interview. Without waiting for the respondent to ask questions, they should introduce themselves. Be sure your interviewers have this part of the process memorized so they can deliver the essential information in 20 to 30 seconds at most. They should state their name and the name of the organization they represent, as well as show their identification badge and the letter that introduces them. You want them to have as legitimate an appearance as possible. If they have a 3-ring binder or clipboard with the logo of your organization, they should have it out and visible. They should assume that the respondent will be interested in participating in an important study.

- *Explaining the study*—At this point, the interviewers have been invited to come in. (After all, they're standing there in the cold, holding an assortment of materials, clearly displaying their credentials, and offering the respondent the chance to participate in an interview; to many respondents, it's a rare and exciting event. They are seldom asked their views about anything, and yet they know that important decisions are made all the time based on input from others.) When the respondent has continued to listen long enough, the interviewer needs to explain the study. There are three rules to this critical explanation: (1) Keep it short, (2) Keep it short, and (3) Keep it short! The respondent doesn't have to or want to know all of the nuances of this study, how it came about, how you convinced your thesis committee to buy into it, and so on. Provide the interviewers with a one- or two-sentence description of the study and have them memorize it. No big words. No jargon. No detail. There will be more than enough time for that later. (Interviewers should bring some written materials to leave at the end for that purpose.) Provide a 25-words-or-less description. What the interviewers *should* spend some time on is disclosing fully the purpose of the study and assuring respondents that they are interviewing them confidentially and that their participation is voluntary.

Asking the Questions The interviewer has gotten in and established an initial rapport with the respondent. It may be that the respondent was in the middle of doing something when the interviewer arrived and needs a few minutes to finish the phone call or send the kids off to do homework. Then it's time to begin the interview itself. Here are some hints you can give your interviewers:

- *Use the questionnaire carefully, but informally.* The interview questionnaire is the interviewer's friend. It was developed with a lot of care and thoughtfulness. Although interviewers have to be ready to adapt to the needs of the setting, their first instinct should always be to trust the instrument that was designed. However, they also need to establish a rapport with the respondent. If they bury their faces in the instrument and read the questions, they'll appear unprofessional and disinterested. Reassure them that even though they may be nervous, the respondent is probably even more nervous. Encourage interviewers to memorize the first few questions, so they need refer to the instrument only occasionally, using eye contact and a confident manner to set the tone for the interview and help the respondent get comfortable.

- *Ask questions exactly as written.* Sometimes, interviewers will think that they could improve on the tone of a question by altering a few words to make it simpler or more friendly. Urge them not to. They should ask the questions as they appear on the instrument. During the training and rehearsals, allow the interviewers to raise any issues they have with the questions. It is important that the interview be as standardized as possible across respondents. (This is true except in certain types of exploratory or interpretivist research, where the explicit goal is to avoid any standardizing.)

- *Follow the order given.* When interviewers know an interview well, they may see a respondent bring up a topic that they know will come up later in the interview. They may be tempted to jump to that section. Urge them not to. This can cause them to lose their place or omit questions that build a foundation for later questions.

- *Ask every question.* Sometimes, interviewers will be tempted to omit a question because they thought they have already heard what the respondent will say. Urge them not to assume. For example, let's say you were conducting an interview with college-age women about the topic of date rape. In an earlier question, the respondent mentioned that she knew of a woman on her dormitory floor who had been raped on a date within the past year. A few questions later, the interviewer is supposed to ask, "Do you know of anyone personally who was raped on a date?" Interviewers might figure they already know that the answer is yes and decide to skip the question. Encourage them to say something like, "I know you may have already mentioned this, but do you know of anyone personally who was raped on a date?" At this point, the respondent may say, "Well, in addition to the woman who lived down the hall in my dorm, I know of a friend from high school who experienced date rape." If the interviewer hadn't asked the question, this detail would have remained undiscovered.

- *Don't finish sentences.* Silence is one of the most effective devices for encouraging respondents to talk. If interviewers finish respondents' sentences for them, they imply that what respondents had to say is transparent or obvious, or that they don't want to give respondents the time to express themselves in their own language.

Obtaining Adequate Responses—The Probe   When the respondent gives a brief, cursory answer, the interviewer needs to probe the respondent to elicit a more thoughtful, thorough response. Teach the following probing techniques:

- *The silent probe*—The most effective way to encourage someone to elaborate is to do nothing at all—just pause and wait. This is referred to as the *silent probe*. It works (at least in certain cultures) because respondents are uncomfortable with pauses or silence. It suggests to respondents that the interviewer is waiting, listening for what they will say next.

- *Overt encouragement*—At times, interviewers can encourage the respondent directly. They should try to do so in a way that does not imply approval or disapproval of what the respondent said (that could bias their subsequent results). Overt encouragement could be as simple as saying "uh-huh" or "okay" after the respondent completes a thought.

- *Elaboration*—Interviewers can encourage more information by asking for elaboration. For instance, it is appropriate to ask questions like "Would you like to elaborate on that?" or "Is there anything else you would like to add?"

- *Ask for clarification*—Sometimes, interviewers can elicit greater detail by asking the respondent to clarify something that was said earlier by saying something like, "A minute ago you were talking about the experience you had in high school. Could you tell me more about that?"

- *Repetition*—This is the old psychotherapist trick. You say something without really saying anything new. For instance, the respondent just described a traumatic childhood experience. The interviewer might say "What I'm hearing you say is that you found that experience very traumatic" and then pause. The respondent is likely to say something like, "Well, yes, and it affected the rest of my family as well. In fact, my younger sister. . . ."

Recording the Response   Although we have the capability to record a respondent in audio and/or video, most interview methodologists don't think it's a good idea. Respondents are often uncomfortable when they know their remarks will be recorded word-for-word. They may strain to say things only in a socially acceptable way. Although you would get a more detailed and accurate record, it is likely to be distorted by the process of obtaining it. This may be more of a problem in some situations than in others. It is increasingly common to be told that your conversation may be recorded during a phone interview, and most focus-group methodologies use unobtrusive recording equipment to capture what's being said. However, in general, personal interviews are still best when recorded by the interviewer using pen and paper. Here, I assume the paper-and-pen approach.

- *Record responses immediately.* The interviewers should record responses as they are being stated. This appropriately conveys the idea that they are interested enough in what the respondent is saying to write it down. The interviewers don't have to write down every single word, but you may want them to record certain key phrases or quotes verbatim. Implement a system for distinguishing what the respondent says verbatim from what interviewers are characterizing (how about quotations, for instance).

- *Include all probes*. The interviewers should indicate every single probe that you use. Develop shorthand for different standard probes. Use a clear form for writing them in (for example, place probes in the left margin). Use abbreviations where possible; abbreviations will help interviewers capture more of the discussion. Develop a standardized system (R = respondent, DK = don't know). If interviewers create an abbreviation on the fly, have them indicate its origin. For instance, if your interviewer decides to abbreviate *Spouse* with an *S*, have them make a notation in the right margin saying S = Spouse.

Concluding the Interview   To bring the interview to closure, interviewers should remember the following:

- *Thank the respondents*. Don't forget to do this. Even if the respondents were troublesome or uninformative, it is important to be polite and thank them for their time.

- *Tell them when you expect to send results*. You owe it to your respondents to show them what they contributed to and what you learned. Now, they may not want your entire 300-page dissertation. It's common practice to prepare a short, readable, jargon-free summary of interviews to send to the respondents.

- *Don't be brusque or hasty*. Interviewers need to allow for a few minutes of winding-down conversation. The respondent may be interested in how the results will be used. While the interviewers are putting away their materials and packing up to go, they should engage the respondent. Some respondents may want to keep on talking long after the interview is over. Provide interviewers with a way to cut off the conversation politely and make their exit. For instance, you might have your interviewers say, "I would love to stay to discuss this more with you, but unfortunately, I have another interview appointment I must keep."

- *Immediately after leaving, the interviewer should write down any notes about how the interview went*. Sometimes, interviewers will have observations about the interview that they didn't want to write down while they were with the respondent. (Perhaps they noticed the respondent becoming upset by a question or detected hostility in a response.) Immediately after the interview, interviewers should go over their notes and make any other comments and observations, but they should be sure to distinguish these from the notes made during the interview (by using a different color pen, for instance).

4-3   SURVEYS

4-3a   Types of Surveys

mail survey (see page 93) A paper-and-pencil survey that is sent to respondents through the mail.

group-administered questionnaire (see page 93)   A survey that is administered to respondents in a group setting. For instance, if a survey is administered to all students in a classroom, we would describe that as a group-administered questionnaire.

household drop-off survey (see page 93)   A paper-and-pencil survey that is administered by dropping it off at the respondent's household and either picking it up at a later time or having the respondent return it directly. The household drop-off method assures a direct personal contact with the respondent, while also allowing the respondent the time and privacy to respond to the survey on his or her own.

Surveys can be divided into two broad categories: the questionnaire and the interview. Questionnaires are typically instruments that the respondent completes. Interviews are typically completed by the interviewer, based on what the respondent says. Sometimes, it's hard to tell the difference between a questionnaire and an interview. Most interviews follow a set script of questions that looks very much like a questionnaire (except that it usually also has instructions for the interviewer and space for the interviewer to record observations about how the interview progressed). Some people think that questionnaires always ask short, closed-ended questions and that interviews always ask broad, open-ended ones, but you will see questionnaires with open-ended questions (although they do tend to be shorter than interview questions), and there will often be a series of closed-ended questions asked in an interview.

Survey research has changed dramatically in the last 10 years. Automated telephone surveys use random dialing methods. Web-based surveys enable people to respond anytime and from anywhere in the world. A new variation of group interview has evolved as focus group methodology. Increasingly, survey research is tightly integrated with the delivery of service—often, so much so that the survey becomes a type of service provision. Your hotel room has a survey on the desk. Your waiter presents a short customer satisfaction survey with your check. You get a call for an interview several days after your last call to a computer company for technical assistance and are asked to complete a short survey when you visit a website. Here, I'll describe the major types of questionnaires and interviews, keeping in mind that technology is leading to rapid evolution of methods. I'll discuss the relative advantages and disadvantages of these different survey types in Section 4-3c, "Advantages and Disadvantages of Survey Methods," later in this chapter.

Questionnaires When most people think of questionnaires, they think of the **mail survey** (Dillman, 1999). All of us have, at some time, probably received a questionnaire in the mail. Mail surveys have many advantages. They are relatively inexpensive to administer. You can send the exact same instrument to a wide number of people. The respondent can fill it out at his or her own convenience. However, there are some disadvantages as well. Response rates from mail surveys are often low, and mail questionnaires are not the best vehicles for asking for detailed written responses.

A second type is the **group-administered questionnaire.** A sample of respondents is brought together and asked to respond to a structured sequence of questions. Traditionally, questionnaires have been administered in group settings for convenience. The researcher can give the questionnaire to those who are present and be fairly sure that there will be a high response rate. If the respondents don't understand the meaning of a question, they can ask for clarification. Additionally, in many organizational settings, it is relatively easy to assemble the group (in a company or business, for instance).

What's the difference between a group-administered questionnaire and a group interview or focus group? In the group-administered questionnaire, each respondent is handed an instrument and asked to complete it while in the room. Each respondent completes an instrument. In the group interview or focus group (see Section 4-2, "Interviews"), the interviewer facilitates the session. People work as a group, listening to each other's comments and answering the questions. Someone takes notes for the entire group; people don't complete the interview individually.

A less familiar type of questionnaire is the **household drop-off survey.** In this approach, a researcher goes to the respondent's home or business and hands the respondent the instrument. In some cases, the respondent is asked to mail it back; in others, the interviewer returns to pick it up. This approach attempts to blend the advantages of the mail survey and the group-administered questionnaire. Like the mail survey, the respondent can work on the instrument in private, when it's convenient. Like the group-administered questionnaire, the interviewers make personal contact with the respondent; they don't just send an impersonal survey instrument. Additionally, respondents can ask questions about the study and get clarification on what they are being asked to do. Generally, this increases the percentage of people willing to respond.

Perhaps the most important change in survey research over the past few decades has been the rise of the **electronic survey** or e-survey (Dillman, 1999). There are a wide and increasing variety of technologies for electronic surveys, but most of them fall into one of two categories: **email surveys** or **web surveys.** Although these two are similar in the technology used for delivery of the survey (email versus web, of course), perhaps the more important difference is that email surveys are "pushed" directly to the respondent's computer, whereas with web surveys, you have to "pull" the respondent to a website. This distinction has important implications for how the respondent perceives the survey and for response rates. Electronic surveys also raise important questions about who can be reached. Although computer access is becoming more ubiquitous, there are still many people who have limited access or none at all. Where this is the case, you may need to conduct **dual-media surveys,** where you make the survey available through multiple channels (for example, e-survey and mail survey) and allow respondents to select their preferred method of response.

Interviews Interviews are a far more personal form of research than questionnaires. In the **personal interview,** the interviewer works directly with the respondent. In contrast to mail surveys, the interviewer has the opportunity to probe or ask follow-up

electronic survey Any survey that is administered to participants through an electronic medium, such as email or the web. An electronic survey is distinguishable from other forms of surveying in that the survey is never printed or completed by hand. Note that if you send a survey to participants via an email attachment but ask them to print it and fax back the results, this would not technically be an electronic survey.

email survey Any survey that is distributed to respondents via email. Generally, the survey is either embedded in the email message and the respondent can reply to complete it, is transmitted as an email attachment that the respondent can complete and return via email, or is reached by providing a link in the email that directs the respondent to a website survey.

web survey A survey that is administered over a website (either intranet or Internet). Respondents use their web browser to reach the website and complete the survey.

dual-media survey A survey that is distributed simultaneously in two ways. For instance, if you distribute a survey to participants as an attachment they can print, complete, and fax back or can complete directly on the web as a web form, you can describe this as a dual-media survey.

personal interview A one-on-one interview between an interviewer and respondent. The interviewer typically uses an interview guide that provides a script for asking questions and follow-up prompts.

questions, and interviews are generally easier for the respondent, especially if you are seeking opinions or impressions. Interviews can be time-consuming, and they are resource intensive. The interviewer is considered a part of the measurement instrument, and interviewers have to be well trained to respond to any possible situation.

An increasingly important type of interview is the **group interview** or **focus group.** In a focus group, the interviewer is essentially a facilitator of the group discussion. Small groups of 5 to 10 people are asked to discuss one or more focus questions. The facilitator strives to assure that each person has an opportunity to give an opinion. Focus groups enable deeper consideration of complex issues than many other survey methods. When people hear the points others make, it often will trigger ideas or responses they wouldn't have thought of by themselves (much like in brainstorming). But you always have to be concerned about how respondents in a group might be constrained from saying what they believe because others are present.

Almost everyone is familiar with the **telephone interview.** Telephone interviews enable a researcher to gather information rapidly. Most of the major public opinion polls that are reported are based on telephone interviews. Like personal interviews, they allow for some personal contact between the interviewer and the respondent. They also allow the interviewer to ask follow-up questions. But they have some major disadvantages: Many people don't have publicly listed telephone numbers, some don't have telephones, people often don't like the intrusion of a call to their homes, and telephone interviews have to be relatively short or people will feel imposed upon.

4-3b Selecting the Survey Method

Selecting the type of survey you are going to use is one of the most critical decisions in many social research contexts. A few simple rules will help you make the decision; you have to use your judgment to balance the advantages and disadvantages of different survey types. Here, all I want to do is give you a number of questions you might ask to guide your decision.

Population Issues   The first set of considerations has to do with the population and its accessibility.

- *Can the population units be identified?* For some populations, you have a complete listing of the units to be sampled. For others, such a list is difficult or impossible to compile. For instance, there are complete listings of registered voters or persons with active drivers' licenses, but no one keeps a complete list of homeless people. If you are doing a study that requires input from homeless persons, it's likely that you'll need to go and find the respondents personally. In such contexts, you can pretty much rule out the idea of mail surveys or telephone interviews.

- *Is the population literate?* Questionnaires require that your respondents read. Although this might seem initially like a reasonable assumption for most adult populations, recent research suggests that the instance of adult illiteracy is alarmingly high. Even if your respondents can read to some degree, your questionnaire might contain difficult or technical vocabulary. Clearly, you would expect some populations to be illiterate. Young children would not be good targets for questionnaires.

- *Are there language issues?* We live in a multilingual world. Virtually every society has members who speak a language other than the predominant language. Some countries (like Canada) are officially multilingual, and our increasingly global economy requires us to do research that spans countries and language groups. Can you produce multiple versions of your questionnaire? For mail instruments, can you know in advance which language your respondent speaks, or do you need to send multiple translations of your instrument? Can you be confident that important connotations in your instrument are not culturally specific? Could some of the important nuances get lost in the process of translating your questions?

group interview   An interview that is administered to respondents in a group setting. For instance, if a survey is administered to all students in a classroom, we would describe that as a group-administered questionnaire. A focus group is a structured form of group interview.

focus group   A qualitative measurement method where input on one or more focus topics is collected from participants in a small-group setting where the discussion is structured and guided by a facilitator.

telephone interview   A personal interview that is conducted over the telephone.

- *Will the population cooperate?* People who do research on illegal immigration have a difficult methodological problem. They often need to speak with illegal immigrants or people who may be able to identify others who are. Why would those respondents cooperate? Although the researcher may mean no harm, the respondents are at considerable risk legally if information they divulge should get into the hands of the authorities. The same can be said for any target group that is engaging in illegal or unpopular activities.

- *What are the geographic restrictions?* Is your population of interest dispersed over too broad a geographic range for you to study feasibly with a personal interview? It may be possible for you to send a mail instrument to a nationwide sample. You may be able to conduct phone interviews with them, but it will almost certainly be less feasible to do research that requires interviewers to visit directly with respondents if they are widely dispersed.

Sampling Issues   The *sample* is the actual group you will have to contact in some way. When doing survey research, you need to consider several important sampling issues.

- *What data is available?* What information do you have about your sample? Do you have current addresses? Current phone numbers? Are your contact lists up to date?

- *Can respondents be found?* Can your respondents be located? Some people are very busy. Some travel a lot. Some work the night shift. Even if you have an accurate phone, address, or email address, you may not be able to locate or make contact with your sample.

- *Who is the respondent?* Who is the respondent in your study? Let's say you draw a sample of households in a small city. A household is not a respondent. Do you want to interview a specific individual? Do you want to talk only to the head of household (how is that person defined)? Are you willing to talk to any member of the household? Do you decide that you will speak to the first adult member of the household who opens the door? What if that person is unwilling to be interviewed but someone else in the house is willing? How do you deal with multifamily households? Similar problems arise when you sample groups, agencies, or companies. Can you survey any member of the organization? Or do you only want to speak to the director of human resources? What if the person you would like to interview is unwilling or unable to participate? Do you use another member of the organization?

- *Can all members of the population be sampled?* If you have an incomplete list of the population (sampling frame), you may not be able to sample every member of the population. Lists of various groups are extremely hard to keep up to date. People move or change their names. Even though they are on your sampling frame listing, you may not be able to get to them. It's also possible they are not even on the list.

- *Are response rates likely to be a problem?* Even if you are able to solve all of the other population and sampling problems, you still have to deal with the issue of response rates. Some members of your sample will simply refuse to respond. Others have the best of intentions but can't seem to find the time to send in your questionnaire by the due date. Still others misplace the instrument or forget about the appointment for an interview. Low response rates are among the most difficult of problems in survey research. They can ruin an otherwise well-designed survey effort.

Question Issues   Sometimes, the nature of what you want to ask respondents determines the type of survey you select.

- *What types of questions can you ask?* Are you going to be asking personal questions? Are you going to need to get lots of detail in the responses? Can you anticipate the most frequent or important types of responses and develop reasonable closed-ended questions?

- *How complex will the questions be?* Sometimes, you are dealing with a complex subject or topic. The questions you want to ask are going to have multiple parts. You may need to branch to subquestions.

- *Will filter questions be needed?* A filter question may be needed to determine whether the respondent is qualified to answer your question(s) of interest. For instance, you wouldn't want to ask for respondents' opinions about a specific computer program without first screening to find out whether they have any experience with the program. Sometimes, you have to filter on several variables (for example, age, gender, and experience). The more complicated the filtering, the less likely it is that you can rely on paper-and-pencil instruments without confusing the respondent.

- *Can question sequence be controlled?* Is your survey one in which you can construct a reasonable sequence of questions in advance? Or are you doing an initial exploratory study in which you may need to ask follow-up questions that you can't easily anticipate?

- *Will lengthy questions be asked?* If your subject matter is complicated, you may need to give the respondent some detailed background for a question. Can you reasonably expect your respondent to sit still long enough in a phone interview to listen to your question?

- *Will long response scales be used?* If you are asking people about the different computer equipment they use, you may have to have a lengthy response list (CD-ROM drive, floppy drive, mouse, touch pad, modem, network connection, external speakers, and so on). Clearly, it may be difficult to ask about each of these in a short phone interview.

Content Issues   The content of your study can also pose challenges for the different survey types you might utilize.

- *Can the respondents be expected to know about the issue?* If respondents do not keep up with the news (for example, by reading the newspaper, watching television news, or talking with others), they may not even know of the news issue you want to ask them about. Or, if you want to do a study of family finances and you are talking to the spouse who doesn't pay the bills on a regular basis, he or she may not have the information to answer your questions.

- *Will the respondent need to consult records?* Even if the respondents understand what you're asking about, you may need to allow them to consult their records to get an accurate answer. For instance, if you ask them how much money they spent on food in the past month, they may need to look up their personal check and credit card records. In this case, you don't want to be involved in an interview where they would have to go look things up while they keep you waiting (and they wouldn't be comfortable with that).

Bias Issues   People come to the research endeavor with their own sets of biases and prejudices. Sometimes, these biases will be less of a problem with certain types of survey approaches.

- *Can social desirability be avoided?* Respondents generally want to look good in the eyes of others. None of us likes to look as if we don't know an answer. We don't want to say anything that would be embarrassing. If you ask people about information that may put them in this kind of position, they may not tell you the truth, or they may spin the response so that it makes them look better. This may be more of a problem in a face-to-face interview situation or a phone interview.

- *Can interviewer distortion and subversion be controlled?* Interviewers may distort an interview as well. They may not ask difficult questions or ones that make them uncomfortable. They may not listen carefully to respondents on topics for which they have strong opinions. They may make the judgment that they already know what the respondent would say to a question based on their prior responses, even though that may not be true.

- *Can false respondents be avoided?* With mail surveys, it may be difficult to know who actually responded. Did the head of household complete the survey or someone else? Did the CEO actually give the responses or instead pass the task off to a subordinate? Are the people you're speaking with on the phone actually who they say they are? At least with personal interviews, you have a reasonable chance of knowing to whom you are speaking. In mail surveys or phone interviews, this may not be the case.

Administrative Issues   Last, but certainly not least, you have to consider the feasibility of the survey method for your study.

- *Costs*—Cost is often the major determining factor in selecting survey type. You might prefer to do personal interviews but can't justify the high cost of training and paying for the interviewers. You may prefer to send out an extensive mailing but can't afford the postage to do so.

- *Facilities*—Do you have the facilities (or access to them) to process and manage your study? In phone interviews, do you have well-equipped phone surveying facilities? For focus groups, do you have a comfortable and accessible room to host the group? Do you have the equipment needed to record and transcribe responses?

- *Time*—Some types of surveys take longer than others. Do you need responses immediately (as in an overnight public opinion poll)? Have you budgeted enough time for your study to send out mail surveys and follow-up reminders and to get the responses back by mail? Have you allowed for enough time to get enough personal interviews to justify that approach?

- *Personnel*—Different types of surveys make different demands of personnel. Interviews require well-trained and motivated interviewers. Group-administered surveys require people who are trained in group facilitation. Some studies may be in a technical area that requires some degree of expertise in the interviewer.

Clearly, there are lots of issues to consider when you are selecting which type of survey to use in your study, and there is no clear and easy way to make this decision in many contexts because it might be that no single approach is clearly the best. You may have to make trade-offs and weigh the advantages and disadvantages discussed in the next section. There is judgment involved. Two expert researchers might, for the same problem or issue, select entirely different survey methods, but if you select a method that isn't appropriate or doesn't fit the context, you can doom a study before you even begin designing the instruments or questions themselves.

4-3c Advantages and Disadvantages of Survey Methods

It's hard to compare the advantages and disadvantages of the major different survey types. Even though each type has some general advantages and disadvantages, there are exceptions to almost every rule. Table 4-1 shows my general assessment.

SUMMARY

A lot of territory was covered in this chapter. You've learned about the different types of surveys—questionnaires and interviews—and how to choose between them. You learned how to construct a questionnaire and address issues of question content, response formats, and question wording and placement. You learned how to train interviewers and the basic steps involved in conducting an interview. Based on this chapter, you should feel pretty confident taking a crack at developing your own survey. The next chapter introduces you to several types of quantitative measurements—scales and indexes—where you attempt to represent a construct with a specific score or value.

TABLE 4-1   Advantages and Disadvantages of Different Survey Methods

Issue	Questionnaire				Interview		
	Group	**Mail**	**Email**	**Drop-Off**	**Personal**	**Phone**	**Focus Group**
Are visual presentations possible?	Yes	Yes	Yes	Yes	Yes	No	Yes
Are long response categories possible?	Yes	Yes	???	Yes	???	No	???
Is privacy a feature?	No	Yes	Yes	No	Yes	???	No
Is the method adaptable on the spot?	No	No	No	No	Yes	Yes	Yes
Are longer open-ended questions feasible?	No	No	No	No	Yes	Yes	Yes
Are reading and writing needed?	???	Yes	Yes	Yes	No	No	No
Can you judge quality of response?	Yes	No	No	???	Yes	???	Yes
Are high response rates likely?	Yes	No	No	Yes	Yes	No	Yes
Can you explain study in person?	Yes	No	No	Yes	Yes	???	Yes
Is it low cost?	Yes	Yes	Yes	No	No	No	No
Are staff and facilities needs low?	Yes	Yes	Yes	No	No	No	No
Does it give access to dispersed samples?	No	Yes	Yes	No	No	No	No
Does respondent have time to formulate answers?	No	Yes	Yes	Yes	No	No	No
Is there personal contact?	Yes	No	No	Yes	Yes	No	Yes
Is a long survey feasible?	No	No	No	No	Yes	No	No
Is there quick turnaround?	No	Yes	Yes	No	No	Yes	???

SUGGESTED WEBSITES

Note: These websites were functional when we went to press. Please access the Online Study Guide Edition for the most up-to-date URLs.

The Survey Research Center
http://www.isr.umich.edu/src/
The Survey Research Center at the University of Michigan conducts a large number of high-quality studies. It is also well known for improving survey methodology and providing training and continuing education in survey research.

The Gallup Organization
http://www.gallup.com/
Nearly everyone has heard of the Gallup Polls. The Gallup website provides insight into how Gallup conducts its studies, as well as access to many publications and reports.

KEY TERMS

dichotomous response format (p. 77)
dual-media survey (p. 93)
electronic survey (p. 93)
email survey (p. 93)
filter or contingency question (p. 78)
focus group (p. 94)
group interview (p. 94)
group-administered questionnaire (p. 93)

household drop-off survey (p. 93)
interval-level response format (p. 78)
Likert response format (p. 78)
mail survey (p. 93)
multioption variable (p. 82)
nominal response format (p. 78)
ordinal response format (p. 78)
personal interview (p. 93)

response brackets (p. 81)
response format (p. 82)
semantic differential (p. 78)
single-option variable (p. 83)
structured response formats (p. 82)
telephone interview (p. 94)
unstructured response formats (p. 83)
web survey (p. 93)

REVIEW QUESTIONS

Note: You can find the correct answers to these questions by taking the quiz and then submitting your answers in the Online Study Guide Edition. The program will automatically score your submission. If you miss a question, the program will provide the correct answer, a rationale for the answer, and the section number in the chapter where the topic is discussed.

1. Which of the following is *not* a type of survey technique?
   a. mail survey
   b. group-administered questionnaire
   c. telephone interview
   d. randomized experiment

2. To determine whether your respondent is qualified to answer your survey questions, you might
   a. ask simple questions to see if the respondent understands.
   b. ask open-ended questions to see what the respondent tells you.
   c. locate data to determine the respondent's knowledge base.
   d. ask a filter or screening question.

3. Researchers and respondents are people who can introduce bias and prejudices into the survey process. The bias that makes us want to look good is called
   a. social desirability.
   b. social bias.
   c. self-esteem.
   d. desirability bias.

4. When a survey question offers two possible responses, it is considered ___.
   a. double-barreled
   b. dichotomous
   c. bipolar
   d. filter or contingency

5. What kind of survey question would change the subsequent question a respondent would be asked to answer?
   a. double-barreled
   b. dichotomous
   c. bipolar
   d. filter or contingency

6. When one survey question can produce two separate answers, it is considered
   a. a question of intensity.
   b. a double-barreled question.
   c. a loaded question.
   d. a question that is too specific.

7. How can you write a survey question to increase the likelihood that the respondent will respond truthfully?
   a. Pose the question in terms of a hypothetical projective respondent.
   b. Specify the responses in as much detail as possible.
   c. Reword the question to appear biased or loaded.
   d. Instruct the respondent that only truthful responses are acceptable.

8. What survey response format would you choose if you wanted to know the types of small electronic appliances the respondent had purchased in the last year?
   a. fill-in-the-blank
   b. check the answer
   c. circle the answer
   d. delete the answer

9. A survey asks respondents to "respond to all that apply" regarding a list of common household items they have used. Those recorded answers would be considered
   a. a single option variable.
   b. multioption variables.
   c. dichotomous variables.
   d. checklist variables.

10. When we ask respondents to state their opinion in written form in a survey, we are asking for what type of response format?
    a. double-barreled
    b. structured
    c. single-option
    d. unstructured

11. A dichotomous response format includes two possible options for response—for example, "True" and "False"
    a. True
    b. False

12. The open-ended comments cards found in many businesses and restaurants are good examples of a structured response format.
    a. True
    b. False

13. The most important items should always be placed last in a survey so that respondents are sufficiently "warmed up" to the topic.
    a. True
    b. False

14. The "Golden Rule" as applied to survey research means that you should always offer compensation to your respondents.
    a. True
    b. False

15. Most methodologists agree that audio or videotaping your respondents is not advisable because most people will be at least a little uncomfortable with being taped and may change their response as a result.
    a. True
    b. False

5

Scales and Indexes

Chapter Outline

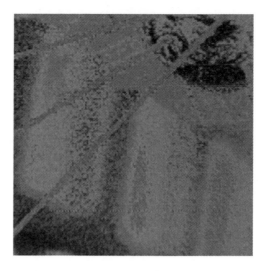

In this chapter, I discuss the two most common approaches for creating quantitative measures of a construct: scaling and indexes. The terms *scale* and *index* are difficult to distinguish, and there are conflicting views in social research about how they should be defined and distinguished. Indexes typically combine different variables into a single score. Often, the variables combined are very different types of constructs and may even be measured in very different ways. So, an index tends to be a composite of differing elements. I consider the basic process in constructing an index and assessing its quality. Scaling evolved from the need to measure abstract or subjective constructs that may seem to be unmeasurable, such as attitudes and beliefs. I discuss general issues in scaling, including the distinction between a scale and a response format. I also explain the difference between multidimensional and unidimensional scaling. Finally, I look in depth at three types of unidimensional scales: Thurstone, Likert, and Guttman. From these discussions, you should not only learn how to use indexes and scales, but you should also learn when each type is most appropriate.

5-1 INDEXES

An **index** is a quantitative score constructed by applying a set of rules to combine two or more variables in order to reflect a more general construct. So, what does this mean? First of all, an index is a score, a numerical value, that purportedly measures something. Second, an index is a composite. It puts different variables together. Often, these variables are very different kinds of things and may even be measured in different ways and on different scales. Third, the variables are put together using a rule or set of rules. Sometimes, the rule is as simple as just adding up or averaging the scores of each variable to get a total index score. Sometimes, the rule is actually a formula or set of procedures for describing how the variables are combined. Finally, we usually construct an index because we want to measure something that none of the individual components alone does a good job of measuring. An index score is typically trying to get at something that cuts across the variables that are combined, that is more general than its composite parts.

index A quantitative score that measures a construct of interest by applying a formula or a set of rules that combines relevant data.

5-1a Some Common Indexes

You are probably already familiar with several famous indexes. One of the best known is the consumer price index, or CPI, that is collected every month by the Bureau of Labor Statistics of the U.S. Department of Labor (U.S. Department of Labor, 2004). Each month, the CPI index is reported and is considered to be a reflection of generally how much consumers have to pay for things. To construct this single score each month, government analysts identified eight major categories of spending for the typical consumer: food and beverages, housing, apparel, transportation, medical care, recreation, education and communication, and other goods and services. They then break down these eight areas into over 200 specific categories. For each of these, they sample from the many items that reflect each category. For example, to represent the "apple" category that is in the "food and beverages" area, they might sample a "particular plastic bag of golden delicious apples, U.S. extra fancy grade, weighing 4.4 pounds" (U.S. Department of Labor, 2004). Each month, people call all over the country to get the current price for over

80,000 items. Through a rather complicated weighting scheme that takes into account things like the location and the probability that the item will be purchased, these prices are combined. That is, there is a series of formulas and rules that are used each month to combine the prices into an index score. Actually, they compute thousands of different CPI scores each month to reflect different groups of consumers and different locations, although one of these is typically reported in the news as the CPI. The CPI is considered an index of consumer costs and, therefore, is a general economic indicator. It illustrates one of the most important reasons for creating an index—to track a phenomenon and its ups and downs over time.

A second well-known type of index is the socioeconomic status index (SES). Unlike the CPI, SES almost always involves the combination of several very different types of variables. Traditionally, SES is a combination of three constructs: income, education, and occupation. Income would typically be measured in dollars. Education might be measured in years or degree achieved. And occupation typically would be classified into categories or levels by status. Then, these very different elements would need to be combined to get the SES score. In one of the early classic studies in this area (Duncan, 1981), the researchers used the degree to which education and income predicted occupation as the basis for constructing the index score. This SES measure is now typically referred to as the Duncan socioeconomic index (SEI). For this index, an SEI score has been created for each of hundreds of occupations. The score is a weighted combination of "occupational education" (the percent of people in that occupation who had one or more years of college education) and "occupational income" (the percentage of people in the occupation who earned more than a specific annual income). With the SEI, all you need to know is the occupation of a person, and you can look up the SEI score that presumably reflects the status of the occupation as related to both education and income. Almost from its inception, the measurement of socioeconomic status has been controversial, and different researchers attempt to accomplish it in a great variety of different ways (Hauser & Warren, 1996; Stevens & Cho, 1985).

5-1b Constructing an Index

There are several steps that are typically followed in constructing an index. I'll go over them briefly here, but you should know that, in practice, each one of these steps is considerably more complex than I'm able to convey in this brief description. Each step can involve sophisticated methods and considerable effort, when accomplished well. Here are the basic steps:

1. *Conceptualize the index.* It probably won't surprise you that the first thing you need to decide is what you would like the index to measure. This may seem like a simple issue at first. However, for almost anything you would like to measure with an index, different people might reasonably disagree about what it means. What is socioeconomic status? Does it include income, education, and occupation? If you measure education and occupation, won't that be highly related to income? If so, do you need a separate component that reflects income or will just the two components be sufficient? If you were trying to measure a construct like "quality of life," what components would you need to include in order to capture the construct? Even with a well-established measure like the CPI, researchers worry about defining basic terms like "consumption by whom" and "prices of what"? To begin composing an index, you need first to identify the construct you are trying to reflect in the index and describe the variables that are components of the construct. There are a wide variety of ways to accomplish this step. You can make it up using your own hunches and intuitions (a surprisingly large amount of social research happens this way). You can review the literature and use current theory as a guide. You can engage experts or key stakeholders in formal processes for conceptualizing, using approaches like brainstorming, concept mapping, or interviewing to identify what the key concept you are trying to measure means to different people. Think about several conceptual issues at this stage. What is the purpose of the index? How will it be used and by whom? Is this a one-time or short-term measure, or one that you would like to use over a long period of time?

2. *Operationalize and measure the components.* It is one thing to say that you would like to measure education and occupation as major components of socioeconomic status. But it is quite another to figure out how to measure each one. If you are trying to measure education as it relates to status, do you simply count the number of years in school? If two people spend the same number of years in college majoring in very different subjects, should they get the same numerical value on educational status? Or should we give more "points" for someone majoring in one field than another. Should all bachelor's degrees be counted the same? If you are trying to look at occupation as it relates to status, how do you even classify occupations? How do you decide the numerical value for each occupation as it relates to status? Over time, do occupations change in status? Are new occupations created? (There weren't any web programmers before the Internet!) If so, how do you accommodate this in an index that tries to measure changes in status over years or decades? What is the unit for which you are measuring? Are you measuring educational levels of individuals? Or are you looking at some other unit like the community or an organization? For example, if you want to measure the educational level of a community and you know the number of years a representative sample of community members went to school, it may be reasonable simply to average the number of years for the community estimate. But if you only have a coding by level of education (for example, 1 = grade school, 2 = some high school, 3 = some college, 4 = associates degree, 5 = bachelor's degree, etc.), you cannot average these values. In this case, you may need to calculate the proportion of the community that achieved a particular level (for example, the proportion of high school graduates) as an estimate of the community educational level. In any event, you need to figure out how you will measure each component of an index before you can move on to calculating the composite index score.

3. *Develop the rules for calculating the index score.* Once you have the components that you think make up the construct of interest, you need to figure out how to combine these component scores to create a single index score. There are many complications here. In the simplest case, you might be able to combine the component scores just by adding or averaging them. In essence, this is what the CPI does. This can be done for the CPI because each consumer item is measured in the same way—its price. But what if each component is measured in entirely different ways? In SES measures, you can't measure income the same way you measure education. So, you're not likely to be able to add or average the scores for income and education in any straightforward way. Even if the components are measured in a similar manner, what if you think different components should be given different emphasis in measuring the construct. For example, what if you believe that income should be considered more important than education when trying to measure socioeconomic status? How much more important? There are several things you can do when combining the components of an index. It helps if you can develop a model of the index that shows the index score, each of the components, and how you think theoretically these are related. You then need to develop precise rules for how to combine the components in the model. Sometimes, these rules can be stated as a set of procedures that you follow to compute the index, almost like a recipe. In other cases, the rules are essentially a formula or set of formulas (a simple average of several components is essentially a formula).

4. One of the most important questions you have to address when constructing an index is whether you are giving each component equal weight or you are constructing a weighted index score. A **weighted index** is one where you combine different components of the index in different amounts or with different emphasis. You're almost certainly familiar with a weighted index because most of you have probably had a teacher that at one time or another used a weighting scheme to come up with your grade for a class. For example, imagine that your teacher measures you on three characteristics: test scores, class participation, and a class project. For the sake of argument (and this is no simple matter in itself), let's assume that you are scored on each of those on a 0-to-100 scale. If you score perfectly on all your tests, you get a 100 on the test score; if your project is perfect, you get 100 on the project score. One

weighted index A quantitative score that measures a construct of interest by applying a formula or a set of rules that combines relevant data where the data components are weighted differently.

way to get a total index score for your course performance would be to average these three components. But what if you (or, more to the point, your professor) believe that these components should not receive equal weight? For instance, maybe participation should only be weighted half as much as the test or project component. You might reason that it doesn't matter how much you participate as long as you can do well on the tests and project. To construct this index score, you would need a formula that weights the test and project components twice as high as the participation. Here's one:

$$\text{Performance} = [(2 \times \text{Test}) + (2 \times \text{Project}) + (1 \times \text{Participation})]/5$$

Why divide by 5? I want the final index score to be on a scale of 1-to-100. Notice that the idea of weighting in index construction can get rather confusing (so what's new?). For example, your professor could have measured both your test and project performance on a 1-to-40 scale (where best performance gets a 40) and your attendance on a 1-to-20 scale. Then, to construct your index score, you might simply add the three component scores! It looks like this is not a weighted index, and technically, it isn't because you're simply adding the scores. But the truth is that you built the weighting into the measurement of each component.

5. *Validate the index score.* Once you have constructed the index, you will need to validate it. This is essentially accomplished in the same way any measure is validated (see Section 3-1, "Construct Validity," in Chapter 3). If the index score is going to be used over time, it is especially important to do periodic validation studies because it's quite possible that the components or how they relate to the index score have changed in important ways over time. For instance, the classification of occupations today differs in important ways from classifications used in 1950. And the selection of consumer goods continually changes over time. Consequently, indexes like the CPI and SES have to be recalibrated or adjusted periodically if they are to be valid reflections of the construct of interest.

Indexes are essential in social research. They range from formal, complex, sophisticated national indexes that track phenomena over years or decades to simple measures developed for use in a single study (or to compute your grade for a course!).

5-2 SCALING

scaling The branch of measurement that involves the construction of an instrument that associates qualitative constructs with quantitative metric units.

Scaling is the branch of measurement that involves the construction of a measure based on associating qualitative judgments about a construct with quantitative metric units. Like an index, a scale is typically designed to yield a single numerical score that represents the construct of interest. In many ways, scaling remains one of the most mysterious and misunderstood aspects of social research measurement. It attempts to do one of the most difficult of research tasks—measure abstract concepts.

Most people don't even understand what scaling is. The basic idea of scaling is described in Section 5-2a, "General Issues in Scaling." The discussion includes the important distinction between a scale and a response format. Scales are generally divided into two broad categories: unidimensional and multidimensional. The unidimensional scaling methods were developed in the first half of the twentieth century and are generally named after their inventors. We'll look at three types of unidimensional scaling methods here:

- Thurstone or equal-appearing interval scaling
- Likert or summative scaling
- Guttman or cumulative scaling

In the late 1950s and early 1960s, measurement theorists developed advanced techniques for creating multidimensional scales. Although these techniques are outside the scope of this text, an understanding of the most common unidimensional scaling methods will provide a good foundation for these more complex variations.

5-2a General Issues in Scaling

S. S. Stevens (1946) came up with what I think is the simplest and most straightforward definition of scaling. He said, "Scaling is the assignment of objects to numbers according to a rule."

What does that mean? In most scaling, the objects are text statements—usually, statements of attitude or belief. In Figure 5-1, three statements describe attitudes toward immigration. To scale these statements, you have to assign numbers to them. Usually, you would like the result to be on at least an interval scale (see Section 3-3, "Levels of Measurement," in Chapter 3), as indicated by the ruler in the figure. What does "according to a rule" mean? If you look at the statements, you can see that as you read down, the attitude toward immigration becomes more restrictive; if people agree with a statement on the list, it's likely that they will also agree with all of the statements higher on the list. In this case, the rule is a cumulative one. So, what is scaling? It's how you get numbers that can be meaningfully assigned to objects; it's a set of procedures. The following paragraphs introduce several approaches to scaling.

First, I have to clear up one of my pet peeves. People often confuse the idea of a scale and a response scale. A **response scale** is the way you collect responses from people on an instrument. You might use a **dichotomous response scale** like Agree/Disagree, True/False, or Yes/No, or you might use an **interval response scale** like a 1-to-5 or 1-to-7 rating. However, if all you are doing is attaching a response scale to an object or statement, you can't call that *scaling*. As you will see, scaling involves procedures that you perform independently of the respondent so that you can come up with a numerical value for the object. In true scaling research, you use a scaling procedure to develop your instrument (scale) and a response scale to collect the responses from participants. Simply assigning a 1-to-5 response scale for an item is *not* scaling! The differences are illustrated in Table 5-1.

response scale A sequential numerical response format, such as a 1-to-5 rating format.

dichotomous response scale A question with two possible responses. The better term to use is dichotomous response *format*.

interval response scale A response measured on an interval level, where the size of the interval between potential response values is meaningful. Most 1-to-5 rating responses can be considered interval level. The better term to use is interval response *format*.

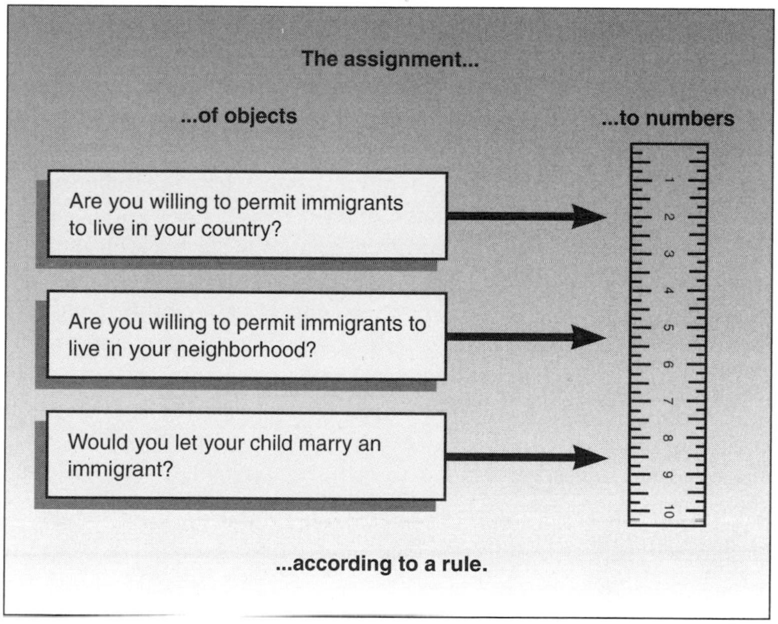

FIGURE 5-1
Scaling as the Assignment of Numbers According to a Rule

Scale	Response Scale
Results from a process	Used to collect the response for an item
Each item on a scale has a scale value	Item not associated with a scale value
Refers to a set of items	Used for a single item

TABLE 5-1

Differences between Scaling and Response Scales

Also, it's important to realize that although a scale is an instrument that can be used alone, it is often integrated into a larger and more complex instrument, such as a survey. Many surveys are designed to assess multiple topics of interest and to collect data that enables us to study the interrelationships of these topics. In many surveys, we will embed one or more scales as separate sections of the survey. When the data is collected, the analyst will compute the various scale scores by combining the responses to items from each scale according to the rules for that scale. However, just because a survey asks a set of questions on a single topic and asks you to respond on a similar response scale (such as a 1-to-5 disagree-agree response scale), you cannot automatically conclude that the set of questions constitute a scale. Got that? Please reread that sentence until you're sure you get the distinction! The set of questions on a survey cannot be considered a scale unless a scaling process was followed to identify the questions and determine how the responses would be combined. So, just because a set of questions on a survey looks like a scale, collects data using the same response scale, and is even analyzed like a scale, it isn't a real scale unless some type of scaling process was used to create it. I'll present several of the most famous scaling processes later in this chapter.

Purposes of Scaling   Why do scaling? Why not just create text statements or questions and use response formats to collect the answers? First, sometimes, you do scaling to test a hypothesis. You might want to know whether the construct or concept is a single dimensional or multidimensional one (more about dimensionality later). Sometimes, you do scaling as part of exploratory research. You want to know what dimensions underlie a set of ratings. For instance, if you create a set of questions, you can use scaling to determine how well they hang together and whether they measure one concept or multiple concepts. But perhaps the most common reason we do scaling is similar to why we construct indexes: We would like to represent a construct using a single score. When a participant gives responses to a set of items, you often want to assign a single number that represents that person's overall attitude or belief. In Figure 5-1, we would like to be able to give a single number that describes a person's attitudes toward immigration, for example. Scaling is a formal procedure that helps you to construct a set of items that can achieve this.

Dimensionality   A scale can have any number of dimensions in it. Most scales that researchers develop have only a few dimensions. What's a dimension? Think of a dimension as a number line, as illustrated in Figure 5-2. If you want to measure a construct, you have to decide whether the construct can be measured well with one number line or whether it may need more. For instance, height is a concept that is unidimensional, or one-dimensional. You can measure the concept of height well with only a single number line (a ruler). Weight is also unidimensional; you can measure it with a scale. Thirst might also be considered a unidimensional concept; you are either more or less thirsty at any given time. It's easy to see that height and weight are unidimensional, but what about a concept like self-esteem? If you think you can measure a person's self-esteem well with a single ruler that goes from low to high, you probably have a unidimensional construct.

FIGURE 5-2
Unidimensional Scales

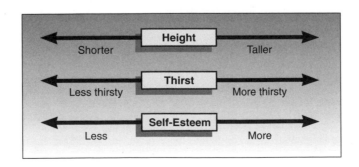

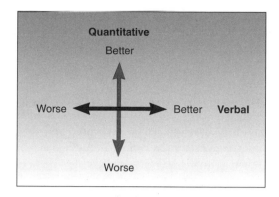

FIGURE 5-3
A Two-Dimensional Scale

What would a two-dimensional concept be? Many models of intelligence or achievement postulate two major dimensions: mathematical and verbal ability. In this type of two-dimensional model, a person can be said to possess two types of achievement, as illustrated in Figure 5-3. Some people will be high in verbal skills and lower in math. For others, it will be the reverse. If a concept is truly two-dimensional, it is not possible to depict a person's level on it by using only a single number line. In other words, to describe achievement, you would need to locate a person as a point in two-dimensional (x, y), space, as shown in Figure 5-3.

Okay, let's push this one step further: How about a three-dimensional concept? Psychologists who study the idea of meaning theorized that the meaning of a term could be well described in three dimensions. Put in other terms, any objects can be distinguished or differentiated from each other along three dimensions. They labeled these three dimensions activity, evaluation, and potency. They called this general theory of meaning the **semantic differential.** Their theory essentially states that you can rate any object along those three dimensions. For instance, think of the idea of ballet. If you like the ballet, you would probably rate it high on activity, favorable on evaluation, and powerful on potency. On the other hand, think about the concept of a book like a novel. You might rate it low on activity (it's passive), favorable on evaluation (assuming you like it), and about average on potency. Now, think of the idea of going to the dentist. Most people would rate it low on activity (it's a passive activity), unfavorable on evaluation, and powerless on potency. (Few routine activities make you feel as powerless!) The theorists who came up with the idea of the semantic differential thought that the meaning of any concepts could be described well by rating the concept on these three dimensions. In other words, to describe the meaning of an object, you have to locate it as a dot somewhere within the cube (three-dimensional space), as shown in Figure 5-4.

semantic differential A scaling method in which the respondent assesses an object on a set of bipolar adjective pairs.

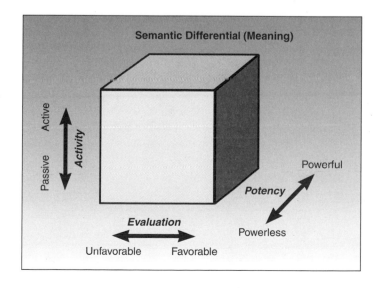

FIGURE 5-4
A Three-Dimensional Scale

Unidimensional versus Multidimensional   What are the advantages of using a unidimensional model? Unidimensional concepts are generally easier to understand. You have either more or less of it, and that's all. You're either taller or shorter, heavier or lighter. It's also important to understand what a unidimensional scale is as a foundation for comprehending the more complex multidimensional concepts. But the best reason to use unidimensional scaling is that you believe the concept you are measuring is unidimensional in reality. As you've seen, many familiar concepts (height, weight, temperature) are actually unidimensional. However, if the concept you are studying is, in fact, multidimensional in nature, a unidimensional scale or number line won't describe it well. If you try to measure academic achievement on a single dimension, you would place every person on a single line, ranging from low to high achievers. How would you score someone who is a high math achiever and terrible verbally, or vice versa? A unidimensional scale can't capture that more general type of achievement; you would need at least two unidimensional scales.

There are three major types of unidimensional scaling methods. They are similar in that they each measure the concept of interest on a number line. However, they differ considerably in how they arrive at scale values for different items. The three methods are Thurstone, or equal-appearing interval scaling; Likert, or summative scaling; and Guttman, or cumulative scaling. Each of these approaches is described in the following sections.

5-2b Thurstone Scaling

Thurstone was one of the first and most productive scaling theorists. He actually invented three different methods for developing a unidimensional scale, which can be considered different ways to do **Thurstone scaling:** the *method of equal-appearing intervals,* the *method of successive intervals,* and the *method of paired comparisons.* The three methods differed in how the scale values for items were constructed, but in all three cases, respondents rated the resulting scale the same way. To illustrate Thurstone's (1925) approach, I'll show you the easiest method of the three to implement: the method of equal-appearing intervals.

> **Developing the Focus**—The method of equal-appearing intervals starts like almost every other scaling method—with a large set of statements to which people respond. Oops! I did it again! You can't start with the set of statements; you have to first define the focus for the scale you're trying to develop. Let this be a warning to all of you: Methodologists like me often start our descriptions with the first objective, methodological step (in this case, developing a set of statements) and forget to mention critical foundational issues like the development of the focus for a project. So, let's try this again. . . .

> The method of equal-appearing intervals starts like almost every other scaling method—with the development of the focus for the scaling project. Because this is a unidimensional scaling method, you have to be able to assume that the concept you are trying to scale is reasonably thought of as one-dimensional. The description of this concept should be as clear as possible so that the person(s) that will create the statements has a clear idea of what you are trying to measure. I like to state the focus for a scaling project in the form of an open-ended statement to give to the people who will create the draft or candidate statements. You want to be sure that everyone who is generating statements has some idea of what you are after in this focus command. You especially want to be sure that technical language and acronyms are spelled out and understood.

Thurstone scaling The process of developing a scale in which the scale items have interval-level numerical values where the final score is the average scale value of all items with which the respondent agreed.

Generating Potential Scale Items—In this phase, you're ready to create statements. Who should create the statements for a scale? That depends. You might have experts who know something about the phenomenon you are studying. Because the people affected are likely to be expert about what they're experiencing, you might sample them to generate statements. For instance, if you are trying to create a scale for quality of life for people who have a certain type of health condition, you might want to ask them to create potential items. Finally, you can make up the items. Obviously, each of these approaches has advantages and disadvantages, so in many situations, you may want to use some or all of them.

You want a large set of candidate statements—usually, as many as 80 to 100—because you are going to select your final scale items from this pool. You also want to be sure that all of the statements are worded similarly—that they don't differ in grammar or structure. For instance, you might want them each to be worded as a statement with which respondents agree or disagree. You don't want some of them to be statements, while others are questions.

Rating the Scale Items—So, now you have a set of items or statements. The next step is to have a group of people called judges rate each statement on a 1-to-11 scale in terms of how much each statement indicates a *favorable* attitude toward the construct of interest. Pay close attention here! You *don't* want the judges to tell you what their attitudes on the statements are, or whether they would agree with the statements. You want them to rate the favorableness of each statement in terms of the construct you are trying to measure, where 1 = extremely unfavorable attitude toward the construct and 11 = extremely favorable attitude towards the construct. One easy way to actually accomplish this is to type each statement on a separate index card and have each judge rate them by sorting them into 11 piles, as shown in Figure 5-5. Who should the judges be? As with generating the items, there is no simple answer. Generally, you want to have people who are "experts" on the construct of interest do this. But there are many kinds of expertise, ranging from academically trained and credentialed experts to the people who are most directly experienced with the phenomenon.

Computing Scale Score Values for Each Item—The next step is to analyze the rating data. For each item or statement, you need to compute the median and the interquartile range. The *median* is the value above and below which 50 percent of the ratings fall. The first quartile (Q1) is the value below which 25 percent of the cases fall and above which 75 percent of the cases fall—in other words, the 25th percentile. The median is the 50th percentile. The third quartile, Q3, is the 75th percentile. The interquartile range is the difference between third and first quartile, or Q3–Q1. Figure 5-6 shows a histogram for a single item and indicates the median and interquartile range.

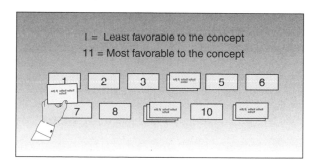

FIGURE 5-5
Rating Statements on a 1-to-11 Scale by Sorting Them Manually

FIGURE 5-6
**Histogram for
a Scale Statement**

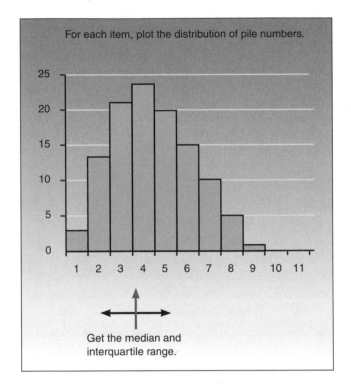

You can compute these values easily with any introductory statistics program or with most spreadsheet programs. To facilitate the final selection of items for your scale, you might want to sort the table of medians and interquartile ranges in ascending order by median and, within that, in descending order by interquartile range.

Selecting the Final Scale Items—Now you have to select the final statements for your scale. You should select statements that are at equal intervals across the range of medians. Ideally, one statement would be selected for each of the 11 median values. Within each value, you should try to select the statement that has the smallest interquartile range (the statement with the least amount of variability across judges). You don't want the statistical analysis to be the only deciding factor here. Look over the candidate statements at each level, and select the statement that makes the most sense. If you find that the best statistical choice is a confusing statement, select the next best choice.

Administering the Scale—You now have a scale—a yardstick you can use for measuring the construct of interest. Each of your final scale items has a scale score—the median value. And the item scores should range across the spectrum of potential attitudes or beliefs on this construct (because you selected items throughout the median range). You can now give the final set of items to respondents and ask them to agree or disagree with each statement. To get an individual's final scale score, average only the scale scores of all the items that person agreed with. When you average the scale items for the statements with which the respondent agreed, you get an average score that has to range between 1 and 11. If they agreed with scale items that were low in favorableness to the construct, then the average of the items they agreed to should be low. If they agreed with items that your judges had said were highly favorable to the construct, then their final score will be on the higher end of the scale.

You should see a couple of things from this discussion. First, you use the judges to create your scale. Think of the scale as a ruler that ranges from 1 to 11 with one scale item or statement at each of the 11 points on the ruler. Second, when you give the set of scale items to a respondent and ask them to tell you which ones they agree with, you are essentially trying to measure them with that ruler. Their scale score—where you would mark the individual on your 11-point ruler—is the average item value for the items the respondent agreed with.

The other Thurstone scaling methods—the method of successive intervals and the method of paired comparisons—are similar to the method of equal-appearing intervals. All of them begin by focusing on a concept that is assumed to be unidimensional and involve generating a large set of potential scale items. All of them result in a scale consisting of relatively few items that the respondent rates on an Agree/Disagree basis. The major differences are in how the data from the judges is collected. For instance, the method of paired comparisons requires each judge to make a judgment about each pair of statements. With lots of statements, this can become time-consuming.

5-2c Likert Scaling

Like Thurstone or Guttman scaling, **Likert scaling** (Murphy and Likert, 1938) is a unidimensional scaling method. Here, I'll explain the basic steps in developing a Likert or summative scale. You may remember learning the term *Likert scale* in Chapter 4, "Survey Research." A Likert scale is a type of response scale and is different from Likert scaling (see the discussion in Section 5-2a, "General Issues in Scaling," and Table 5-1 for the differences between response scales and scaling).

Likert scaling The process of developing a scale in which the ratings of the items are summed to get the final scale score. Ratings are usually done using a 1-to-5 Disagree-to-Agree response format. Likert scales are also sometimes called summated scales.

> **Defining the Focus**—As in all scaling methods, the first step is to define what it is you are trying to measure. Because this is a unidimensional scaling method, it is assumed that the concept you want to measure is one-dimensional in nature. You might operationalize the definition as an instruction to the people who are going to create or generate the initial set of candidate items for your scale.
>
> **Generating the Items**—Next, you have to create the set of potential scale items. These should be items that can be rated on a 1-to-5 or 1-to-7 Disagree-Agree response scale. Sometimes, you can create the items by yourself based on your intimate understanding of the subject matter. More often than not, though, it's helpful to engage a number of people in the item creation step. For instance, you might use some form of brainstorming to create the items. It's desirable to have as large a set of potential items as possible at this stage; about 80 to 100 would be best.
>
> **Rating the Items**—The next step is to have a group of judges rate the items. Usually, you would use a 1-to-5 rating scale where:
>
> 1 = Strongly unfavorable to the concept
>
> 2 = Somewhat unfavorable to the concept
>
> 3 = Undecided
>
> 4 = Somewhat favorable to the concept
>
> 5 = Strongly favorable to the concept
>
> Notice that, as in other scaling methods, the judges are not telling you what they believe; they are judging how favorable each item is with respect to the construct of interest.
>
> Who should the judges be? As in any scaling method, that's not an easy question to answer. Some argue that experts familiar with the process should be used. Others suggest that you should use a random sample of the same types of people who are ultimately your respondents of interest for the scale. There are advantages and disadvantages to each.
>
> **Selecting the Items**—The next step is to compute the intercorrelations between all pairs of items, based on the ratings of the judges. In making judgments about which items to retain for the final scale, there are several analyses you can perform:

- Throw out any items that have a low correlation with the total (summed) score across all items. In most statistics packages, it is relatively easy to compute this type of item-total correlation. First, you create a new variable that is the sum of all of the individual items for each respondent. Then, you include this variable in the correlation-matrix computation. (If you include it as the last variable in the list, the resulting item-total correlations will all be the last line of the correlation matrix and will be easy to spot.) How low should the correlation be for you to throw out the item? There is no fixed rule here; you might eliminate all items that have a correlation with the total score less than .6, for example. (The idea of correlation is covered in Section 11-3d, "Correlation," in Chapter 11.)

- For each item, get the average rating for the top quarter of judges and the bottom quarter. Then, do a *t*-test of the differences between the mean value for the item for the top and bottom quarter judges. (An in-depth discussion of *t*-tests appears in Chapter 11, "Analysis.") Higher *t*-values mean that there is a greater difference between the highest and lowest judges. In more practical terms, items with higher *t*-values are better discriminators, so you want to keep these items. In the end, you will have to use your judgment about which items are most sensibly retained. You want a relatively small number of items on your final scale (from 10 to 15), and you want them to have high item-total correlations and high discrimination (that is, high *t*-values).

Administering the Scale—You're now ready to use your Likert scale. Each respondent is asked to rate each item on some response scale. For instance, respondents could rate each item on a 1-to-5 response scale where:

1 = Strongly disagree

2 = Disagree

3 = Undecided

4 = Agree

5 = Strongly agree

There are a variety of possible response scales (1-to-7, 1-to-9, 0-to-4). All of these odd-numbered scales have a middle value, which is often labeled *neutral* or *undecided*. It is also possible to use a forced-choice response scale with an even number of responses and no middle neutral or undecided choice. In this situation, respondents are forced to decide whether they lean more toward the "agree" or "disagree" end of the scale for each item.

The final score for the respondent on the scale is the sum of his or her ratings for all of the items. (This is why this is sometimes called a *summated scale*.) On some scales, you will have items that are reversed in meaning from the overall direction of the scale. These are called *reversal items*. You will need to reverse the response value for each of these items before summing for the total. That is, if the respondent gave a 1, you make it a 5; if a respondent gave a 2, you make it a 4; 3 = 3; 4 = 2; and 5 = 1. Researchers disagree about whether you should have a "neutral" or "undecided" point on the scale (an odd number of responses) or whether the response scale should be a "forced choice" one with no neutral point and an even number of responses (as in a 1-to-4 scale).

Table 5-2 shows an example of a hypothetical 10-item Likert scale that attempts to estimate the level of self-esteem (Rosenberg, 1965) a person has on the job. Notice that this instrument has no center or neutral point in the response scale; the respondent has to declare whether he or she is in agreement or disagreement with the item.

TABLE 5-2

The Employment Self-Esteem Likert Scale

Strongly disagree	Somewhat disagree	Somewhat agree	Strongly agree	1. I feel good about my work on the job.
Strongly disagree	Somewhat disagree	Somewhat agree	Strongly agree	2. On the whole, I get along well with others at work.
Strongly disagree	Somewhat disagree	Somewhat agree	Strongly agree	3. I am proud of my ability to cope with difficulties at work.
Strongly disagree	Somewhat disagree	Somewhat agree	Strongly agree	4. When I feel uncomfortable at work, I know how to handle it.
Strongly disagree	Somewhat disagree	Somewhat agree	Strongly agree	5. I can tell that other people at work are glad to have me there.
Strongly disagree	Somewhat disagree	Somewhat agree	Strongly agree	6. I know I'll be able to cope with work for as long as I want.
Strongly disagree	Somewhat disagree	Somewhat agree	Strongly agree	7. I am proud of my relationship with my supervisor at work.
Strongly disagree	Somewhat disagree	Somewhat agree	Strongly agree	8. I am confident that I can handle my job without constant assistance.
Strongly disagree	Somewhat disagree	Somewhat agree	Strongly agree	9. I feel like I make a useful contribution at work.
Strongly disagree	Somewhat disagree	Somewhat agree	Strongly agree	10. I can tell that my coworkers respect me.

5-2d Guttman Scaling

Guttman scaling (Guttman, 1950) is also sometimes known as *cumulative scaling* or *scalogram analysis*. In Chapter 4, "Survey Research," I introduced the term *Guttman scale* in Section 4-1a, "Types of Questions." A Guttman scale is a type of response scale and is different from Guttman scaling (see the discussion in Section 5-2a, "General Issues in Scaling," and Table 5-1 for the differences between response scales and scaling). The purpose of Guttman scaling is to establish a one-dimensional continuum for a concept you want to measure. What does that mean? Essentially, you would like a set of items or statements so that a respondent who agrees with any specific question in the list will also agree with all previous questions. Put more formally, you would like to be able to predict item responses perfectly knowing only the total score for the respondent. For example, imagine a 10-item cumulative scale. If the respondent scores a four, it should mean that he or she agreed with the first four statements. If the respondent scores an eight, it should mean he or she agreed with the first eight. The object is to find a set of items that perfectly matches this pattern. In practice, you would seldom expect to find this cumulative pattern perfectly. So, you use scalogram analysis to examine how closely a set of items corresponds with this idea of cumulativeness. Here, I'll explain how you develop a Guttman scale.

> **Guttman scaling** The process of developing a scale in which the items are assigned scale values that allow them to be placed in a cumulative ordering with respect to the construct being scaled.

Define the Focus—As in all of the scaling methods, you begin by defining the focus for your scale. Let's imagine that you want to develop a cumulative scale that measures U.S. citizen attitudes toward immigration. You would want to be sure to specify in your definition whether you are talking about any type of immigration (legal and illegal) from anywhere (Europe, Asia, Latin and South America, Africa).

Develop the Items—Next, as in all scaling methods, you would develop a large set of items that reflect the concept. You might do this yourself, or you might engage a knowledgeable group to help. Of course, as with all scaling methods, you would want to come up with many more statements (about 80 to 100 is desirable) than you will ultimately need.

Rate the Items—Next, you would want to have a group of judges rate the statements or items in terms of how favorable they are to the concept of interest. They would give a *Yes* if the item is favorable toward construct and a *No* if it is not. Notice that you are not asking the judges whether they personally agree with the statement. Instead, you're asking them to make a judgment about how the statement is related to the construct of interest.

Develop the Cumulative Scale—The key to Guttman scaling is in the analysis. You construct a matrix or table that shows the responses of all the judges on all of the items. You then sort this matrix so that judges who agree with more statements are listed at the top and those who agree with fewer are at the bottom. For judges with the same number of agreements, sort the statements from left to right from those that most agreed to, to those that fewest agreed to. You might get a table something like the one in Figure 5-7. Notice that the scale is nearly cumulative when you read from left to right across the columns (items). Specifically, a person who agreed with item 7 always agreed with item 2. Someone who agreed with item 5 always agreed with items 7 and 2. The matrix shows that the cumulativeness of the scale is not perfect, however. While, in general, a person agreeing with item 3 tended to also agree with 5, 7, and 2, there are several exceptions to that rule.

Although you can examine the matrix if there are only a few items in it, if there are many items, you need to use a data analysis called *scalogram analysis* to determine the subsets of items from the pool that best approximate the cumulative property. Then, you review these items and select your final scale elements. There are several statistical techniques for examining the table to find a cumulative scale. Because there is seldom a perfectly cumulative scale, you usually have to test how good it is. These statistics also estimate a scale score value for each item. This scale score is used in the final calculation of a respondent's score.

FIGURE 5-7

Developing a Cumulative Scale with Guttman Scaling

When sorted by row and column, it will show whether there is a cumulative scale.

Respondent	Item 2	Item 7	Item 5	Item 3	Item 8	Item ...
7	Y	Y	Y	Y	Y	Y
15	Y	Y	Y	–	(Y)	–
3	Y	Y	Y	Y	–	–
29	Y	Y	Y	Y	–	–
19	Y	Y	Y	–	–	–
32	Y	Y	–	(Y)	–	–
41	Y	Y	–	–	–	–
6	Y	Y	–	–	–	–
14	Y	–	–	(Y)	–	–
33	–	–	–	–	–	–

Exceptions

Administering the Scale—After you've selected the final scale items, it's relatively simple to administer the scale. You simply present the items and ask respondents to check items with which they agree.

Each scale item has a scale value associated with it (obtained from the scalogram analysis). To compute a respondent's scale score, you simply sum the scale values of every item the respondent agrees with. In this example, the final value should be an indication of the respondent's view on the construct of interest.

5-3 INDEXES AND SCALES

At this point, you should have a much clearer sense of how indexes and scales are similar to and different from each other. One clear commonality is that both an index and a scale yield a single numerical score or value that is designed to reflect the construct of interest.

But there are lots of ways in which scales and indexes are different. Indexes very often are used to combine component scores that are very different from each other and are measured in different ways, like income, occupation, and education in SES. Scales typically involve rating a set of similar items on the same response scale, as in the 1-to-5 Likert response format. Indexes often combine numerical values that are counts or are more objectively observable (like prices). Scales very often are constructed to get at more subjective and judgmental constructs like attitudes or beliefs.

Needless to say, there's considerable disagreement among researchers about whether and how indexes and scales can be defined and distinguished. Some researchers argue that a scale is a particular type or subset of an index. Others argue that they are very different things altogether. Some maintain that a unique feature of scaling is the sophistication of the methodology used to select the items; others contend that good index development can get as sophisticated and advanced as any scaling procedure. And so it goes. However we define them, it should be clear to you that both indexes and scales are essential tools in social research.

SUMMARY

A lot of territory was covered in this chapter. We began by learning about indexes. We briefly looked at two of the most famous indexes: the consumer price index (CPI) and socioeconomic status (SES). I then went through the basic steps for how to construct an index score. Next, I showed you what a scale is and described the basic univariate scale types: Thurstone, Likert, and Guttman. You saw that scales can be used as stand-alone instruments, but they can also be integrated into a larger survey. Based on this chapter, you should have a feel for what would be involved in creating and using either an index or scale. The next chapter introduces you to several very different forms of measurement—qualitative and unobtrusive—that aren't geared to generating a single score like an index or scale does, but that are at least as important for social research.

SUGGESTED WEBSITES

The U.S. Department of Labor Bureau of Labor Statistics
http://www.bls.gov/cpi/home.htm
Visit this website to see the data used in determining the consumer price indexes, as well as to explore many related issues.

National Center for Health Statistics
http://www.cdc.gov/nchs/products/pubs/pubd/other/clrhouse/clrhouse.htm
If you have any interest in health, you might like to peruse the bibliographic resources compiled annually by the Centers for Disease Control on construction of health indexes for the U.S. population.

KEY TERMS

dichotomous response scale (p. 105) *Likert scaling (p. 111)* *Thurstone scaling (p. 108)*
Guttman scaling (p. 113) *response scale (p. 105)* *weighted index (p. 103)*
index (p. 101) *scaling (p. 104)*
interval response scale (p. 105) *semantic differential (p. 107)*

REVIEW QUESTIONS

Note: You can find the correct answers to these questions by taking the quiz and then submitting your answers in the Online Study Guide Edition. The program will automatically score your submission. If you miss a question, the program will provide the correct answer, a rationale for the answer, and the section number in the chapter where the topic is discussed.

1. The Thurstone, Likert, and Guttman scales are all
   a. unidimensional scales.
   b. multidimensional scales.
   c. based on the exact same procedures.
   d. qualitative and unobtrusive forms of measurement.

2. A/An _____ is a quantitative score constructed by applying a set of rules to combine two or more variables in order to reflect a more general construct.
   a. variable
   b. scale
   c. index
   d. attitude

3. The four steps in developing a new index, in order, are
   a. conceptualization, validation, calculation, operationalization.
   b. operationalization, conceptualization, calculation, validation.
   c. calculation, validation, operationalization, conceptualization.
   d. conceptualization, operationalization, calculation, validation.

4. A teacher who uses a formula like (total score = .3 (quiz scores) + .4 (term paper) + .1 (class participation) + .2 (class presentation)) is using which kind of index?
   a. Likert scale
   b. weighted index
   c. scalogram index
   d. Guttman or cumulative scaling

5. According to S. S. Stevens, "_____ is the assignment of objects to numbers according to a rule."
   a. Science
   b. Empiricism
   c. Scaling
   d. Quantitative analysis

6. When a researcher is involved in such activities as brainstorming, using hunches and intuitions, and reviewing the way constructs have been described in the literature, the researcher is involved in which step in index construction?
   a. conceptualization
   b. operationalization
   c. calculation
   d. validation

7. Thurstone's method of equal-appearing intervals allows the researcher to
   a. identify whether a construct is unidimensional or multidimensional.
   b. determine the attitudes of students toward fraternities and sororities.
   c. follow a well-defined set of steps to construct a unidimensional scale.
   d. determine the internal consistency of a set of scale items.

8. Which method of scale construction includes studying the item-total correlations in order to make decisions about which items best reflect the construct?
   a. Thurstone's method of equal-appearing intervals
   b. Likert scales
   c. Guttman's scalogram analysis
   d. semantic differential

9. Which scaling method is based on the idea that attitudes can be measured as cumulative?
   a. Thurstone's method of equal-appearing intervals
   b. Likert scales
   c. Guttman's scalogram analysis
   d. semantic differential

10. All scaling methods require first and foremost that you
    a. understand the concept of correlation.
    b. are able to calculate internal reliability.
    c. generate a large pool of scale items.
    d. define the focus.

11. The terms *scale* and *index* are synonymous.
    a. True
    b. False

12. Construction of indexes of socioeconomic status has eliminated the problems of measurement in this complex and important area.
    a. True
    b. False

13. The operationalization step in index construction basically involves figuring out how to translate the construct in specific observables.
    a. True
    b. False

14. If a survey asks a set of questions on a single topic and asks you to respond on a similar response scale (such as a 1-to-5 disagree-agree response scale), you can automatically conclude that the set of questions constitutes a scale.
    a. True
    b. False

15. A Likert scale is any scale that has the respondent rate things from 1 to 7.
    a. True
    b. False

6

Qualitative and Unobtrusive Measures

Chapter Outline

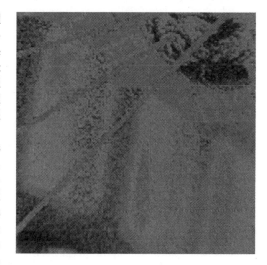

his chapter presents two broad areas of measurement—qualitative measurement and unobtrusive measurement. Each of them is distinct from traditional survey methods described in Chapter 4, "Survey Research," and from scaling and index measures described in Chapter 5, "Scales and Indexes."

Qualitative measurement comes from a long tradition of field research, originally in anthropology and then subsequently in psychology, sociology, and the other social sciences. This tradition is extremely complex and diverse, and there is probably as much variation and dispute within the tradition as there is in more quantitative traditions. Even the simple notion that qualitative means nonquantitative has begun to break down as we recognize the intimate interconnectedness between the two. This chapter introduces the qualitative tradition, the idea of qualitative data and the different approaches to collecting it, the different types of qualitative methods, and the standards for judging the *validity* of qualitative measurement.

Unobtrusive measures are ones that are collected without interfering in the lives of the respondents (Webb et al., 1981). They also represent a broad tradition of measurement in social research. They range from traditional content analysis of existing text documents and secondary analysis of existing data to some of the cleverest and most indirect methods of measurement you'll see.

6-1 QUALITATIVE MEASURES

Qualitative research is a vast and complex area of methodology that can easily take up whole textbooks on its own. The purpose of this section is to introduce you to the idea of qualitative research (and how it is related to quantitative research) and show you the major types of qualitative research data, approaches, and methods.

So, what is qualitative research, and what are qualitative measures? **Qualitative measures** are any measures where the data is not recorded in numerical form. (I know, it's a pain to define something by telling you what it is not, but this really is the most accurate way to look at the breadth of qualitative measures.) Qualitative measures include brief written responses on surveys, interviews, anthropological field research, video and audio data recording, and many other approaches, all of which are characterized by a non-numerical format. Qualitative research is any research that relies primarily or exclusively on qualitative measures.

qualitative measures Data not recorded in numerical form.

6-1a When to Use Qualitative Research

Qualitative research is typically the approach of choice in circumstances that have one or more of the following four characteristics:

- For generating new theories or hypotheses
- For achieving a deep understanding of the issues
- For developing detailed stories to describe a phenomenon
- For mixed methods research

These are addressed in the sections that follow.

Generating New Theories or Hypotheses   One of the major reasons for doing qualitative research is to understand a phenomenon well enough to be able to form some initial theories, hypotheses, or hunches about how it works. Too often in applied social research (especially in economics and psychology), graduate students jump from doing a quick literature review of a topic of interest to writing a research proposal complete with theories and *hypotheses* based on their own thinking. What they miss is the direct experience of the phenomenon. Before mounting a study, all students should probably be required to spend some time living with the phenomenon they are studying. If they do, they are likely to approach the existing literature on the topic with a fresh perspective born of their direct experience, as well as formulate their own ideas about what causes what to happen. This is where the more interesting and valuable new theories and hypotheses originate, and good qualitative research can play a major role in such theory development.

Achieving Deeper Understanding of the Phenomenon   Qualitative research enables us to get at the rich complexity of the phenomenon, to deepen our understanding of how things work. Although quantitative research can describe a phenomenon generally, across a group of respondents, it is very difficult to learn from a quantitative study how the phenomenon is understood and experienced by the respondents, how it interacts with other issues and factors that affect their lives. In addition, in social research, there are many complex and sensitive issues that almost defy simple quantitative summarization. For example, if you are interested in how people view topics like religion, human sexuality, the death penalty, gun control, and so on, my guess is that you would be hard pressed to develop a quantitative methodology that would do anything more than summarize a few key positions on these issues. Although this does have its place (and it's done all the time), if you really want to try to achieve a deep understanding of how people think about these topics, some type of in-depth interviewing or observation is almost certainly required.

Developing Detailed Stories to Describe a Phenomenon   Qualitative research excels at generating detailed information to tell stories. We can see how that is important when we look at how social research is used in policy development and decision making. There's an informal saying among social research that goes something like "one good personal story trumps pages of quantitative results." In legislative hearings and organizational boardrooms, the well-researched anecdote is often what compels decision makers. I'm not suggesting that all we need to do in social research is produce stories. There is a persuasiveness to a pattern of evidence based on quantitative assessment. But if that is all we present, the numbers in our case may not translate well for decision makers because impersonal numbers may not connect to their experience. Illustrating the implications of quantitative data through well-researched qualitative anecdotes and stories is essential to effective use of social research.

Qualitative research, and the stories it can generate, enables you to describe the phenomenon of interest with great richness, often in the original language of the research participants. Because of its complexity, some of the best qualitative research is published in book form, often in a style that almost approaches a narrative story. One of my favorite writers (and, I daresay, one of the finest qualitative researchers) is Studs Terkel. He has written intriguing accounts of the Great Depression (*Hard Times*), World War II (*The Good War*), and socioeconomic divisions in America (*The Great Divide*), among others. In each book, he follows a similar qualitative methodology, identifying informants who directly experienced the phenomenon in question, interviewing them at length, and then editing the interviews so that the collection tells a rich and multilayered story that addresses the question of interest in a way that no one story alone would convey.

mixed methods research   Any research that uses multiple research methods to take advantage of the unique advantages that each method offers. For instance, a study that combines case study interviews with an experimental design can be considered mixed methods.

Mixed Methods Research   One of the most important areas in applied social research these days is called **mixed methods research.** In mixed methods research, we simultaneously conduct both qualitative and quantitative research to achieve the advantages of each and mitigate their weaknesses. There are several different ways to accomplish the mixing of methods. These tend to differ in how and at what stage of the research you bring the quantitative and qualitative traditions together. For instance, you can conduct qualitative and quantitative substudies as though they are independent of each other on separate parallel tracks where you bring together the results of each at the end in a synthesis or summary. Or you can mix quantitative and qualitative data collection methods throughout, analyzing the results together and examining the similarities and contrasts. Or you can integrate the qualitative and quantitative approaches into a new synthetic method, such as when we combine qualitative brainstorming and quantitative rating approaches into a single method. Or you can integrate the paradigmatic perspectives of qualitative and quantitative traditions at all stages of a research project, repeatedly and dynamically using each to question and improve the results of the other.

Quantitative research excels at summarizing large amounts of data and reaching generalizations based on statistical estimations. Qualitative research excels at telling the story from the participant's viewpoint, providing the rich, descriptive detail that sets quantitative results into their human context. We are only beginning to learn about how we can best integrate these great traditions of qualitative and quantitative research, and many of today's social research students will spend much of their careers exploring this idea.

6-1b Qualitative and Quantitative Data

It may seem odd that I would argue that there is little difference between qualitative and quantitative data. After all, qualitative data typically consists of words, whereas quantitative data consists of numbers. Aren't these fundamentally different? I don't think so, for the following reasons:

- All qualitative data can be coded quantitatively.
- All quantitative data is based on qualitative judgment.

I'll consider each of these reasons in turn.

All Qualitative Data Can Be Coded Quantitatively

What I mean here is simple. Anything that is qualitative can be assigned meaningful numerical values. These values can then be manipulated numerically or quantitatively to help you achieve greater insight into the meaning of the data so you can examine specific hypotheses. Consider an example. Many surveys have one or more short, open-ended questions that ask the respondent to supply text responses. The most familiar instance is probably the sentence that is often tacked onto a short survey: "Please add any additional comments." The immediate responses are text-based and qualitative, but you can always (and usually will) perform some type of simple classification of the text responses. You might sort the responses into simple categories, for example. Often, you'll give each category a short label that represents the theme in the response. What you don't often recognize is that even the simple act of categorizing can be viewed as a quantitative one. For instance, let's say that you develop five themes that the respondents express in their open-ended responses. Assume that you have ten respondents. You could easily set up a simple coding table like the one in Table 6-1 to represent the coding of the ten responses into the five themes.

This is a simple qualitative thematic coding analysis. But you can represent exactly the same information quantitatively as in Table 6-2.

Notice that this is exactly the same data. The first table (Table 6-1) would probably be called a qualitative coding, while the second (Table 6-2) is clearly quantitative. The quantitative coding gives you additional useful information and makes it possible to do analyses that you couldn't do with the qualitative coding. For instance, simply by adding down the columns in Table 6-2, you can say that Theme 4 was the most frequently mentioned, and by adding across the rows, you can say that all respondents touched on two or three of the five themes.

The point is that the line between qualitative and quantitative is less distinct than we sometimes imagine. All qualitative data can be quantitatively coded in an almost infinite variety of ways. This doesn't detract from the qualitative information. You can still

TABLE 6-1	Person	Theme 1	Theme 2	Theme 3	Theme 4	Theme 5
Coding of Qualitative Data into Five Themes for Ten Respondents	1	✓	✓		✓	
	2	✓		✓		
	3	✓	✓		✓	
	4		✓		✓	
	5		✓		✓	✓
	6	✓	✓			✓
	7			✓	✓	✓
	8		✓		✓	
	9			✓		✓
	10				✓	✓

do any judgmental syntheses or analyses you want, but recognizing the similarities between qualitative and quantitative information opens up new possibilities for interpretation that might otherwise go unutilized. Now to the other side of the coin. . . .

All Quantitative Data Is Based on Qualitative Judgment   Numbers in and of themselves can't be interpreted without understanding the assumptions that underlie them. Take, for example, a simple 1-to-5 rating variable, shown in Figure 6-1.

Here, the respondent answered 2 = Disagree. What does this mean? How do you interpret the value 2 here? You can't really understand this quantitative value unless you dig into some of the judgments and assumptions that underlie it:

- Did the respondent understand the term *capital punishment?*
- Did the respondent understand that 2 means that he or she is disagreeing with the statement?
- Does the respondent have any idea about alternatives to capital punishment (otherwise, how can he or she judge what's best)?
- Did the respondent read carefully enough to determine that the statement was limited only to convicted murderers (for instance, rapists were not included)?
- Does the respondent care, or was he or she just circling anything arbitrarily?

TABLE 6-2	**Quantitative Coding of the Data in Table 6-1**					
Person	Theme 1	Theme 2	Theme 3	Theme 4	Theme 5	Totals
1	1	1	0	1	0	3
2	1	0	1	0	0	2
3	1	1	0	1	0	3
4	0	1	0	1	0	2
5	0	1	0	1	1	3
6	1	1	0	0	1	3
7	0	0	1	1	1	3
8	0	1	0	1	0	2
9	0	0	1	0	1	2
10	0	0	0	1	1	2

> Capital punishment is the best way to deal with convicted murderers.
>
> | 1 | ② | 3 | 4 | 5 |
> | Strongly disagree | Disagree | Neutral | Agree | Strongly agree |

FIGURE 6-1
A 1-to-5 Rating Variable

A rating illustrates that quantitative data is based on qualitative judgments.

- How was this question presented in the context of the survey (for example, did the questions immediately before this one bias the response in any way)?
- Was the respondent mentally alert (especially if this is late in a long survey or the respondent had other things going on earlier in the day)?
- What was the setting for the survey (lighting, noise, and other distractions)?
- Was the survey anonymous? Was it confidential?
- In the respondent's mind, is the difference between a 1 and a 2 the same as between a 2 and a 3 (meaning, is this an interval scale)?

I could go on and on, but my point should be clear. All numerical information involves numerous judgments about what the number means. Quantitative and qualitative data are, at some level, virtually inseparable. Neither exists in a vacuum; neither can be considered totally apart from the other. To ask which is better or more valid or has greater verisimilitude or whatever ignores the intimate connection between them. To do the highest quality research, you need to incorporate both the qualitative and quantitative approaches.

6-1c Qualitative Data

Qualitative data is extremely varied in nature. It includes virtually any information that can be captured that is not numerical in nature (Miles & Huberman, 1994). Here are some of the major categories or types of qualitative data:

- *In-depth interviews*—These include both individual interviews (one-on-one) as well as group interviews (including focus groups). The data can be recorded in numerous ways, including stenography, audio recording, video recording, and written notes. In-depth interviews differ from direct observation primarily in the nature of the interaction. In interviews, it is assumed that there is a questioner and one or more interviewees. The purpose of the interview is to probe the ideas of the interviewees about the phenomenon of interest.

- *Direct observation*—I use the term *direct observation* broadly here. It differs from interviewing in that the observer does not actively query the respondent. It can include everything from field research, where one lives in another context or culture for a period of time, to photographs that illustrate some aspect of the phenomenon. The data can be recorded in many of the same ways as interviews (stenography, audio, and video) and through pictures (photos or drawings). (For example, courtroom drawings of witnesses are a form of direct observation.)

- *Written documents*—Usually, this refers to existing documents (as opposed to transcripts of interviews conducted for the research). It can include newspapers, magazines, books, websites, memos, transcripts of conversations, annual reports, and so on. Usually, written documents are analyzed with some form of content analysis (see Section 6-2b, "Content Analysis").

qualitative data Data in which the variables are not in a numerical form, but are in the form of text, photographs, sound bytes, and so on.

6-1d Qualitative Traditions

A qualitative tradition is a general way of thinking about conducting qualitative research. It describes, either explicitly or implicitly, the purpose of the qualitative research, the role of the researcher(s), the stages of research, and the method of data analysis. Here, four of the major qualitative traditions are introduced: ethnography, phenomenology, field research, and grounded theory.

ethnography Study of a culture using qualitative field research.

Ethnography

The ethnographic approach to qualitative research comes largely from the field of anthropology. The emphasis in **ethnography** is on studying a phenomenon in the context of its culture. Originally, the idea of a culture was tied to the notion of ethnicity and geographic location, but it has been broadened to include virtually any group or organization.

Ethnography is an extremely broad area with a great variety of practitioners and methods. However, the most common ethnographic approach is participant observation as a part of field research. The ethnographer becomes immersed in the culture as an active participant and records extensive field notes. As in grounded theory, there is no preset limiting of what will be observed and no obvious ending point in an ethnographic study.

phenomenology A philosophical perspective as well as an approach to qualitative methodology that focuses on people's subjective experiences and interpretations of the world.

Phenomenology

The **phenomenology** tradition emphasizes the study of how the phenomenon is experienced by respondents or research participants. It has a long history in several social research disciplines, including psychology, sociology, and social work. Phenomenology is a school of thought that focuses on people's subjective experiences and interpretations of the world. That is, the phenomenologist wants to understand how the world appears to others.

field research A research method in which the researcher goes into the field to observe the phenomenon in its natural state.

Field Research

Field research can also be considered either a broad tradition of qualitative research or a method of gathering qualitative data. The essential idea is that the researcher goes into the field to observe the phenomenon in its natural state or "in situ" (on site). As such, it is probably most related to the method of participant observation. The field researcher typically takes extensive field notes that are subsequently coded and analyzed for major themes.

grounded theory An iterative qualitative approach that includes initial generative questions, gathering qualitative data, identifying theoretical concepts, verifying emerging concepts in data, reconsidering theoretical concepts, and so on, until a detailed theory that is grounded in observation is achieved.

Grounded Theory

Grounded theory is a qualitative research tradition that was originally developed by Glaser and Strauss (1967). The self-defined purpose of grounded theory is to develop theory about phenomena of interest, but Glaser and Strauss are not talking about abstract theorizing. Instead, the theory needs to be grounded or rooted in observations—hence, the term.

Grounded theory is a complex dynamic iterative process in which the development of a theory and the collection of data related to that theory build on each other. The research begins with the raising of generative questions that help guide the research but are not intended to be either static or confining. As the researcher begins to gather data, core theoretical concept(s) are identified. Tentative linkages are developed between the theoretical core concepts and the data. This early phase of the research tends to be open and can take months. Later on, the researcher is more engaged in verification and summary. The effort tends to evolve toward one core category that is central. Eventually, you approach a conceptually dense theory as each new observation leads to new linkages that lead to revisions in the theory and more data collection. The core concept or category is identified and fleshed out in detail.

What do you have when you're finished? Presumably, you have an extremely well-considered explanation for some phenomenon of interest—the grounded theory. This theory can be explained in words and is usually presented along with much of the contextually relevant detail.

6-1e Qualitative Methods

A variety of methods are common in qualitative measurement. In fact, the methods are limited primarily by the imagination of the researcher. Here, I discuss a few of the more common methods.

Participant Observation   One of the most common methods for qualitative data collection—**participant observation**—is also one of the most demanding. It requires that the researcher become a participant in the culture or context being observed. The literature on participant observation discusses how to enter the context, the role of the researcher as a participant, the collection and storage of field notes, and the analysis of field data. Participant observation often requires months or years of intensive work because the researcher needs to become accepted as a natural part of the culture to ensure that the observations are of the natural phenomenon.

> **participant observation**
> A method of qualitative observation in which the researcher becomes a participant in the culture or context being observed.

Direct Observation   **Direct observation** is distinguished from participant observation in a number of ways. First, a direct observer doesn't typically try to become a participant in the context. However, the direct observer does strive to be as unobtrusive as possible so as not to bias the observations. Second, direct observation suggests a more detached perspective. The researcher is watching, rather than both watching and taking part. Consequently, technology can be a useful part of direct observation. For instance, you can videotape the phenomenon or observe from behind one-way mirrors. Third, direct observation tends to be more structured than participant observation. The researcher is observing certain sampled situations or people, rather than trying to become immersed in the entire context. Finally, direct observation tends not to take as long as participant observation. For instance, one might observe mother-child interactions under specific circumstances in a laboratory setting, looking especially for the nonverbal cues being used.

> **direct observation**   The process of observing a phenomenon to gather information about it. This process is distinguished from participant observation in that a direct observer does not typically try to become a participant in the context and does strive to be as unobtrusive as possible so as not to bias the observations.

Unstructured Interviewing   **Unstructured interviewing** involves direct interaction between the researcher and a respondent or group. It differs from traditional structured interviewing in several important ways. First, although the researcher may have some initial guiding questions or core concepts to ask about, there is no formal structured instrument or protocol. Second, the interviewer is free to move the conversation in any direction of interest that may come up. Consequently, unstructured interviewing is particularly useful for exploring a topic broadly. However, there is a price for this lack of structure. Because each interview tends to be unique with no predetermined set of questions asked of all respondents, it is usually more difficult to analyze unstructured interview data, especially when synthesizing across respondents.

> **unstructured interviewing**
> An interviewing method that uses no predetermined interview protocol or survey and in which the interview questions emerge and evolve as the interview proceeds.

Unstructured interviewing may very well be the most common form of data collection of all. You could say it is the method being used whenever anyone asks someone else a question! It is especially useful when conducting site visits or casual focus groups designed to explore a context or situation.

Case Studies   A **case study** is an intensive study of a specific individual or specific context. For instance, Freud developed case studies of several individuals as the basis for the theory of psychoanalysis, and Piaget did case studies of children to study developmental phases. There is no single way to conduct a case study, and a combination of methods (such as unstructured interviewing and direct observation) is often used.

> **case study**   An intensive study of a specific individual or specific context.

6-1f The Quality of Qualitative Research

Some qualitative researchers reject the framework of validity that is commonly accepted in more quantitative research in the social sciences. They reject the idea that there is a single reality that exists separate from our perceptions. In their view, each of us sees a different reality because we see it from a different perspective and through different experiences. They don't think research can be judged using the criteria of validity. Research is less about getting at the truth than it is about reaching meaningful conclusions, deeper understanding, and useful results. These qualitative researchers argue for different standards of judging the quality of qualitative research.

For instance, Guba and Lincoln (1981) proposed four criteria for judging the soundness of qualitative research and explicitly offered these as an alternative to the four

TABLE 6-3	Traditional Criteria for Judging Quantitative Research	Alternative Criteria for Judging Qualitative Research
Criteria for Judging Research Quality from a More Qualitative Perspective	Internal validity	Credibility
	External validity	Transferability
	Reliability	Dependability
	Objectivity	Confirmability

criteria often used in the quantitative tradition (Cook & Campbell, 1979). They felt that their four criteria better reflected the underlying assumptions involved in much qualitative research. Their proposed criteria and the analogous quantitative criteria are listed in Table 6-3.

Credibility   The credibility criteria involve establishing that the results of qualitative research are credible or believable from the perspective of the participant in the research. Since from this perspective the purpose of qualitative research is to describe or understand the phenomena of interest from the participants' eyes, the participants are the only ones who can legitimately judge the credibility of the results.

Transferability   Transferability refers to the degree to which the results of qualitative research can be generalized or transferred to other contexts or settings. From a qualitative perspective, transferability is primarily the responsibility of the one doing the generalizing. The qualitative researcher can enhance transferability by doing a thorough job of describing the research context and the assumptions that were central to the research. The person who wishes to transfer the results to a different context is then responsible for making the judgment of how sensible the transfer is.

Dependability   The traditional quantitative view of *reliability* is based on the assumption of replicability or repeatability (see Section 3-2, "Reliability," in Chapter 3). Essentially, it is concerned with whether you would obtain the same results if you could observe the same thing twice. However, you can't actually measure the same thing twice; by definition, if you are measuring twice, you are measuring two different things. This thinking goes back at least to the ancient Greek Democritus, who argued that we can never step into the same river twice because the river is constantly changing. To estimate reliability, quantitative researchers construct various hypothetical notions (for example, *true score theory* as described in Section 3-2a in Chapter 3) to try to get around this fact.

The idea of dependability, on the other hand, emphasizes the need for the researcher to account for the ever-changing context within which research occurs. The researcher is responsible for describing the changes that occur in the setting and how these changes might affect the conclusions that are reached. Reliability emphasizes the researcher's responsibility to develop measures that, in the absence of any real change, would yield consistent results. Dependability emphasizes the researcher's responsibility to describe the ever-changing research context.

data audit A systematic assessment of data and data collection procedures conducted to establish and document the credibility of data collection processes and potential inaccuracies in the data.

Confirmability   Qualitative research tends to assume that each researcher brings a unique perspective to the study. Confirmability refers to the degree to which others can confirm or corroborate the results. There are a number of strategies for enhancing confirmability. The researcher can actively search for and describe negative instances that contradict prior observations. After the study, a researcher can conduct a **data audit** that examines the data collection and analysis procedures and makes judgments about the potential for bias or distortion.

6-2 UNOBTRUSIVE MEASURES

Unobtrusive measures are measures that allow the researcher to gather data without becoming involved in respondents' interaction with the measure used (Webb et al., 1981). In all of the methods I've presented to this point, researchers have some interaction with respondents in the course of conducting studies. For example, direct observation and participant observation require the researcher to be physically present. This can lead the respondents to alter their behavior to look good in the eyes of the researcher or to conform to what they think the researcher would like to see. A questionnaire is an interruption in the natural stream of behavior. Respondents may tire of filling out a survey or become resentful of the questions asked.

Unobtrusive measurement presumably reduces the biases that result from the intrusion of the researcher or measurement instrument. However, unobtrusive measures depend on the context and, in many situations, are simply not available or feasible. For some constructs, there may not be any sensible way to develop unobtrusive measures.

Three approaches to unobtrusive measurement are discussed here: indirect measures, content analysis, and secondary analysis of data.

6-2a Indirect Measures

An **indirect measure** is an unobtrusive measure that occurs naturally in a research context. The researcher is able to collect data without the respondent being aware of it.

The types of indirect measures that may be available are limited only by the researcher's imagination and inventiveness. For instance, let's say you would like to measure the popularity of various exhibits in a museum. It may be possible to set up some type of mechanical measurement system that is invisible to the museum patrons. In one study, the system was simple. The museum installed new floor tiles in front of each exhibit it wanted a measurement on, and after a period of time, researchers measured the wear-and-tear on the tiles as an indirect measure of patron traffic and interest. You might be able to improve on this approach considerably by using more contemporary electronic instruments. For instance, you might construct an electrical device that senses movement in front of an exhibit or place hidden cameras and code patron interest based on videotaped evidence.

One of my favorite indirect measures occurred in a study of radio station listening preferences. Rather than conducting an obtrusive, costly, and time-consuming survey or interviewing people about favorite radio stations, the researchers went to local auto dealers and garages and checked all cars that were being serviced to see what station the radios were tuned to when the cars were brought in for servicing. In a similar manner, if you want to know magazine preferences, you might observe magazine sales rates, rather than trying to survey readers to ask which magazines they buy. Of course, we need to be careful about how we interpret indirect measures. Just checking radio stations of cars brought in for servicing can be deceptive. We can't automatically conclude that the driver of the car was the one who actually preferred that station (wait till you have kids!), or when it was being listened to, or how often it was tuned in.

These examples illustrate one of the most important points about indirect measures: You have to be careful about ethics when using this type of measurement. In an indirect measure, you are, by definition, collecting information without the respondents' knowledge. In doing so, you may be violating their right to privacy, and you are certainly not using informed consent. Of course, some types of information may be public and therefore do not involve an invasion of privacy, but you should be especially careful to review the ethical implications of the use of indirect measures.

6-2b Content Analysis

Content analysis is the systematic analysis of text (Krippendorff, 2004). The analysis can be quantitative, qualitative, or both. Typically, the major purpose of content analysis is to

unobtrusive measures Methods used to collect data without interfering in the lives of the respondents.

indirect measure An unobtrusive measure that occurs naturally in a research context.

content analysis The analysis of text documents. The analysis can be quantitative, qualitative, or both. Typically, the major purpose of content analysis is to identify patterns in text.

identify patterns in text. Content analysis is an extremely broad area of research. It includes the following types of analysis:

- *Thematic analysis of text*—The identification of themes or major ideas in a document or set of documents. The documents can be any kind of text, including field notes, newspaper articles, technical papers, or organizational memos.

- *Indexing*—A variety of automated methods for rapidly indexing text documents exists. For instance, Key Words in Context (KWIC) analysis is a computer analysis of text data. A computer program scans the text and indexes all key words. A key word is any term in the text that is not included in an exception dictionary. Typically, an **exception dictionary** would exclude all nonessential words like *is, and,* and *of*. All remaining key words in the text are alphabetized and listed with the text that precedes and follows it, so the researcher can see the word in the context in which it occurred in the text. In an analysis of interview text, for instance, you could easily identify all uses of the term *abuse* and the context in which it was used.

- *Quantitative descriptive analysis*—Here, the purpose is to describe features of the text quantitatively. For instance, you might want to find out which words or phrases were used most frequently in the text. Again, this type of analysis is most often done directly with computer programs.

exception dictionary
A dictionary that includes all nonessential words like *is, and,* and *of,* in a content analysis study.

unitizing   In content analysis, the process of breaking continuous text into separate units that can subsequently be coded.

coding   The process of categorizing qualitative data.

Content analysis typically includes several important steps or phases. First, when there are many texts to analyze (for example, newspaper stories, organizational reports), the researcher often has to begin by *sampling* from the population of potential texts to select the ones that will be used. Second, the researcher usually needs to identify and apply the rules that are used to divide each text into segments or "chunks" that will be treated as separate units of analysis in the study, a process referred to as **unitizing.** For instance, you might extract each identifiable assertion from a longer interview transcript. Third, the content analyst constructs and applies one or more codes to each unitized text segment, a process called **coding.** The development of a coding scheme is based on the themes that you are searching for or uncover as you classify the text. Finally, you analyze the coded data, very often both quantitatively and qualitatively, to determine which themes occur most frequently, in what contexts, and how they might be correlated.

Content analysis has several potential limitations that you should keep in mind. First, you are limited to the types of information available in text form. If you were studying the way a news story is being handled by the news media, you probably would have a ready population of news stories from which you could *sample*. However, if you are interested in studying people's views on capital punishment, you are less likely to find an archive of text documents that would be appropriate. Second, you have to be especially careful with sampling to avoid bias. For instance, a study of current research on methods of treatment for cancer might use the published research literature as the population. This would leave out both the writing on cancer that was not published for one reason or another (publication bias), as well as the most recent work that has not yet been published. Finally, you have to be careful about interpreting results of automated context analyses. A computer program cannot always determine what someone meant by a term or phrase. It is relatively easy in a large analysis to misinterpret a result because you did not take into account the subtleties or context of meaning.

However, content analysis has the advantage of being unobtrusive and, depending on whether automated methods exist, can be a relatively rapid method for analyzing large amounts of text.

6-2c Secondary Analysis of Data

Secondary analysis, like content analysis, makes use of already existing data sources. However, secondary analysis typically refers to the reanalysis of quantitative data, rather than text.

In our modern world, an unbelievable mass of data is routinely collected by governments, businesses, schools, and other organizations. Much of this information is stored in electronic databases that can be accessed and analyzed. In addition, many research projects store raw data in electronic form in computer archives so that others can also analyze the data. Examples of data available for secondary analysis include:

- Census Bureau data
- Crime records
- Standardized testing data
- Economic data
- Consumer data

Secondary analysis often involves combining information from multiple databases to examine research questions. For example, you might join crime data with census information to assess patterns in criminal behavior by geographic location and group.

Secondary analysis has several advantages. First, it is efficient. It makes use of data that was already collected by someone else. It is the research equivalent of recycling. Second, it often allows you to extend the scope of your study considerably. In many small research projects, it is impossible to consider taking a national sample because of the costs involved. Many archived databases are already national in scope, and by using them, you can leverage a relatively small budget into a much broader study than if you collected the data yourself.

However, secondary analysis is not without difficulties. Frequently, it is no trivial matter to access and link data from large complex databases. Often, you have to make assumptions about which data to combine and which variables are appropriately aggregated into indexes (see Chapter 5, "Scales and Indexes"). Perhaps more importantly, when you use data collected by others, you often don't know what problems occurred in the original data collection. Large, well-financed national studies are usually documented thoroughly, but even detailed documentation of procedures is often no substitute for direct experience collecting data.

One of the most important and least utilized purposes of secondary analysis is to replicate prior research findings. In any original data analysis, there is the potential for errors. In addition, data analysts tend to approach the analysis from their own perspective, using the analytic tools with which they are familiar. In most research, the data is analyzed only once by the original research team. It seems an awful waste. Data that might have taken months or years to collect is only examined once in a relatively brief way and from one analyst's perspective. In social research, we generally do a terrible job of documenting and archiving the data from individual studies and making it available in electronic form for others to reanalyze, and we tend to give little professional credit to studies that are reanalyzed. Nevertheless, in the hard sciences, the tradition of replicability of results is a critical one, and we in the applied social sciences could benefit by directing more of our efforts to secondary analysis of existing data.

> **secondary analysis** Analysis that makes use of already existing data sources.

SUMMARY

This chapter began by comparing qualitative and quantitative data. I made the point that each type of data has its strengths and weaknesses, and that they are often best when used together. Qualitative data can always be quantified, and quantitative data is always based on qualitative assumptions.

Qualitative data can be collected through a variety of methods, including in-depth interviews, direct observation, and written documents. Standards for judging the quality of qualitative data include credibility, transferability, dependability, and confirmability.

Unobtrusive measures are ways of collecting data that don't require researcher interaction with the population of interest. Indirect measures require the researcher to set up conditions so that those being studied are unaware that they are being studied. Content analysis involves the systematic assessment of existing texts and, because it does not require original data collection, is typically considered unobtrusive. Similarly, by definition, the secondary analysis of existing data makes use of information that was previously collected and, as such, does not intrude on respondents.

SUGGESTED WEBSITES

Note: These websites were functional when we went to press. Please access the Online Study Guide Edition for the most up-to-date URLs.

The Association for Qualitative Research
http://www.latrobe.edu.au/aqr/
The Association for Qualitative Research is an international association of qualitatively oriented researchers. The website gives you a sense of the interests and activities of researchers who favor qualitative methods.

QualPage: Resources for Qualitative Research
http://www.qualitativeresearch.uga.edu/QualPage/
This website has a large number of links. It is well organized and covers the field in a broad and comprehensive way.

KEY TERMS

case study (p. 125)
coding (p. 128)
content analysis (p. 127)
data audit (p. 126)
direct observation (p. 125)
ethnography (p. 124)
exception dictionary (p. 128)

field research (p. 124)
grounded theory (p. 124)
indirect measure (p. 127)
mixed methods research (p. 120)
participant observation (p. 125)
phenomenology (p. 124)
qualitative data (p. 123)

qualitative measures (p. 119)
secondary analysis (p. 129)
unitizing (p. 128)
unobtrusive measures (p. 127)
unstructured interviewing (p. 125)

REVIEW QUESTIONS

Note: You can find the correct answers to these questions by taking the quiz and then submitting your answers in the Online Study Guide Edition. The program will automatically score your submission. If you miss a question, the program will provide the correct answer, a rationale for the answer, and the section number in the chapter where the topic is discussed.

1. Which of the following statements is correct?
   a. Qualitative data can only be coded qualitatively.
   b. Quantitative data is based on qualitative judgment.
   c. Quantitative data is often collected in text format for content analysis.
   d. Qualitative data is the primary type of unobtrusive measure.

2. Which of the following is *not* an approach to qualitative research?
   a. ethnography
   b. field research
   c. diagramming
   d. grounded theory

3. What type of qualitative approach to data collection begins with a set of generative questions, then identifies core concepts as data is gathered, with linkages developed between the core concepts and the data?
   a. ethnography
   b. field research
   c. diagramming
   d. grounded theory

4. In general, what is the most demanding qualitative method?
   a. direct observation
   b. analyzing existing documents
   c. participant observation
   d. case studies

5. For which of the following purposes is qualitative research *not* well suited?
   a. generating new theories or hypotheses
   b. achieving a deep understanding of complex and sensitive issues
   c. generalizing themes across a population
   d. generating information that is very detailed

6. According to Guba and Lincoln, the alternative criterion for judging the "internal validity" of qualitative research is
   a. credibility.
   b. confirmability.
   c. transferability.
   d. dependability.

7. According to Guba and Lincoln, the alternative criterion for judging the "objectivity" of qualitative research is
   a. credibility.
   b. confirmability.
   c. transferability.
   d. dependability.

8. When assessing the confirmability of qualitative research results, a researcher can
   a. actively search for and describe negative instances that contradict prior observations.
   b. do a data audit after the fact to make judgments about potential bias.
   c. have another researcher play devil's advocate with respect to the results, documenting the process.
   d. All of the above will increase the confirmability of qualitative research results.

9. Which of the following is *not* an unobtrusive measure?
   a. indirect measure
   b. content analysis
   c. participant observation
   d. secondary analysis

10. Which unobtrusive measure involves the systematic analysis of text?
    a. indirect measure
    b. content analysis
    c. participant observation
    d. secondary analysis

11. Qualitative measures are any measures where the data is not recorded in numerical form.
    a. True
    b. False

12. Quantitative research is better than qualitative research for generating new theories.
    a. True
    b. False

13. All qualitative data can be coded quantitatively.
    a. True
    b. False

14. One of the best ways to reduce the impact of measurement procedures or the presence of researchers as observers is known as unobtrusive measurement.
    a. True
    b. False

15. Like content analysis, secondary analysis employs existing data sources but is different in that the data analyzed in secondary analysis is typically quantitative.
    a. True
    b. False

DESIGN

7

Design

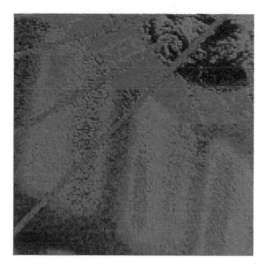

esearch design provides the glue that holds the research project together. A design is used to structure the research, to show how all of the major parts of the research project— the *samples* or groups, measures, treatments or programs, and methods of assignment—work together to address the central research questions. In this chapter, I begin by showing that research design is most related to assessing cause-effect questions like whether a program or intervention caused a result or outcome. I discuss internal validity first because it is concerned with causal inference and is therefore closely connected with the topic of research design. I then describe the major threats to the internal validity of a study and how research designs are used to address them. Next, I'll show you the basic components of research designs and how to classify the major types of designs. You'll see that a major distinction is made between the experimental designs that use random assignment to groups or programs and the quasi-experimental designs that don't use random assignment. (People often confuse random selection with the idea of random assignment. You should make sure that you understand the distinction between random selection and random assignment as described in Chapter 8, "Experimental Design.") Understanding the relationships among designs is important when you need to make design choices.

7-1 INTERNAL VALIDITY

Why begin a chapter on research design with a discussion of internal validity? Because I like tormenting readers with irrelevant abstract philosophical discussions? No! Because the two topics are inextricably linked. Research designs are typically constructed to address or eliminate threats to internal validity. So, you can't really understand why certain designs might be better than others until you understand how the designs try to address internal validity concerns. If I only taught you the standard research designs, you could probably learn to apply them. But you would never really understand them, and you certainly would not know how to adapt them to address the specific concerns in your study. If you learn about internal validity and how threats to it shape research design, you'll not only be able to use a few standard designs, but you'll also better understand how to tailor designs to the specific needs of your study. I'll spend some time on internal validity at the beginning of this chapter, and we'll link this to research designs later in the chapter.

Internal validity is the approximate truth about inferences regarding cause-effect or *causal* relationships (Cook & Campbell, 1979). What does this mean? Why should you care? If you are doing a study where you would like to say that something—a program, treatment, or event—caused something else to happen, you are dealing with causal relationships. At the end of the study, you would like to be able to draw some inferences about the cause being responsible for the effect. Internal validity is only relevant in studies that try to establish a causal relationship. It's not relevant in most observational or descriptive studies, for instance. However, for studies that assess the effects of social programs or interventions, internal validity is perhaps the primary consideration. In such studies, you want to be able to conclude that your program or treatment made a

internal validity The approximate truth of inferences regarding cause-effect or causal relationships.

FIGURE 7-1

**A Schematic View
of the Conceptual Context
for Internal Validity**

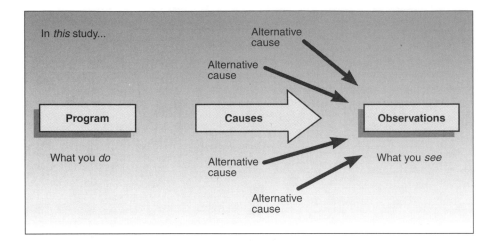

difference—it improved test scores or reduced symptomology, as shown in Figure 7-1. However, there are likely to be many reasons, other than your program, that explain why test scores improve or symptoms are reduced. The key question of internal validity is whether observed changes can be attributed to your program or intervention (the cause) and not to other possible causes (sometimes described as alternative explanations for the outcome).

One of the things that's most difficult to grasp about internal validity is that it is only relevant to the specific study in question. That is, you can think of internal validity as a zero-generalizability concern. Internal validity doesn't care about whether the cause-effect relationship would be found in any other context outside the current study. All that internal validity means is that you have evidence that what you did in your immediate study (for example, the program) caused what you observed (the outcome) to happen. It doesn't tell you whether the program you implemented was what you wanted to implement or whether what you observed was what you wanted to observe; those are *construct validity* concerns (see Chapter 3, "The Theory of Measurement"). It is possible to have internal validity in a study and not have construct validity. For instance, imagine a study in which you are looking at the effects of a new computerized tutoring program on math performance in first-grade students. Imagine that the tutoring is unique in that it has a heavy computer-game component, and you think that will really improve math performance. Finally, imagine that you were wrong. (Hard, isn't it?) Let's say that it turns out that math performance did improve and that it was because of something you did in the study, but that it had nothing to do with the computer program. For example, perhaps what caused the improvement was the individual attention that the adult tutor gave to the child; the computer program didn't make any difference. This study would have internal validity because something you did affected something that you observed. (You did cause *something* to happen.) The study would not have construct validity because the label "computer-math program" does not accurately describe the actual cause. A more accurate label for the cause that actually influenced the effect might be "personal adult attention."

Because the key issue in internal validity is the causal one, I'll begin by discussing the criteria you need to meet to show that a cause-effect relationship happened in your research project. Then I'll discuss the different threats to internal validity—the kinds of criticisms your critics will raise when you try to conclude that your program caused the outcome. For convenience, I divide the threats to validity into three categories. The first involves the *single-group threats*—criticisms that apply when you are only studying a single group that receives your program. The second consists of the *multiple-group threats*—criticisms that are likely to be raised when you have several groups in your study (such as a program and a comparison group). Finally, I'll discuss the *social interaction threats* to internal validity—threats that arise because social research is conducted in real-world human contexts, where people react to not only what affects them but also to what is happening to others around them.

7-1a Establishing Cause and Effect

How do you establish a cause-effect (causal) relationship? What criteria do you have to meet? Generally, you must meet three criteria before you can say that you have evidence for a **causal relationship:**

- Temporal precedence
- Covariation of the cause and effect
- No plausible alternative explanations

causal relationship A cause-effect relationship. For example, when you evaluate whether your treatment or program causes an outcome to occur, you are examining a causal relationship.

Temporal Precedence   To establish **temporal precedence,** you have to show that your cause happened *before* your effect. Sounds easy, huh? Of course, my cause has to happen before the effect. Did you ever hear of an effect happening before its cause? Before you get lost in the logic here, consider a classic example from economics: Does inflation cause unemployment? It certainly seems plausible that as inflation increases, more employers find that, to meet costs, they have to lay off employees. So, it seems that inflation could, at least partially, be a cause for unemployment. However, both inflation and employment rates are occurring together on an ongoing basis. Is it possible that fluctuations in employment can affect inflation? If employment in the workforce increases (lower unemployment), there is likely to be more demand for goods, which would tend to drive up the prices (that is, inflate them), at least until supply can catch up. So, which is the cause and which the effect—inflation or unemployment? It turns out that this kind of cyclical situation involves ongoing processes that interact and that both may cause and, in turn, be affected by the other (see Figure 7-2). It is hard to establish a single causal relationship in this situation because it's likely that the *variables* influence each other causally.

temporal precedence One criterion for establishing a causal relationship that holds that the cause must occur before the effect.

Covariation of the Cause and Effect   What does **covariation of the cause and effect** mean? Before you can show that you have a causal relationship, you have to show that you have a relationship at all. For instance, consider the syllogism:

If X, then Y.

If not X, then not Y.

If you observe that whenever X is present, Y is also present, and whenever X is absent, Y is, too, you have demonstrated that there is a relationship between X and Y. I don't know about you, but sometimes I find it's not easy to think about Xs and Ys. Let's put this same syllogism in program evaluation terms:

If program, then outcome.

If not program, then not outcome.

covariation of the cause and effect A criterion for establishing a causal relationship that holds that the cause and effect must be related or co-vary.

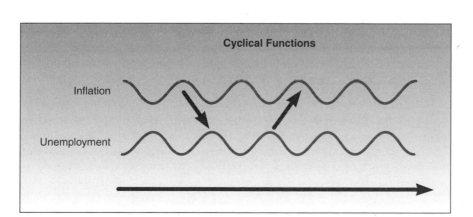

FIGURE 7-2
The Difficulty in Establishing Temporal Precedence in a Causal Relationship

Or in everyday terms: When you give the program, you observe the outcome, but when you don't give the program, you don't observe the outcome. This provides evidence that the program and outcome are related. Notice, however, that this syllogism doesn't provide evidence that the program caused the outcome; perhaps, some other factor present with the program caused the outcome rather than the program. The relationships described so far are simple binary relationships. Sometimes, you want to know whether different amounts of the program lead to different amounts of the outcome—a continuous relationship:

If more of the program, then more of the outcome.

If less of the program, then less of the outcome.

No Plausible Alternative Explanations   Just because you show there's a relationship doesn't mean it's a causal one. It's possible that some other variable or factor is causing the outcome. This is sometimes referred to as the *third-variable* or *missing-variable* problem, and it's at the heart of the internal-validity issue. What are some of the possible **plausible alternative explanations?** Later in this chapter, when I discuss the threats to internal validity (see Section 7-1b, "Single-Group Threats"; Section 7-1c, "Multiple-Group Threats"; and Section 7-1d, "Social Interaction Threats"), you'll see that each threat describes a type of alternative explanation.

To argue that you have internal validity—that you have shown there's a causal relationship—you have to rule out the plausible alternative explanations. How do you do that? One of the major ways is with research design. Consider a simple single-group threat to internal validity (an example of a history threat). Let's assume you measure your program group before you begin the program (to establish a baseline), you give the group the program, and then you measure the group's performance afterward in a posttest. You see a marked improvement in the group's performance, which you would like to infer is caused by your program. One of the plausible alternative explanations is that it's not your program that caused the gain but some other specific (historical) event. For instance, your antismoking campaign did not cause the reduction in smoking, but rather, the surgeon general's latest report was issued between the time you gave your pretest and posttest and that caused the effect. How do you rule this out with your research design? One of the simplest ways would be to incorporate the use of a **control group**—a group comparable to your program group that differed only because it didn't receive your program. However, both groups experienced the surgeon general's latest report. If you find that your program group shows a reduction in smoking greater than the control group, this can't be because of the surgeon general's report because both groups experienced that. You have effectively "ruled out" the surgeon general's report as a plausible alternative explanation for the outcome, thereby improving the internal validity of your causal inference.

In most applied social research that involves evaluating programs, temporal precedence is not a difficult criterion to meet because you administer the program before you measure effects. Establishing covariation is relatively simple because you have some control over the program and can set things up so you have some people who get it and some who don't (if X and if not X). Typically, the most difficult criterion to meet is the third—ruling out alternative explanations for the observed effect. That is why research design is such an important issue and why it is intimately linked to the idea of internal validity.

7-1b Single-Group Threats

What is meant by a **single-group threat?** Let's consider two single-group designs and then consider the threats that are most relevant with respect to internal validity. The top design in Figure 7-3 shows a posttest-only single-group design. Here, a group of people receives your program and afterward is given a posttest. In the bottom part of the figure, you see a pretest-posttest, single-group design. In this case, the participants receive a pretest or baseline measure, the program or treatment, and then a posttest.

---

plausible alternative explanation
Any other cause that can bring about an effect that is different from your hypothesized or manipulated cause.

control group   A group, comparable to the program group, that did not receive the program.

single-group threat   A threat to internal validity that occurs in a study that uses only a single program or treatment group and no comparison or control.

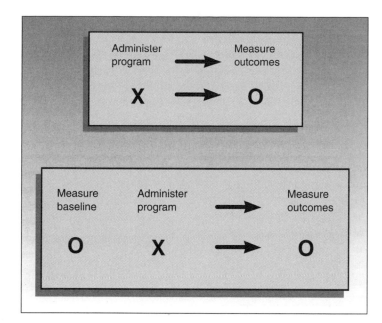

FIGURE 7-3
**Single-Group Threats
to Internal Validity**

To help make this a bit more concrete, let's imagine that you are studying the effects of a program on an outcome measure. In the post-only design, you would give the program and then give a posttest. You might choose not to give them a baseline measure because you have reason to believe that, prior to the program, they would have no basis for performance on the outcome. It wouldn't make sense to pretest them if they would have no idea what you're pretesting them about. In the pre-post design, you are not willing to assume that your group members have no prior knowledge. You measure the baseline to determine where the participants start out on the outcome. You might hypothesize that the change or gain from pretest to posttest is due to your program.

With this scenario in mind, consider what would happen if you observe a certain level of posttest performance or a change or gain from pretest to posttest. You want to conclude that the observed outcome is due to your program. How could you be wrong? Here are some of the threats to internal validity that your critics might raise, some of the plausible alternative explanations for your observed effect:

- *History threat*—When some event other than your program affects the outcome, we say there is a **history threat** to internal validity. It's not your program that caused the outcome—it's something else, some other event that occurred. We refer to this other event as an *historical* one because it is something that happens during the course of your study.

- *Maturation threat*—When the outcome level or change over time is due to normal maturation or growth on the outcome rather than to your program, we say there is a **maturation threat** to internal validity. How is this maturation explanation different from a history threat? In general, if a specific event or chain of events could cause the outcome, it is a history threat. A maturation threat consists of all the events that typically transpire in your life that could cause the outcome (without being specific as to which ones are the active causal agents). For instance, children typically improve in language skills as they move from infancy to adulthood. Some of this improvement is natural maturation that occurs simply because the children live in context with others who also use language. Some of it may be due to education or to programs designed to provide the children with greater skill. The maturation threat reminds us that we cannot attribute all change in an outcome like language skill to a program or intervention we might be studying. Even without any intervention, kids would improve in language naturally.

history threat A threat to internal validity that occurs when some historical event affects the study outcome.

maturation threat A threat to validity that is a result of natural maturation that occurs between pre- and postmeasurement.

testing threat A threat to internal validity that occurs when taking the pretest affects how participants do on the posttest.

instrumentation threat A threat to internal validity that arises when the instruments (or observers) used on the posttest and the pretest differ.

mortality threat A threat to validity that occurs because a significant number of participants drop out.

regression threat, regression artifact, or **regression to the mean** A statistical phenomenon that causes a group's average performance on one measure to regress toward or appear closer to the mean of that measure than anticipated or predicted. Regression occurs whenever you have a nonrandom sample from a population and two measures that are imperfectly correlated. A regression threat will bias your estimate of the group's posttest performance and can lead to incorrect causal inferences.

- *Testing threat*—This threat only occurs in a pre-post design. What if the pretest made some of the respondents more aware of what you are measuring? Perhaps it primed them for the program so that when they received it, they were ready for it in a way that they wouldn't have been without the pretest. This is what is meant by a **testing threat** to internal validity; it is taking the pretest, not participating in the program, that affects how respondents do on the posttest.

- *Instrumentation threat*—Like the testing threat, the **instrumentation threat** operates only in a pretest-posttest situation. What if the change from pretest to posttest is due not to your program, but rather, to a change in the way you measured the outcome? The term *instrumentation* refers to any type of outcome measure—from observations to paper-and-pencil tests to direct index scores. Perhaps part or all of any pre-post gain is attributable to the change in instrument, rather than to your program. Instrumentation threats are especially likely when the instrument is essentially a human observer. The observers may get tired over time or bored with the observations. Conversely, they might get better at making the observations as they practice. In either event, the change in instrumentation, not the program, leads to the outcome.

- *Mortality threat*—A **mortality threat** to internal validity doesn't mean that people in your study are dying (although if they are, it would certainly be considered a mortality threat!). *Mortality* is used metaphorically here. It means that people are dropping out of your study. What's wrong with that? Let's assume that, in your program, you have a considerable number of people who drop out between pretest and posttest. Assume also that the participants who are dropping out had lower pretest scores than those who remained. If you look at the average gain from pretest to posttest, using all of the scores available to you on each occasion, you would include these low-pretest subsequent dropouts in the pretest and not in the posttest. You'd be dropping out the potential low scorers from the posttest, or you'd be artificially inflating the posttest average over what it would have been if no respondents had dropped out. You won't necessarily solve this problem by comparing pre-post averages for only those who stayed in the study. This subsample would certainly not be representative even of the original entire sample, much less of the population. When mortality is a threat, the researcher can often estimate the degree of the threat by comparing the dropout group against the nondropout group on pretest measures. If there are no major differences, it may be more reasonable to assume that mortality was happening across the entire sample and is not biasing results greatly. However, if the pretest differences are large, you must be concerned about the potential biasing effects of mortality.

- *Regression threat*—A **regression threat** to internal validity, also known as a **regression artifact** or **regression to the mean,** is a statistical phenomenon that falsely makes it appear that your group changed to be more like the overall population between the pretest and posttest (Campbell & Kenny, 1999). If your group members were above average on the pretest, they will look like they lost ground on the posttest. If they were below average on the pretest, they will falsely appear to have improved. Regression occurs whenever you have a nonrandom sample from a population and two measures that are imperfectly correlated. Okay, for most of you that explanation was probably gibberish. Let me try again. Assume that your two measures are a pretest and posttest. You can certainly bet these aren't perfectly correlated with each other—they would only be perfectly correlated if the highest scorer on the pretest was the highest on the posttest, the next highest pretest scorer was second highest on the posttest, and so on down the line. Furthermore, assume that your sample consists of pretest scorers who, on average, score lower than the population average. The regression threat means that the pretest average for the group in your study will appear to increase or improve (relative to the overall population), even if you don't do anything to them, even if you never give them a treatment. Regression is a confusing threat to understand at first. I like to think about it as the *you can only go up (or down) from here* phenomenon. If you include in your program only the participants who constituted the lowest 10 percent on the pretest, what are the chances that they would constitute exactly the lowest 10 percent on the posttest? Virtually none. That could only happen in the unlikely event that the pretest and posttest are perfectly correlated. Although most of them would score low on the posttest, it is very unlikely that the lowest 10 percent on the pretest would be exactly the lowest 10 percent on the posttest. This purely statistical phenomenon is what we mean by a regression threat.

How do you deal with these single-group threats to internal validity? Although you can rule out threats in several ways, one of the most common approaches to ruling them out is through your research design. For instance, instead of doing a single-group study, you could incorporate a second group, typically called a control group. In such a study, you would have two groups: one receives your program, and the other one doesn't. In fact, the only difference between these groups should be the presence or absence of the program. When that's the case, the control group would experience all the same history and maturation threats, have the same testing and instrumentation issues, and have similar rates of mortality and regression to the mean. In other words, a good control group is one of the most effective ways to rule out all of the single-group threats to internal validity. Of course, when you add a control group, you no longer have a single-group design, and you still have to deal with two major types of threats to internal validity: the multiple-group threats to internal validity and the social interaction threats to internal validity.

7-1c Multiple-Group Threats

A multiple-group design typically involves at least two groups and before-after measurements. Most often, one group receives the program or treatment, while the other (the control or comparison group) does not. However, sometimes, one group gets the program, and the other gets either the standard program or another program you would like to compare. In this case, you would be comparing two programs for their relative outcomes. Typically, you would construct a multiple-group design so that you could compare the groups directly. In such designs, the key internal validity issue is the degree to which the groups are comparable before the study. If they are comparable, and the only difference between them is the program, posttest differences can be attributed to the program, but that's a big *if*. If the groups aren't comparable to begin with, you won't know how much of the outcome to attribute to your program or to the initial differences between groups.

There really is only one **multiple-group threat** to internal validity: that the groups were not comparable before the study. This threat is called a **selection bias** or **selection threat.** A selection threat is *any* factor other than the program that leads to posttest differences between groups. Whenever you suspect that outcomes differ between groups not because of your program but because of prior group differences, you are suspecting a selection bias. Although the term *selection bias* is used as the general category for all prior differences, when you know specifically what the group difference is, you usually hyphenate it with the selection term. The multiple-group selection threats directly parallel the single-group threats. For instance, whereas history is a single-group threat, selection-history is its multiple-group analogue.

Here are the major multiple-group threats to internal validity:

- *Selection-history threat*—A **selection-history threat** is any other event that occurs between pretest and posttest that the groups experience differently. Because this is a selection threat, the groups differ in some way. Because it's a history threat, the way the groups differ is with respect to their reactions to historical events. For example, what if the prior characteristics of one group differ from those in the other group? It may be that a higher average posttest for the program group doesn't indicate the effect of your program; it's really an effect of the two groups experiencing a relevant event differentially between the pretest and posttest.

multiple-group threat An internal validity threat that occurs in studies that use multiple groups—for instance, a program and a comparison group.

selection bias or **selection threat** Any factor other than the program that leads to posttest differences between groups.

selection-history threat A threat to internal validity that results from any other event that occurs between pretest and posttest that the groups experience differently.

- *Selection-maturation threat*—A **selection-maturation threat** results from differential rates of normal growth between pretest and posttest for the groups. It's important to distinguish between history and maturation threats. In general, history refers to a discrete event or series of events, whereas maturation implies the normal, ongoing developmental process that takes place. In any case, if the groups are maturing at different rates with respect to the outcome, you cannot assume that posttest differences are due to your program; they may be selection-maturation effects.

- *Selection-testing threat*—A **selection-testing threat** occurs when a *differential* effect of taking the pretest exists between groups on the posttest. Perhaps the test primed the respondents in each group differently, or they may have learned differentially from the pretest. In these cases, an observed posttest difference can't be attributed to the program. It could be the result of selection testing.

- *Selection-instrumentation threat*—A **selection-instrumentation threat** refers to any differential change in the test used for each group from pretest to posttest. In other words, the test changes differently for the two groups. Perhaps the instrument is based on observers who rate outcomes for the two groups. What if the program group observers, for example, become better at doing the observations, while, over time, the comparison group observers become fatigued and bored. Differences on the posttest could easily be due to this differential instrumentation—selection-instrumentation—and not to the program.

- *Selection-mortality threat*—A **selection-mortality threat** arises when there is differential nonrandom dropout between pretest and posttest. Different types of participants might drop out of each group, or more may drop out of one than the other. Posttest differences might then be due to the different types of dropouts—the selection-mortality—and not to the program.

- *Selection-regression threat*—Finally, a **selection-regression threat** occurs when there are different rates of regression to the mean in the two groups. This might happen if one group were more extreme on the pretest than the other. It may be that the program group had a disproportionate number of low pretest scorers. Its mean regresses a greater distance toward the overall population posttest mean, and its group members appear to gain more than their comparison-group counterparts. This is not a real program gain; it's a selection-regression artifact.

When you move from a single group to a multiple group study, what advantages do you gain from the rather significant investment in a second group? If the second group is a control group and is comparable to the program group, you can rule out entirely the single-group threats to internal validity because those threats will all be reflected in the comparison group and cannot explain why posttest group differences would occur. But the key is that the groups must be comparable. How can you possibly hope to create two groups that are truly comparable? The best way to do that is to randomly assign persons in your sample into the two groups—that is, you conduct a randomized or true experiment (see the discussion of experimental designs in Chapter 8, "Experimental Design").

However, in many applied research settings, you can't randomly assign, either because of logistical or ethical factors. In those cases, you typically try to assign two groups nonrandomly so that they are as equivalent as you can make them. You might, for instance, have one preexisting group assigned to the program and another to the comparison group. In this case, you would hope the two are equivalent, and you may even have reasons to believe that they are. Nonetheless, they may not be equivalent. Therefore, you have to take extra care to look for preexisting differences and adjust for them in the analysis because you did not use a procedure like random assignment to at least ensure that they are probabilistically equivalent. If you measure the groups on a pretest, you can examine whether they appear to be similar on key measures before the study begins and make some judgment about the plausibility that a selection bias or preexisting difference exists. There are also ways to adjust statistically for preexisting differences between groups if they are present, although these procedures are notoriously assumption-laden and fairly complex. Research designs that look like randomized or true experiments (they have multiple groups and pre-post measurement) but use nonrandom assignment to choose the groups are called *quasi-experimental designs* (see the discussion of quasi-experimental designs in Chapter 9, "Quasi-Experimental Design").

Even if you move to a multiple-group design and have confidence that your groups are comparable, you cannot assume that you have strong internal validity. There would still remain a number of social threats to internal validity that arise from the human interaction in applied social research, and you will need to address them.

7-1d Social Interaction Threats

Applied social research is a human activity. The results of such research are affected by the human interactions involved. The **social interaction threats** to internal validity refer to the social pressures in the research context that can lead to posttest differences not directly caused by the treatment itself. Most of these threats occur because the various groups (for example, program and comparison) or key people involved in carrying out the research are aware of each other's existence and of the role they play in the research project or are in contact with one another. Isolating the two groups from each other can minimize many of these threats, but this leads to other problems. For example, it's often hard within organizational or institutional constraints to both randomly assign and then subsequently isolate the groups from each other; this is likely to reduce generalizability or *external validity* (see Chapter 2, "Sampling"). Here are the major social interaction threats to internal validity:

social interaction threats Threats to internal validity that arise because social research is conducted in real-world human contexts where people react to not only what affects them, but also to what is happening to others around them.

- *Diffusion or imitation of treatment*—**Diffusion or imitation of treatment** occurs when a comparison group learns about the program either directly or indirectly from program group participants. Participants from different groups within the same organization might share experiences when they meet casually. Or comparison group participants, seeing what the program group is getting, might set up their own experience to try to imitate that of the program group. In either case, if the diffusion or imitation affects the posttest performance of the comparison group, it can jeopardize your ability to assess whether your program is causing the outcome. Notice that this threat to validity tends to equalize the outcomes between groups, minimizing the chance of seeing a program effect even if there is one.

diffusion or imitation of treatment A social threat to internal validity that occurs because a comparison group learns about the program either directly or indirectly from program group participants.

- *Compensatory rivalry*—In the **compensatory rivalry** case, the comparison group knows what the program group is getting and develops a competitive attitude with the program group. The participants in the comparison group might see the program the other group is getting and feel jealous. This could lead them to compete with the program group "just to show" how well they can do. Sometimes, in contexts like these, the participants are even encouraged by well-meaning administrators to compete with each other. (Although this might make organizational sense as a motivation for the participants in both groups to work harder, it works against the ability of researchers to see the effects of their program.) If the rivalry between groups affects posttest performance, it could make it more difficult to detect the effects of the program. As with diffusion and imitation, this threat generally equalizes the posttest performance across groups, increasing the chance that you won't see a program effect, even if the program is effective.

compensatory rivalry A social threat to internal validity that occurs when one group knows the program another group is getting and, because of that, develops a competitive attitude with the other group.

- *Resentful demoralization*—**Resentful demoralization** is almost the opposite of compensatory rivalry. Here, participants in the comparison group know what the program group is getting and instead of developing a rivalry, the group members become discouraged or angry and give up. Or if the program group is assigned to an especially difficult or uncomfortable condition, group members can rebel in the form of resentful demoralization. Unlike the previous two threats, this one is likely to exaggerate posttest differences between groups, making your program look even more effective than it actually is.

resentful demoralization A social threat to internal validity that occurs when the comparison group knows what the program group is getting and becomes discouraged or angry and gives up.

compensatory equalization of treatment A social threat to internal validity that occurs when the control group is given a program or treatment (usually, by a well-meaning third party) designed to make up for or "compensate" for the treatment the program group gets.

- *Compensatory equalization of treatment*—**Compensatory equalization of treatment** is the only threat of the four that primarily involves the people who help manage the research context, rather than the participants themselves. When program and comparison group participants are aware of each other's conditions, they might wish they were in the other group (depending on the perceived desirability of the program, it could work either way). They might pressure the administrators to have them reassigned to the other group. The administrators may begin to feel that the allocation of goods to the groups is not fair and may compensate one group for the perceived advantage of the other. If the program is a desirable one, you can bet that the participants assigned to the comparison group will pressure the decision makers to equalize the situation. Perhaps these decision makers will give the comparison group members something to compensate for their not getting the desirable program. If these compensating programs equalize the groups on posttest performance, they will tend to work against your detecting an effective program even when it does work.

As long as people engage in applied social research, you have to deal with the realities of human interaction and its effect on the research process. The threats described here can often be minimized by constructing multiple groups that are unaware of each other (for example, a program group from one organization or department and a comparison group from another) or by training administrators in the importance of preserving group membership and not instituting equalizing programs. However, researchers will never be able to eliminate entirely the possibility that human interactions are making it more difficult to assess cause-effect relationships.

7-2 INTRODUCTION TO DESIGN

Research design can be thought of as the *structure* of research; the research design tells you how all the elements in a research project fit together (Spector, 1981). Researchers often use concise notations to describe a design, which enables them to summarize a complex design structure efficiently. A design includes the following elements:

- *Observations or measures*—These are symbolized by an O in design notation. An O can refer to a single measure (a measure of body weight), a single instrument with multiple items (a 10-item, self-esteem scale), a complex multipart instrument (a survey), or a whole battery of tests or measures given out on one occasion. If you need to distinguish among specific measures, you can use subscripts with the O, as in O_1, O_2, and so on.

- *Treatments or programs*—These are symbolized with an X in design notation. The X can refer to a simple intervention (such as a one-time surgical technique) or to a complex hodgepodge program (such as an employment-training program). Usually, a no-treatment control or comparison group has no symbol for the treatment (although some notational systems use X+ and X– to indicate the treatment and control, respectively.) As with observations, you can use subscripts to distinguish different programs or program variations.

- *Groups*—Each group in a design is given its own line in the design structure. For instance, if the design notation has three lines, the design contains three groups.

- *Assignment to group*—Assignment to group is designated by a letter at the beginning of each line (or group) that describes how the group was assigned. The major types of assignment are:

    R = random assignment
    N = nonequivalent groups
    C = assignment by cutoff

FIGURE 7-4
A Detailed Example of Design Notation

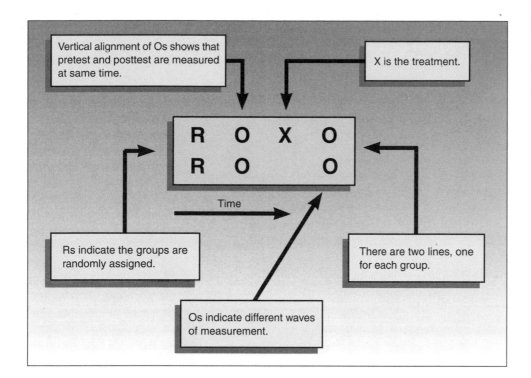

Vertical alignment of Os shows that pretest and posttest are measured at same time.

X is the treatment.

R O X O
R O O

Time

Rs indicate the groups are randomly assigned.

There are two lines, one for each group.

Os indicate different waves of measurement.

Don't worry at this point if you don't know what some of these are; each of these assignment strategies characterizes a different type of design and will be described later when discussing that design type.

- *Time*—Time moves from left to right. Elements that are listed on the left occur before elements that are listed on the right.

It's always easier to explain design notation through examples than it is to describe it in words. Figure 7-4 shows the design notation for a pretest-posttest (or before-after) treatment versus comparison group randomized experimental design. Let's go through each of the parts of the design. There are two lines in the notation, so you should realize that the study has two groups. There are four Os in the notation: two on each line and two for each group. When the Os are stacked vertically on top of each other, it means they are collected at the same time. In the notation, the two Os taken before (to the left of) the treatment are the pretest. The two Os taken after the treatment is given are the posttest. The R at the beginning of each line signifies that the two groups are randomly assigned (making it an experimental design as described in Chapter 8, "Experimental Design").

The design is a treatment-versus-comparison-group one, because the top line (treatment group) has an X, whereas the bottom line (control group) does not. You should be able to see why many of my students call this type of notation the tic-tac-toe method of design notation; there are lots of Xs and Os! Sometimes, you have to use more than simply the Os or Xs. Figure 7-5 shows the identical research design with some subscripting of the Os. What does this mean? Because all of the Os have a subscript of 1, some measure or set of measures was collected for both groups on both occasions. But the design also has two Os with a subscript of 2, both taken at the posttest. This means that some additional measure or set of measures was collected *only* at the posttest.

With this simple set of rules for describing a research design in notational form, you can concisely explain even complex design structures. Additionally, using a notation helps to show common design substructures across different designs that you might not recognize as easily without the notation. For example, three of the designs I'll show you are the analysis of covariance randomized experimental design (Chapter 8, "Experimental

FIGURE 7-5
An Example of a Design Notation That Includes Subscripts

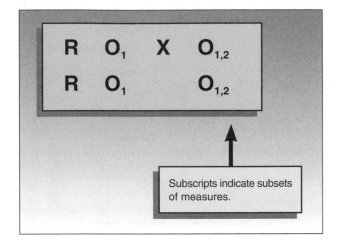

Design"), the nonequivalent groups design, and the regression discontinuity design (Chapter 9, "Quasi-Experimental Design"). From their titles and even their written descriptions, it is not immediately apparent what these designs have in common. But one glance at their design notation immediately shows that all three are similar in that they have two groups and before-and-after measurement and that the only key difference between the designs is in their assignment to groups.

7-3 TYPES OF DESIGNS

What are the different major types of research designs? You can classify designs into a simple threefold classification by asking some key questions, as shown in Figure 7-6.

First, does the design use random assignment to groups? (Don't forget that random *assignment* is not the same thing as *random selection* of a sample from a population!) If random assignment is used, the design is a randomized experiment or *true* experiment. If random assignment is not used, ask a second question: Does the design use *either* multiple groups or multiple waves of measurement? If the answer is yes, label it a quasi-experimental design. If no, call it a nonexperimental design.

This threefold classification is especially useful for describing the design with respect to internal validity. A randomized experiment generally is the strongest of the three

FIGURE 7-6
Basic Questions That Distinguish the Major Types of Designs

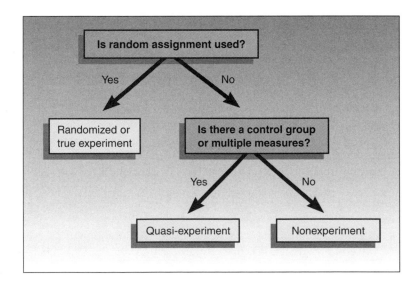

designs when your interest is in establishing a cause-effect relationship. A nonexperiment is generally the weakest in this respect. I have to hasten to add here that I don't mean that a nonexperiment is the weakest of the three designs *overall*, but only with respect to internal validity or causal assessment. In fact, the simplest form of nonexperiment is a one-shot survey design that consists of nothing but a single observation O. This is probably one of the most common forms of research and for some research questions—especially descriptive ones—is clearly a strong design. When I say that the nonexperiment is the weakest with respect to internal validity, all I mean is that it isn't a particularly good method for assessing the cause-effect relationships that you think might exist between a program and its outcomes.

To illustrate the different types of designs, consider one of each in design notation, as shown in Figure 7-7. The first design is a **posttest-only randomized experiment.** You can tell it's a randomized experiment because it has an R at the beginning of each line, indicating random assignment. The second design is a **pre-post nonequivalent groups quasi-experiment.** You know it's not a randomized experiment because random assignment wasn't used. Additionally, you know it's not a nonexperiment because both multiple groups and multiple waves of measurement exist. That means it must be a quasi-experiment. You add the label *nonequivalent* because, in this design, you do not explicitly control the assignment, and the groups may be nonequivalent or not similar to each other (see Section 9-1, "The Nonequivalent-Groups Design," in Chapter 9). Finally, you see a **posttest-only nonexperimental design.** You might use this design if you want to study the effects of a natural disaster like a flood or tornado and you want to do so by interviewing survivors. Notice that, in this design, you don't have a comparison group (for example, you didn't interview in a town down the road that didn't have the tornado to see what differences the tornado caused), and you don't have multiple waves of measurement (a pre-tornado level of how people in the ravaged town were doing before the disaster). Does it make sense to do the nonexperimental study? Of course! You could gain valuable information by well-conducted post-disaster interviews. However, you may have a hard time establishing which of the things you observed are due to the disaster, rather than to other factors like the peculiarities of the town or pre-disaster characteristics.

posttest-only randomized experiment An experiment in which the groups are randomly assigned and receive only a posttest.

pre-post nonequivalent groups quasi-experiment A research design in which groups receive both a pre- and posttest, and group assignment is not randomized, and therefore, the groups may be nonequivalent, making it a quasi-experiment.

posttest-only nonexperimental design A research design in which only a posttest is given. It is referred to as nonexperimental because no control group exists.

Posttest-only randomized experiment	R X O R O
Pre-post nonequivalent groups quasi-experiment	N O X O N O O
Posttest-only nonexperiment	X O

FIGURE 7-7
Notation for Examples of Each of the Three Major Classes of Research Design

SUMMARY

Research design helps you to put together all of the disparate pieces of your research project: the participants or sample, the measures, and the data analysis. This chapter showed that research design is intimately connected with the topic of internal validity because the type of research design you construct determines whether you can address causal questions, such as whether your treatment or program made a difference on outcome measures. There are three major types of problems—threats to validity—that occur when trying to assure internal validity. Single-group threats occur when you have only a single program group in your study.

Researchers typically try to avoid single-group threats by using a comparison group, but this leads to multiple-group threats or selection threats when the groups are not comparable. Because all social research involves human interaction, you must also be concerned about social interaction threats to internal validity that can make your groups perform differently but are unrelated to the treatment or program. Research designs can get somewhat complicated. To keep them straight and describe them succinctly, researchers use design notation that describes the design in abstract form.

SUGGESTED WEBSITES

Note: These websites were functional when we went to press. Please access the Online Study Guide Edition for the most up-to-date URLs.

Centre for Evidence-Based Medicine
http://www.cebm.net/index.asp
This website shows you the impact of research design on modern medicine. You can see the relationship of research design to the "levels of evidence" used to make decisions about the effectiveness of medical treatments. There are also some handy tools for study planners.

Institutional Review Board Guidebook
http://www.hhs.gov/ohrp/irb/irb_chapter4.htm
This website, sponsored by the U.S. Office for Human Research Protections, was designed primarily to help members of institutional review boards to understand the relationship of research design to ethics. As noted in the introductory paragraph, "The value of research depends upon the integrity of study results." This basically means that if you are going to do a study, it should be designed so that it answers the research question in as valid a manner as possible, while protecting the rights of all participants.

KEY TERMS

causal relationship (p. 137)
compensatory equalization
  of treatment (p. 144)
compensatory rivalry (p. 143)
control group (p. 138)
covariation of the cause and effect (p. 137)
diffusion or imitation of treatment (p. 143)
history threat (p. 139)
instrumentation threat (p. 140)
internal validity (p. 135)
maturation threat (p. 139)
mortality threat (p. 140)

multiple-group threat (p. 141)
plausible alternative explanation (p. 138)
posttest-only nonexperimental design (p. 147)
posttest-only randomized experiment (p. 147)
pre-post nonequivalent groups
  quasi-experiment (p. 147)
regression artifact (p. 140)
regression threat (p. 140)
regression to the mean (p. 140)
resentful demoralization (p. 143)
selection bias (p. 141)
selection threat (p. 141)

selection-history threat (p. 141)
selection-instrumentation threat (p. 142)
selection-maturation threat (p. 142)
selection-mortality threat (p. 142)
selection-regression threat (p. 142)
selection-testing threat (p. 142)
single-group threat (p. 138)
social interaction threats (p. 143)
temporal precedence (p. 137)
testing threat (p. 140)

REVIEW QUESTIONS

Note: You can find the correct answers to these questions by taking the quiz and then submitting your answers in the Online Study Guide Edition. The program will automatically score your submission. If you miss a question, the program will provide the correct answer, a rationale for the answer, and the section number in the chapter where the topic is discussed.

1. What term reflects the accuracy of any cause-effect relationship you might infer as a result of a study?
   a. generalizability
   b. conclusion validity
   c. internal validity
   d. construct validity

2. When studying the effectiveness of interventions or programs, what allows you to conclude that research results were achieved because of the intervention itself and not some other factor?
   a. generalizability
   b. conclusion validity
   c. internal validity
   d. construct validity

3. If the results of a study determine that an intervention worked, though not for the reason anticipated, the study would have _____ validity but not _____ validity.
   a. internal, construct
   b. construct, internal
   c. construct, causal
   d. conclusion, construct

4. When considering a "What came first—the chicken or the egg?" question in an attempt to establish cause and effect, a researcher is reflecting on
   a. construct validity.
   b. internal validity.
   c. temporal precedence.
   d. single-group threats.

5. Which of the following is *not* a criterion for establishing a cause-effect relationship?
   a. Determine that there is a relationship between the cause and effect.
   b. Determine that the cause comes before the effect.
   c. Determine that no other possible explanations exist for the relationship.
   d. Determine that the effect as measured reflects the construct of the effect.

6. Consider a study evaluating the usefulness of a phonics program. A pretest is given on the first day of kindergarten, and the same instrument is used as a posttest, which is given on the first day of first grade on the same subjects. What alternative explanation could explain a positive effect of the phonics program?
   a. testing threat
   b. history threat
   c. instrumentation threat
   d. mortality threat

7. The threat to cause-effect conclusions that results from a change in the test instrument used between the time of the pretest and the time of the posttest is called
   a. a testing threat.
   b. a history threat.
   c. an instrumentation threat.
   d. a mortality threat.

8. What are the two conditions that will create "regression toward the mean"?
   a. an accurate random sample but imperfectly correlated pretests and posttests
   b. a nonrandom sample and imperfectly correlated pretests and posttests
   c. a random sample and highly correlated pretests and posttests
   d. a nonrandom sample and highly correlated pretests and posttests

9. Regression toward the mean is a phenomenon that affects a(n) ___ score.
   a. individual
   b. group
   c. statistical
   d. variable

10. Which of the following is a social interaction threat to internal validity?
    a. resentful demoralization
    b. funding disputes
    c. regression to the mean
    d. overgeneralization of findings by the media

11. Mortality is a threat to internal validity because the people who drop out of the study might be different in important ways from the ones who complete the study.
    a. True
    b. False

12. The three conditions needed to establish a cause-effect relationship are: (1) temporal precedence, (2) independence of the cause and effect, and (3) plausible alternative explanations.
    a. True
    b. False

13. If a researcher studies children at the beginning and end of the school year, there is really no need to worry about maturation as a threat to validity because children really do not mature that much in one year.
    a. True
    b. False

14. The main reason that researchers use a control group is to be able to estimate the effects of various threats to validity and thereby make a valid inference about the group that received the treatment, program, or "active ingredient" of the study.
    a. True
    b. False

15. If random assignment is used, the design is a randomized experiment or *true* experiment.
    a. True
    b. False

Experimental Design

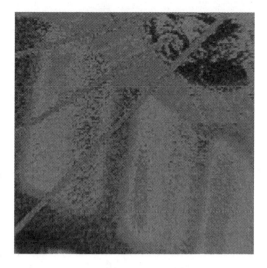

Experimental designs are often touted as the most rigorous of all research designs, or as the gold standard against which all other designs are judged. In one sense, they probably are. If you can implement an experimental design well (and that is a big *if*, indeed), the experiment is probably the strongest design with respect to internal validity (see Chapter 7, "Design").

This chapter introduces the idea of an experimental design and describes why it is strong in internal validity. I show that the key distinguishing feature of experimental design—random assignment to group—depends on the idea of probabilistic equivalence and explain what that means. I then try to head off one of the biggest sources of confusion to most students—the distinction between random selection and random assignment. Then I get into the heart of the chapter, describing how to classify the different experimental designs, presenting each type in turn.

8-1 INTRODUCTION TO EXPERIMENTAL DESIGN

8-1a Experimental Designs and Internal Validity

Experimental designs are usually considered the strongest of all designs in internal validity (see the discussion on internal validity and research design in Chapter 7, Section 7-3, " Types of Designs"). Why? Recall that internal validity is at the center of all *causal* or cause-effect inferences. When you want to determine whether some program or treatment causes some outcome or outcomes to occur, you are interested in having strong internal validity. Essentially, you want to assess the proposition:

If X, then Y.

Or in everyday terms:

If the program is given, then the outcome occurs.

Unfortunately, it's not enough to show that when the program or treatment occurs, the expected outcome also happens because many reasons, other than the program, might account for why you observed the outcome. To show that there is a causal relationship, you have to simultaneously address the two propositions:

If X, then Y.
and
If not X, then not Y.

Or once again more informally:

If the program is given, then the outcome occurs.
and
If the program is *not* given, then the outcome does *not* occur.

If you are able to provide evidence for both of these propositions, you've in effect isolated the program from all of the other potential causes of the outcome. You've shown that when the program is present, the outcome occurs, and when it's not present, the outcome doesn't occur. That points to the causal effectiveness of the program.

Think of all this like a fork in the road. Down one path, you implement the program and observe the outcome. Down the other path, you don't implement the program, and the outcome doesn't occur. But can you take both paths in the road in the same study? How can you be in two places at once? Ideally, what you want is to have the same conditions—the same people, context, time, and so on—and see whether when the program is given, you get the outcome and when the program is not given, you don't. Obviously, you can never achieve this hypothetical situation. If you give the program to a group of people, you can't simultaneously *not* give it! So, how do you get out of this apparent dilemma?

Perhaps, you just need to think about the problem a little differently. What if you could create two groups or contexts that are as similar as you can possibly make them? If you could be confident that the two situations are comparable, you could administer your program in one (and see whether the outcome occurs) and not give the program in the other (and see whether the outcome doesn't occur). If the two contexts are comparable, this is like taking both forks in the road simultaneously. You can have your cake and eat it, too, so to speak.

That's exactly what an experimental design tries to achieve. In the simplest type of experiment, you create two groups that are equivalent to each other. One group (the program or treatment group) gets the program, and the other group (the comparison or *control group*) does not. In all other respects, the groups are treated the same. They have similar people who live in similar contexts, have similar backgrounds, and so on. Now, if you observe differences in outcomes between these two groups, the differences must be due to the only thing that differs between them—that one received the program and the other didn't.

Okay, so how do you create two equivalent groups? The approach used in experimental design is to assign people randomly from a common pool of people into the two groups. The experiment relies on this idea of *random assignment* to groups (Fisher, 1925) as the basis for obtaining two similar groups. Then, you give one the program or treatment, and you don't give it to the other. You observe the same outcomes in both groups.

The key to the success of the experiment is in the random assignment. In fact, even with random assignment, you never expect the groups you create to be exactly the same. How could they be, when they are made up of different people? You rely on the idea of probability and assume that the two groups are probabilistically equivalent or equivalent within known probabilistic ranges.

If you randomly assign people to two groups, and you have enough people in your study to achieve the desired probabilistic equivalence, you can consider the experiment strong in *internal validity*, and you probably have a good shot at assessing whether the program causes the outcome(s). (See the discussion of statistical power and sample size in Chapter 11, Section 11-1a "Threats to Conclusion Validity.")

However, many things can go wrong. You may not have a large enough sample. Some people might refuse to participate in your study or drop out partway through. You might be challenged successfully on ethical grounds. (After all, to use this approach, you have to deny the program to some people who might be as equally deserving of it as others.) You might meet resistance from the staff members in your study who would like some of their favorite clients to get the program or treatment.

The bottom line here is that experimental design is intrusive and difficult to carry out in most real-world contexts, and because an experiment is often an intrusion, you are setting up an artificial situation so that you can assess your causal relationship with high internal validity. As a result, you are limiting the degree to which you can generalize your results to real contexts where you haven't set up an experiment. That is, you have reduced your external validity to achieve greater internal validity.

In the end, there is no simple answer (no matter what anyone tells you). If the situation is right, an experiment is a strong design, but it isn't automatically so.

Experimental design is a complex subject in its own right. In this chapter, you'll explore the basic two-group posttest-only experimental design, look at the major variations, and learn the principles that underlie all experimental-design strategies.

8-1b Two-Group Experimental Designs

The simplest of all experimental designs is the **two-group posttest-only randomized experiment** (see Figure 8-1). In design notation, it has two lines—one for each group—with an R at the beginning of each line to indicate that the groups were randomly assigned.

One group gets the treatment or program (the X), and the other group is the comparison group and doesn't get the program. (Note that you could alternatively have the comparison [control] group receive the standard or typical treatment—in which case, this study would be a relative comparison.)

Notice that a pretest is not required for this design. In many two-group designs, you include a pretest to determine whether groups are comparable prior to the program. However, because this design uses random assignment, you can assume that the two groups are probabilistically equivalent to begin with, and the pretest is not required (although you'll see with covariance designs later in this chapter that a pretest may still be desirable in this context).

In this design, you are most interested in determining whether the two groups are different after the program. Typically, you measure the groups on one or more measures (the Os in the notation), and you compare them by testing for the differences between the means using a *t*-test or one-way **analysis of variance (ANOVA),** which is covered in Chapter 12, Section 12-3a, "The Two-Group Posttest-Only Randomized Experiment."

The posttest-only randomized experiment is the strongest of all research designs with respect to the threats to internal validity, as shown in Figure 8-2. The figure indicates (with a check mark) that it is strong against all the *single-group threats to internal validity* because it's not a single group design! (Tricky, huh?) It's also strong against the *multiple-group threats* except for the **selection-mortality threat.** For instance, it's strong against the *selection-testing* and *selection-instrumentation threats* because it doesn't use repeated measurement. The selection-mortality threat can be a problem if there are differential rates of dropouts in the two groups. This could result if the treatment or program is a noxious or negative one (such as a painful medical procedure like chemotherapy) or if the control group condition is painful or intolerable. This design is susceptible to all of the *social threats to internal validity.* Because the design requires random assignment, in some institutional settings such as schools, it is more likely to utilize persons who would be aware of each other and of the conditions to which you have assigned them.

The posttest-only randomized experimental design is, despite its simple structure, one of the best research designs for assessing cause-effect relationships. It is relatively easy to execute and, because it uses only a posttest, is relatively inexpensive. However, there are many variations on this simple experimental design. You can begin to explore these by looking at how you classify the various experimental designs (see Section 8-2, "Classifying Experimental Designs," later in this chapter).

8-1c Probabilistic Equivalence

What do I mean by the term **probabilistic equivalence,** and why is it important to experimental design? Well, to begin with, I certainly *don't* mean that two groups are equal to each other. When you deal with human beings, it is impossible to say that any two individuals or groups are equal or equivalent. Clearly, the important word in the phrase is *probabilistic.* This means that the type of equivalence you have is based on the notion of probabilities. In more concrete terms, probabilistic equivalence means that you know *perfectly* the odds of finding a difference between two groups. Notice, it doesn't mean that the means of the two groups will be equal. It just means that you know the odds that they won't be equal. Figure 8-3 shows two groups, one with a mean of 49 and the other with a mean of 51. Could these two groups be probabilistically equivalent even though their averages are different? Certainly!

You achieve probabilistic equivalence through the mechanism of random assignment to groups. When you randomly assign to groups, you can calculate the chance that the

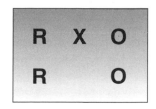

F I G U R E   8 - 1
Notation for the Basic Two-Group Posttest-Only Randomized Experimental Design

two-group posttest-only randomized experiment
A research design in which two randomly assigned groups participate. Only one group receives the program, and both groups receive a posttest.

analysis of variance (ANOVA)
An analysis that estimates the difference between groups on a posttest. The ANOVA could estimate the difference between a treatment and control group (thus being equivalent to the *t*-test) or can examine both main and interaction effects in a factorial design.

selection-mortality threat
A threat to internal validity that arises when there is differential nonrandom dropout between groups during the study.

probabilistic equivalence
The notion that two groups, if measured infinitely, would on average perform identically. Note that two groups that are probabilistically equivalent would seldom obtain the exact same average score in a real setting.

√ History
√ Maturation
√ Testing
√ Instrumentation
√ Mortality
√ Regression to the mean
√ Selection
√ Selection—history
√ Selection—maturation
√ Selection—testing
√ Selection—instrumentation
✗ Selection—mortality
√ Selection—regression
✗ Diffusion or imitation
✗ Compensatory equalization
✗ Compensatory rivalry
✗ Resentful demoralization

FIGURE 8-2
Threats to Internal Validity for the Posttest-Only Randomized Experimental Design

random assignment Process of assigning your sample into two or more subgroups by chance. Procedures for random assignment can vary from flipping a coin to using a table of random numbers to using the random number capability built into a computer.

FIGURE 8-3
Probabilistic Equivalence

Probabilistic equivalence does not mean that two randomly selected groups will obtain the exact same average score.

two groups will differ just because of the random assignment (that is, by chance alone). Let's say you are assigning people to two groups. Further, let's assume that the average test scores for these two groups (where the population mean is 50) were 49 and 51, respectively. You might conduct a *t*-test to see whether the means of the two randomly assigned groups are statistically different. Through random assignment and the law of large numbers, the chance that they will be different is 5 out of 100 when you set the significance level to .05 (that is, $\alpha = .05$). In other words, 5 times out of every 100, when you randomly assign two groups, you can expect to get a significant difference at the .05 level of significance.

When you assign subjects to groups randomly, groups can only differ due to chance because their assignment is entirely based on the randomness of assignment. If, by chance, the groups differ on one variable, you have no reason to believe that they will automatically be different on any other. Even if you find that the groups differ on a pretest, you have no reason to suspect that they will differ on a posttest. Why? Because their pretest difference had to be due to chance. So, when you randomly assign, you are able to assume that the groups do have a form of equivalence. You don't expect them to be equal, but you can expect them to be probabilistically equal.

8-1d Random Selection and Assignment

Random selection is how you draw the sample of people for your study from a population. **Random assignment** is how you assign the sample that you draw to different groups or treatments in your study.

It is possible to have both random selection and assignment in a study. Let's say you drew a random sample of 100 clients from a population list of 1,000 current clients of your organization. That is random sampling. Now, let's say you randomly assign 50 of these clients to get some new additional program and the other 50 to be controls. That's random assignment.

It is also possible to have only one of these (random selection or random assignment) but not the other in a study. For instance, if you do not randomly draw the 100 cases from your list of 1,000 but instead just take the first 100 on the list, you do not have random selection. You could, however, still randomly assign this nonrandom sample to treatment versus control. Or you could randomly select 100 from your list of 1,000 and then nonrandomly assign them to treatment or control groups.

It's also possible to have neither random selection nor random assignment. In a typical nonequivalent-groups design (see Chapter 9, "Quasi-Experimental Design"), you might choose two intact preexisting groups to be in your study. This is nonrandom selection. Then, you could arbitrarily assign one group to get the new program and the other to be the comparison group. This is nonrandom (or nonequivalent) assignment.

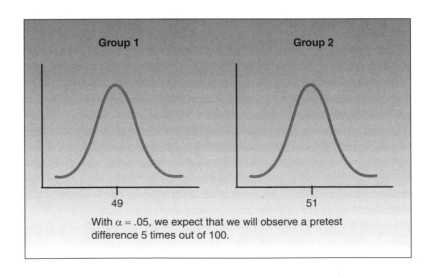

With $\alpha = .05$, we expect that we will observe a pretest difference 5 times out of 100.

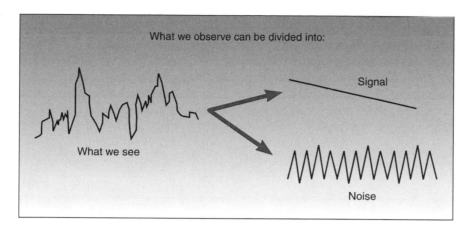

FIGURE 8-4
Observed Time Series

An observed time series can be thought of as being made up of two components—its signal and noise.

Random selection is related to *sampling* (see Chapter 2, "Sampling"). Therefore, it is most closely related to the *external validity* (or generalizability) of your results. After all, researchers randomly sample so that their research participants better represent the larger group from which they're drawn. Random assignment is most closely related to design. In fact, when you randomly assign participants to treatments, you have, by definition, an experimental design. Therefore, random assignment is most related to internal validity (see Chapter 7, "Design"). Researchers randomly assign to help ensure that their treatment groups are similar to each other (probabilistically equivalent) prior to the treatment.

8-2 CLASSIFYING EXPERIMENTAL DESIGNS

Although many experimental design variations exist, you can classify and organize them using a simple signal-to-noise ratio metaphor. In this metaphor, assume that what you observe or see in a research study can be divided into two components: the signal and the noise. (By the way, this is directly analogous to the discussion of signal and noise in the *true-score theory* of measurement discussed in Chapter 3, "The Theory of Measurement.") Figure 8-4 shows a time series with a slight downward slope. However, because there is so much **variability** or noise in the series, it is difficult even to detect the downward slope. When you divide the series into its two components, you can clearly see the slope.

In most research, the signal is related to the key variable of interest—the construct you're trying to measure, or the program or treatment that's being implemented. The noise consists of all of the random factors in the situation that make it harder to see the signal: the lighting in the room, local distractions, how people felt that day, and so on. You can construct a ratio of these two by dividing the signal by the noise (see Figure 8-5). In research, you want the signal to be high relative to the noise. For instance, if you have a powerful treatment or program (meaning a strong signal) and good measurement (that is, low noise), you have a better chance of seeing the effect of the program than if you have either a strong program and weak measurement, or a weak program and strong measurement.

You can further classify the experimental designs into two categories: signal enhancers or noise reducers. Doing either of these things—enhancing signal or reducing noise—improves the quality of the research. The *signal-enhancing experimental designs* are called the **factorial designs.** In these designs, the focus is almost entirely on the setup of the program or treatment, its components, and its major dimensions. In a typical factorial design, you would examine several different variations of a treatment. Factorial designs are discussed in Section 8-3 of this chapter.

The two major types of *noise-reducing experimental designs* are covariance designs and blocking designs. In these designs, you typically use information about the makeup of the sample or about preprogram variables to remove some of the noise in your study. Covariance and blocking designs are discussed in Section 8-4, "Randomized Block Designs," and Section 8-5, "Covariance Designs."

variability The extent to which the values measured or observed for a variable differ.

factorial designs Designs that focus on the program or treatment, its components, and its major dimensions and enable you to determine whether the program has an effect, whether different subcomponents are effective, and whether there are interactions in the effects caused by subcomponents.

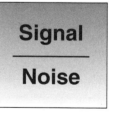

FIGURE 8-5
Signal-to-Noise Ratio

The signal-to-noise ratio is simply a fraction where signal is divided by noise.

8-3 FACTORIAL DESIGNS

Factorial designs (Keppel, 1991) focus on the signal in your research by directly manipulating your program or features of your program or treatment. Factorial designs are especially efficient because they enable you to examine which features or combinations of features of your program or treatment have an effect. I'll start with the simplest factorial design, show you why it is such an efficient approach, explain how to interpret the results, and then move on to more advanced variations.

8-3a The Basic 2 × 2 Factorial Design

Probably the easiest way to begin understanding factorial designs is by looking at an example (see Figure 8-6). Imagine a design where you have an educational program in which you would like to look at a variety of program variations to see which works best. For instance, you would like to vary the amount of time the children receive instruction, with one group getting 1 hour of instruction per week and another getting 4 hours per week. Additionally, you'd like to vary the setting so that one group gets the instruction in class (probably pulled off into a corner of the classroom), and the other group is pulled out of the classroom for instruction in another room. You could think about having separate studies to do this, but when you vary the amount of time in instruction, which setting would you use: in-class or pull-out? And when you study setting, what amount of instruction time would you use: 1 hour, 4 hours, or something else? To do this right, you would need a separate study to compare each possible combination.

With factorial designs, you don't have to compromise when answering these questions. You can have it both ways if you cross each of your two times in instruction conditions with each of your two settings. Let's begin by doing some defining of terms. In factorial designs, a **factor** is a major independent variable. This example has two factors: time in instruction and setting. A **level** is a subdivision of a factor. In this example, time in instruction has two levels and setting has two levels.

Sometimes, you depict a factorial design with a numbering notation. In this example, you can say that you have a 2 × 2 (spoken two-by-two) factorial design. In this notation, the *number of numbers* tells you how many factors there are, and the *number values* tell you how many levels. A 3 × 4 factorial design has 2 factors, where one factor has 3 levels and the other has 4. The order of the numbers makes no difference, and you could just as easily term this a 4 × 3 factorial design. You can easily determine the number of

> **factor**   A major independent variable in an experimental design.

> **level**   In an experimental design, a subdivision of a factor into components or features.

FIGURE 8-6

An Example of a Basic 2 × 2 Factorial Design

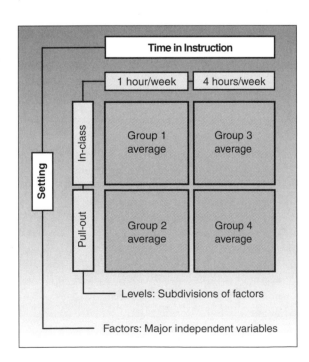

different treatment groups that you have in any factorial design by multiplying through the number notation. For instance, the school study example has 2 × 2 = 4 groups. A 3 × 4 factorial design requires 3 × 4 = 12 groups.

You can also depict a factorial design in design notation. Because of the treatment-level combinations, it is useful to use subscripts on the treatment (X) symbol. Figure 8-7 shows that there are four groups, one for each combination of levels of factors. It also shows that the groups were randomly assigned and that this is a posttest-only design.

Now, let's look at a variety of different results you might get from this simple 2 × 2 factorial design. Each of the graphs in Figure 8-8 (see pages 158–160) describes a different possible outcome. Each outcome is shown in table form (the 2 × 2 table with the row and column averages) and in graphic form (with each factor taking a turn on the horizontal axis). Take the time to understand how and why the information in the tables agrees with the information in both of the graphs. Also study the graphs and figures to verify that the pair of graphs in each figure show the exact same information graphed in two different ways. The lines in the graphs are technically not necessary; they are a visual aid that enables you to track where the averages for a single level go across levels of another factor. Keep in mind that the values in the tables and graphs are group averages on the outcome variable of interest. In this example, the outcome might be a test of achievement in the subject being taught. Assume that scores on this test range from 1 to 10, with higher values indicating greater achievement. You should study carefully the outcomes in each figure to understand the differences between these cases.

The Null Outcome   The **null case** is a situation in which the treatments have no effect. Figure 8-8a assumes that even if you didn't give the training, you would expect students to score a 5 on average on the outcome test. You can see in this hypothetical case that all four groups score an average of 5, and therefore, the row and column averages must be 5. The lines for both levels in the graphs overlap each other.

The Main Effects   A **main effect** is an outcome that is a consistent difference between levels of a factor. For instance, you would say there's a main effect for setting if you find a statistical difference between the averages for the in-class and pull-out groups *at all levels* of time in instruction. Figure 8-8b depicts a main effect of time. For all settings, the 4-hour/week condition worked better than the 1-hour/week condition. It is also possible to have a main effect for setting (and none for time).

In the second main effect graph, shown in Figure 8-8c, you see that in-class training was better than pull-out training for all amounts of time.

Finally, it is possible to have a main effect on both variables simultaneously, as depicted in the third main effect (see Figure 8-8d). In this instance, 4 hours/week always works better than 1 hour/week, and in-class setting always works better than the pull-out setting.

Interaction Effects   If you could look at only main effects, factorial designs would be useful. But, because of the way you combine levels in factorial designs, they also enable you to examine the **interaction effect** that exists between factors. An interaction effect exists when differences on one factor depend on which level you are on in another factor. It's important to recognize that an interaction is between factors, not levels. You wouldn't say there's an interaction between 4 hours/week and in-class treatment. Instead, you would say that there's an interaction between time and setting, and then you would describe the specific levels involved.

How do you know whether there is an interaction in a factorial design? There are three ways you can determine whether an interaction exists. First, when you run the statistical analysis, the statistical table will report on all main effects and interactions. Second, you know there's an interaction when you can't talk about an effect on one factor without mentioning the other factor. If you can say at the end of your study that time in instruction makes a difference, you know that you have a main effect and not an interaction (because you did not have to mention the setting factor when describing the

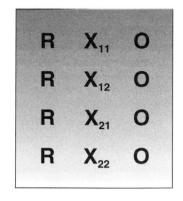

FIGURE 8-7
Design Notation for a 2 × 2 Factorial Design

null case   A situation in which the treatment has no effect.

main effect   An outcome that shows consistent differences between all levels of a factor.

interaction effect   An effect that occurs when differences on one factor depend on which level you are on another factor.

FIGURE 8-8a
Factorial Design

The null effects case in a 2 × 2
factorial design.

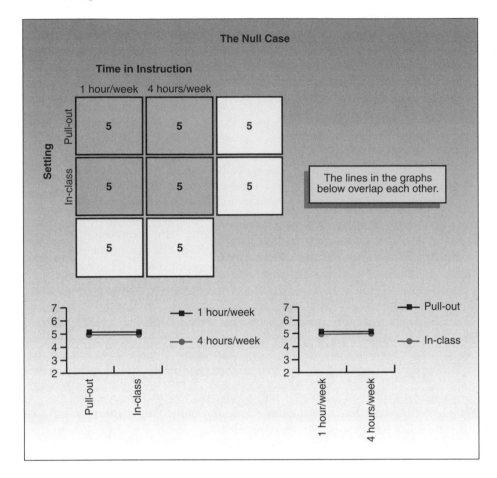

FIGURE 8-8b
Factorial Design

A main effect of time in
instruction in a 2 × 2 factorial
design.

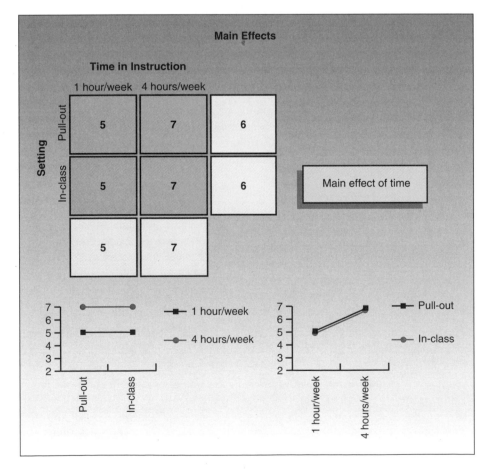

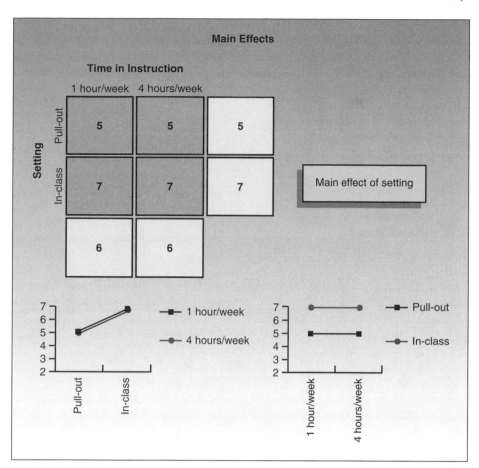

FIGURE 8-8c
Factorial Design

A main effect of setting in a 2 × 2 factorial design.

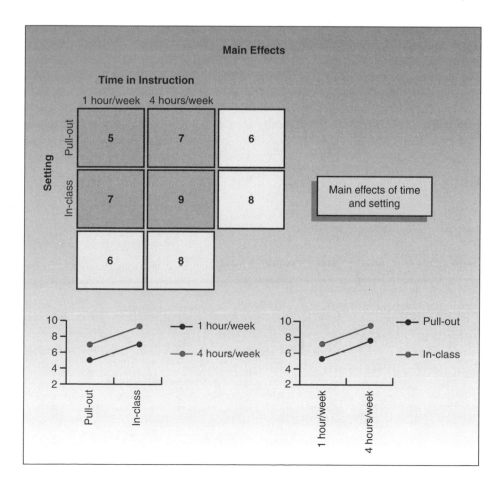

FIGURE 8-8d
Factorial Design

Main effects of both time and setting in a 2 × 2 factorial design.

FIGURE 8-8e
Factorial Design

An interaction in a 2 × 2 factorial design.

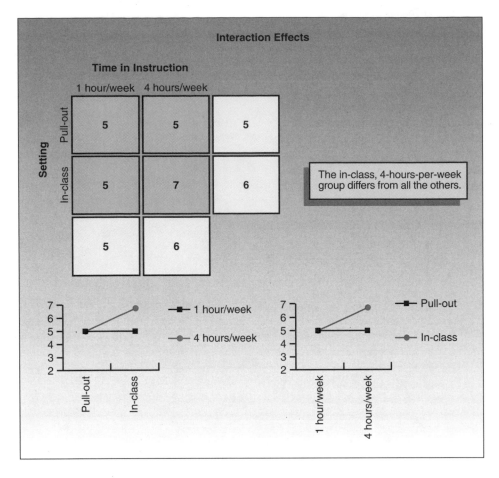

FIGURE 8-8f
Factorial Design

A crossover interaction in a 2 × 2 factorial design.

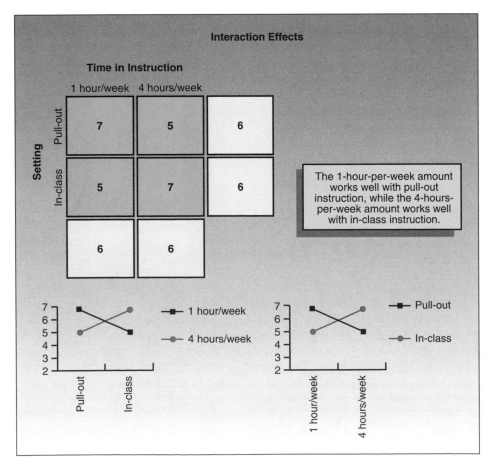

results for time). On the other hand, when you have an interaction, it is impossible to describe your results accurately without mentioning both factors. Finally, you can always spot an interaction in the graphs of group means; whenever lines are not parallel, an interaction is present! If you check out the main effect graphs in Figure 8-8c, you will notice that all of the lines within a graph are parallel. In contrast, for all of the interaction graphs, you will see that the lines are not parallel.

In the first interaction effect graph (see Figure 8-8e—page 160), one combination of levels—4 hours/week and in-class setting—shows better results than the other three.

The second interaction (see Figure 8-8f—page 160) shows more complex crossover interaction. Here, at 1 hour/week, the pull-out group does better than the in-class group, whereas at 4 hours/week, the reverse is true. Furthermore, both of these combinations of levels do equally well.

Factorial design has several important features. First, it gives you great flexibility for exploring or enhancing the signal (treatment) in your studies. Whenever you are interested in examining treatment variations, factorial designs should be strong candidates as the designs of choice. Second, factorial designs are efficient. Instead of conducting a series of independent studies, you are effectively able to combine these studies into one. Finally, factorial designs are the only effective way to examine interaction effects.

8-3b Factorial Design Variations

So far, you have only looked at a simple 2 × 2 factorial design structure. This section discusses a number of different factorial designs. I'll begin with a two-factor design where one of the factors has more than two levels. Then I'll introduce the three-factor design. Finally, I'll present the idea of the incomplete factorial design.

A 2 × 3 Example   For these examples, I'll construct an example designed to study the effect of different treatment combinations for cocaine abuse. Here, the dependent measure is a severity-of-illness rating performed by the treatment staff. The outcome ranges from 1 to 10, where higher scores indicate more severe illness—in this case, more severe cocaine addiction. Furthermore, assume that the levels of treatment are as follows:

- Factor 1: Treatment
  - Psychotherapy
  - Behavior modification
- Factor 2: Setting
  - Inpatient
  - Day treatment
  - Outpatient

Note that the setting factor in this example has three levels.

Figure 8-9a shows what an effect for the setting outcome might look like. You have to be careful when interpreting these results because higher scores mean the patient is doing *worse*. It's clear that inpatient treatment works best, day treatment is next best, and outpatient treatment is worst of the three. It's also clear that there is no difference between the two treatment levels (psychotherapy and behavior modification). Even though both graphs in the figure depict the exact same data, it's easier to see the main effect for setting in the graph on the lower left, where setting is depicted with different lines on the graph rather than at different points along the horizontal axis.

Figure 8-9b shows a main effect for treatment, with psychotherapy performing better (remember the direction of the outcome variable) in all settings than behavior modification. The effect is more clear in the graph on the lower right, where treatment levels are used for the lines. Note that in both this and Figure 8-9a, the lines in all graphs are parallel, indicating that there are no interaction effects.

FIGURE 8-9a
Factorial Design

Main effect of setting in a 2 × 3 factorial design.

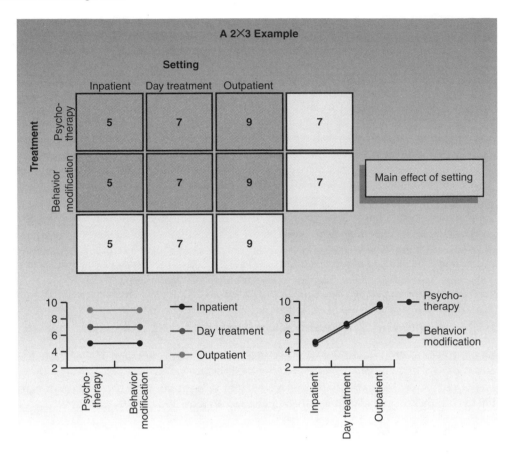

FIGURE 8-9b
Factorial Design

Main effect of treatment in a 2 × 3 factorial design.

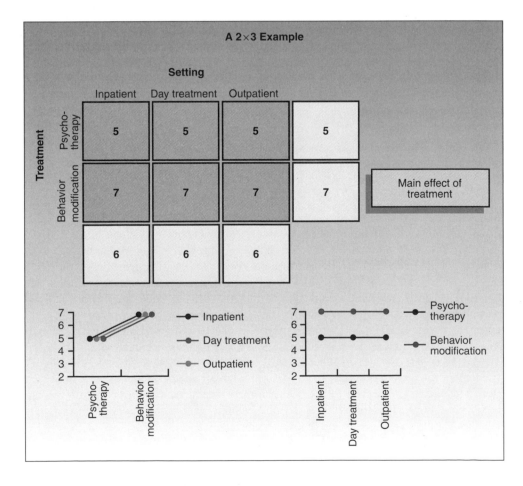

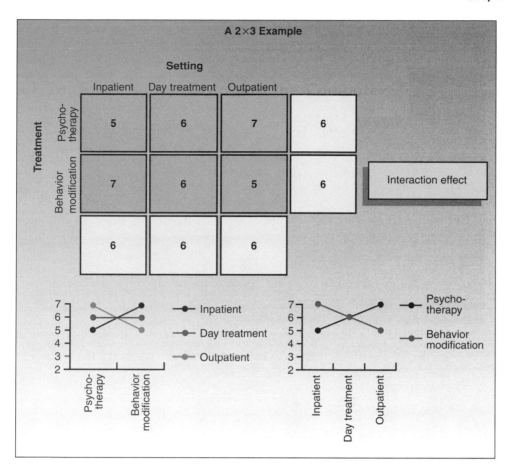

F I G U R E   8 - 9 c
Factorial Design

An interaction effect in a 2 × 3 factorial design.

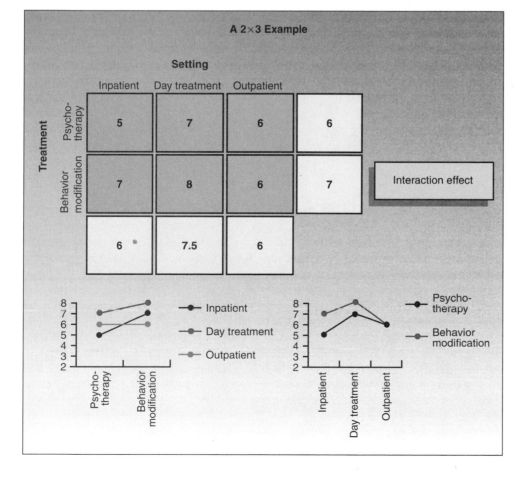

F I G U R E   8 - 9 d
Factorial Design

An interaction effect in a 2 × 3 factorial design.

Figure 8-9c (see page 163) shows one possible interaction effect: Day treatment is never the best condition. Furthermore, you see that psychotherapy works best with inpatient care, and behavior modification works best with outpatient care.

The other interaction effect shown in Figure 8-9d (see page 163) is a bit more complicated. Although there may be some main effects mixed in with the interaction, what's important here is that there is a unique combination of levels of factors that stands out as superior: psychotherapy done in the inpatient setting. After you identify a best combination like this, the main effects are virtually irrelevant.

A Three-Factor Example   Now let's examine what a three-factor study might look like. I'll use the same factors as in the previous example for the first two factors, but here I'll include a new factor for dosage that has two levels. The factor structure in this $2 \times 2 \times 3$ factorial experiment is as follows:

- Factor 1: Dosage
  - 100 mg
  - 300 mg
- Factor 2: Treatment
  - Psychotherapy
  - Behavior modification
- Factor 3: Setting
  - Inpatient
  - Day treatment
  - Outpatient

Notice that in this design, you have $2 \times 2 \times 3 = 12$ groups (see Figure 8-10). Although it's tempting in factorial studies to add more factors, the number of groups always increases multiplicatively. Notice also that to show the tables of means, you have to have two tables that both show a two-factor relationship. It's also difficult to graph the results in a study like this because there will be many different possible graphs. In the statistical analysis, you can look at the main effects for each of your three factors, the three two-way interactions (for example, treatment vs. dosage, treatment vs. setting, and setting vs. dosage), and the one three-way interaction. Whatever else may be happening, it is clear that one combination of three levels works best: 300 mg and psychotherapy in an inpatient setting. Thus, this study has a three-way interaction. If you were an administrator having to make a choice among the different treatment combinations, you would be best advised to select that one (assuming your patients and setting are comparable to the ones in this study).

Incomplete Factorial Design   It's clear that factorial designs can become cumbersome and have too many groups, even with only a few factors. In much research, you won't be interested in a **fully crossed factorial design** like the ones shown previously that pair every combination of levels of factors. Some of the combinations may not make sense from a policy or administrative perspective, or you simply may not have the funds to implement all combinations. In this case, you may decide to implement an incomplete factorial design. In this variation, some of the cells are intentionally left empty; you don't assign people to get those combinations of factors.

One of the most common uses of **incomplete factorial design** is to allow for a control or placebo group that receives no treatment. In this case, it is actually impossible to implement a group that simultaneously has several levels of treatment factors and receives no treatment at all. So, you consider the control group to be its own cell in an incomplete factorial table, which allows you to conduct both relative and absolute treatment comparisons within a single study and to get a fairly precise look at different treatment combinations (see Figure 8-11).

fully crossed factorial design
A design that includes the pairing of every combination of factor levels.

incomplete factorial design
A design in which some cells or combinations in a fully crossed factorial design are intentionally left empty.

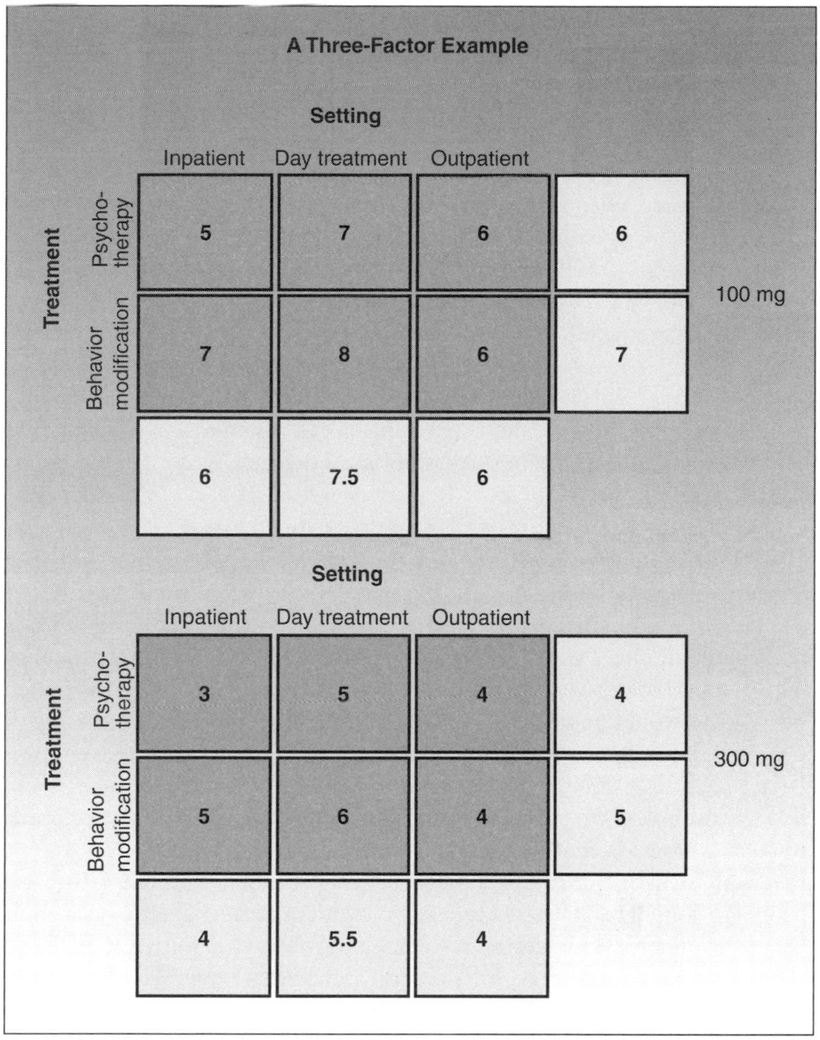

FIGURE 8-10
**Example of a 2 × 2 × 3
Factorial Design**

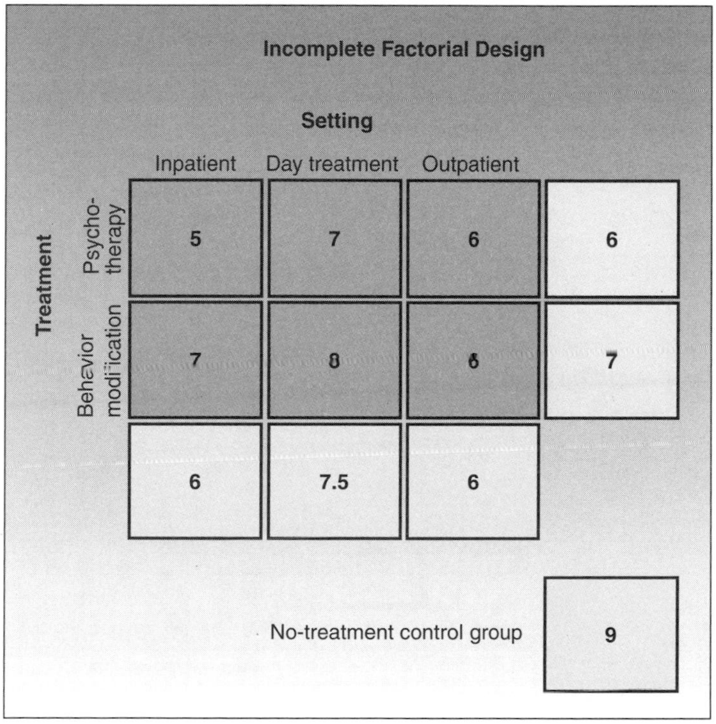

FIGURE 8-11
**An Incomplete Factorial
Design**

8-4 RANDOMIZED BLOCK DESIGNS

The **randomized block design** is research design's equivalent to *stratified random sampling* (see Chapter 2, "Sampling"). Like stratified sampling, randomized block designs are constructed to reduce noise or variance in the data (see Section 8-2, "Classifying Experimental Designs,"). How do they do it? They require you to divide the sample into relatively homogeneous subgroups or blocks (analogous to strata in stratified sampling). Then, the experimental design you want to apply is implemented within each block or homogeneous subgroup. The key idea is that the variability within each block is less than the variability of the entire sample. Thus, each estimate of the treatment effect within a block is more efficient than estimates across the entire sample. When you pool these more efficient estimates across blocks, you should get a more efficient estimate overall than you would without blocking.

Figure 8-12 shows a simple example. Let's assume that you originally intended to conduct a simple posttest-only randomized experimental design, but you recognized that your sample has several intact or homogeneous subgroups. For instance, in a study of college students, you might expect that students are relatively homogeneous with respect to class or year. So, you decide to block the sample into four groups: freshman, sophomore, junior, and senior. If your hunch is correct—that the variability within class is less than the variability for the entire sample—you will probably get more powerful estimates of the treatment effect within each block (see the discussion on statistical power in Chapter 11, Section 11-1a, "Threats to Conclusion Validity"). Within each of your four blocks, you would implement the simple post-only randomized experiment.

Notice a couple of things about this strategy. First, to an external observer, it may not be apparent that you are blocking. You implement the same design in each block, and there is no reason that the people in different blocks need to be segregated or separated physically from each other. In other words, blocking doesn't necessarily affect anything that you do with the research participants. Instead, blocking is a strategy for grouping people in your data analysis to reduce noise; it is an *analysis* strategy. Second, you will only benefit from a blocking design if you are correct in your hunch that the blocks are more homogeneous than the entire sample is. If you are wrong—if different college-level classes aren't relatively homogeneous with respect to your measures—you will actually be

FIGURE 8-12
The Basic Randomized Block Design

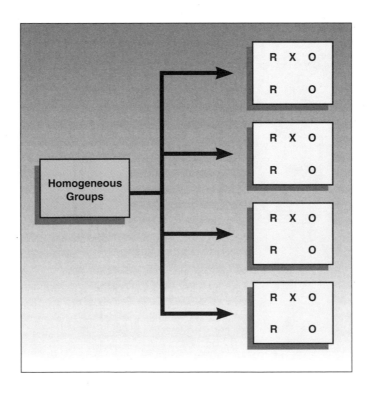

hurt by blocking. (You'll get a less powerful estimate of the treatment effect.) How do you know whether blocking is a good idea? You need to consider carefully whether the groups are relatively homogeneous. If you are measuring political attitudes, for instance, is it reasonable to believe that freshmen are more like each other than they are like sophomores or juniors? Would they be more homogeneous with respect to measures related to drug abuse? Ultimately, the decision to block involves judgment on the part of the researcher.

8-5 COVARIANCE DESIGNS

The basic **analysis of covariance** design (**ANCOVA** or **ANACOVA**) is a pretest-posttest randomized experimental design. The notation shown in Figure 8-13 suggests that the preprogram measure is the same one as the postprogram measure (otherwise you would use subscripts to distinguish the two), and so you would call this a pretest. Note however that the preprogram measure doesn't have to be a pretest; it can be any variable measured prior to the program intervention. It is also possible for a study to have more than one covariate.

The preprogram measure or pretest is sometimes also called a *covariate* because of the way it's used in the data analysis; you co-vary it with the outcome variable or posttest to remove variability or noise. Thus, the ANCOVA design falls in the class of a noise-reduction experimental design (see Section 8-2, "Classifying Experimental Designs").

In social research, you frequently hear about statistical adjustments that attempt to control for important factors in your study. For instance, you might read that an analysis examined posttest performance after *adjusting for* the income and educational level of the participants. In this case, *income* and *education level* are covariates. **Covariates** are the variables you *adjust for* in your study. Sometimes, the language that will be used is that of *removing the effects* of one variable from another. For instance, you might read that an analysis examined posttest performance after *removing the effect of* income and educational level of the participants.

How does a covariate reduce noise? One of the most important ideas in social research is how you make a statistical adjustment—adjust one variable based on its covariance with another variable. The adjustment for a covariate in the ANCOVA design is accomplished with the statistical analysis, not through rotation of graphs. See Section 12-3d, "Analysis of Covariance," in Chapter 12 for details. The ANCOVA design is a noise-reducing experimental design. It *adjusts* posttest scores for variability on the covariate (pretest); this is what it means to *adjust* for the effects of one variable on another in social research. You can use *any* continuous variable as a covariate, but a pretest is usually best. Why? Because the pretest is usually the variable that is most highly correlated with the posttest. (A variable should correlate highly with itself, shouldn't it?) Because it's so highly correlated, when you subtract it out or remove it, you're removing extraneous variability from the posttest. The rule in selecting covariates is to select the measure(s) that correlate most highly with the outcome and, for multiple covariates, have little intercorrelation. (Otherwise, you're simply adding redundant covariates, and you actually lose precision by doing that.) For example, you probably wouldn't want to use both gross and net income as two covariates in the same analysis because they are highly related and therefore redundant as adjustment variables.

8-6 SWITCHING REPLICATIONS EXPERIMENTAL DESIGNS

The **switching replications design** is one of the strongest of the experimental designs. When the circumstances are right for this design, it addresses one of the major problems in experimental designs: the need to deny the program through random assignment of some participants to a no-program comparison group. The design notation (see Figure 8-14) indicates that this is a two-group design with three waves of measurement. You might think of this as two pre-post treatment-control designs grafted together. That is, the implementation of the treatment is repeated or *replicated*. In the repetition of the treatment, the two groups *switch* roles: The original control group becomes the treatment

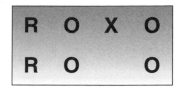

FIGURE 8-13

Notation for the Basic Analysis of Covariance Design

analysis of covariance (ANCOVA or ANACOVA) An analysis that estimates the difference between the groups on the posttest after adjusting for differences on the pretest.

covariates Variables you adjust for in your study.

switching replications design A two-group design in two phases defined by three waves of measurement. The implementation of the treatment is repeated in both phases. In the repetition of the treatment, the two groups switch roles: The original control group in phase 1 becomes the treatment group in phase 2, whereas the original treatment acts as the control. By the end of the study, all participants have received the treatment.

FIGURE 8-14
Notation for the Switching Replications, Randomized Experimental Design

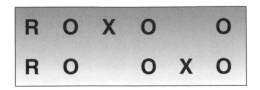

group in phase 2, whereas the original treatment acts as the control. By the end of the study, all participants have received the treatment.

The switching replications design is most feasible in organizational contexts where programs are repeated at regular intervals. For instance, it works especially well in schools that are on a semester system. All students are pretested at the beginning of the school year. During the first semester, Group 1 receives the treatment, and during the second semester, Group 2 gets it. The design also enhances organizational efficiency in resource allocation. Schools need to allocate only enough resources to give the program to half of the students at a time.

Let's look at two possible outcomes. In the first example, the program is given to the first group, and the recipients do better than the controls (see Figure 8-15). In the second phase, when the program is given to the original controls, they catch up to the original program group. Thus, you have a converge-diverge-reconverge outcome pattern. You might expect a result like this when the program covers specific content that the students master in the short term and when you don't expect them to continue improving as a result.

Now, look at the other example result (see Figure 8-16). During the first phase, you see the same result as before: The program group improves while the control group does not. As before, during the second phase, the original control group—in this case, the program group—improved as much as the first program group did. This time, however, during phase 2, the original program group continued to increase even after it no longer received the program. Why would this happen? It could happen in circumstances where the program has continuing effects. For instance, if the program focused on learning skills, students might continue to improve even after the formal program period because they continue to apply the skills and improve in them.

What specific internal validity threats does the switching replications design address? Remember that in randomized experiments, especially when the groups are aware of each other, there is the potential for social threats to internal validity. Compensatory rivalry, compensatory equalization, and resentful demoralization are all likely to be present in educational contexts where programs are given to some students and not to others. The switching replications design helps lessen these threats because it ensures that everyone will eventually get the program. Additionally, it allocates who gets the program first in the fairest possible manner: through the lottery of random assignment.

FIGURE 8-15
Switching Replications Design with a Short-Term Persistent Treatment Effect

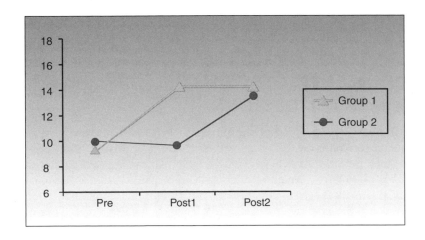

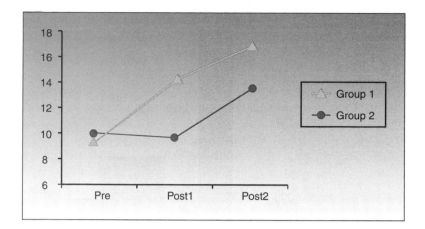

FIGURE 8-16

Switching Replications Design with a Long-Term Continuing Treatment Effect

SUMMARY

This chapter introduced experimental designs. The basic idea of a randomized experiment was presented, along with consideration of how it addresses internal validity, the key concepts of probabilistic equivalence, and the distinction between random selection and random assignment. Experimental designs can be classified as signal enhancers or noise reducers. Factorial designs were presented as signal enhancers that emphasize studying different combinations of treatment (signal) features. Two types of noise-reducing strategies—randomized blocks and covariance designs—were presented, along with descriptions of how each acts to reduce noise in the data. Finally, a hybrid experimental design—the switching replications design—was presented to illustrate the versatility of experimental designs and the ability to tailor designs that address specific threats to internal validity.

SUGGESTED WEBSITES

Note: These websites were functional when we went to press. Please access the Online Study Guide Edition for the most up-to-date URLs.

Research Design and Methods

http://www.niaid.nih.gov/ncn/grants/write/write_m1.htm
On this website, sponsored by The National Institutes of Health, is a concise description of how reviewers of grant applications to the federal government critique the design section of a grant application. There is a nice checklist linked to the main page with a thorough list of critical issues to be addressed when writing about your design.

Choosing an Experimental Design

http://www.itl.nist.gov/div898/handbook/pri/section3/pri3.htm
This website, sponsored by the National Institute of Standards and Technology, features links to the most commonly used research designs in engineering. As you peruse the various options, note the similarities and differences in language and purpose to those you have read in the text.

KEY TERMS

analysis of covariance (ANCOVA or ANACOVA) (p. 167)
analysis of variance (ANOVA) (p. 153)
covariates (p. 167)
factor (p. 156)
factorial designs (p. 155)
fully crossed factorial design (p. 164)

incomplete factorial design (p. 164)
interaction effect (p. 157)
level (p. 156)
main effect (p. 157)
null case (p. 157)
probabilistic equivalence (p. 153)
random assignment (p. 154)

randomized block design (p. 166)
selection-mortality threat (p. 153)
switching replications design (p. 167)
two-group posttest-only randomized experiment (p. 153)
variability (p. 155)

REVIEW QUESTIONS

1. The randomized experiment is considered the strongest design when you are interested in which validity type?
   a. conclusion
   b. internal
   c. construct
   d. external

2. Subjects randomly assigned to a treatment and/or control group are assumed
   a. to be similar.
   b. to be probabilistically equivalent.
   c. to share common backgrounds.
   d. to have similar personalities.

3. The creation of an "artificial" laboratory experiment designed to increase _____ validity often decreases _____ validity.
   a. construct, internal
   b. construct, external
   c. internal, external
   d. external, internal

4. Which of the following is *not* a way to determine whether an interaction exists in a 2 × 2 factorial design?
   a. The levels of factors are exhaustive and mutually exclusive.
   b. The statistical results that list all main effects and interactions.
   c. It is impossible to describe your results accurately without discussing both factors.
   d. The graphs of group means contain nonparallel lines.

5. A researcher randomly assigns subjects to two groups, administers a pretest, and then performs a *t*-test to assess their equivalence. What are the chances that they can have different means yet still be probabilistically equivalent if this researcher sets his or her alpha level at .05?
   a. They will be the same 5 times out of 100.
   b. They will be the same 95 times out of 100.
   c. They are different, nonequivalent groups if they have different means.
   d. You cannot tell anything about the groups by administering a *t*-test on pretest measures.

6. Random selection is to _____ validity as random assignment is to _____ validity.
   a. internal, external
   b. external, internal
   c. construct, internal
   d. external, construct

7. Random selection involves _____, while random assignment is most related to _____.
   a. sampling, research design
   b. research design, research design
   c. sampling, sampling
   d. research design, sampling

8. Which two-group experimental design would increase the quality of research by "enhancing" the study of treatment effects?
   a. factorial design
   b. covariance design
   c. blocking design
   d. both covariance and blocking design

9. Which two-group experimental design would increase the quality of research results by "reducing the noise" that would surround the treatment effects?
   a. factorial design
   b. covariance design
   c. blocking design
   d. either covariance or blocking design

10. How many factors are in a 2 × 3 factorial design?
    a. one
    b. two
    c. three
    d. four

11. The switching replications design is a strong design both in terms of internal validity and ethics.
    a. True
    b. False

12. Random selection and random assignment are equivalent terms.
    a. True
    b. False

13. An interaction effect is an outcome that is a consistent difference between levels of a factor.
    a. True
    b. False

14. The null case is a situation in which the treatments have no effect.
    a. True
    b. False

15. A 2 × 3 factorial design would have six groups of subjects or participants.
    a. True
    b. False

Quasi-Experimental Design

Chapter Outline

A **quasi-experimental design** is one that looks a bit like an experimental design but lacks the key ingredient—*random assignment*. My mentor, Don Campbell, often referred to these designs as "queasy" experiments because they give the experimental purists a queasy feeling. With respect to *internal validity*, they often appear to be inferior to randomized experiments. However, there is something compelling about these designs; taken as a group, they are more frequently implemented than their randomized cousins.

I'm not going to try to cover the quasi-experimental designs comprehensively. Instead, I'll present two of the classic quasi-experimental designs in some detail. Probably the most commonly used quasi-experimental design (and it may be the most commonly used of all designs) is the nonequivalent-groups design (NEGD). In its simplest form, it requires a pretest and posttest for treatment and control groups. It's identical to the *analysis of covariance (ANCOVA)* randomized experimental design (see Chapter 8, "Experimental Design"), except that the groups are not created through random assignment. You will see that the lack of random assignment and the potential nonequivalence between the groups complicates the statistical analysis of the nonequivalent-groups design (as covered in the discussion of analysis in Chapter 11, "Analysis").

The second design I'll focus on is the regression-discontinuity design. I'm not including it just because I did my dissertation on it and wrote a book about it (Trochim, 1984), although those were certainly factors weighing in its favor. I include it because I believe it is an important (and often misunderstood) alternative to randomized experiments. Its distinguishing characteristic—assignment to treatment using a cutoff score on a pretreatment variable—allows you to assign to the program those who need or deserve it most. At first glance, the regression-discontinuity design strikes most people as biased because of regression to the mean (discussed in Chapter 7, "Design"). After all, you're assigning low scorers to one group and high scorers to the other. In the discussion of the statistical analysis of the regression-discontinuity design (see Chapter 12, "Analysis for Research Design"), I'll show you why this isn't the case.

Finally, I'll briefly present an assortment of other quasi-experiments that have specific applicability or noteworthy features, including the proxy-pretest design, double-pretest design, nonequivalent dependent-variables design, pattern-matching design, and the regression point displacement design.

9-1 THE NONEQUIVALENT-GROUPS DESIGN

The **nonequivalent-groups design (NEGD)** is probably the most frequently used design in social research. Why? Because it is one of the most intuitively sensible designs around. If you want to study the effects of your program, you probably recognize the need to have a group of people receive the program. That's your program group, and you probably see that it would be sensible to measure that group before and after the program so you can see how much the program improved or changed them. That's the pre-post measurement. Once you understand the basic problem of *internal validity* (see Chapter 7, "Design"), you will readily admit that it would be nice to have a comparable group that differs from your

quasi-experimental designs
Research designs that have several of the key features of randomized experimental designs, such as pre-post measurement and treatment-control group comparisons, but lack random assignment to a treatment group.

nonequivalent-groups design (NEGD) A pre-post two-group quasi-experimental design structured like a pretest-posttest randomized experiment, but lacking random assignment to group.

program group in only one respect—it doesn't get the program. That's your *control group*. Put all of these elements together, and you have the basic NEGD. Although the design is intuitively straightforward, it is not without its difficulties or challenges. The major challenge stems from the term *nonequivalent* in its title. If your comparison group is really similar to the program group in all respects—except for receiving the program—this design is an excellent one. But how do you assure that the groups are equivalent? And what do you do if they are not? That's the central challenge for this design, and I'll take some time here to address this issue.

9-1a The Basic Design

The NEGD is structured like a pretest-posttest randomized experiment, but it lacks the key feature of the randomized designs—*random assignment*. The design notation for the basic NEGD is shown in Figure 9-1.

In the NEGD, you most often use intact groups that you think are similar as the treatment and control groups. You try to select groups that are as similar as possible, so you can fairly compare the treated one with the comparison one, but you can never be sure the groups are comparable. Put another way, it's unlikely that the two groups would be as similar as they would if you assigned them through a random lottery. Because it's often likely that the groups are not equivalent, this design was named the nonequivalent-groups design to remind us of that. The design notation (refer to Figure 9-1) uses the letter N to indicate that the groups are nonequivalent.

So, what does the term *nonequivalent* mean? In one sense, it means that assignment to group was not random. In other words, the researcher did not control the assignment to groups through the mechanism of random assignment. As a result, the groups may be different prior to the study. That is, the NEGD is especially susceptible to the internal validity threat of selection (see Chapter 7, Section 7-1c, "Multiple-Group Threats"). Any prior differences between the groups may affect the outcome of the study. Under the worst circumstances, this can lead you to conclude that your program didn't make a difference when in fact it did, or that it did make a difference when in fact it didn't.

9-1b The Bivariate Distribution

Let's begin our exploration of the NEGD by looking at some hypothetical results. Figure 9-2a shows a bivariate distribution in the simple pre-post, two-group study. The *treated cases* are indicated with plusses, and the *comparison cases* are indicated with circles. A couple of things should be obvious from the graph. To begin, you don't even need statistics to see that there is a whopping treatment effect (although statistics would help you estimate the size of that effect more precisely). The program cases (plusses) consistently score better on the posttest than the comparison cases (circles) do. If positive scores on the posttest are better, you can conclude that the program improved things. Second, in the NEGD, the biggest threat to internal validity is selection—that the groups differed before the program. Does that appear to be the case here? Although it may be harder to see, the program group does appear to be a little further to the right, on average. This suggests that program group participants did have an initial advantage on the pretest and that the positive results may be due in whole or in part to this initial difference.

You can see the initial difference—the *selection bias*—when you look at the graph in Figure 9-2b. The two vertical lines in the graph show that the program group scored about 5 points higher than the comparison group on the pretest. The comparison group had a pretest average of about 50, whereas the program group averaged about 55. The two horizontal lines on the graph show that the program group scored about 15 points higher than the comparison group on the posttest. That is, the comparison group posttest score was again about 50, whereas this time, the program group scored around 65. These observations suggest that there is a potential selection threat, although the initial 5-point difference doesn't explain why you observe a 15-point difference on the posttest. It may be that there is still a legitimate treatment effect here, even given the initial advantage of the program group.

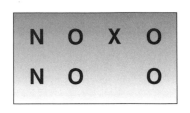

FIGURE 9-1

Notation for the Nonequivalent-Groups Design (NEGD)

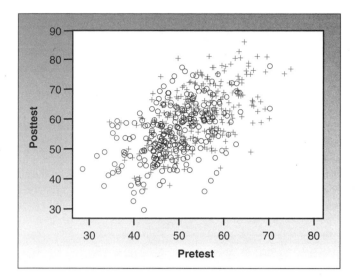

FIGURE 9-2a
Graphs of the Basic Nonequivalent-Groups Design

Bivariate distribution for a hypothetical example of a nonequivalent-groups design.

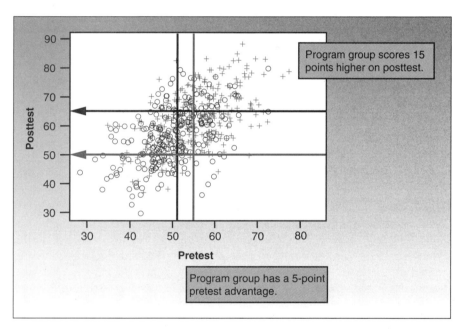

Program group scores 15 points higher on posttest.

Program group has a 5-point pretest advantage.

FIGURE 9-2b
Graphs of the Basic Nonequivalent-Groups Design

Nonequivalent-groups design with pretest and posttest averages marked for each group.

Possible Outcome 1[1]   Let's take a look at several different possible outcomes from a NEGD to see how they might be interpreted. The important point here is that each of these outcomes has a different storyline. Some are more susceptible to **threats to internal validity** than others. Before you read each of the descriptions, take a good look at the associated graph and try to figure out how you would explain the results. If you were a critic, what kinds of problems would you be looking for? Then, read the synopsis and see if it agrees with your perception.

Sometimes, it's useful to look at the means for the two groups. Figure 9-3 shows the means for the distribution in which the pre-post means of the program group are joined with a dashed line, and the pre-post means of the comparison group are joined with a solid one. This first outcome shows the situation in the two bivariate plots. Here, you can see much more clearly both the original pretest difference of 5 points and the larger 15-point posttest difference.

threat to internal validity Any factor that can lead you to reach an incorrect conclusion about whether there is a causal relationship in your study.

---

[1]The discussion of the five possible outcomes is based on the discussion in Cook and Campbell (1979, pp. 103–112).

FIGURE 9-3
Plot of Pretest and Posttest Means for Possible Outcome 1

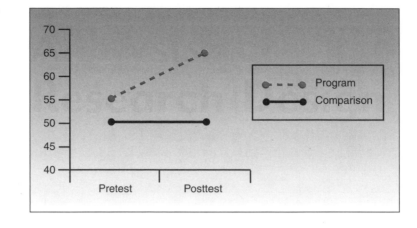

How might you interpret these results? To begin, you need to recall that with the NEGD, you are usually most concerned about **selection threats.** Which selection threats might be operating here? The key to understanding this outcome is that the comparison group did not change between the pretest and the posttest. Therefore, it would be hard to argue that that the outcome is due to a *selection-maturation threat*. Why? Remember that a selection-maturation threat means that the groups are maturing at different rates and that this creates the illusion of a program effect when there is not one. However, because the comparison group didn't mature (change) at all, it's hard to argue that differential maturation produced the outcome. What could have produced the outcome? A *selection-history threat* certainly seems plausible. Perhaps, some event occurred (other than the program) that the program group reacted to and the comparison group didn't. Maybe a local event occurred for the program group but not for the comparison group. Notice how much more likely it is that outcome pattern 1 is caused by such a history threat than by a maturation difference. What about the possibility of *selection regression?* This one actually works a lot like the selection-maturation threat. If the jump in the program group is due to *regression to the mean*, it would have to be because the program group was below the overall population pretest average and consequently regressed upward on the posttest. However, if that's true, it should be even more the case for the comparison group, which started with an even lower pretest average. The fact that it doesn't appear to regress at all helps rule out the possibility that outcome 1 is the result of regression to the mean.

Possible Outcome 2   The second hypothetical outcome (see Figure 9-4) presents a different picture. Here, both the program and comparison groups gain from pre to post, with the program group gaining at a slightly faster rate. This is almost the definition of a selection-maturation threat. The fact that the two groups differed to begin with suggests that they may already be maturing at different rates. The posttest scores don't do anything to help rule out that possibility. This outcome might also arise from a selection-history

FIGURE 9-4
Plot of Pretest and Posttest Means for Possible Outcome 2

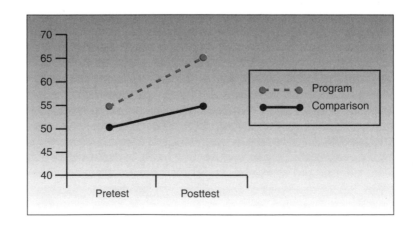

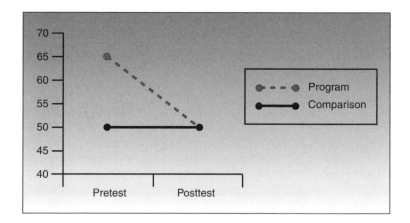

threat. If the two groups, because of their initial differences, react differently to some historical event, you might obtain the outcome pattern shown. Both *selection testing* and *selection instrumentation* are also possibilities, depending on the nature of the measures used. This pattern could indicate a *selection-mortality* problem if there are more low-scoring program cases that drop out between testings. What about selection regression? It doesn't seem likely, for much the same reasoning as for outcome 1. If there were an upward regression to the mean from pre to post, you would expect that regression to be greater for the comparison group because it has the lower pretest score.

Possible Outcome 3 This third possible outcome (see Figure 9-5) cries out selection regression! Or at least it would if it could cry out. The regression scenario is that the program group was selected so that it was extremely high (relative to the population) on the pretest. The fact that the group scored lower, approaching the comparison group on the posttest, may simply be due to its regressing toward the population mean. You might observe an outcome like this when you study the effects of giving a scholarship or an award for academic performance. You give the award because students did well (in this case, on the pretest). When you observe the group's posttest performance, relative to an average group of students, it appears to perform worse. Pure regression! Notice how this outcome doesn't suggest a selection-maturation threat. What kind of maturation process would have to occur for the highly advantaged program group to decline while a comparison group evidences no change?

Possible Outcome 4 The fourth possible outcome also suggests a selection-regression threat (see Figure 9-6). Here, the program group is disadvantaged to begin with. The fact that it appears to pull closer to the comparison group on the posttest may be due to regression. This outcome pattern may be suspected in studies of compensatory programs—programs designed to help address some problem or deficiency. For instance,

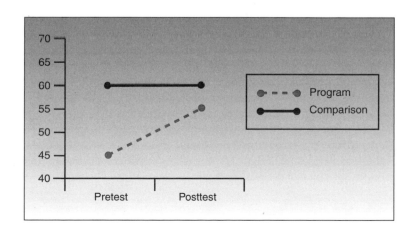

FIGURE 9-7
Plot of Pretest and Posttest Means for Possible Outcome 5

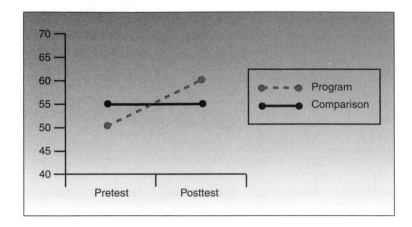

compensatory education programs are designed to help children who are doing poorly in some subject. They are likely to have lower pretest performance than more average comparison children. Consequently, they are likely to regress to the mean in a pattern similar to the one shown in outcome 4.

Possible Outcome 5   This last hypothetical outcome (see Figure 9-7) is sometimes referred to as a *crossover pattern*. Here, the comparison group doesn't appear to change from pre to post, but the program group does, starting out lower than the comparison group and ending up above it. This is the clearest pattern of evidence for the effectiveness of the program of all five of the hypothetical outcomes. It's hard to come up with a threat to internal validity that would be plausible here. Certainly, there is no evidence for selection maturation here unless you postulate that the two groups are involved in maturational processes that tend to start and stop, and just coincidentally, you caught the program group maturing while the comparison group had gone dormant. However, if that were the case, why would the program group actually cross over the comparison group? Why didn't it approach the comparison group and stop maturing? How likely is this outcome as a description of normal maturation? Not very. Similarly, this isn't a selection-regression result. Regression might explain why a low-scoring program group approaches the comparison group posttest score (as in outcome 4), but it doesn't explain why it crosses over.

Although this fifth outcome is the strongest evidence for a program effect, you can't very well construct your study expecting to find this kind of pattern. It would be a little bit like giving your program to the toughest cases and seeing whether you can improve them so much that they not only become like average cases, but actually outperform them. That's an awfully big expectation with which to saddle any program. Typically, you wouldn't want to subject your program to that kind of expectation. If you do happen to find that kind of result, you really have a program effect that beats the odds.

9-2 THE REGRESSION-DISCONTINUITY DESIGN

What a terrible name for a research design! In everyday language, both parts of the term *regression-discontinuity* have primarily negative connotations. To most people, *regression* implies a reversion backward or a return to some earlier, more primitive state; *discontinuity* suggests an unnatural jump or shift in what might otherwise be a smoother, more continuous process. To a research methodologist, however, the term carries no such negative meaning. Instead, the **regression-discontinuity (RD) design** is seen as a useful method for determining whether a program or treatment is effective.

In its simplest and most traditional form, the RD design is a pretest-posttest program-comparison group strategy. The unique characteristic that sets RD designs apart from other pre-post group designs is the method by which research participants are assigned to conditions. In RD designs, participants are assigned to program or comparison groups

regression-discontinuity (RD) design   A pretest-posttest program-comparison group quasi-experimental design in which a cutoff criterion on the preprogram measure is the method of assignment to group.

solely on the basis of a cutoff score on a preprogram measure. Thus, the RD design is distinguished from randomized experiments (or randomized clinical trials) and from other quasi-experimental strategies by its unique method of assignment. This cutoff criterion implies the major advantage of RD designs; they are appropriate when you want to target a program or treatment to those who most need or deserve it. Thus, unlike its randomized or quasi-experimental alternatives, the RD design does not require you to assign potentially needy individuals to a no-program comparison group to evaluate the effectiveness of a program.

From a methodological point of view, inferences drawn from a well-implemented RD design are comparable in internal validity to conclusions from randomized experiments. Thus, the RD design is a strong competitor to randomized designs when *causal* hypotheses are being investigated. From an ethical perspective, RD designs are compatible with the goal of getting the program to those most in need. It is not necessary to deny the program from potentially deserving recipients simply for the sake of a scientific test. From an administrative viewpoint, the RD design is often directly usable with existing measurement efforts, such as the regularly collected statistical information typical of most management-information systems.

9-2a The Basic RD Design

The basic RD design is a pretest-posttest two-group design. The term *pretest-posttest* implies that the same measure (or perhaps alternate forms of the same measure) is administered before and after some program or treatment. In fact, the RD design does not require that the pre and post measures be the same. In the RD design, I'll use the term *preprogram measure* instead of *pretest*. The term *preprogram measure* indicates that the before and after measures may be the same or different. The term *pretest* suggests that it is the same "test" that is in the "posttest," only it is given before the program (that is, *pre*). It is assumed that a cutoff value on the pretest or preprogram measure is being used to assign persons or other units to the program. Two-group versions of the RD design might imply either that some treatment or program is being contrasted with a no-program condition or that two alternative programs are being compared. The description of the basic design as a two-group design implies that a single pretest-cutoff score is used to assign participants to either the program or comparison group. The term *participants* refers to the units assigned. In many cases, participants are individuals, but they could be any definable units such as hospital wards, hospitals, counties, and so on. The term *program* is used in this discussion of the RD design to refer to any program, treatment, or manipulation whose effects you want to examine. In notational form, the basic RD design might be depicted as shown Figure 9-8:

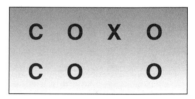

FIGURE 9-8
Notation for the Regression-Discontinuity (RD) Design

- C indicates that groups are assigned by means of a cutoff score.
- An O stands for the administration of a measure to a group.
- An X depicts the implementation of a program.
- Each group is described on a single line (for example, program group on top and control group on the bottom).

To make this initial presentation more concrete, imagine a hypothetical study examining the effect of a new treatment protocol for inpatients with a particular diagnosis. For simplicity, assume that you want to try the new protocol on patients who are considered most ill and that for each patient you have a continuous *quantitative* indicator of health that is a composite rating that takes values from 1 to 100, where high scores indicate greater health. Furthermore, assume that a pretest cutoff score of 50 was (more or less arbitrarily) chosen as the assignment criterion, or that all those scoring lower than 50 on the pretest are to be given the new treatment protocol, while those with scores greater than or equal to 50 are given the standard treatment.

FIGURE 9-9a

Graphs of the Basic Regression-Discontinuity Design

Pre-post distribution for an RD design with no treatment effect.

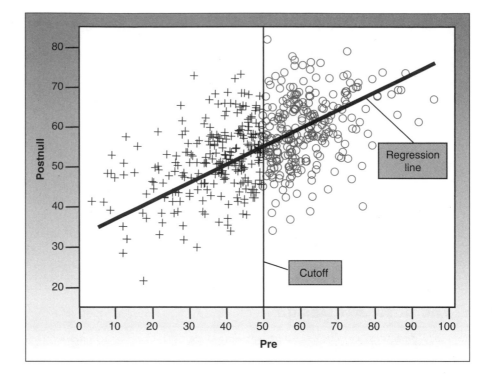

FIGURE 9-9b

Graphs of the Basic Regression-Discontinuity Design

The RD design with 10-point treatment effect.

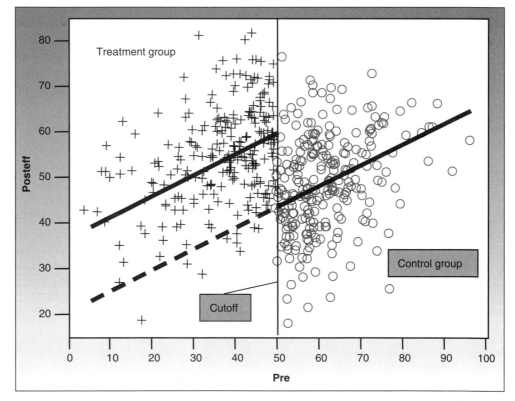

It is useful to begin by considering what the data might look like if you did not administer the treatment protocol but instead only measured all participants at two points in time. Figure 9-9a shows the hypothetical bivariate distribution for this situation. Each circle on the figure indicates a single person's pretest and posttest scores. The plusses to the left of the cutoff show the program cases. Patients are more severely ill on both the pretest and posttest. The circles show the comparison group that is comparatively healthy on both measures. The vertical line at the pretest score of 50 indicates the cutoff point. (In Figure 9-9a, the assumption is that no treatment has been given.) The

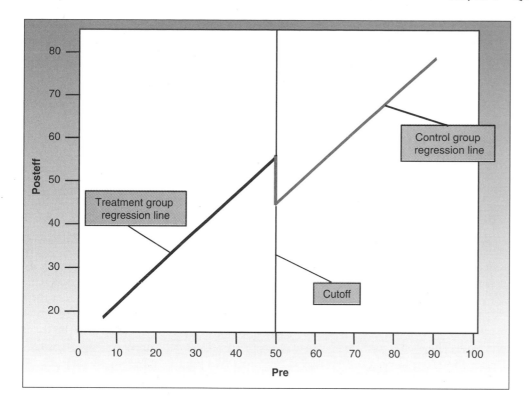

FIGURE 9-9c

Graphs of the Basic Regression-Discontinuity Design

Regression lines for the data shown in Figure 9-9b.

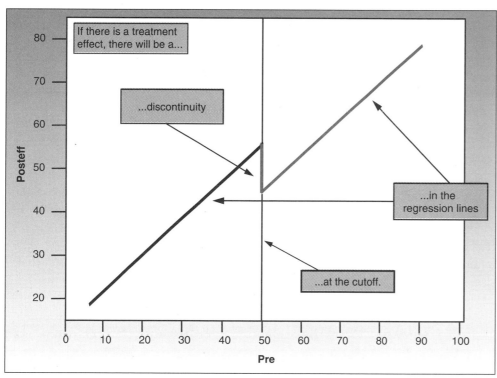

FIGURE 9-9d

Graphs of the Basic Regression-Discontinuity Design

How the RD design got its name.

solid line through the bivariate distribution is the linear regression line. The distribution depicts a strong positive relationship between the pretest and posttest; in general, the more healthy a person is at the pretest, the more healthy he or she is on the posttest, and the more severely ill a person is at the pretest, the more ill that person is on the posttest.

Consider what the outcome might look like if the new treatment protocol is administered and has a positive effect (see Figure 9-9b). For simplicity, assume that the treatment had a constant effect that raised each treated person's health score by 10 points.

Figure 9-9*b* is identical to Figure 9-9*a* except that all points to the left of the cutoff (that is, the treatment group) have been raised by 10 points on the posttest. The dashed line in Figure 9-9*b* shows what you would expect the treated group's regression line to look like if the program had no effect (as was the case in Figure 9-9*a*).

It is sometimes difficult to see the forest for the trees in these types of bivariate plots. So, let's remove the individual data points and look only at the regression lines. The plot of regression lines for the treatment effect case of Figure 9-9*b* is shown in Figure 9-9*c* (see page 181).

On the basis of Figure 9-9*c*, you can now see how the RD design got its name; a program effect is suggested when you observe a *jump* or *discontinuity* in the regression lines at the cutoff point. This is illustrated in Figure 9-9*d* (see page 181).

The Role of the Comparison Group in RD Designs In experimental or other quasi-experimental designs, you either assume or try to provide evidence that the program and comparison groups are equivalent prior to the program so that postprogram differences can be attributed to the manipulation. The RD design involves no such assumption. Instead, with RD designs, you assume that in the absence of the program, the pre-post relationship would be equivalent for the two groups. Thus, the strength of the RD design is dependent on two major factors. The first is the assumption that there is no artificial discontinuity in the pre-post relationship that happens to coincide with the cutoff point. The second factor concerns the degree to which you can know and correctly model the pre-post relationship and constitutes the major problem in the statistical analysis of the RD design, which will be discussed in Chapter 11, "Analysis."

The Internal Validity of the RD Design Although the RD design might initially seem susceptible to threats to internal validity, and especially to selection biases, it is not. Only factors that would naturally induce a discontinuity in the pre-post relationship could be considered threats to the internal validity of inferences from the RD design. For instance, a selection-maturation threat would mean that the groups on either side of the cutoff point differed noncontinuously in maturation rates. It's likely that people differ in natural maturation and even that this is related to preprogram levels. But it's hard to imagine that maturation rates would differ abruptly between groups and coincidentally differ at the cutoff. In principle then, the RD design is as strong in internal validity as its randomized experimental alternatives. In practice, however, the validity of the RD design depends directly on how well you can model the true pre-post relationship, certainly a serious statistical problem.

9-2b Statistical Power and the RD Design

The previous discussion argues that the RD design is strong in internal validity, certainly stronger than the NEGD design and perhaps as strong as the randomized experimental design, but the RD designs are not as statistically powerful as randomized experiments (see Chapter 11, "Analysis," for a discussion of statistical power). That is, to achieve the same level of statistical accuracy, an RD design needs as much as 2.75 times the number of participants as a randomized experiment. For instance, if a randomized experiment needs 100 participants to achieve a certain level of power, the RD design might need as many as 275.

9-2c Ethics and the RD Design

So, why would you ever use the RD design instead of a randomized one? The real allure of the RD design is that it allows you to assign the treatment or program to those who most need or deserve it. Thus, the real attractiveness of the design is ethical; you don't have to deny the program or treatment to participants who might need it, as you do in randomized studies.

9-3 OTHER QUASI-EXPERIMENTAL DESIGNS

There are many different types of quasi-experimental designs that have a variety of applications in specific contexts. Here, I'll briefly present a number of the more interesting or important quasi-experimental designs. By studying the features of these designs, you can gain a deeper understanding of how to tailor design components to address threats to internal validity in your own research contexts.

9-3a The Proxy-Pretest Design

The **proxy-pretest design** (see Figure 9-10) looks like a standard pre-post design with an important difference. The pretest in this design is collected after the program is given! But how can you call it a pretest if it's collected after the program? Because you use a proxy variable to estimate where the groups would have been on the pretest. There are essentially two variations of this design. In the first, you ask the participants to estimate where their pretest level would have been. This can be called the *recollection proxy-pretest design*. For instance, you might ask participants to complete your measures by estimating how they would have answered the questions 6 months ago. This type of proxy pretest is not good for estimating actual pre-post changes because people may forget where they were at some prior time, or they may distort the pretest estimates to make themselves look better. However, at times, you might be interested not so much in where they were on the pretest but rather in where they think they were. The recollection proxy pretest would be a sensible way to assess participants' perceived gain or change.

The other proxy-pretest design uses archived records to stand in for the pretest. This design is called the *archived proxy-pretest design*. For instance, imagine that you are studying the effects of an educational program on the math performance of eighth graders. Unfortunately, you were brought in to do the study after the program had already been started (a too-frequent case, I'm afraid). You are able to construct a posttest that shows math ability after training, but you have no pretest. Under these circumstances, your best bet might be to find a proxy variable that would estimate pretest performance. For instance, you might use the students' grade point averages in math from the seventh grade as the proxy pretest.

The proxy-pretest design is not one you should ever select by choice, but if you find yourself in a situation where you have to evaluate a program that has already begun, it may be the best you can do and would almost certainly be better than relying only on a posttest-only design.

9-3b The Separate Pre-Post Samples Design

The basic idea in the **separate pre-post samples** design (and its variations) is that the people you use for the pretest are not the same as the people you use for the posttest (see Figure 9-11). Take a close look at the design notation for the first variation of this design. There are four groups (indicated by the four lines), but two of the groups come from a single nonequivalent group, and the other two also come from a single nonequivalent group (indicated by the subscripts next to N). Imagine that you have two agencies or organizations that you think are similar. You want to implement your study in one agency and use the other as a control. The program you are looking at is an agency-wide one, and you expect the outcomes to be most noticeable at the agency level. For instance, let's say the program is designed to improve customer satisfaction. Because customers routinely cycle through your agency, you can't measure the same customers pre-post. Instead, you measure customer satisfaction in each agency at one point in time, implement your program, and then measure customer satisfaction in the agency at another point in time after the program. Notice that the customers will be different within each agency for the pretest and posttest. This design is not a particularly strong one because you cannot match individual participant responses from pre to post; you can only look at the change in average customer satisfaction. Here, you always run the risk that you have nonequivalence not only between the agencies but also within the pre and post groups. For instance, if you

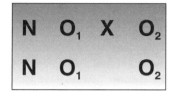

proxy-pretest design A post-only design in which, after the fact, a pretest measure is constructed from preexisting data. This is usually done to make up for the fact that the research did not include a true pretest.

$$
\begin{array}{cccc}
N & O_1 & X & O_2 \\
N & O_1 & & O_2
\end{array}
$$

FIGURE 9-10
The Proxy-Pretest Design

separate pre-post samples A design in which the people who receive the pretest are not the same as the people who take the posttest.

$$
\begin{array}{cccc}
N_1 & O & & \\
N_1 & & X & O \\
N_2 & O & & \\
N_2 & & & O
\end{array}
$$

FIGURE 9-11
The Separate Pre-Post Samples Design

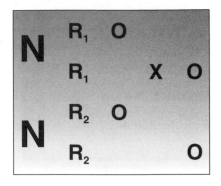

FIGURE 9-12

The Separate Pre-Post Sample Design with Random Sampling

double-pretest design   A design that includes two waves of measurement prior to the program.

have different types of clients at different times of the year, this could bias the results. Another way of looking at this is as a proxy pretest on a different group of people.

The second example of the separate pre-post sample design is shown in design notation in Figure 9-12. Again, there are four groups in the study. This time, however, you are taking random samples from your agency or organization at each point in time. This is essentially the same design as the one in Figure 9-11, except for the random sampling. Probably the most sensible use of this design would be in situations where you routinely do sample surveys in an organization or community. For instance, assume that every year two similar communities do a community-wide survey of residents to ask about satisfaction with city services. Because of costs, you randomly sample each community each year. In one of the communities, you decide to institute a program of community policing, and you want to see whether residents feel safer and have changed in their attitudes toward police. You would use the results of last year's survey as the pretest in both communities and this year's results as the posttest. Again, this is not a particularly strong design. Even though you are taking random samples from each community each year, it may still be the case that the community changes fundamentally from one year to the next and that the random samples within a community cannot be considered equivalent.

9-3c The Double-Pretest Design

The double-pretest design (see Figure 9-13) is a strong quasi-experimental design with respect to internal validity. Why? Recall that the pre-post NEGD is especially susceptible to selection threats to internal validity. In other words, the nonequivalent groups may be different in some way before the program is given, and you may incorrectly attribute posttest differences to the program. Although the pretest helps you assess the degree of preprogram similarity, it does not determine whether the groups are changing at similar rates prior to the program. Thus, the NEGD is especially susceptible to selection-maturation threats.

The **double-pretest design** includes two measures prior to the program. Consequently, if the program and comparison group are maturing at different rates, you should detect this as a change from pretest 1 to pretest 2. Therefore, this design explicitly controls for selection-maturation threats. The design is also sometimes referred to as a *dry-run quasi-experimental design* because the double pretests simulate what would happen in the *null case*.

9-3d The Switching Replications Design

The switching replications quasi-experimental design is also strong with respect to internal validity, and because it allows for two independent implementations of the program, it may enhance external validity or generalizability (see Figure 9-14). The *switching repli-*

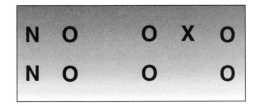

FIGURE 9-13
The Double-Pretest Design

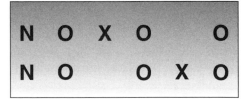

FIGURE 9-14
The Switching Replications Design

cations design has two groups and three waves of measurement. In the first phase of the design, both groups are given pretests, one is given the program, and both are posttested. In the second phase of the design, the original comparison group is given the program, while the original program group serves as the control. This design is identical in structure to its randomized experimental version (described in Chapter 8, "Experimental Design") but lacks the random assignment to group. It is certainly superior to the simple NEGD. In addition, because it ensures that all participants eventually get the program, it is probably one of the most ethically feasible quasi-experiments.

9-3e The Nonequivalent Dependent Variables (NEDV) Design

The **nonequivalent dependent variables (NEDV) design** is a deceptive one. In its simple form, it is an extremely weak design with respect to internal validity. However, in its **pattern-matching** variations (covered later in this chapter), it opens the door to an entirely different approach to causal assessment that is extremely powerful. The design notation shown in Figure 9-15 is for the simple two-variable case. Notice that this design has only a single group of participants. The two lines in the notation indicate separate *variables*, not separate groups.

The idea in this design is that you have a program designed to change a specific outcome. For instance, assume you are training first-year high-school students in algebra. Your training program is designed to affect algebra scores, but it is not designed to affect geometry scores. You reasonably expect pre-post geometry performance to be affected by other internal validity factors, such as history or maturation. In this case, the pre-post geometry performance acts like a control group; it models what would likely have happened to the algebra pre-post scores if the program hadn't been given. The key is that the control variable has to be similar enough to the target variable to be affected in the same way by history, maturation, and the other single group internal validity threats, but not so similar that it is affected by the program.

Figure 9-16 shows the results you might get for the two-variable, algebra-geometry example. Note that this design only works if the geometry variable is a reasonable alternative for what would have happened on the algebra scores in the absence of the program. The real allure of this design is the possibility that you don't need a control group; you can give the program to your entire sample. The problem is that in its two-variable simple version, the assumption of the control variable is a difficult one to meet. (Note that a double-pretest version of this design would be considerably stronger.)

The Pattern-Matching NEDV Design   Although the two-variable NEDV design is quite weak, you can make it considerably stronger by adding multiple outcome variables. In this variation, you need many outcome variables and a theory that tells *how affected* (from most to least) each variable will be by the program. Let's reconsider the example from the algebra program in the previous discussion. Now, instead of having only an algebra and geometry score, imagine you have 10 measures that you collect pre and

nonequivalent dependent variables (NEDV) design A single-group pre-post quasi-experimental design with two outcome measures, where only one measure is theoretically predicted to be affected by the treatment and the other is not.

pattern-matching   The degree of correspondence between two data items. For instance, you might look at a pattern match of a theoretical expectation pattern with an observed pattern to see if you are getting the outcomes you expect.

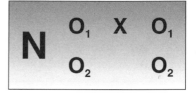

FIGURE 9-15
The Nonequivalent Dependent Variables Design

FIGURE 9-16
Example of a Two-Variable Nonequivalent Dependent Variables Design

FIGURE 9-17

Example of a Pattern-Matching Variation of the NEDV Design

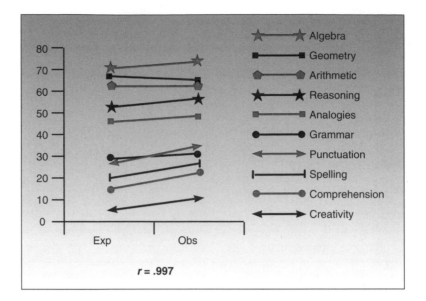

post. You would expect the algebra measure to be most affected by the program (because that's what the program was most designed to affect). However, in this variation, you recognize that geometry might also be affected because training in algebra might be relevant, at least tangentially, to geometry skills. On the other hand, you might theorize that creativity would be much less affected, even indirectly, by training in algebra and so you predict the creativity measure to be the least affected of the 10 measures.

Now, line up your theoretical expectations against your pre-post gains for each variable. You can see in Figure 9-17 that the expected order of outcomes (on the left) is mirrored well in the actual outcomes (on the right).

Depending on the circumstances, the **pattern-matching NEDV design** can be quite strong with respect to internal validity. In general, the design is stronger if you have a larger set of variables and your expectation pattern matches well with the observed results. What are the threats to internal validity in this design? Only a factor (such as an historical event or maturational pattern) that would yield the same outcome pattern can act as an alternative explanation. Furthermore, the more complex the predicted pattern, the less likely it is that some other factor would yield it. The problem is, the more complex the predicted pattern, the less likely it is that you will find it matches your observed data as well.

The pattern-matching notion implicit in the NEDV design requires an entirely different approach to causal assessment, one that depends on detailed prior explication of the program. It suggests a much richer model for causal assessment than one that relies only on a simplistic dichotomous treatment-control model.

9-3f The Regression Point Displacement (RPD) Design

The **regression point displacement (RPD) design** is a simple quasi-experimental strategy that has important implications, especially for community-based research. The problem with community-level interventions is that it is difficult to do causal assessment to determine whether your program made a difference as opposed to other potential factors. Typically, in community-level interventions, program costs limit implementation of the program in more than one community. You look at pre-post indicators for the program community and see whether there is a change. If you're relatively enlightened, you seek out another similar community and use it as a comparison. However, because the intervention is at the community level, you only have a single unit of measurement for your program and comparison groups.

pattern-matching NEDV design A single-group pre-post quasi-experimental design with multiple outcome measures where there is a theoretically specified pattern of expected effects across the measures. To assess the treatment effect, the theoretical pattern of expected outcomes is correlated or matched with the observed pattern of outcomes as measured.

regression point displacement (RPD) design A pre-post quasi-experimental research design where the treatment is given to only one unit in the sample, with all remaining units acting as controls. This design is particularly useful to study the effects of community-level interventions, where outcome data is routinely collected at the community level.

The RPD design (see Figure 9-18) attempts to enhance the single program unit situation by comparing the performance on that single unit with the performance of a large set of comparison units. In community research, you would compare the pre-post results for the intervention community with a large set of other communities. The advantage of doing this is that you don't rely on a single nonequivalent community; you attempt to use results from a heterogeneous set of nonequivalent communities to model the comparison condition and then compare your single site to this model. For typical community-based research, such an approach may greatly enhance your ability to make causal inferences.

I'll illustrate the RPD design with an example of a community-based AIDS education program to be implemented in one particular community in a state, perhaps a county. The state routinely publishes annual HIV-positive rates by county for the entire state. So, the remaining counties in the state function as control counties. Instead of averaging all the control counties to obtain a single control score, you use them as separate units in the analysis. Figure 9-19a shows the bivariate pre-post distribution of HIV-positive rates per 1,000 people for all the counties in the state. The program county—the one that gets the AIDS education program—is shown as a plus, and the remaining control counties are shown as circles. You compute a regression line for the control cases to model your predicted outcome for a county with any specific pretest rate. To estimate the effect of the program, you test whether the displacement of the program county from the control county regression line is statistically significant.

Figure 9-19b (see page 188) shows why the RPD design was given its name. In this design, you know you have a treatment effect when there is a significant *displacement* of the program *point* from the control group *regression* line.

The RPD design is especially applicable in situations where a treatment or program is applied in a single geographical unit (such as a state, county, city, hospital, or hospital unit) instead of an individual, where many other units are available as control cases, and where there is routine measurement (for example, monthly or annually) of relevant outcome variables.

The analysis of the RPD design turns out to be a variation of the analysis of covariance model.

FIGURE 9-18
The Regression Point Displacement (RPD) Design

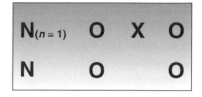

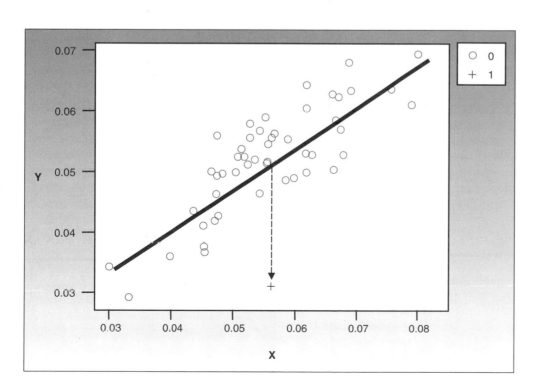

FIGURE 9-19a
Graphs of the Basic Regression Point Displacement (RPD) Design

An example of the RPD design.

FIGURE 9-19b

Graphs of the Basic Regression Point Displacement (RPD) Design

How the RPD design got its name.

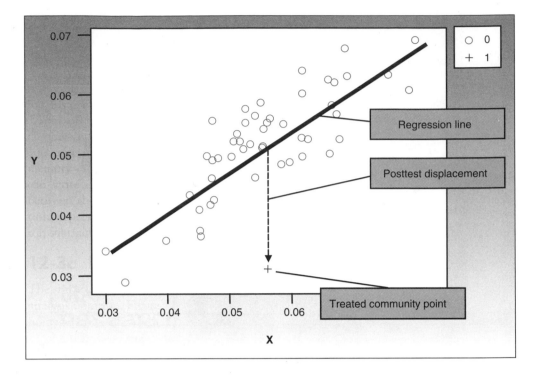

SUMMARY

This chapter introduced the idea of quasi-experimental designs. These designs look a bit like their randomized or true experimental relatives (described in Chapter 8, "Experimental Design"), but they lack their random assignment to groups. Two major types of quasi-experimental designs were explained in detail. Both are pre-post two-group designs, and they differ primarily in the manner used to assign the groups. In the NEGD, groups are assigned naturally or are used intact; the researcher does not control the assignment. In RD designs, participants are assigned to groups solely on the basis of a cutoff score on the preprogram measure; the researcher explicitly controls this assignment. Because assignment is explicitly controlled in the RD design and not in NEGD, the former is considered stronger with respect to internal validity, perhaps comparable in strength to randomized experiments. Finally, the versatility and range of quasi-experimental design was illustrated through the brief presentation of a number of lesser-known designs that illustrate various combinations of sampling, measurement, and analysis strategies.

SUGGESTED WEBSITES

Note: These websites were functional when we went to press. Please access the Online Study Guide Edition for the most up-to-date URLs.

The American Evaluation Association
http://www.eval.org/
Program evaluators are among the most enthusiastic users of quasi-experimental designs. You might be interested in getting a sense of this profession by visiting the website of the main program evaluation organization in the country. You can find out about their professional meetings, publications, training, and job opportunities. You should also get a sense of the real-world importance of the many forms of quasi-experimental design.

Human Services Policy: Children and Youth
http://aspe.hhs.gov/hsp/hspyoung.htm
This website, sponsored by the Office of the Assistant Secretary for Planning and Evaluation within the U.S. Department of Health and Human Services, has pages that summarize the results of studies on key issues. For example, the page on the effects of pre-kindergarten specifically summarizes the results of quasi-experimental studies and puts them in the context of an integrative summary along with other research designs. As you browse the pages, you can see the kinds of studies of young children that have been done with quasi-experimental designs, as well as the implications of these studies for public policy.

KEY TERMS

double-pretest design (p. 184)
nonequivalent dependent variables (NEDV)
   design (p. 185)
nonequivalent-groups design (NEGD)
   (p. 173)

pattern-matching (p. 185)
pattern-matching NEDV design (p. 186)
proxy-pretest design (p. 183)
quasi-experimental designs (p. 173)
regression-discontinuity (RD) design (p. 178)

regression point displacement (RPD)
   design (p. 186)
selection threats (p. 176)
separate pre-post samples (p. 183)
threats to internal validity (p. 175)

REVIEW QUESTIONS

Note: You can find the correct answers to these questions by taking the quiz and then submitting your answers in the Online Study Guide Edition. The program will automatically score your submission. If you miss a question, the program will provide the correct answer, a rationale for the answer, and the section number in the chapter where the topic is discussed.

1. When a researcher uses two groups that already exist (such as two classrooms of students), gives a treatment to one and not the other, and compares the groups' pre-post gain, the researcher is using a
   a. true experimental design.
   b. nonequivalent-groups design.
   c. randomized quasi-experimental design.
   d. nonexperimental design.

2. One of the greatest threats to internal validity in a quasi-experimental design is the likelihood that
   a. one is comparing equivalent groups.
   b. one is comparing nonequivalent groups.
   c. both groups will have similar pretest scores.
   d. both groups will demonstrate regression toward the mean.

3. In general, the "nonequivalent" in "nonequivalent-groups design" means that
   a. the groups are not equivalent.
   b. research participants were not assessed to determine if they were equivalent.
   c. research participants were not randomly assigned to groups.
   d. the groups were haphazardly selected.

4. Which of the following is the greatest threat to the internal validity of a quasi-experimental design?
   a. selection bias (that the groups differed initially)
   b. inadequate statistical power (not enough participants to see a difference)
   c. inadequate preoperation explication of constructs (poor job of determining what is to be studied and why)
   d. mortality (loss of participants during the course of the study)

5. If two group pretest means in a quasi-experiment are analyzed and determined to be different, then there is likely a
   a. maturation bias.
   b. instrumentation bias.
   c. selection bias.
   d. testing bias.

6. Which quasi-experimental design is generally considered as strong with respect to internal validity as a randomized experiment?
   a. bivariate distribution design
   b. regression-discontinuity design
   c. proxy-pretest design
   d. switching replications design

7. In which research design is a program given to the persons most in need?
   a. bivariate distribution design
   b. regression-discontinuity design
   c. proxy-pretest design
   d. switching replications design

8. In the regression-discontinuity design, a positive treatment effect can be inferred from
   a. continuity between expected versus observed regression lines.
   b. discontinuity between expected versus observed regression lines.
   c. continuity between regression lines and additional knowledge, such as who received what treatment and how to interpret the outcome measures.
   d. discontinuity between regression lines and additional knowledge, such as who received what treatment and how to interpret the outcome measures.

9. Which of the following quasi-experimental designs could be used if a researcher is brought into a study after a program has been implemented and the researcher needs a pretest measure?
   a. proxy-pretest design
   b. double-pretest design
   c. regression point displacement design
   d. nonequivalent dependent variables design

10. Which of the following quasi-experimental designs is particularly well designed to give researchers information about selection-maturation threats?
    a. proxy-pretest design
    b. double-pretest design
    c. regression point displacement design
    d. nonequivalent dependent variables design

11. The term *nonequivalent* in the nonequivalent-groups design refers to the fact that a pretest has determined that the groups are significantly different.
    a. True
    b. False

12. Examining the bivariate distribution in a graph is useful because it allows you to see the relationship between two variables. When studying groups, as in a quasi-experimental design, the bivariate distribution in a graph allows you to readily see whether there may be a treatment effect even before you calculate any statistical results.
    a. True
    b. False

13. The regression-discontinuity design may be as strong as the randomized experiment in terms of internal validity, but the true experiment provides more statistical power (that is, you need fewer participants to determine with the same level of confidence whether there is an effect).
    a. True
    b. False

14. The nonequivalent dependent variables (NEDV) design can be a particularly powerful design with regard to causal analysis if viewed from the pattern-matching perspective and assuming that the dependent variables are reasonably well known in terms of how they should behave under various conditions (that is, they can be expected to respond in predictable ways to the independent variable).
    a. True
    b. False

15. If the groups in a nonequivalent-groups quasi-experiment seem to respond at different rates to a program, but in fact are maturing at different rates so that the apparent program effect is an illusion, we would say that the design suffers from a selection-mortality threat to validity.
    a. True
    b. False

10

Designing Designs

This chapter encourages you to think deeply about how you go about designing a research design for your own research project. It tries to take you from being a research design user to being a research design creator. The typical social science methodology textbook (which this book is not, I dare-say) usually presents a dizzying array of research designs and the alternative explanations these designs rule out or minimize. This tends to foster a "cookbook" approach to research design—an emphasis on the selection of an available design off the shelf, as it were. Although standard designs may sometimes fit real-life situations, top-notch researchers (which I'm sure you aspire to be) learn how to tailor a research design to fit the particular needs of the research context and minimize the relevant threats to validity. Furthermore, even if standard textbook designs are used, an understanding of the logic of design construction in general will improve your comprehension of these standard approaches. In this chapter, I present a simple approach to how to design a research design (Trochim & Land, 1982). Although this is by no means the only strategy for constructing research designs, it helps to clarify some of the basic principles of design logic.

10-1 DESIGNING DESIGNS FOR RESEARCH

Here's some important stuff to review before we discuss designing designs for research. In Chapter 7, "Design," I mentioned that three conditions must be met before you can infer that a cause-effect relationship exists:

1. *Covariation*—Changes in the presumed cause must be related to changes in the presumed effect. Thus, if you introduce, remove, or change the level of a treatment or program, you should observe some change in the outcome measures.

2. *Temporal precedence*—The presumed cause must occur prior to the presumed effect.

3. *No plausible alternative explanations*—The presumed cause must be the only reasonable explanation for changes in the outcome measures. If other factors could be responsible for changes in the outcome measures, you cannot be confident that the presumed cause-effect relationship is correct.

In most social research, the third condition is the most difficult to meet. Any number of factors other than the treatment or program could cause changes in outcome measures. Chapter 7, "Design," lists a number of common plausible alternative explanations (or *threats to internal validity*). For example, it may be that some historical event that occurs at the same time that the program or treatment is instituted was responsible for the change in the outcome measures, or changes in record keeping or measurement systems that occur at the same time as the program might be falsely attributed to the program.

10-1a Minimizing Threats to Validity

Before we get to constructing designs themselves, it would help to think about what designs are designed to accomplish. Good research designs minimize the plausible alternative explanations for the hypothesized cause-effect relationship. But research design is not the only way you can rule out threats. Here, I present five alternative ways to minimize any threats to any type of validity, only one of which is by research design:

1. *By argument*—The most straightforward way to rule out a potential threat to validity is simply to argue that the threat in question is not a reasonable one. Such an argument may be made either *a priori* or *a posteriori*. (That's before the fact or after the fact, for those of you who never studied dead languages.) The former is usually more convincing than the latter. For example, depending on the situation, you might argue that an instrumentation threat is not likely because the same test is used for pre- and posttest measurements and did not involve observers who might improve or change over time. In most cases, ruling out a potential threat to validity by argument alone is weaker than using the other following approaches. As a result, the most plausible threats in a study should not, except in unusual cases, be ruled out by argument alone.

2. *By measurement or observation*—In some cases, it is possible to rule out a threat by measuring it and demonstrating that either it does not occur at all or occurs so minimally as to not be a strong alternative explanation for the cause-effect relationship. Consider, for example, a study of the effects of an advertising campaign on subsequent sales of a particular product. In such a study, history (meaning the occurrence of other events than the advertising campaign that might lead to an increased desire to purchase the product) would be a plausible alternative explanation. For example, a change in the local economy, the removal of a competing product from the market, or similar events could cause an increase in product sales. You can attempt to minimize such threats by measuring local economic indicators and the availability and sales of competing products. If there were no changes in these measures coincident with the onset of the advertising campaign, these threats would be considerably minimized. Similarly, if you are studying the effects of special mathematics training on math achievement scores of children, it might be useful to observe everyday classroom behavior to verify that students were not receiving any math training in addition to that provided in the study.

3. *By design*—Here, the major emphasis is on ruling out alternative explanations by adding treatment or control groups, waves of measurement, and the like. I've already covered how you do this in Chapters 8 and 9.

4. *By analysis*—Statistical analysis offers you several ways to rule out alternative explanations. For instance, you could study the plausibility of an attrition or *mortality threat* by conducting a two-way factorial experimental design (see Chapter 8, "Experimental Design"). One factor in this study might be the original treatment group designations (for example, program vs. comparison group), while the other factor would be attrition (for example, dropout vs. nondropout group). The dependent measure could be the pretest or other available preprogram measures. A *main effect* on the attrition factor would be indicative of a threat to external validity or generalizability; an interaction between group and attrition factors would point to a possible threat to *internal validity*. Where both effects occur, it is reasonable to infer that there is a threat to both internal and *external validity*.

    The plausibility of alternative explanations might also be minimized using covariance analysis (see the discussion of covariance in Chapter 8, Section 8-5, "Covariance Designs"). For example, in a study of the effects of workfare programs on social welfare caseloads, one plausible alternative explanation might be the status of local economic conditions. Here, it might be possible to construct a measure of economic conditions and include that measure as a covariate in the statistical analysis in order to adjust for or remove this factor from the outcome scores. You must be careful when using covariance adjustments of this type; perfect covariates do not exist in most social research, and the use of imperfect covariates does not completely adjust for potential alternative explanations. Nevertheless, demonstrating that treatment effects occur even after adjusting on a number of good covariates strengthens causal assertions.

5. *By preventive action*—When you anticipate potential threats, you can often rule them out by taking some type of preventive action. For example, if the program is a desir-

able one, it is likely that the comparison group would feel jealous or demoralized. You can take several actions to minimize the effects of these attitudes, including offering the program to the comparison group upon completion of the study or using program and comparison groups that have little opportunity for contact and communication. In addition, you can use auditing methods and quality control to track potential experimental dropouts or to insure the standardization of measurement.

These five methods for reducing the threats to internal validity should not be considered mutually exclusive. The inclusion of measurements designed to minimize threats to validity will obviously be related to the design structure and is likely to be a factor in the analysis. A good research plan should, wherever possible, make use of multiple methods for reducing threats. In general, reducing a particular threat by design or preventive action is stronger than by using one of the other three approaches. Choosing which strategy to use for any particular threat is complex and depends at least on the cost of the strategy and on the potential seriousness of the threat.

10-1b Building a Design

Here is where the rubber meets the road, design-wise. In the next few sections, I'll take a look at the different elements or pieces in a design and then show you how you might think about putting them together to create a tailored design to address your own research context.

Basic Design Elements   Most research designs can be constructed from four basic elements:

1. *Time*—A *causal* relationship, by its very nature, implies that some time has elapsed between the occurrence of the cause and the consequent effect. Although for some phenomena, the elapsed time is measured in microseconds and is therefore unnoticeable to a casual observer, you normally assume that the cause and effect in social science arenas do not occur simultaneously. In design notation, you indicate the passage of time horizontally. You place the symbol used to indicate the presumed cause to the left of the symbol that indicates measurement of the effect. Thus, as you read from left to right in design notation, you are reading across time. Complex designs might involve a lengthy sequence of observations and programs or treatments across time.

2. *Program(s) or treatment(s)*—The presumed cause may be a program or treatment under the explicit control of the researcher or the occurrence of some natural event or program not explicitly controlled. Recall from Chapter 7, "Design," that in design notation, you usually depict a presumed cause with the symbol X. When multiple programs or treatments are being studied using the same design, you keep the programs distinct by using subscripts such as X_1 or X_2. For a comparison group (one that does not receive the program under study), no X is used.

3. *Observation(s) or measure(s)*—Measurements are typically depicted in design notation with the symbol O. If the same measurement or observation is taken at every point in time in a design, this O is sufficient. Similarly, if the same set of measures is given at every point in time in this study, the O can be used to depict the entire set of measures. However, if you give different measures at different times, it is useful to subscript the O to distinguish between measurements and points in time.

4. *Groups or individuals*—The final design element consists of the intact groups or the individuals who participate in various conditions. Typically, there will be one or more program and comparison groups. In design notation, each group is indicated on a separate line. Furthermore, the manner in which groups are assigned to the conditions can be indicated by an appropriate symbol at the beginning of each line. In these cases, R represents a randomly assigned group, N depicts a nonrandomly assigned group (a nonequivalent group or cohort), and C indicates that the group was assigned using a cutoff score on a measurement.

FIGURE 10-1
The Simplest Causal Design with the Cause and Its Observed Effect

In Chapters 7 through 9, I've shown you a variety of experimental and quasi-experimental design notations that use the components summarized here.

Expanding a Design   With this brief review of design notation, you are now ready to understand one of the basic procedures you can use to create a tailored design—the idea of expanding basic design elements. Expanding involves adding design components from the four basic design elements to arrive at an initial research design—one that is probably more complex than you will require in the end. As a starting point for constructing your design, begin by thinking of the simplest design that includes both a cause and its observed effect (see Figure 10-1).

This is the simplest design in causal research and serves as a starting point for the development of tailored strategies. When you add to this basic design, you are essentially expanding one of the four basic elements described previously. Each possible expansion has implications both for the cost of the study and for the threats that might be ruled out. Here are the four most common ways to expand on this simple design.

Expanding across Time   You can add to the basic design by including additional observations either before or after the program, or by adding or removing the program or different programs. For example, you might add one or more preprogram measurements and achieve the design shown in Figure 10-2.

The addition of such pretests provides a baseline that, for instance, helps to assess the potential of a maturation or testing threat. If a change occurs between the first and second preprogram measures, it is reasonable to expect that similar changes might take place between the second pretest and the posttest even in the absence of the program. However, if no change occurs between the two pretests, you might more confidently assume that maturation or testing is not a likely alternative explanation for the cause-effect relationship you hypothesized. Similarly, you could add additional postprogram measures, which would be useful for determining whether an immediate program effect decays over time, or whether there is a lag in time between the initiation of the program and the occurrence of an effect.

You might also add and remove the program over time, as shown in Figure 10-3. This design is what is sometimes called the *ABAB design,* which is frequently used in clinical psychology and psychiatry. The design is particularly strong against a *history threat* because when you repeat the program, it is less likely that unique historical events are responsible for replicated outcome patterns.

Expanding across Programs   You have just seen that you can expand the program by adding it or removing it across time. Another way to expand the program would be to

FIGURE 10-2
A Double-Pretest Single-Group Design Created by Expanding across Time

FIGURE 10-3
An Add-Remove Design Formed by Expanding Program and Observation Elements over Time

divide it into different levels of treatment. For example, in a study of the effect of a novel drug on subsequent behavior, you might use more than one dosage of the drug (see the design notation in Figure 10-4).

This design is an example of a simple factorial design with one factor having two levels. Notice that group assignment is not specified, indicating that any type of assignment might have been used. This is a common strategy in a sensitivity or parametric study where the primary focus is on the effects obtained at various program levels. In a similar manner, you might expand the program by varying specific components of it across groups, which might be useful if you wanted to study different modes of the delivery of the program, different sets of program materials, and the like. Finally, you can expand the program by using theoretically polarized or opposite treatments. A comparison group is one example of such a polarization. Another might involve use of a second program that you expect to have an opposite effect on the outcome measures. A strategy of this sort provides evidence that the outcome measure is sensitive enough to differentiate between different programs.

Expanding across Observations At any point in time in a research design, it is usually desirable to collect multiple or redundant measurements. For example, you might add a number of measures that are similar to each other to determine whether their results converge. Or you might want to add measurements that theoretically should not be affected by the program in question to demonstrate that the program discriminates between effects. Strategies of this type are useful for achieving convergent and discriminant validity of measures, as discussed in Chapter 3, "The Theory of Measurement." Another way to expand the observations is by proxy measurements (see the discussion of proxy pretest designs in Chapter 9, Section 9-3a, "The Proxy-Pretest Design"). Assume that you wanted to study a new educational program but neglected to take preprogram measurements. You might use a standardized achievement test for the posttest and grade-point-average records as a proxy measure of student achievement prior to the initiation of the program. Finally, you might also expand the observations through the use of "recollected" measures. Again, if you were conducting a study and had neglected to administer a pretest or desired information in addition to the pretest information, you might ask participants to recall how they felt or behaved prior to the study and use this information as an additional measure. Different measurement approaches obviously yield data of different quality. What is advocated here is the use of multiple measurements, rather than reliance on only a single strategy.

Expanding across Groups Often, it will be to your advantage to add additional groups to a design to rule out specific threats to validity. For example, consider the pre-post two-group randomized experimental design in Figure 10-5.

If this design were implemented within a single institution where members of the two groups were in contact with each other, one might expect intergroup communication, group rivalry, or demoralization of a group denied a desirable treatment or given an undesirable one to pose threats to the validity of the causal inference. (Social threats to internal validity are covered in Chapter 7, Section 7-1d, "Social Interaction Threats.") In such a case, you might add an additional nonequivalent group from a similar institution that consists of persons unaware of the original two groups (see Figure 10-6).

In a similar manner, whenever you use nonequivalent groups in a study it is usually advantageous to have multiple replications of each group. The use of many nonequivalent groups helps minimize the potential of a particular selection bias affecting the results. In some cases, it may be desirable to include the norm group as an additional group in the design. Norming group averages are available for most standardized achievement tests, for example, and might comprise an additional nonequivalent control group. You can also use cohort groups in a number of ways. For example, you might use a single measure of a cohort group to help rule out a testing threat (see Figure 10-7).

In this design, the randomized groups might be sixth-graders from the same school year, and the cohort might be the entire sixth grade from the previous academic year. This cohort group did not take the pretest, and if it were similar to the randomly selected control group,

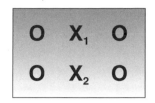

FIGURE 10-4
A Two-Treatment Design Formed by Expanding across Programs

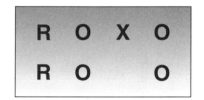

FIGURE 10-5
The Basic Pre-Post Randomized Experimental Design

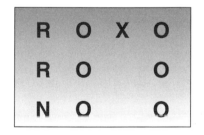

FIGURE 10-6
A Randomized Experiment Expanded with a Nonequivalent Control Group

FIGURE 10-7

A Randomized Experiment Expanded with a Non-equivalent Group to Help Rule Out a Testing Threat

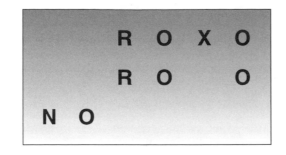

FIGURE 10-8

A Nonequivalent Group Design Expanded with an Additional Nonequivalent Group

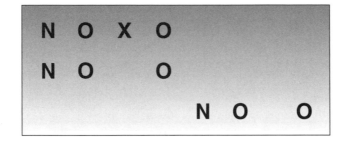

it would provide evidence for or against the notion that taking the pretest had an effect on posttest scores. You might also use pre-post cohort groups (see Figure 10-8).

Here, the treatment group consists of sixth-graders, the first comparison group of seventh-graders in the same year, and the second comparison group consists of the following year's sixth-graders (the fifth-graders during the study year). Strategies of this sort are particularly useful in nonequivalent designs, where *selection bias* is a potential problem and where routinely collected institutional data is available. Finally, one other approach for expanding the groups involves partitioning groups with different assignment strategies. For example, you might randomly divide nonequivalent groups or select nonequivalent subgroups from randomly assigned groups. An example of this sort, involving the combination of *random assignment* and assignment by a cutoff, is discussed in detail in Section 10-1c, "A Simple Strategy for Design Construction."

10-1c A Simple Strategy for Design Construction

It is not sufficient to consider only the basic elements of a research design and the different possibilities for expansion. You need to be able to integrate these into an overall strategy. Additionally, you need to decide which potential threats are best handled by design rather than by argument, measurement, analysis, or preventive action.

Although no definitive approach for designing designs exists, I offer here a tentative strategy based on the notion of expansion discussed in Section 10-1b, "Building a Design." First, you begin the designing task by setting forth a design that depicts the simple hypothesized causal relationship. Second, you deliberately overexpand this basic design by expanding across time, program, observations, and groups. At this step, the emphasis is on accounting for as many likely alternative explanations or threats to validity as possible using the design. Finally, you scale back this overexpanded version, taking into account the effect of eliminating each design component. It is at this point that you face the difficult decisions concerning the costs of each design component and the advantages of ruling out specific threats using other approaches.

Several advantages result from using this type of approach to design construction. First, you are forced to be clear about the decisions you create. Second, the approach is conservative in nature. The strategy minimizes the chance of your overlooking a major threat to validity in constructing your design. Third, you arrive at a design that is tailored to the situation at hand. Finally, the strategy is cost-efficient. Threats you can account for by some other, less costly approach need not be accounted for in the design itself.

10-1d An Example of a Hybrid Design

Let's assume that you want to study the effects of a new compensatory education program on subsequent student achievement. The program is designed to help students who are poor in reading improve reading skills. You can begin with the simple hypothesized cause-effect relationship (see Figure 10-9).

Here, the X represents the reading program and the O stands for a reading achievement test. Assume you decide that it is desirable to add a preprogram measure so that you might investigate whether the program improves reading test scores. You also decide to expand across groups by adding a comparison group. At this point, you have the typical notation shown in Figure 10-10.

The next problem concerns how to assign the two groups. Because the program is specifically designed to help students who need special assistance in reading, you rule out random assignment because it would require denying the program to students in need. You considered the possibility of offering the program to one randomly assigned group in the first year and to the control group in the second, but ruled that out on the grounds that it would require two years of program expenses and the denial of a potentially helpful program for half of the students for a period of a year. Instead, you decide to assign students by means of a cutoff score on the pretest. All students scoring below a preselected percentile on the reading pretest would be given the program while those above that percentile would act as controls. (The RD design is covered in Chapter 9, "Quasi-Experimental Design.") However, previous experience with this strategy shows that it is difficult to adhere to a single cutoff score for assignment to a group. Of special concern is the fact that teachers or administrators might allow students who score slightly above the cutoff point into the program because they have little confidence in the ability of the achievement test to make fine distinctions in reading skills for children who score close to the cutoff. To deal with this potential problem, you decide to partition the groups using a particular combination of assignment by a cutoff and random assignment, as shown in Figure 10-11.

This design has two cutoff points. All those scoring below a certain percentile are assigned to the program group automatically by this cutoff. All those scoring above another higher percentile are automatically assigned to the comparison group by this cutoff. Finally, all those who fall in the interval between the cutoffs on the pretest are randomly assigned to either the program or comparison group.

This strategy has several advantages. It directly addresses the concern of teachers and administrators that the test may not be able to discriminate well between students who score immediately above or below a cutoff point. For example, a student whose true ability in reading would place him or her near the cutoff might have a bad day and therefore might be placed into the treatment or comparison group by chance factors. The design outlined in Figure 10-11 is defensible. You can agree with the teachers and administrators that the test is fallible. Nevertheless, because you need some criterion to assign students to the program, you can argue that the fairest approach would be to assign borderline cases by lottery. In addition, by combining two excellent strategies (the randomized experiment and the regression discontinuity), you can analyze results separately for each and address the possibility that design factors might bias results.

Many other worthwhile strategies are not mentioned in the previous scenario. For example, instead of using simple randomized assignment within the cutoff interval, you might use a weighted random assignment so that students scoring lower in the interval have a greater probability of being assigned to the program. In addition, you might consider expanding the design in a number of other ways, by including double pretests or multiple posttests, multiple measures of reading skills, additional replications of the program or variations of the programs, and additional groups, such as norming groups, controls from other schools, and the like. Nevertheless, this brief example serves to illustrate the advantages of constructing a research design to meet the specific needs of a particular situation.

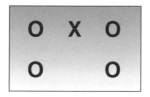

FIGURE 10-9

The Cause-Effect Relationship: The Starting Point for Tailoring a Design

FIGURE 10-10

A Pre-Post Two-Group Design

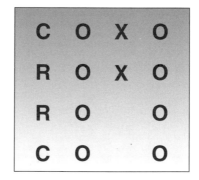

FIGURE 10-11

A Randomized Experimental Design Nested within a Regression-Discontinuity Design

SUMMARY

This chapter describes several ways to guide your thinking about research. Because research can be viewed as a process for reaching valid conclusions from data, a paramount concern is how to minimize the threats to validity. There are really just a few ways to minimize threats to validity: through the arguments you make, by measuring or observing the threat, through your research design, by the analyses you use, or by trying to prevent the threat from occurring. Of course, in any research project, you are likely to use a combination of these strategies. Research design is where you pull together the various components in your study. It's where you integrate the basic design elements: measures, groups, program, and time. This chapter outlined a general approach to putting these elements together to create your own design. You begin with the key causal relationship of interest and then expand across time, programs, observations, and groups to address threats to validity. Then, you scale back to a final design that is feasible and that fits within the resources you have to spend. This approach enables you to move beyond the preset research designs and create a tailored or hybrid design that meets the specific needs of your research.

SUGGESTED WEBSITES

Note: These websites were functional when we went to press. Please access the Online Study Guide Edition for the most up-to-date URLs.

The National Institute on Alcohol Abuse and Alcoholism: Advanced Research Program
http://www.niaaa.nih.gov/extramural/advanced-text.htm
The Advanced Research Program at the National Institute on Alcohol Abuse and Alcoholism is looking for innovative approaches to overcome many of the validity threats common to traditional research designs. The website describes what the prior validity threats are and invites creative approaches to overcoming them. This is a "thinking outside the box" approach to research design. Perhaps you'll come up with a good idea!

Center for System Reliability (CSR): Design of Experiments
http://reliability.sandia.gov/Manuf_Statistics/Design_of_Experiments/design_of_experiments.html
The U.S. Department of Energy supports research in many areas. One way is through contracts with private research companies, such as Sandia's Center for System Reliability. Sandia is a collection of national research and development laboratories operated for the Department of Energy by Sandia Corporation, a Lockheed Martin company. Sandia's primary mission is to ensure that the U.S. nuclear weapons stockpile is safe, secure, and reliable. At this website, you can see examples of how the experimental design ideas you have studied in this chapter are central to this important and sensitive area of research. Scroll down to examine the figure that describes a study of soldering techniques.

REVIEW QUESTIONS

Note: You can find the correct answers to these questions by taking the quiz and then submitting your answers in the Online Study Guide Edition. The program will automatically score your submission. If you miss a question, the program will provide the correct answer, a rationale for the answer, and the section number in the chapter where the topic is discussed.

1. Which of the following is a condition that must be met in order to assume a cause-effect relationship between a treatment and an outcome?
   a. Changes in the presumed cause must not be related to changes in the presumed effect.
   b. The presumed cause must occur after the effect is measured.
   c. There are no plausible explanations for the presumed effect other than your hypothesized cause.
   d. You are able to demonstrate that you have both discrimination and convergence of the presumed cause and effect.

2. Which of the following is *not* a way to minimize threats to the validity of research?
   a. Establish a convincing argument against alternative explanations.
   b. Establish a working relationship with individuals who share your hypothesis.
   c. Rule out alternative explanations using statistical analyses.
   d. Rule out alternative explanations by adding preventative features to the research design.

3. What are the four basic elements of research design?
   a. time, treatments, observations, and participants
   b. time, observations, measurements, and participants
   c. programs, treatments, observations, and measurements
   d. programs, treatments, observations, and time

4. Which of the following strategies would help rule out social threats to internal validity?
   a. expanding across time
   b. expanding across programs
   c. expanding across groups
   d. expanding across observations

5. Which of the following strategies would help achieve convergent and discriminant validity of measures?
   a. expanding across time
   b. expanding across programs
   c. expanding across groups
   d. expanding across observations

6. When a researcher studies whether differences in attrition from a study are related to changes observed in a treatment and comparison group, the goal of the analysis is probably to
   a. rule out plausible alternative explanations for the results with a logical argument.
   b. rule out the possibility that the comparison group received some unintended benefits from participating in the study.
   c. rule out a threat to the internal validity of the study via statistical analysis.
   d. see if the participant recruiting plans were effective.

7. In simplest terms, a good research design does which of the following?
   a. guarantees statistical significance
   b. minimizes the need for further studies
   c. minimizes the plausible alternative explanations for the hypothesized cause-effect relationship
   d. includes multiple measures of every theoretically related construct

8. Which feature would most improve the internal validity of the regression-discontinuity design?
   a. adding more observations
   b. adding random assignment in addition to cutoff intervals
   c. adding more participants
   d. adding more waves of measurement

9. For which design is the assignment to a group based on a pretest cutoff score?
   a. randomized experiment design
   b. regression-discontinuity design
   c. nonequivalent-groups design
   d. nonequivalent dependent variables design

10. Redundancy in research design is a good thing because
    a. if you can include more measures, groups, etc., you will need a larger budget, and larger grants are helpful in the researcher's career development.
    b. including multiple measures, for example, can minimize bias due to a particular form of measurement.
    c. as in Murphy's Law, what can go wrong probably will go wrong, and redundancy in design is the best way to prepare for this.
    d. Actually, redundancy is a bad thing in research design.

11. Generally speaking, the best strategies to use in attempting to control threats to validity are to try preventing them in the first place or by design.
    a. True
    b. False

12. The purpose of overexpanding the components of the basic factorial design is to be sure you have enough statistical power to identify the presence of effects.
    a. True
    b. False

13. Covariation and causation mean the same thing.
    a. True
    b. False

14. Controlling threats to validity on the basis of a good argument done in an *a priori* manner is usually sufficient to account for nearly all threats to validity.
    a. True
    b. False

15. It is necessary to have at least two time points in research that attempts to study a causal relationship.
    a. True
    b. False

ANALYSIS

11

Analysis

By the time you get to the analysis of your data, most of the really difficult work has been done. It's much harder to define the research problem; develop and implement a sampling plan; conceptualize, operationalize, and test your measures; and develop a design structure. If you have done this work well, the analysis of the data is usually straightforward.

In most social research, data analysis involves three major steps, performed in roughly this order:

- Data preparation involves checking or logging the data in, checking the data for accuracy, entering the data into the computer, transforming the data, and developing and documenting a database structure that integrates the various measures.

- Descriptive statistics describe the basic features of the data in a study. They provide simple summaries about the sample and the measures. Together with simple graphics analysis, they form the basis of virtually every quantitative analysis of data. With descriptive statistics, you are simply describing what is—what the data shows.

- Statistical analysis of the research design (that is, inferential statistics) tests your research hypotheses. In experimental and quasi-experimental designs, you use statistics to determine whether the program or treatment has a statistically detectable effect.

You should note that the term **statistics** encompasses both descriptive analyses of your data and inferential analyses designed to test formal hypotheses. In most research projects, the descriptive statistics that you actually look at can be voluminous. In most write-ups, you carefully select and organize these statistics into summary tables and graphs that show only the most relevant or important information. After you describe the data, you construct specific analyses for each of the research questions or hypotheses raised in your research design. In most analysis write-ups, it's especially critical that you not miss the forest for the trees. If you present too much detail, the reader may not be able to follow the central line of the results. Often, extensive analysis details are appropriately relegated to appendices, reserving only the most critical analysis summaries for the body of the report itself.

This chapter discusses the basics of descriptive data analysis. I save the topic of data analysis for your research design for Chapter 12. However, I'll warn you right now that this is not a statistics text. I'll cover lots of statistics, some elementary and some advanced, but I'm not trying to teach you statistics here. Instead, I'm trying to get you to think about data analysis and how it fits into the broader context of your research.

I'll begin this chapter by discussing *conclusion validity*, the validity of inferences you draw from your data analyses. This will give you an understanding of some of the key principles involved in any research analysis. Then I'll cover the often-overlooked issue of data preparation. This includes all of the steps involved in cleaning and organizing the data for analysis. I then introduce the basic descriptive statistics and consider some general analysis issues that set the stage for consideration of the analysis of the major research designs in Chapter 12, "Analysis for Research Design."

11-1 CONCLUSION VALIDITY

Of the four types of validity (see also *internal validity*, *construct validity*, and *external validity*), **conclusion validity** is undoubtedly the least considered and most misunderstood—probably due to the fact that it was originally labeled *statistical conclusion validity* (Cook

statistics A branch of mathematics dealing with the collection, analysis, interpretation, and presentation of quantitative data.

conclusion validity The degree to which conclusions you reach about relationships in your data are reasonable.

& Campbell, 1979), and you know how even the mere mention of the word *statistics* will scare off most of the human race!

In many ways, conclusion validity is the most important of the four validity types because it is relevant whenever you are trying to decide whether there is a relationship in your observations (and that's one of the most basic aspects of any analysis). Perhaps I should start with an attempt at a definition:

> Conclusion validity is the degree to which conclusions you reach about relationships in your data are reasonable.

For instance, if you're doing a study that looks at the relationship between socioeconomic status (SES) and attitudes about capital punishment, you eventually want to reach some conclusion. Based on your data, you might conclude that there is a positive relationship—that persons with higher SES tend to have a more positive view of capital punishment, whereas those with lower SES tend to be more opposed. Conclusion validity in this case is the degree to which that conclusion or inference is credible or believable.

Although conclusion validity was originally thought to be primarily a quantitative and statistical issue, it is also relevant in qualitative research. For example, in an observational field study of homeless adolescents, a researcher might, on the basis of field notes, see a pattern that suggests that teenagers on the street who use drugs are more likely to be involved in more complex social networks and to interact with a more varied group of people than the nondrug users. Although this conclusion or inference may be based entirely on qualitative observational data, you can ask whether it has conclusion validity; that is, whether it is a reasonable conclusion about the relationship inferred from the observations.

Conclusion validity is an issue whenever you are talking about a relationship, even when the relationship is between some program (or treatment) and some outcome. In other words, conclusion validity also pertains to *causal* relationships. How do you distinguish it from internal validity, which is also involved with causal relationships? Conclusion validity is only concerned with whether there is a relationship; internal validity assumes you have demonstrated a relationship and is concerned with whether that relationship is causal. For instance, in a program evaluation, you might conclude that there is a positive relationship between your educational program and achievement test scores; students in the program get higher scores, and students not in the program get lower ones. Conclusion validity is essentially concerned with whether that relationship is a reasonable one or not, given the data. However, it is possible to conclude that, while a relationship exists between the program and outcome, the program itself didn't cause the outcome. Perhaps, some other factor, and not your program, was responsible for the outcome in this study. For instance, the observed differences in the outcome could be due to the fact that the program group was smarter than the comparison group to begin with. Your observed posttest differences between these groups could be due to this initial difference and not be the result of your program. This issue—the possibility that some factor other than your program caused the outcome—is what internal validity is all about. So, it is possible that in a study you can conclude that your program and outcome are related (conclusion validity) and also conclude that the outcome was caused by some factor other than the program (you don't have internal validity).

I'll begin this discussion by considering the major threats to conclusion validity—the different reasons you might be wrong in concluding that there is or isn't a relationship. You'll see that there are several key reasons why reaching conclusions about relationships is so difficult. One major problem is that it is often hard to see a relationship because your measures or observations have low *reliability*; they are too weak relative to all of the noise in the environment. Another issue is that the relationship you are looking for may be a weak one, and seeing it is a bit like looking for a needle in the haystack. Sometimes, the problem is that you just didn't collect enough information to see the relationship even if it is there. All of these problems are related to the idea of statistical power, and so I'll spend some time trying to explain what power is in this context. Finally, you need to recognize that you have some control over your ability to detect relationships, and I'll conclude with some suggestions for improving conclusion validity.

11-1a Threats to Conclusion Validity

A **threat to conclusion validity** is any factor that can lead you to reach an incorrect conclusion about a relationship in your observations. You can essentially make two kinds of errors about relationships:

- You can conclude that there is a relationship when in fact there is not. (You're seeing things that aren't there!) This error is known as Type I error.

- You can conclude that there is no relationship when in fact there is. (You missed the relationship or didn't see it.) This error is known as Type II error.

Most threats to conclusion validity have to do with the second problem. Why? Maybe it's because it's so hard in most research to find relationships in data in the first place that it's not as big or frequent a problem; researchers tend to have more problems finding the needle in the haystack than seeing things that aren't there! So, I'll divide the threats by the type of error with which they are associated.

Type I Error: Finding a Relationship When There Is Not One (or Seeing Things That Aren't There)   In anything but the most trivial research study, the researcher spends a considerable amount of time analyzing the data for relationships. Of course, it's important to conduct a thorough analysis, but most people are well aware of the fact that if you torture the data long enough, you can usually turn up results that support or corroborate your hypotheses. In more everyday terms, you are "fishing" for a specific result by analyzing the data repeatedly under slightly differing conditions or assumptions.

In statistical analysis, you attempt to determine the probability that your finding is either a real one or a chance event. In fact, you often use this probability to decide whether to accept the statistical result as evidence that there is a relationship. In the social sciences, researchers often use the rather arbitrary value, known as the **0.05 level of significance,** to decide whether their result is credible or could be considered a fluke. Essentially, the value 0.05 means that the result you got could be expected to occur by chance at least 5 times out of every 100 times you ran the statistical analysis. The level of significance is also called the **alpha level**—they are essentially two terms for the same thing.

A major assumption that underlies most statistical analyses is that each analysis is independent of the other. However, that is usually not true when you conduct multiple analyses of the same data in the same study. For instance, let's say you conduct 20 statistical tests and for each one you use the 0.05 level criterion for deciding whether you are observing a relationship. For each test, the odds are 5 out of 100 that you will see a relationship even if there is not one there. (That's what it means to say that the result could be due to chance.) Odds of 5 out of 100 are equal to the fraction 5/100, which is also equal to 1 out of 20. Now, in this study, you conduct 20 separate analyses. Let's say that you find that of the 20 results, only one is statistically significant at the 0.05 level. Does that mean you have found a real relationship? If you had only done the one analysis, you might conclude that you found a relationship in that result. However, if you did 20 analyses, you would expect to find one of them significant by chance alone, even if no real relationship exists in the data. This threat to conclusion validity is called **fishing and the error rate problem.** The basic problem is that you were fishing by conducting multiple analyses and treating each one as though it was independent. Instead, when you conduct multiple analyses, you should adjust the error rate (the significance level or alpha level) to reflect the number of analyses you are doing. The bottom line here is that you are more likely to see a relationship when there isn't one when you keep reanalyzing your data and don't take your fishing into account when drawing your conclusions.

Type II Error: Finding No Relationship When There Is One (or Missing the Needle in the Haystack)   When you're looking for the needle in the haystack, you essentially have two basic problems: the tiny needle and too much hay. You

threat to conclusion validity Any factor that can lead you to reach an incorrect conclusion about a relationship in your observations.

0.05 level of significance or **alpha level**   The significance level. Specifically, alpha is the Type I error, or the probability of concluding that there is a treatment effect when, in reality, there is not.

fishing and the error rate problem A problem that occurs as a result of conducting multiple analyses and treating each one as independent.

can think of this as a signal-to-noise ratio problem. What you are observing in research is composed of two major components: the signal (or the relationship you are trying to see) and the noise (or all of the factors that interfere with what you are looking at). If the noise is too great, it's hard to see the signal. There's too much hay in the haystack to see the needle. This ratio of the signal to the noise (or needle to haystack) in your research is often called the *effect size*.

There are several important sources of noise, each of which can be considered a threat to conclusion validity. One important threat is *low reliability of measures* (see Section 3-2, "Reliability," in Chapter 3). This can be caused by many factors, including poor question wording, bad instrument design or layout, illegibility of field notes, and so on. In studies where you are evaluating a program, you can introduce noise through *poor reliability of treatment implementation*. If the program doesn't follow the prescribed procedures or is inconsistently carried out, it will be harder to see relationships between the program and other factors like the outcomes. Noise caused by *random irrelevancies in the setting* can also obscure your ability to see a relationship. For example, in a classroom context, the traffic outside the room, disturbances in the hallway, and countless other irrelevant events can distract the researcher or the participants. The types of people you have in your study can also make it harder to see relationships. The threat here is due to the *random heterogeneity of respondents*. If you have a diverse group of respondents, group members are likely to vary more widely on your measures or observations. Some of their variability may be related to the phenomenon you are looking at, but at least part of it is likely to constitute individual differences that are irrelevant to the relationship you observe. All of these threats add variability into the research context and contribute to the noise relative to the signal of the relationship you are looking for, but noise is only one part of the problem. You also have to consider the issue of the signal—the true strength of the relationship.

Statistical Power   The concept of statistical power (Cohen, 1988) is central to conclusion validity and is related to both Type I and Type II errors. Statistical power is affected by both the strength of the signal of what you are observing and the noise caused by extraneous factors that might obscure that signal. The threat of *low statistical power* is almost always relevant to conclusion validity and encompasses many of the threats described here. Statistical power is technically definable as the probability or odds that you will conclude there is a relationship when in fact there *is* one. In other words, power is the odds of correctly finding the needle in the haystack. Like any probability, statistical power can be described as a number between 0 and 1. For instance, if we have statistical power of .8, that means that the odds are 80 out of 100 that we will detect a relationship when it is really there. Or it's the same as saying that the chances are 80 out of 100 that we will find the needle that's in the haystack. We want statistical power to be as high as possible. Power will be lower in our study if there is either more noise (a bigger haystack), a smaller needle (a weaker signal), or both. So, improving statistical power in your study usually involves important trade-offs and additional costs.

Problems That Can Lead to Either Conclusion Error   Every analysis is based on a variety of assumptions about the nature of the data, the procedures you use to conduct the analysis, and the match between these two. If you are not sensitive to the assumptions behind your analysis, you are likely to draw incorrect conclusions about relationships. In *quantitative* research, this threat is referred to as the *violated assumptions of statistical tests*. For instance, many statistical analyses are based on the assumption that the data is distributed normally—that the population from which it is drawn would be distributed according to a normal or bell-shaped curve. If that assumption is not true for your data and you use that statistical test, you are likely to get an incorrect estimate of the true relationship. It's not always possible to predict what type of error you might make—seeing a relationship that isn't there or missing one that is.

I believe that the same problem can occur in *qualitative* research as well. There are assumptions, some of which you may not even realize, behind all qualitative methods. For instance, in interview situations, you might assume that the respondents are free to say anything they wish. If that is not true—if the respondent is under covert pressure from supervisors to respond in a certain way—you may erroneously see relationships in the responses that aren't real and/or miss ones that are.

Section 11-1b, "Improving Conclusion Validity," illustrates the threats involved when you try to decide whether there is a relationship in your data or observations; this section details several strategies for improving conclusion validity through minimizing or eliminating these threats.

11-1b Improving Conclusion Validity

So, let's say you have a potential problem ensuring that you reach credible conclusions about relationships in your data. What can you do about it? Here are some general guidelines you can follow in designing your study that will help improve conclusion validity.

- *Good statistical power*—The rule of thumb in social research is that you want **statistical power** to be greater than 0.8 in value. That is, you want to have at least 80 chances out of 100 of finding a relationship when there *is* one. Several factors interact to affect power. One thing you can usually do is collect more information—use a larger sample size. Of course, you have to weigh the gain in power against the time and expense of having more participants or gathering more data. The second thing you can do is increase your risk of making a Type I error—increase the chance that you will find a relationship when it's not there. In practical terms, you can do that statistically by raising the alpha level or level of significance. For instance, instead of using a 0.05 significance level, you might use 0.10 as your cutoff point. Finally, you can increase the effect size. Since the effect size is a ratio of the signal of the relationship to the noise in the context, there are two broad strategies here. To raise the signal, you can increase the salience of the relationship itself. This is especially true in experimental studies where you are looking at the effects of a program or treatment. If you increase the dosage of the program (for example, increase the hours spent in training or the number of training sessions), it should be easier to see an effect. The other option is to decrease the noise (or, put another way, increase reliability).

> **statistical power** The probability of correctly concluding that there is a treatment or program effect in your data.

- *Good reliability*—Reliability (see discussion in Chapter 3, Section 3-2, "Reliability") is related to the idea of noise or error that obscures your ability to see a relationship. In general, you can improve reliability by doing a better job of constructing measurement instruments, by increasing the number of questions on a scale, or by reducing situational distractions in the measurement context. When you improve reliability, you reduce noise, which increases your statistical power and improves conclusion validity.

- *Good implementation*—When you are studying the effects of interventions, treatments, programs, or measures, you can improve conclusion validity by ensuring good implementation. You accomplish this by training program operators and standardizing the protocols for administering the program and measuring the results.

11-2 DATA PREPARATION

Data preparation involves checking or logging the data in, checking the data for accuracy, entering the data into the computer, transforming the data, and developing and documenting a database structure that integrates the various measures.

11-2a Logging the Data

In any research project, you might have data coming from several different sources at different times, as in the following examples:

- Mail survey returns
- Coded-interview data

- Pretest or posttest data
- Observational data

In all but the simplest of studies, you need to set up a procedure for logging the information and keeping track of it until you are ready to do a comprehensive data analysis. Different researchers differ in how they keep track of incoming data. In most cases, you will want to set up a database that enables you to assess, at any time, which data is already entered and which still needs to be entered. You could do this with any standard computerized database program (such as Microsoft Access or Filemaker), although this requires familiarity with such programs, or you can accomplish this using standard statistical programs (for example, SPSS, SAS, Minitab, or Datadesk) and running simple descriptive analyses to get reports on data status. It is also critical that the data analyst retain the original data records—returned surveys, field notes, test protocols, and so on—for a reasonable period of time. Most professional researchers retain such records for at least 5 to 7 years. For important or expensive studies, the original data might be stored in a data archive. The data analyst should always be able to trace a result from a data analysis back to the original forms on which the data was collected. A database for logging incoming data is a critical component in good research record keeping.

11-2b Checking the Data for Accuracy

As soon as you receive the data, you should screen it for accuracy. In some circumstances, doing this right away allows you to go back to the sample to clarify any problems or errors. You should ask the following questions as part of this initial data screening:

- Are the responses legible/readable?
- Are all important questions answered?
- Are the responses complete?
- Is all relevant contextual information included (for example, data, time, place, and researcher)?

In most social research, quality of data collection is a major issue. Ensuring that the data collection process does not contribute inaccuracies helps ensure the overall quality of subsequent analyses.

11-2c Developing a Database Structure

The database structure is the manner in which you intend to store the data for the study so that it can be accessed in subsequent data analyses. You might use the same structure you used for logging in the data, or in large complex studies, you might have one structure for logging data and another for storing it. There are generally two options for storing data on computer: database programs and statistical programs. Usually database programs are the more complex of the two to learn and operate, but they allow you greater flexibility in manipulating the data.

codebook A written description of the data that describes each variable and indicates where and how it can be accessed.

In every research project, you should generate a printed **codebook** that describes the data and indicates where and how it can be accessed. Minimally, the codebook should include the following items for each variable:

- Variable name
- Variable description
- Variable format (number, data, text)
- Instrument/method of collection
- Date collected
- Respondent or group
- Variable location (in database)
- Notes

The codebook is an indispensable tool for the analysis team. Together with the database, it should provide comprehensive documentation that enables other researchers who might subsequently want to analyze the data to do so without any additional information.

11-2d Entering the Data into the Computer

You can enter data into a computer in a variety of ways. Probably the easiest is to just type the data in directly. To ensure a high level of data accuracy for quantitative data, you should generally use a procedure called **double entry.** In this procedure, you enter the data once. Then, you use a special program that allows you to enter the data a second time and checks the second entries against the first. If there is a discrepancy, the program notifies you and enables you to determine which is the correct entry. This double-entry procedure significantly reduces entry errors. However, these double-entry programs are not widely available and require some training. An alternative is to enter the data once and set up a procedure for checking the data for accuracy. For instance, you might spot-check records on a random basis.

After you enter the data, you will typically summarize the data so that you can check that all the data falls within acceptable limits and boundaries. For instance, simple summary reports would enable you to spot whether there are persons whose age is 601 or whether anyone entered a "7" where you expect a 1-to-5 response.

double entry An automated method for checking data-entry accuracy in which you enter data once and then enter it a second time, with the software automatically stopping each time a discrepancy is detected until the data enterer resolves the discrepancy. This procedure assures extremely high rates of data entry accuracy, although it requires twice as long for data entry.

11-2e Data Transformations

After the data is entered, it is often necessary to transform the original data into variables that are more usable. There are a variety of transformations that you might perform. The following are some of the more common ones:

- *Missing values*—Many analysis programs automatically treat blank values as missing. In others, you need to designate specific values to represent missing values. For instance, you might use a value of –99 to indicate that the item is missing. You need to check the specific program you are using to determine how to handle missing values.

- *Item reversals*— On scales and surveys, the use of reversal items (see Chapter 5, "Scales and Indexes") can help reduce the possibility of a response set. When you analyze the data, you want all scores for questions or scale items to be in the same direction where high scores mean the same thing and low scores mean the same thing. In such cases, you may have to reverse the ratings for some of the scale items to get them in the same direction as the others. For instance, let's say you had a 5-point response scale for a self-esteem measure, where 1 meant strongly disagree and 5 meant strongly agree. One item is "I generally feel good about myself." If respondents strongly agree with this item, they will put a 5, and this value would be indicative of higher self-esteem. Alternatively, consider an item like "Sometimes, I feel like I'm not worth much as a person." Here, if a respondent strongly agrees by rating this a 5, it would indicate low self-esteem. To compare these two items, you would reverse the scores. (Probably, you'd reverse the latter item so that high values always indicate higher self-esteem.) You want a transformation where if the original value was 1, it's changed to 5, 2 is changed to 4, 3 remains the same, 4 is changed to 2, and 5 is changed to 1. Although you could program these changes as separate statements in most programs, it's easier to do this with a simple formula like the following:

$$\text{New Value} = (\text{High Value} + 1) - \text{Original Value}$$

In our example, the *high value* for the scale is 5, so to get the new (transformed) scale value, you simply subtract the *original value* on each reversal item from 6 (that is, 5 + 1).

- *Scale totals*—After you transform any individual scale items, you will often want to add or average across individual items to get a total score for the scale.

- *Categories*—You may want to collapse one or more variables into categories. For instance, you may want to collapse income estimates (in dollar amounts) into income ranges.

11-3 DESCRIPTIVE STATISTICS

descriptive statistics Statistics used to describe the basic features of the data in a study.

Descriptive statistics describe the basic features of the data in a study. They provide simple summaries about the sample and the measures. Together with simple graphics analysis, they form the basis of virtually every quantitative analysis of data.

Descriptive statistics present quantitative descriptions in a manageable form. In a research study, you may have many measures, or you might measure a large number of people on any given measure. Descriptive statistics help you summarize large amounts of data in a sensible way. Each descriptive statistic reduces data into a simpler summary. For instance, consider a simple number used to summarize how well a batter is performing in baseball, the batting average. This single number is the number of hits divided by the number of times at bat (reported to three significant digits). A batter who is hitting .333 is getting a hit one time in every three at bats. One batting .250 is hitting one time in four. The single number describes a large number of discrete events. Or consider the scourge of many students: the grade point average (GPA). This single number describes the general performance of a student across a potentially wide range of course experiences.

Every time you try to describe a large set of observations with a single indicator, you run the risk of distorting the original data or losing important detail. The batting average doesn't tell you whether batters hit home runs or singles. It doesn't tell whether they've been in a slump or on a streak. The GPAs don't tell you whether the students were in difficult courses or easy ones, or whether the courses were in their major field or in other disciplines. Even given these limitations, descriptive statistics provide a powerful summary that enables comparisons across people or other units.

A single variable has three major characteristics that are typically described as

- The distribution
- The central tendency
- The dispersion

In most situations, you would describe all three of these characteristics for each of the variables in your study.

11-3a The Distribution

distribution The manner in which a variable takes different values in your data.

The **distribution** is a summary of the frequency of individual values or ranges of values for a variable. The simplest distribution lists every value of a variable and the number of persons who had each value. For instance, a typical way to describe the distribution of college students is by year in college, listing the number or percent of students at each of the four years. Or you describe gender by listing the number or percent of males and females. In these cases, the variable has few enough values that you can list each one and summarize how many sample cases had the value. But what do you do for a variable like income or GPA? These variables have a large number of possible values, with relatively few people having each one. In this case, you group the raw scores into categories according to ranges of values. For instance, you might look at GPA according to the letter grade ranges, or you might group income into four or five ranges of income values.

frequency distribution A summary of the frequency of individual values or ranges of values for a variable.

One of the most common ways to describe a single variable is with a **frequency distribution.** Depending on the particular variable, all of the data values might be represented, or you might group the values into categories first. (For example, with age, price, or temperature variables, it is usually not sensible to determine the frequencies for each value. Rather, the values are grouped into ranges and the frequencies determined.) Frequency distributions can be depicted in two ways, as a table or as a graph. Figure 11-1a shows an age frequency distribution with five categories of age ranges defined. The same frequency distribution can be depicted in a graph, as shown in Figure 11-1b. This type of graph is often referred to as a histogram or bar chart.

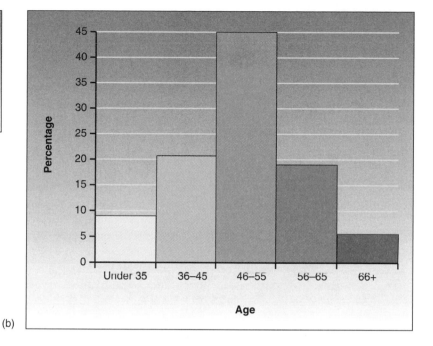

Category	Percent
Under 35	9%
36–45	21%
46–55	45%
56–65	19%
66+	6%

(a)

(b)

FIGURE 11-1

Frequency Distributions

(a) A frequency distribution in table form. *(b)* A frequency distribution bar chart.

Distributions can also be displayed using percentages. For example, you could use percentages to describe the following:

- Percentage of people in different income levels
- Percentage of people in different age ranges
- Percentage of people in different ranges of standardized test scores

11-3b Central Tendency

The **central tendency** of a distribution is an estimate of the center of a distribution of values. There are three major types of estimates of central tendency:

- Mean
- Median
- Mode

The **mean** or average is probably the most commonly used method of describing central tendency. To compute the mean, all you do is add up all the values and divide by the number of values. For example, the mean or average quiz score is determined by summing all the scores and dividing by the number of students taking the exam. Consider the test score values:

15, 20, 21, 20, 36, 15, 25, 15

The sum of these eight values is 167, so the mean is 167/8 = 20.875.

The **median** is the score found at the exact middle of the set of values. One way to compute the median is to list all scores in numerical order and then locate the score in the center of the sample. For example, if there are 500 scores in the list, score number 250 would be the median. If you order the eight scores shown previously, you would get

15, 15, 15, 20, 20, 21, 25, 36

There are eight scores, and score number 4 and number 5 represent the halfway point. Because both of these scores are 20, the median is 20. If the two middle scores had different values, you find the value midway between them to determine the median.

central tendency An estimate of the center of a distribution of values. The most usual measures of central tendency are the mean, median, and mode.

mean A description of the central tendency in which you add all the values and divide by the number of values.

median The middle number in a series of numbers or the score found at the exact middle or fiftieth percentile of the set of values. One way to compute the median is to list all scores in numerical order and then locate the score in the center of the sample.

mode The most frequently occurring value in the set of scores.

The **mode** is the most frequently occurring value in the set of scores. To determine the mode, you might again order the scores as shown previously and then count each one. The most frequently occurring value is the mode. In our example, the value 15 occurs three times and is the mode. In some distributions, there is more than one modal value. For instance, in a bimodal distribution, two values occur most frequently.

Notice that for the same set of eight scores, we got three different values—20.875, 20, and 15—for the mean, median, and mode, respectively. If the distribution is truly normal (bell-shaped), the mean, median, and mode are all equal to each other.

11-3c Dispersion or Variability

dispersion The spread of the values around the central tendency. The two common measures of dispersion are the range and the standard deviation.

range The highest value minus the lowest value.

standard deviation The spread or variability of the scores around their average in a *single sample*. The standard deviation, often abbreviated SD, is mathematically the square root of the variance. The standard deviation and variance both measure dispersion, but because the standard deviation is measured in the same units as the original measure and the variance is measured in squared units, the standard deviation is usually more directly interpretable and meaningful.

Dispersion refers to the spread of the values around the central tendency. The two common measures of dispersion are the range and the standard deviation. The **range** is simply the highest value minus the lowest value. In the previous example distribution, the high value is 36 and the low is 15, so the range is 36 – 15 = 21.

The **standard deviation** is a more accurate and detailed estimate of dispersion because an outlier can greatly exaggerate the range (as was true in this example, where the single outlier value of 36 stands apart from the rest of the values). The standard deviation shows the relation that set of scores has to the mean of the sample. Again, let's take the set of scores:

15, 20, 21, 20, 36, 15, 25, 15

To compute the standard deviation, you first find the distance between each value and the mean. You know from before that the mean for the data in this example is 20.875. So, the differences from the mean are

$$15 - 20.875 = -5.875$$
$$20 - 20.875 = -0.875$$
$$21 - 20.875 = +0.125$$
$$20 - 20.875 = -0.875$$
$$36 - 20.875 = 15.125$$
$$15 - 20.875 = -5.875$$
$$25 - 20.875 = +4.125$$
$$15 - 20.875 = -5.875$$

Notice that values that are below the mean have negative discrepancies and values above it have positive ones. Next, you square each discrepancy:

$$-5.875 \times -5.875 = 34.515625$$
$$-0.875 \times -0.875 = 0.765625$$
$$+0.125 \times +0.125 = 0.015625$$
$$-0.875 \times -0.875 = 0.765625$$
$$15.125 \times 15.125 = 228.765625$$
$$-5.875 \times -5.875 = 34.515625$$
$$+4.125 \times +4.125 = 17.015625$$
$$-5.875 \times -5.875 = 34.515625$$

Now, you take these squares and sum them to get the sum of squares (SS) value. Here, the sum is 350.875. Next, you divide this sum by the number of scores minus 1.

$$\sqrt{\frac{\Sigma(X-\bar{X})^2}{(n-1)}}$$

where:

X = Each score

$\bar{X}$ = The mean or average

n = The number of values

Σ = Means we sum across the values

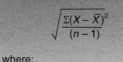

FIGURE 11-2

Formula for the Standard Deviation

Here, the result is 350.875 / 7 = 50.125. This value is known as the **variance.** To get the standard deviation, you take the square root of the variance (remember that you squared the deviations earlier). This would be $\sqrt{50.125}$ = 7.079901129253.

Although this computation may seem convoluted, it's actually quite simple. To see this, consider the formula for the standard deviation, shown in Figure 11-2.

In the top part of the ratio, the numerator, notice that each score has the mean subtracted from it, the difference is squared, and the squares are summed. In the bottom part, you take the number of scores minus 1. The ratio is the variance, and the square root is the standard deviation. In English, the standard deviation is described as follows:

> The square root of the sum of the squared deviations from the mean divided by the number of scores minus one

Although you can calculate these univariate statistics by hand, it becomes quite tedious when you have more than a few values and variables. Every statistics program is capable of calculating them easily for you. For instance, I put the eight scores into SPSS and got the results shown in Table 11-1. This table confirms the calculations I did by hand previously.

The standard deviation allows you to reach some conclusions about specific scores in your distribution. Assuming that the distribution of scores is normal or bell-shaped (or close to it), you can reach the following conclusions:

- Approximately 68 percent of the scores in the sample fall within one standard deviation of the mean.
- Approximately 95 percent of the scores in the sample fall within two standard deviations of the mean.
- Approximately 99 percent of the scores in the sample fall within three standard deviations of the mean.

For instance, because the mean in our example is 20.875 and the standard deviation is 7.0799, you can use the statement listed previously to estimate that approximately 95 percent of the scores will fall in the range of 20.875 − (2 × 7.0799) to 20.875 + (2 × 7.0799)

variance A statistic that describes the variability in the data for a variable. The variance is the spread of the scores around the mean of a distribution. Specifically, the variance is the sum of the squared deviations from the mean divided by the number of observations minus 1.

N	8
Mean	20.8750
Median	20.0000
Mode	15.00
Standard deviation	7.0799
Variance	50.1250
Range	21.00

TABLE 11-1

Table of Descriptive Statistics

or between 6.7152 and 35.0348. This kind of information is critical in enabling you to compare the performance of individuals on one variable with their performance on another, even when the variables are measured on entirely different scales.

11-3d Correlation

correlation A single number that describes the degree of relationship between two variables.

The correlation is one of the most common and most useful statistics. A **correlation** is a single number that describes the degree of relationship between two variables. Let's work through an example to show you how this statistic is computed.

Correlation Example   Let's assume that you want to look at the relationship between two variables: height (in inches) and self-esteem. Perhaps you have a hypothesis that how tall you are affects your self-esteem. (Incidentally, I don't think you have to worry about the direction of causality here; it's not likely that self-esteem causes your height.) Let's say you collect some information on 20 individuals—all male. (The average height differs for males and females; to keep this example simple, I'll just use males.) Height is measured in inches. Self-esteem is measured based on the average of 10, 1-to-5 rating items (where higher scores mean higher self-esteem). See Table 11-2 for the data for the 20 cases. (Don't take this too seriously; I made this data up to illustrate what a correlation is.)

Now, let's take a quick look at the histogram for each variable (see Figure 11-3 and Figure 11-4). Table 11-3 shows the descriptive statistics. Finally, look at the simple bivariate (two-variable) plot (see Figure 11-5).

You should immediately see in the bivariate plot that the relationship between the variables is a positive one because if you were to fit a single straight line through the dots it would have a positive slope or move up from left to right. (If you can't see the positive relationship, review Section 1-1e, "Types of Relationships," in Chapter 1.)

TABLE 11-2	Person	Height (inches)	Self-Esteem
Hypothetical Data to Demonstrate the Correlation between Height and Self-Esteem	1	68	4.1
	2	71	4.6
	3	62	3.8
	4	75	4.4
	5	58	3.2
	6	60	3.1
	7	67	3.8
	8	68	4.1
	9	71	4.3
	10	69	3.7
	11	68	3.5
	12	67	3.2
	13	63	3.7
	14	62	3.3
	15	60	3.4
	16	63	4.0
	17	65	4.1
	18	67	3.8
	19	63	3.4
	20	61	3.6

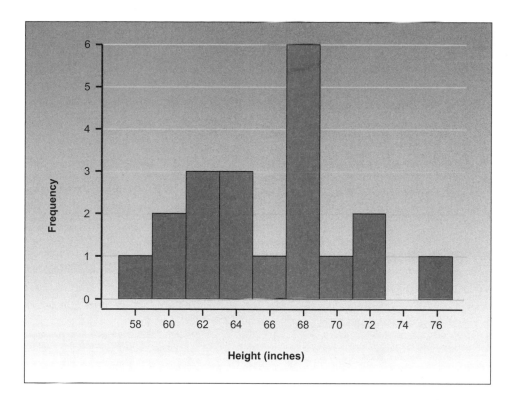

FIGURE 11-3
Histogram for the Height Variable in the Example Correlation Calculation

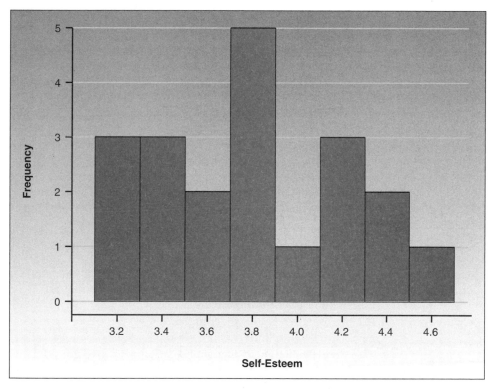

FIGURE 11-4
Histogram for the Self-Esteem Variable in the Example Correlation Calculation

TABLE 11-3   Descriptive Statistics for Correlation Calculation Example

Variable	Mean	Standard Deviation	Variance	Sum	Minimum	Maximum	Range
Height	65.4	4.40574	19.4105	1308	58	75	17
Self-Esteem	3.755	0.426090	0.181553	75.1	3.1	4.6	1.5

FIGURE 11-5
**Bivariate Plot for the
Example Correlation
Calculation**

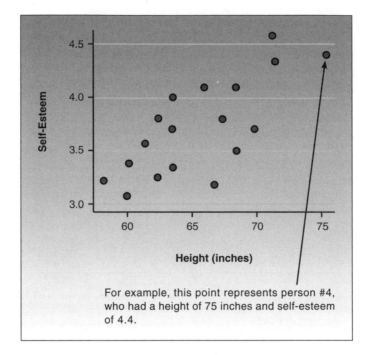

For example, this point represents person #4,
who had a height of 75 inches and self-esteem
of 4.4.

Because the correlation is nothing more than a quantitative estimate of the relationship, you would expect a positive correlation.

What does a positive relationship mean in this context? It means that, in general, higher scores on one variable tend to be paired with higher scores on the other and that lower scores on one variable tend to be paired with lower scores on the other. You should confirm visually that this is generally true in the plot in Figure 11-5.

Calculating the Correlation   Now you're ready to compute the correlation value. The formula for the correlation is shown in Figure 11-6.

The symbol r stands for the correlation. Through the magic of mathematics, it turns out that r will always be between −1.0 and +1.0. If the correlation is negative, you have a negative relationship; if it's positive, the relationship is positive. (Pretty clever, huh?) You don't need to know how I came up with this formula unless you want to be a statistician. But you probably will need to know how the formula relates to real data—how you can use the formula to compute the correlation. Let's look at the data you need for the formula. Table 11-4 shows the original data with the other necessary columns.

The first three columns are the same as those in Table 11-2. The next three columns are simple computations based on the height and self-esteem data in the first three columns. The bottom row consists of the sum of each column. The information contained in this table is all the information you need to compute the correlation. Figure 11-7 (see page 220) shows the values from the bottom row of the table (where N is 20 people) as they are related to the symbols in the formula.

Now, when you plug these values into the formula in Figure 11-6, you get what is shown rather tediously, one step at a time, in Figure 11-8 (see page 220). The correlation for the 20 cases is .73, which is a fairly strong positive relationship. I guess there is a relationship between height and self-esteem, at least in this made-up data!

Testing the Significance of a Correlation   After you've computed a correlation, you can determine the probability that the observed correlation occurred by chance. That is, you can conduct a significance test. Most often, you are interested in determining the probability that there is a correlation. When you are interested in that, you are testing the mutually exclusive hypotheses:

$$H_0: r = 0$$

$$H_1: r \neq 0$$

$$r = \frac{N\Sigma xy - (\Sigma x)(\Sigma y)}{\sqrt{[N\Sigma x^2 - (\Sigma x)^2][N\Sigma y^2 - (\Sigma y)^2]}}$$

where:

N = Number of pairs of scores

Σxy = Sum of the products of paired scores

Σx = Sum of the x scores

Σy = Sum of the y scores

Σx^2 = Sum of squared x scores

Σy^2 = Sum of squared y scores

FIGURE 11-6
The Formula for the Correlation

In effect, you are testing whether the real correlation is zero or not. The easiest way to test this hypothesis is to find a statistics book that has a table of critical values of r. (Most introductory statistics texts would have a table like this.) As in all hypothesis testing, you need to first determine the significance level you will use for the test. Here, I'll use the common significance level of $\alpha = .05$. This means that I am conducting a test where the odds that the correlation occurred by chance are no more than 5 out of 100. Before I look up the critical value in a table, I also have to compute the **degrees of freedom (df).** The df for a correlation is simply equal to $N - 2$ or, in this example, $20 - 2 = 18$. Finally, I have to decide whether I am doing a one-tailed or two-tailed test (see the discussion in Chapter 1, Section 1-1f, "Hypotheses"). In this example, because I have no strong prior theory to suggest whether the relationship between height and

degrees of freedom (df)
A statistical term that is a function of the sample size. In the t-test formula, for instance, the df is the number of persons in both groups minus 2.

Person	Height (x)	Self-Esteem (y)	xy	x²	y²
1	68	4.1	278.8	4624	16.81
2	71	4.6	326.6	5041	21.16
3	62	3.8	235.6	3844	14.44
4	75	4.4	330.5	625	19.36
5	58	3.2	185.6	3364	10.24
6	60	3.1	186.3	600	9.61
7	67	3.8	254.6	4489	14.44
8	68	4.1	278.8	4624	16.81
9	71	4.3	305.3	5041	18.49
10	69	3.7	255.3	4761	13.69
11	68	3.5	238.4	624	12.25
12	67	3.2	214.4	4489	10.24
13	63	3.7	233.1	3969	13.69
14	62	3.3	204.6	3844	10.89
15	60	3.4	204.0	3600	11.56
16	63	4.0	252.0	3969	16.00
17	65	4.1	266.5	4225	16.81
18	67	3.8	254.6	4489	14.44
19	63	3.4	214.2	3969	11.56
20	61	3.6	219.6	3721	12.96
Sum =	1308	75.1	4937.6	85912	285.45

TABLE 11-4

Computations for the Example Correlation Calculation

$$N = 20$$
$$\Sigma xy = 4937.6$$
$$\Sigma x = 1308$$
$$\Sigma y = 75.1$$
$$\Sigma x^2 = 85912$$
$$\Sigma y^2 = 285.45$$

FIGURE 11-7

The Parts of the Correlation Formula with the Numerical Values from the Example

correlation matrix A table of correlations showing all possible relationships among a set of variables. The diagonal of a correlation matrix (the numbers that go from the upper-left corner to the lower right) always consists of 1s because these are the correlations between each variable and itself (and a variable is always perfectly correlated with itself). Off-diagonal elements are the correlations of variables represented by the relevant row and column in the matrix.

self-esteem would be positive or negative, I'll opt for the two-tailed test. With these three pieces of information—the significance level (alpha = .05), degrees of freedom (df = 18), and type of test (two-tailed)—I can now test the significance of the correlation I found. When I look up this value in the handy little table at the back of my statistics book, I find that the critical value is .4438. This means that if my correlation is greater than .4438 or less than −.4438 (remember, this is a two-tailed test), I can conclude that the odds are less than 5 out of 100 that this is a chance occurrence. Because my correlation of .73 is actually quite a bit higher, I conclude that it is not a chance finding and that the correlation is statistically significant (given the parameters of the test). I can reject the null hypothesis and accept the alternative—I have a statistically significant correlation.

The Correlation Matrix   All I've shown you so far is how to compute a correlation between two variables. In most studies, you usually have more than two variables. Let's say you have a study with 10 interval-level variables, and you want to estimate the relationships among all of them (between all possible pairs of variables). In this instance, you have 45 unique correlations to estimate (more later on how I knew that). You could do the computations just completed 45 times to obtain the correlations, or you could use just about any statistics program to automatically compute all 45 with a simple click of the mouse.

I used a simple statistics program to generate random data for 10 variables with 20 cases (persons) for each variable. Then, I told the program to compute the correlations among these variables. The results are shown in Table 11-5.

This type of table is called a **correlation matrix.** It lists the variable names (in this case, C1 through C10) down the first column and across the first row. The diagonal of a correlation matrix (the numbers that go from the upper-left corner to the lower right) always consists of ones because these are the correlations between each variable and itself (and a variable is always perfectly correlated with itself). The statistical program I used shows only the lower triangle of the correlation matrix. In every correlation matrix, there are two triangles: the values below and to the left of the diagonal (lower triangle) and above and to the right of the diagonal (upper triangle). There is no reason to print both triangles because the two triangles of a correlation matrix are always mirror images of each other. (The correlation of variable *x* with variable *y* is always equal to the correlation of variable *y* with variable *x*.) When a matrix has this mirror-image quality above

FIGURE 11-8

Example of the Computation of the Correlation

$$r = \frac{20(4937.6) - (1308)(75.1)}{\sqrt{[20(85912) - (1308 * 1308)][20(285.45) - (75.1 * 75.1)]}}$$

$$r = \frac{20(4937.6) - (1308)(75.1)}{\sqrt{[1718240 - 1710864][5709 - 5640.01]}}$$

$$r = \frac{521.2}{\sqrt{[7376][68.99]}}$$

$$r = \frac{521.2}{\sqrt{508870.2}}$$

$$r = \frac{521.2}{713.3514}$$

$$r = .73$$

TABLE 11-5			Hypothetical Correlation Matrix for 10 Variables						
C1	**C2**	**C3**	**C4**	**C5**	**C6**	**C7**	**C8**	**C9**	**C10**
C1 1.000									
C2 0.274	1.000								
C3 −0.134	−0.269	1.000							
C4 0.201	−0.153	0.075	1.000						
C5 −0.129	−0.166	0.278	−0.011	1.000					
C6 −0.095	0.280	−0.348	−0.378	−0.009	1.000				
C7 0.171	−0.122	0.288	0.086	0.193	0.002	1.000			
C8 0.219	0.242	−0.380	−0.227	−0.551	0.324	−0.082	1.000		
C9 0.518	0.238	0.002	0.082	−0.015	0.304	0.347	−0.013	1.000	
C10 0.299	0.568	0.165	−0.122	−0.106	−0.169	0.243	0.014	0.352	1.000

and below the diagonal, it is referred to as a **symmetric matrix.** A correlation matrix is always a symmetric matrix.

To locate the correlation for any pair of variables, find the value in the table for the row and column intersection for those two variables. For instance, to find the correlation between variables C5 and C2, look for where row C2 and column C5 is (in this case, it's blank because it falls in the upper triangle area) and where row C5 and column C2 is, and in the second case, the correlation is −.166.

Okay, so how did I know that there are 45 unique correlations when there are 10 variables? There's a simple little formula that tells how many pairs (correlations) there are for any number of variables (see Figure 11-9). N is the number of variables. In the example, I had 10 variables, so I know I have $(10 \times 9)/2 = 90/2 = 45$ pairs.

Other Correlations   The specific type of correlation I've illustrated here is known as the **Pearson product moment correlation.** It is appropriate when both variables are measured at an interval level (see the discussion of level of measurement in Chapter 3, Section 3-3, "Levels of Measurement"). However, there are other types of correlations for other circumstances. For instance, if you have two ordinal variables, you could use the Spearman rank order correlation (*rho*) or the Kendall rank order correlation (*tau*). When one measure is a continuous, interval-level one and the other is dichotomous (two-category), you can use the point-biserial correlation. The formulas for these various correlations differ because of the type of data you're feeding into the formulas, but the idea is the same; they estimate the relationship between two variables as a number between −1 and +1.

symmetric matrix   A square (as many rows as columns) table of numbers that describes the relationships among a set of variables, where each variable represents a row or column. Each value in the table represents the relationship between the row and column variable for that cell of the table. The table is "symmetric" when the relationship between a specific row and column variable is identical to the relationship between the same column and row. A correlation matrix is a symmetric matrix.

Pearson product moment correlation   A particular type of correlation used when both variables can be assumed to be measured at an interval level of measurement.

$$\frac{N * (N - 1)}{2}$$

FIGURE 11-9
Formula for Determining the Number of Unique Correlations, Given the Number of Variables

SUMMARY

This chapter introduced the basics involved in data analysis. *Conclusion validity* is the degree to which inferences about relationships in data are reasonable. Conclusions from data involve accepting one *hypothesis* and thereby rejecting its mutually exclusive and exhaustive alternative, and in reaching a conclusion, you can either be correct or incorrect. You can make two types of errors. A Type I error occurs when you conclude there is a relationship when in fact there is not (seeing something that's not there). A Type II error occurs when you conclude there is no effect when in fact there is (missing the needle in the haystack). Data preparation involves checking or logging the data in, checking the data for accuracy, entering the data into the computer, transforming the data, and developing and documenting a database structure that integrates the various measures. Descriptive statistics describe the basic features of the data in a study. The basic descriptive statistics include descriptions of the data distributions, measures of central tendency and dispersion or variability, and the different forms of correlation.

SUGGESTED WEBSITES

Note: These websites were functional when we went to press. Please access the Online Study Guide Edition for the most up-to-date URLs.

Java Applets for Power and Sample Size
http://www.stat.uiowa.edu/~rlenth/Power/
Professor Russ Lenth at the University of Iowa has developed a number of applets to allow you to estimate power for various designs. There are also some good references and links related to power.

The UCLA Department of Statistics
http://www.stat.ucla.edu/
This website has a large number of resources, including a nice set of online calculators.

KEY TERMS

0.05 level of significance (p. 207)
alpha level (p. 207)
central tendency (p. 213)
codebook (p. 210)
conclusion validity (p. 205)
correlation (p. 216)
correlation matrix (p. 220)
degrees of freedom (df) (p. 219)
descriptive statistics (p. 212)

dispersion (p. 214)
distribution (p. 212)
double entry (p. 211)
fishing and the error rate problem (p. 207)
frequency distribution (p. 212)
mean (p. 213)
median (p. 213)
mode (p. 214)
Pearson product moment correlation (p. 221)

range (p. 214)
standard deviation (p. 214)
statistical power (p. 209)
statistics (p. 205)
symmetric matrix (p. 221)
threat to conclusion validity (p. 207)
variance (p. 215)

REVIEW QUESTIONS

Note: You can find the correct answers to these questions by taking the quiz and then submitting your answers in the Online Study Guide Edition. The program will automatically score your submission. If you miss a question, the program will provide the correct answer, a rationale for the answer, and the section number in the chapter where the topic is discussed.

1. Which of the following is *not* one of the three steps involved in data analysis?
   a. data preparation
   b. data generation
   c. descriptive statistics
   d. statistical analysis of the research design
2. Conclusion validity involves the degree to which researchers
   a. draw accurate conclusions regarding relationships in the data.
   b. can accurately infer a relationship between treatment and outcome variables.
   c. can generalize individual research results to the population of interest.
   d. accurately conclude that a measure reflects what it is intended to measure.
3. Conclusion validity is
   a. only a statistical inference issue.
   b. only a judgmental, qualitative issue.
   c. relevant in both quantitative and qualitative research.
   d. unnecessary except in the most complex research designs.
4. Conclusion validity is separate from internal validity in that conclusion validity
   a. does not apply to causal relationships.
   b. is concerned only with generalizing.
   c. is not concerned with whether a program or treatment caused an outcome.
   d. is only relevant in observational studies.
5. A researcher can improve conclusion validity by using
   a. measures with strong construct validity.
   b. reliable measures.
   c. quantitative measures.
   d. qualitative measures.
6. Which of the following is *not* related to statistical power?
   a. sample size
   b. treatment group
   c. effect size
   d. significance level
7. The probability of concluding that there is a relationship when, in fact, there is not is called
   a. Type I error.
   b. Type II error.
   c. the confidence level.
   d. power.

8. What type of condition(s) may create a threat to conclusion validity?
   a. poor reliability of measures
   b. poor implementation of program procedures
   c. irrelevant events that distract participants
   d. anything that adds variability to the research context (that is, all of the above)
9. What threat to conclusion validity occurs when a researcher "fishes" for a specific result, using a series of statistical techniques on the same data, while assuming each analysis is independent?
   a. finding no relationship when there is one
   b. finding a relationship when there is none
   c. This does not present a threat to conclusion validity.
   d. low statistical power
10. What kind of error is committed when a researcher reports that no relationship exists when, in fact, there is one?
   a. Type I error
   b. Type II error
   c. Type III error
   d. the third variable error
11. The value 0.05 means that the result you got could be expected to occur by chance at least 5 times out of every 100 times you run the statistical analysis.
   a. True
   b. False
12. The alpha level and level of significance refer to the same thing.
   a. True
   b. False
13. In research, as in life, it is best to be patient when "fishing" for a good result.
   a. True
   b. False
14. Power will be lower in a study if there is more noise (a bigger haystack), a smaller needle (a weaker signal), or both.
   a. True
   b. False
15. The rule of thumb in social research is that you want statistical power to be greater than 0.8 in value.
   a. True
   b. False

12

Analysis for Research Design

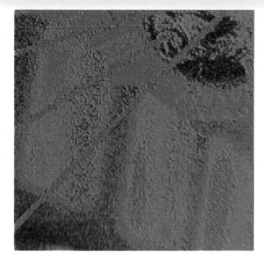

The heart of the data analysis—the part where you answer the major research questions—is inextricably linked to the research design. Especially in *causal* research, the research design frames the entire endeavor, specifying how the measures and participants are brought together. So, it shouldn't surprise you that the research design also frames the data analysis, determining the types of analysis that you can and cannot do.

This chapter describes the relationship between design and analysis. I begin by briefly describing inferential statistics, which differ from *descriptive statistics* in that they are explicitly constructed to address a research question or *hypothesis*. I then present the general linear model (GLM). Even though each specific design has its own unique design quirks and idiosyncrasies, things aren't as confusing or complicated as they may at first seem. The GLM underlies all of the analyses presented here and is the major framework for statistical modeling in social research, so if you get a good understanding of what that's all about, the rest should be a little easier to handle. (Note that I said a *little* easier. I didn't say it was going to be easy.) I then move on to consider the basic randomized experimental designs, starting with the simplest—the two-group posttest-only experiment—and moving to more complex designs. Finally, I briefly discuss the world of quasi-experimental analysis, where the quasi nature of the design leads to all types of analytic problems (some of which may even make you queasy). By the time you're through with all of this, you'll have a pretty firm grasp on how analysis is crafted to your research design and about the perils of applying the analysis that seems most obvious to the wrong design structure.

12-1 INFERENTIAL STATISTICS

Inferential statistics is the process of trying to reach conclusions that extend beyond the immediate data. Inferential statistics approaches are used when you are trying to use the data as the basis for drawing broader inferences (thus, the name). For instance, you use inferential statistics to try to infer from the sample data what the population might think. Or you use inferential statistics to make judgments about the probability that an observed difference between groups is a dependable one or one that might have happened by chance in your study. Thus, you use inferential statistics to draw conclusions from your data to the more general case; you use descriptive statistics simply to describe what's going on in the data.

In this chapter, I concentrate on inferential statistics, which are useful in experimental and *quasi-experimental research design* or in program-outcome evaluation. To understand how inferential statistics are used to analyze data for various research designs, there are two foundational issues we need to take up.

First, you need to understand what is meant by the **general linear model (GLM).** Virtually all the major inferential statistics come from the general family of statistical models known as the GLM. Given the importance of the GLM, it's a good idea for any serious social researcher to become familiar with the basic idea of it. The discussion of the GLM here is elementary and only considers the simplest of these models, but it will familiarize you with the idea of the linear model and how it is adapted to meet the analysis needs of different research designs.

Second, one of the keys to understanding how the GLM is adapted for the analysis of specific research designs is to learn what a dummy variable is and how it is used. The name doesn't suggest that you are using *variables* that aren't smart or, even worse, that the analyst who uses them is a dummy! Perhaps these variables would be better described as *stand-in*

dummy variable A variable that uses discrete numbers, usually 0 and 1, to represent different groups in your study. Dummy variables are often used in the equations.

variables. Essentially, a **dummy variable** is one that uses discrete numbers, usually 0 and 1, to represent different groups in your study in the equations of the GLM. The concept of dummy variables is a simple one that enables some complicated things to happen. For instance, by including a simple dummy variable in a model, you can model two separate groups (for example, a treatment and comparison group) within a single equation.

12-2 THE GENERAL LINEAR MODEL

The GLM underlies most of the statistical analyses that are used in applied and social research. It is the foundation for the *t*-test, ANOVA (Iversen & Norpoth, 1976), ANCOVA, regression analysis, and many of the multivariate methods, including factor analysis, cluster analysis, multidimensional scaling, discriminant function analysis, canonical correlation, and others. That is, all of the analyses I just mentioned can be described using the same family of equations known as the GLM. Who cares? Well, have you ever wondered why the best quantitative researchers seem to know so much about different types of analyses? Sure, they spent years slogging away in advanced statistics classes in graduate school. But the real reason they can address so many different situations with some authority statistically is that they are really learning one basic approach, the GLM, which has lots of variations. Learn the general approach and you will understand, at least intuitively, the range of analyses (and more) described here. Now, don't get me wrong. This text only introduces the idea of the GLM. This is not a statistics text. There are hundreds of books around that are entirely devoted to the GLM or to one or more of its specific forms. But what I can do here is describe the idea of GLM in nonstatistical language and suggest how it is adapted to address the major research designs.

12-2a The Two-Variable Linear Model

Let's begin by trying to understand the simplest variation of the GLM, the two-variable case. Figure 12-1a shows a bivariate plot of two variables. These may be any two continuous variables, but in the discussion that follows, think of them as a pretest (on the *x*-axis) and a posttest (on the *y*-axis). Each dot on the plot represents the pretest and posttest score for an individual. The pattern clearly shows a positive relationship because, in general, people with higher pretest scores also have higher posttests, and vice versa.

The goal in data analysis is to summarize or describe accurately what is happening in the data. The bivariate plot shows the data. How might you best summarize this data? Figure 12-1b shows that a straight line through the cloud of data points would effectively describe the pattern in the bivariate plot. Although the line does not perfectly describe any specific point (because no point falls precisely on the line), it does accurately describe the pattern in the data. When you fit a line to data, you are using a **linear model.** The word *linear* refers to the fact that you are fitting a line. The word *model* refers to the equation that summarizes the line that you fit. A line like the one shown in Figure 12-1b is often referred to as a **regression line** (a description of the relationship between two variables) and the analysis that produces it is often called **regression analysis.**

Figure 12-1c shows the equation for a straight line. You may recognize this equation from your high school algebra classes, where it is often stated in the form $y = mx + b$. This is exactly the same as the equation in Figure 12-1c. It just uses b in place of b_0, and m instead of b_1. The equation in Figure 12-1c has the following components:

$$y = \text{the } y\text{-axis variable, the outcome or posttest}$$

$$x = \text{the } x\text{-axis variable, the pretest}$$

$$b_0 = \text{the intercept (value of } y \text{ when } x = 0)$$

$$b_1 = \text{the slope of the line}$$

The slope of the line can be described as the change in the posttest given in pretest units. As mentioned previously, this equation does not perfectly fit the cloud of points in Figure 12-1a. If it did, every point would fall on the line. You need one more component to describe the way this line fits to the bivariate plot.

linear model Any statistical model that uses equations to estimate lines.

regression line A line that describes the relationship between two or more variables.

regression analysis A general statistical analysis that enables us to model relationships in data and test for treatment effects. In regression analysis, we model relationships that can be depicted in graphic form with lines that are called *regression lines.*

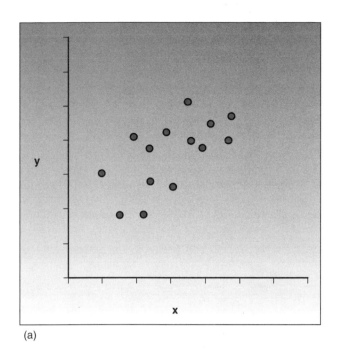

(a)

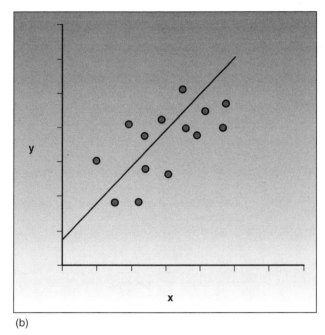

(b)

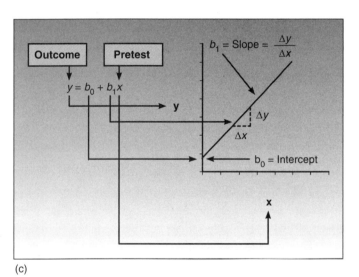

(c)

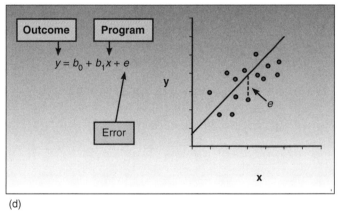

(d)

(e)

FIGURE 12-1
The Two-Variable Linear Model

(a) A bivariate plot.
(b) A straight-line summary of the data. (c) The straight-line model. (d) The two variable linear model. (e) What the model estimates.

Figure 12-1*d* (see page 227) shows this equation for the two-variable or bivariate linear model. The piece added to the equation in Figure 12-1*d* is an **error term** that describes the vertical distance from the straight line to each point. This component is called *error* because it is the degree to which the line is in error in describing each point. When you fit the two-variable linear model to your data, you have an *x* and *y* score for each person in your study. You input these value pairs into a computer program. The program estimates the b_0 and b_1 values as indicated in Figure 12-1*e* (see page 227). You actually get two numbers back in the computer results for those two values.

You can think of the two-variable regression line like any other descriptive statistic; it simply describes the relationship between two variables much as a *mean* describes the central tendency of a single variable. Just as the mean does not accurately represent every value in a distribution, the regression line does not accurately represent every value in the bivariate distribution. You use regression lines as summaries because they show the general patterns in your data and allow you to describe these patterns in more concise ways than showing the entire distribution of points. In one simple equation, you can summarize the pattern of hundreds or thousands of points in a scatter plot.

12-2b The "General" in the General Linear Model

Now, let's extend the two-variable case to the multiple variable one—the GLM. Essentially the GLM looks similar to the two-variable model shown in Figure 12-1*e*; it is an equation. The big difference is that each of the four terms in the GLM stands for a whole set of variables instead of representing only a single variable. So, the GLM can be written as follows:

$$y = b_0 + bx + e$$

where

y = a set of outcome variables

x = a set of preprogram variables or covariates

b_0 = the set of intercepts (value of each y when each $x = 0$)

b = a set of coefficients, one each for each x

This model allows you to summarize an enormous amount of information. In an experimental or quasi-experimental study, you would represent the program or treatment with one or more dummy-coded variables (see Section 12-2c, "Dummy Variables"), each represented in the equation as an additional *x*-value. (However, the convention is to use the symbol *z* to indicate that the variable is a dummy-coded *x*.) If your study has multiple outcome variables, you can include them as a set of *y*-values. If you have multiple pretests, you can include them as a set of *x*-values. For each *x*-value (and each *z*-value), you estimate a *b*-value that represents an *x,y* relationship. The estimates of these *b*-values and the statistical testing of these estimates are what enable you to test specific research hypotheses about *relationships* between variables or differences between groups.

The GLM allows you to summarize a wide variety of research outcomes. The major problem for the researcher who uses the GLM is **model specification,** how to identify the equation that best summarizes the data for a study. If the model is misspecified, the estimates of the coefficients (the *b*-values) that you get from the analysis are likely to be biased (wrong), and the resulting equation will not describe the data accurately. In complex situations, this model specification problem can be a serious and difficult one.

The GLM is one of the most important tools in the statistical analysis of data. It represents a major achievement in the advancement of social research in the twentieth century. All of the analyses described in this chapter will be expressed using specific forms of the GLM.

12-2c Dummy Variables

A *dummy variable* is a numerical variable used in the GLM (especially in regression analysis) to represent subgroups of the sample in your study. It is not a variable used by dummies. In fact, you have to be pretty smart to figure out how to use dummy variables. In research design, a dummy variable is typically used to distinguish different treatment or program groups. In the simplest case, you would use a 0,1 dummy variable where a person is given a value of 1 if in the treated group or a 0 if placed in the *control group*.

Dummy variables are useful because they enable you to use a single regression equation to represent multiple groups. This means that you don't need to write out separate equation models for each subgroup. The dummy variables act like *switches* that turn various values on and off in an equation. Another advantage of a 0,1 dummy-coded variable is that even though it is a nominal-level variable, you can treat it statistically like an interval-level variable. (If this made no sense to you, you probably should refresh your memory on levels of measurement covered in Chapter 3, Section 3-3, "Levels of Measurement.") For instance, if you take an interval-level analysis like computing an average of a 0,1 variable, you will get a meaningful result—the proportion of 1s in the distribution.

To illustrate how dummy variables work, consider a simple regression model that could be used for analysis of a posttest-only two-group randomized experiment, shown in Figure 12-2. Because this is a posttest-only design, there is no pretest variable in the model. Instead, there is a dummy variable, z, that represents the two groups and there is the posttest variable, y. The key term in the model is β_1, the estimate of the difference between the groups. To see why this is the case, and how dummy variables work, I'll use this simple model to show you how dummy variables can be used to pull out the separate subequations for each subgroup. Then I'll show how to estimate the difference between the subgroups by subtracting their respective equations. You'll see that you can pack an enormous amount of information into a single equation using dummy variables. In the end, you should be able to understand why β_1 is actually the difference between the treatment and control groups in this model.

To begin understanding how dummy variables work, let's develop an equation specifically for the control group, using the model in Figure 12-2. For the control group, the β_0 term drops out of the equation because β_0 times 0 (which is what z is for the control group) equals 0. Furthermore, we always assume that the error term e_i averages to 0 (that there will be as many errors above the line as below it), so the e_i term drops out. So, when we take the equation in Figure 12-2 and use it to determine a specific equation for the control group, we see that the predicted value for the control group is β_1 as shown in Figure 12-3.

Now, to figure out the treatment-group line, you substitute the value of 1 for z, again recognizing that by assumption, the error term averages to 0. The equation for the treatment group indicates that the treatment group value is the sum of the two beta values.

Now you're ready to move on to the second step—computing the difference between the groups. How do you determine that? Well, the difference must be the difference between the equations for the two groups that you worked out previously. In other words,

$$y_i = \beta_0 + \beta_1 z_i + e_i$$

where:

y_i = Outcome score for the *i*th unit

β_0 = Coefficient for the *intercept*

β_1 = Coefficient for the *slope*

z_i = 1 if *i*th unit is in the treatment group
　　 0 if *i*th unit is in the control group

e_i = Residual for the *i*th unit

FIGURE 12-2

Use of a Dummy Variable in a Regression Equation

FIGURE 12-3

Using a Dummy Variable to Create Separate Equations for Each Dummy Variable Value

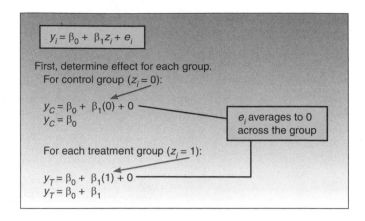

$$y_i = \beta_0 + \beta_1 z_i + e_i$$

First, determine effect for each group.
For control group ($z_i = 0$):

$$y_C = \beta_0 + \beta_1(0) + 0$$
$$y_C = \beta_0$$

e_i averages to 0 across the group

For each treatment group ($z_i = 1$):

$$y_T = \beta_0 + \beta_1(1) + 0$$
$$y_T = \beta_0 + \beta_1$$

FIGURE 12-4

Determining the Difference between Two Groups by Subtracting the Equations Generated through Their Dummy Variables

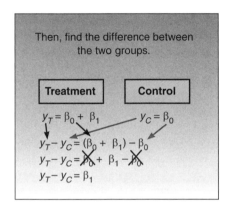

Then, find the difference between the two groups.

| Treatment | Control |

$$y_T = \beta_0 + \beta_1 \qquad y_C = \beta_0$$
$$y_T - y_C = (\beta_0 + \beta_1) - \beta_0$$
$$y_T - y_C = \cancel{\beta_0} + \beta_1 - \cancel{\beta_0}$$
$$y_T - y_C = \beta_1$$

to find the difference between the groups, you find the difference between the equations for the two groups! It should be obvious from Figure 12-4 that the difference is β_1. Think about what this means. The difference between the groups is β_1. Okay, one more time just for the sheer heck of it: The difference between the groups in this model is β_1! Now take a look back at Figure 12-2. You should see that β_1 is the term in the equation that is next to the z value. So, that's what a dummy variable does—within one equation, it lets us see what the difference is between two equations.

Whenever you have a regression model with dummy variables, you can always see how the variables are being used to represent multiple subgroup equations by following the two steps described in Figures 12-3 and 12-4, as follows:

- Create separate equations for each subgroup by substituting the dummy values (as in Figure 12-3).

- Find the difference between groups by finding the difference between their equations (as in Figure 12-4).

12-2d The *t*-Test

Okay, here's where I'll try to pull together the previous sections on the general linear model and the use of dummy variables. I'll show you how the general linear model uses dummy variables to create one of the simplest tests in research analysis, the *t*-test. If you can understand how this works, you're well on your way to grasping how all the research designs discussed here can be analyzed. That is, the general linear model is a general tool you can use to analyze virtually all of the major research designs. Learn it and you have a general tool (and understanding) for research.

The **t-test** (Brown & Melamed, 1990) assesses whether the means of two groups are *statistically* different from each other. Why is it called the *t*-test? Because when the statistician who invented this analysis first wrote out the formula, he used the letter "t" to symbolize the value that describes the difference between the groups. Why? Beats me. You remember the formula for the straight line from your high school algebra? You know, the

t-test A statistical test of the difference between the means of two groups, often a program and comparison group. The *t*-test is the simplest variation of the one-way analysis of variance (ANOVA).

one that goes *y* = *mx* + *b*? Well, using the name *t*-test is like calling that formula the *y*-formula. Maybe the statisticians decided they would come up with more interesting names later. Maybe they were in the same fix as the astronomers who had so many stars to name they just assigned temporary numbers until someone noteworthy enough came along. Whatever the reason, don't lose any sleep over it. The *t*-test is just a name, and as the bard says, what's in a name?

Before you can proceed to the analysis itself, it is useful to understand what the difference means in the question, "Is there a *difference* between the groups?" Each group can be represented by a bell-shaped curve that describes the group's distribution on a single variable. You can think of the **bell curve** as a smoothed histogram or bar graph describing the frequency of each possible measurement response.

Figure 12-5 shows the distributions for the treated and control groups in a study. Actually, the figure shows the idealized or smoothed *distribution*—the actual distribution would usually be depicted with a histogram or bar graph. The figure indicates where the control and treatment group means are located. The question the *t*-test addresses is whether the means are statistically different.

What does it mean to say that the averages for two groups are statistically different? Consider the three situations shown in Figure 12-6. The first thing to notice about the three situations is that *the difference between the means is the same in all three*. But you should also notice that the three situations don't look the same; they tell different stories. The top example shows a case with moderate variability of scores within each group (variability is reflected in the spread, width, or range of the distribution). The second situation

bell curve Smoothed histogram or bar graph describing the expected frequency for each value of a variable. The name comes from the fact that such a distribution often has the shape of a bell.

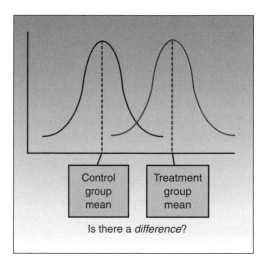

Control group mean

Treatment group mean

Is there a *difference*?

FIGURE 12-5
Idealized Distributions for Treated and Control Group Posttest Values

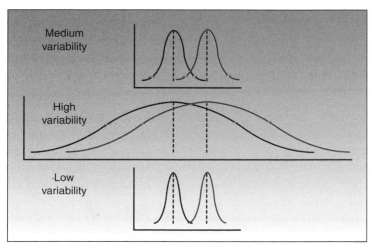

Medium variability

High variability

Low variability

FIGURE 12-6
Three Scenarios for Differences between Means

FIGURE 12-7

Formula for the *t*-Test

(a) How the *t*-test formula relates to the distribution of the data for the groups. *(b)* Formula for the *standard error* of the difference between the means. *(c)* Formula for the *t*-test.

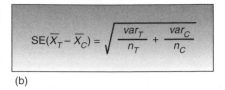

(b)

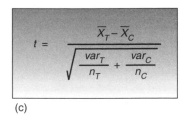

(c)

(a)

t-value   The estimate of the difference between the groups relative to the variability of the scores in the groups.

standard error of the difference A statistical estimate of the standard deviation one would obtain from the distribution of an infinite number of estimates of the difference between the means of two groups.

shows the high-variability case. The third shows the case with low variability. Clearly, you would conclude that the two groups appear most different or distinct in the bottom or low-variability case. Why? Because there is relatively little overlap between the two bell-shaped curves. In the high-variability case, the group difference appears least striking (even though it is identical) because the two bell-shaped distributions overlap so much.

This leads to an important conclusion: When you are looking at the differences between scores for two groups, you have to judge the difference between their means relative to the spread or variability of their scores. The *t*-test does just this.

So, how does the *t*-test work? The traditional formula for the *t*-test is expressed as a ratio or fraction. The top part of the ratio is the difference between the two means or averages. The bottom part is a measure of the variability or dispersion of the scores. This formula is essentially another example of the signal-to-noise metaphor in research. The top part of the formula, the difference between the means, is the signal that, in this case, you think your program or treatment introduced into the data. The bottom part of the formula is a measure of variability that is essentially noise that might make it harder to see the group difference. The ratio that you compute is called a **t-value** and describes the difference between the groups relative to the variability of the scores in the groups. Figure 12-7*a* shows the formula for the *t*-test and how the numerator and denominator are related to the distributions.

The top part of the formula is easy to compute—just find the difference between the means. The bottom part is called the **standard error of the difference.** To compute it, take the *variance* (see Chapter 11, Section 11-3c, "Dispersion or Variability") for each group and divide it by the number of people in that group. You add these two values and then take their square root. The specific formula is given in Figure 12-7*b*. Remember, that the variance is simply the square of the *standard deviation*. The final formula for the *t*-test is shown in Figure 12-7*c*.

The *t*-value will be positive if the first mean is larger than the second value and negative if it is smaller. After you compute the *t*-value, you have to look it up in a table of significance to test whether the ratio is large enough to say that the difference between the groups is not likely to have been a chance finding. To test the significance, you need to set a risk level (called the *alpha level*, as described in Chapter 11, Section 11-1a, "Threats to Conclusion Validity"). In most social research, the rule of thumb is to set the alpha level at .05. This means that five times out of a hundred, you would find a statistically significant difference between the means even if there were none (meaning by chance). You also need to determine the *degrees of freedom (df)* for the test. In the *t*-test, the df is the number of persons in both groups minus 2. Given the alpha level, the df, and

$$y_i = \beta_0 + \beta_1 z_i + e_i$$

where:

y_i = Outcome score for the ith unit

β_0 = Coefficient for the *intercept*

β_1 = Coefficient for the *slope*

z_i = 1 if ith unit is in the treatment group

0 if ith unit is in the control group

e_i = Residual for the ith unit

FIGURE 12-8

The Regression Formula for the *t*-Test (and Also the Post-Test Only Two-Group One-Way Analysis of Variance or ANOVA Model)

the *t*-value, you can look the *t*-value up in a standard table of significance to determine whether the *t*-value is large enough to be significant. If it is, you can conclude that the difference between the means for the two groups is different (given the variability). Fortunately, statistical computer programs routinely print the significance test results and save you the trouble of looking them up in a table.

Now that you understand the basic idea of the *t*-test, I want to show you how it relates to the general linear model, regression analysis, and dummy variables. Why? If you can understand the *t*-test, probably one of the simplest versions of the general linear model, you will be able to understand how you can change the model to address more complex research designs. One tool, the general linear model, can open the door to understanding how almost all research designs are analyzed. At least that's the theory. Let's see if we can achieve this level of understanding.

Okay, so here's the statistical model for the *t*-test in regression form (see Figure 12-8). Remember that regression is just one subclass of the general linear model.

Look familiar? It is identical to the formula I showed in Figure 12-2 to introduce dummy variables. Also, you may not realize it (although I hope against hope that you do), but essentially this formula is the equation from high school for a straight line with a random error term (e_i) thrown in. Remember high school algebra? Remember high school? Okay, for those of you with faulty memories, you may recall that the equation for a straight line is often given as follows:

$$y = mx + b$$

which, when rearranged, can be written as follows:

$$y = b + mx$$

(The complexities of the commutative property make you nervous? If this gets too tricky, you may need to stop for a break. Have something to eat, make some coffee, or take the poor dog out for a walk.) Now you should see that, in the statistical model, y_i is the same as y in the straight-line formula, β_0 is the same as b, β_1 is the same as m, and z_i is the same as x. In other words, in the statistical formula, β_0 is the intercept and β_1 is the slope (see Figure 12-9).

Wait a minute. β_1 is the same thing as the slope? Earlier, I said that β_1 was the difference between the two groups. How can it be the slope of a line? What line? How can a slope also be a difference between means? To see this, you have to look at the graph of what's going on in Figure 12-9. The graph shows the measure on the vertical axis. This is exactly the same as the two bell-shaped curves shown in Figures 12-5 and 12-6 except that here they're turned on their sides and are graphed on the vertical dimension. On the horizontal axis, the z variable, our dummy variable, is plotted. This variable has only two possible values: a 0 if the person is in the control group or a 1 if the person is in the program group. This kind of variable is a dummy variable because with its two values it is a stand-in variable that represents the two groups that received the different program

FIGURE 12-9

The Elements of the Equation in Figure 12-8 in Graphic Form

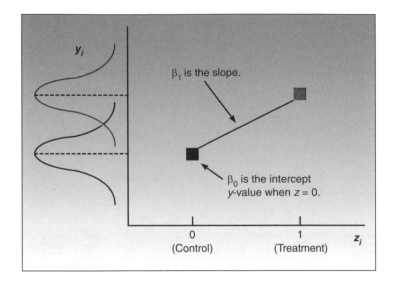

slope The change in y for a change in x of one unit.

analysis of variance (ANOVA) An analysis that estimates the difference between groups on a posttest. The ANOVA could estimate the difference between a treatment and control group (thus being equivalent to the t-test) or can examine both main and interaction effects in a factorial design.

or treatment conditions (see Section 12-2c, "Dummy Variables"). The two points in the graph indicate the average (posttest) value for the control ($z = 0$) and treated ($z = 1$) cases. The line that connects the two dots is only included for visual enhancement purposes; because there are no z values between 0 and 1, there can be no values plotted where the line is. Nevertheless, you can speak meaningfully about the slope of this line—the line that would connect the posttest means for the two values of z. Do you remember the definition of slope? (Here we go again, back to high school!) The **slope** is the change in y over the change in x (or, in this case, z). Stated differently, it is the change in y for a single unit change in x (which in this example is z). But because it is a dummy variable, the change in z between the groups is always equal to 1. Therefore, the slope of the line must be equal to the difference between the average y-values for the two groups. That's what I set out to show (reread the first three sentences of this paragraph). β_1 is the same value that you would get if you subtracted the two means from each other. (In this case, because the treatment group equals 1, you are subtracting the control group out of the treatment group value. A positive value implies that the treatment-group mean is higher than the control-group mean; a negative value means it's lower.)

But remember at the beginning of this discussion, I pointed out that just knowing the difference between the means was not good enough for estimating the treatment effect because it doesn't take into account the variability or spread of the scores. So, how do you do that here? Every regression analysis program will give, in addition to the ß values, a report on whether each ß value is statistically significant. They report a t-value that tests whether the ß value differs from zero. It turns out that the t-value for the β_1 coefficient is the exact same number that you would get if you did a t-test for independent groups. And it's the same as the square root of the F value in the traditional two-group one-way **analysis of variance (ANOVA)** because $t^2 = F$.

Here's a few conclusions from all this:

- The t-test, one-way ANOVA, and regression analysis are mathematically equivalent and yield the *same* results in this case.

- The regression analysis method of the t-test utilizes a dummy variable (z) for treatment.

- Regression analysis is the most useful model of the three because of its generality. Remember that regression analysis is a part of the general linear model. If you understand how it works for the t-test, you should be able to grasp that by adding more terms to the t-test version of the regression formula you can create more complex analyses that address virtually all of the major research designs.

12-3 EXPERIMENTAL ANALYSIS

Now we're ready to turn to the discussion of the major experimental designs and how they are analyzed. The simplest experimental design, two-group posttest-only randomized experiment, is usually analyzed with the simple *t*-test (which is also the simplest variation of the one-way ANOVA). The factorial experimental designs are usually analyzed with the ANOVA model. *Randomized block designs (RD)* use a special form of the ANOVA-blocking model that uses dummy-coded variables to represent the blocks. The analysis of covariance experimental design uses, not surprisingly, the analysis of covariance statistical model. Each of these analyses can be expressed with a single equation that is a variation of the general linear model.

12-3a The Two-Group Posttest-Only Randomized Experiment

To analyze the two-group posttest-only randomized experimental design, you need an analysis that meets the following requirements:

- Has two groups
- Uses a post-only measure
- Has two distributions (measures), each with an average and variation
- Assesses treatment effect as the statistical (nonchance) difference between the groups

You can estimate the treatment effect for the posttest-only randomized experiment in three ways. All three yield mathematically equivalent results, a fancy way of saying that they give you the exact same answer. So, why are there three different ones? In large part, these three approaches evolved independently and only after that was it clear that they are essentially three ways to do the same thing. So, what are the three ways? First, you can compute an independent *t*-test. Second, you could compute a one-way ANOVA between two independent groups. Finally, you can use regression analysis to regress the posttest values onto a dummy-coded treatment variable. Of these three, the regression analysis approach is the most general. In fact, I describe the statistical models for all the experimental and quasi-experimental designs in regression-model terms. You just need to be aware that the results from all three methods are identical. So, the analysis model for the simple two-group posttest-only randomized experimental design is the *t*-test, which is expressed as a regression formula in Figure 12-8.

12-3b Factorial Design Analysis

Now that you have some understanding of the GLM and dummy variables, I can present the models for other more complex experimental designs rather easily. Figure 12-10 shows the regression model for a simple 2×2 factorial design.

$$y_i = \beta_0 + \beta_1 z_{1i} + \beta_2 z_{2i} + \beta_3 z_{1i} z_{2i} + e_i$$

where:
y_i = Outcome score for the *i*th unit
β_0 = Coefficient for the intercept
β_1 = Mean difference on factor 1
β_2 = Mean difference on factor 2
β_3 = Interaction of factor 1 and factor 2
z_{1i} = Dummy variable for factor 1
　　(0 = 1 hour/week, 1 = 4 hours/week)
z_{2i} = Dummy variable for factor 2
　　(0 = in-class, 1 = pull-out)
e_i = Residual for the *i*th unit

FIGURE 12-10
Regression Model for a 2 × 2 Factorial Design

In this simplest of factorial designs, you have two factors, each of which has two levels. The model uses a dummy variable (represented by a z) for each factor. In two-way factorial designs like this, you have two *main effects* and one *interaction effect*. In this model, the main effects are the statistics associated with the beta values that are adjacent to the z-variables. The interaction effect is the statistic associated with β_3 (that is, the t-value for this coefficient) because it is adjacent in the formula to the multiplication of (interaction of) the dummy-coded z-variables for the two factors. Because there are two dummy-coded variables, and each has two values, you can write out $2 \times 2 = 4$ separate equations from this one general model. (Go ahead, I dare you. If you need to refresh your memory, check back to Section 12-2c, "Dummy Variables.") You might want to see if you can write out the equations for the four cells. Then, look at some of the differences between the groups. You can also write two equations for each z-variable. These equations represent the main effect equations. To see the difference between levels of a factor, subtract the equations from each other.

12-3c Randomized Block Analysis

The statistical model for the randomized block design can also be presented in regression analysis notation. Figure 12-11 shows the model for a case where there are four blocks or homogeneous subgroups.

Notice that a number of dummy variables are used to specify this model. The dummy variable z_1 represents the treatment group. The dummy variables z_2, z_3, and z_4 indicate blocks 2, 3, and 4, respectively. Analogously, the beta values (β_s) reflect the treatment and blocks 2, 3, and 4. What happened to block 1 in this model? To see what the equation for the block 1 comparison group is, fill in your dummy variables and multiply through. In this case, all four zs are equal to 0, and you should see that the intercept (β_0) is the estimate for the block 1 control group. For the block 1 treatment group, $z_1 = 1$ and the estimate is equal to $\beta_0 + \beta_1$. By substituting the appropriate dummy variable switches, you should be able to figure out the equation for any block or treatment group.

The data that is entered into this analysis would consist of five columns and as many rows as you have participants: the posttest data and one column of 0s or 1s for each of the four dummy variables.

12-3d Analysis of Covariance

The statistical model for the analysis of covariance or ANCOVA, which estimates the difference between the groups on the posttest after adjusting for differences on the pretest, can also be given in regression analysis notation. The model shown in Figure 12-12 is for a case where there is a single covariate, a treated group, and a control group.

FIGURE 12-11

Regression Model for a Randomized Block Design

$$y_i = \beta_0 + \beta_1 z_{1i} + \beta_2 z_{2i} + \beta_3 z_{3i} + \beta_4 z_{4i} + e_i$$

where:

y_i = Outcome score for the ith unit

β_0 = Coefficient for the intercept

β_1 = Mean difference for treatment

β_2 = Blocking coefficient for block 2

β_3 = Blocking coefficient for block 3

β_4 = Blocking coefficient for block 4

z_{1i} = Dummy variable for treatment
   (0 = control, 1 = treatment)

z_{2i} = 1 if block 2, 0 otherwise

z_{3i} = 1 if block 3, 0 otherwise

z_{4i} = 1 if block 4, 0 otherwise

e_i = Residual for the ith unit

The dummy variable z_i represents the treatment group. The beta values(s) are the parameters being estimated. The value β_0 represents the intercept. In this model, it is the predicted posttest value for the control group for a given x value (and when $x = 0$, it is the intercept for the control-group regression line). Why? Because a control group case has a $z = 0$, and because the z variable is multiplied with β_2, that whole term would drop out.

The data that is entered into this analysis would consist of three columns—the posttest data y_i, one column, z_i of 0s or 1s to indicate which treatment group the participant is in, and the *covariate* score, x_i—and as many rows as you have participants.

This model assumes that the data in the two groups are well described by straight lines that have the same slope. If this does not appear to be the case, you have to modify the model appropriately. How do you do that? Well, I'll tell you the short answer, but for the complete one you need to take an advanced statistics course. The short answer is that you add the term $\beta_i x_i z_i$ to the model in Figure 12-12. If you've been following along, you should be able to create the separate equations for the different values of the dummy variable z_i and convince yourself that the addition of this term will allow for the two groups to have different slopes.

12-4 QUASI-EXPERIMENTAL ANALYSIS

The quasi-experimental designs differ from the experimental ones in that they don't use *random assignment* to assign units (people) to program groups. The lack of random assignment in these designs tends to complicate their analysis considerably, but the principles are the same and the general linear model is still used. For example, to analyze the *nonequivalent-groups design (NEGD)*, you have to adjust the pretest scores for **measurement error** in what is often called a *reliability-corrected analysis of covariance model*. In the simplest case of the RD design, you use a variation of the ANCOVA model. The *regression point displacement design (RPD)* has only a single treated unit. Nevertheless, the analysis of the RPD design is based directly on the traditional ANCOVA model.

The experimental designs discussed previously have comparatively straightforward analysis models. You'll see here that you pay a price for not using random assignment like they do; the analyses generally become more complex.

12-4a Nonequivalent Groups Analysis

The nonequivalent-groups design (NEGD) has two groups—a program and comparison group—each measured pre and post (Figure 12-13). The statistical model that you might intuitively expect to be used in this situation would include pretest variable, posttest variable, and a dummy variable that describes which group the person is in. These three variables would be the input for the statistical analysis.

In this example, assume you are interested in estimating the difference between the groups on the posttest after adjusting for differences on the pretest. This is essentially the ANCOVA model as described in connection with randomized experiments. (Review how to adjust for pretest differences in Chapter 8, Section 8-5, "Covariance Designs.") There's only one major problem with this model when used with the NEGD; it doesn't work! If you fit the traditional ANCOVA model, you are likely to get the wrong answer because the model is biased when nonrandom assignment is used. Why? Well, the detailed story is too complex to go into here, but I can skip to the conclusion. It turns out that the bias is due to two major factors: measurement error in the pretest coupled with the initial nonequivalence between the groups on the pretest. It does not occur in randomized experiments because there is no pretest nonequivalence. The bias will be greater with greater nonequivalence between groups; the less similar the groups, the bigger the problem.

How do we fix the problem? A simple way is to adjust the pretest for the amount of measurement error. Because *reliability* is related to measurement error—the higher the reliability the lower the error, and vice versa—we use an estimate of reliability to do the correction. The formula for the adjustment is simple (see Figure 12-14).

$$y_i = \beta_0 + \beta_1 x_i + \beta_2 z_i + e_i$$

where:
y_i = Outcome score for the ith unit
β_0 = Coefficient for the intercept
β_1 = Pretest coefficient
x_i = Covariate
β_2 = Mean difference for treatment
z_i = Dummy variable for treatment
     (0 = control, 1 = treatment)
e_i = Residual for the ith unit

FIGURE 12-12
**Regression Model
for the ANCOVA**

measurement error   Any influence on an observed score not related to what you are attempting to measure.

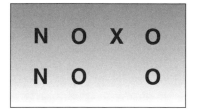

N O X O
N O   O

FIGURE 12-13
**Design Notation
for the NEGD**

$$x_{adj} = \overline{x} + r(x - \overline{x})$$

where:

x_{adj} = Adjusted pretest value

$\overline{x}$ = Original pretest value

r = Reliability

FIGURE 12-14

Formula for Adjusting Pretest Values for Unreliability in the Reliability-Corrected ANCOVA

The idea in this formula is that you are going to construct new pretest scores for each person. These new scores will be adjusted for pretest unreliability by an amount proportional to the reliability.

Once you've made this adjustment, all you need to do is substitute this adjusted pretest score for the original pretest score in the ANCOVA model (see Figure 12-15).

Notice that the only difference is that the x in the original ANCOVA is changed to the term x_{adj}. Of course, things are never as simple as they seem. There are some complications even for this simple reliability-corrected ANCOVA model. For example, in the reliability adjustment formula I did not tell you which of the many methods for estimating reliability should be used (see Chapter 3, Section 3-2d, "Types of Reliability"). Because they are likely to differ and we never know which is the "correct" estimate, we often run the analysis several ways using different reliability estimates each time to try to bracket the "correct" answer. But don't let all of these details get in your way. The important point here is that this design, like all of the others discussed in this chapter, uses the same basic approach to analysis, a variation of the general linear model.

12-4b Regression-Discontinuity Analysis

The basic RD design is also a two-group pretest-posttest model. As in other versions of this design structure (see Section 12-3d, "Analysis of Covariance," and Section 12-4a, "Nonequivalent Groups Analysis"), you will need a statistical model that includes a term for the pretest, one for the posttest, and a dummy-coded variable to represent the program.

For the simplest case where we can assume that a straight line with the same slope fits well the pre-post data for both groups, the only analysis complication has to do with the cutoff point, which is unique to the RD design. The fix is fairly straightforward. As with the NEGD, all you need to do is adjust the pretest scores, in this case by subtracting the cutoff value from each one, as shown in the formula in Figure 12-16. This transformation has the effect of "centering" the regression model on the pretest cutoff, because by subtracting the cutoff we are effectively setting the intercept of the model to the cutoff value. (Don't get that? Don't worry! That's for a more advanced discussion than we're doing here.)

$$y_i = \beta_0 + \beta_1 x_{adj} + \beta_2 z_i + e_i$$

where:

y_i = Outcome score for the ith unit

β_0 = Coefficient for the intercept

β_1 = Pretest coefficient

β_2 = Mean difference for treatment

x_{adj} = Transformed pretest

z_i = Dummy variable for treatment
(0 = control, 1 = treatment)

e_i = Residual for the ith unit

FIGURE 12-15

The Regression Model for the Reliability-Corrected ANCOVA for the Nonequivalent Groups Design (NEGD)

$$\tilde{x}_i = x_i - x_c$$

where:

$\tilde{x}_i$ = Pretest – cutoff value

x_i = Pretest

x_c = Cutoff value

FIGURE 12-16

Adjusting the Pretest by Subtracting the Cutoff in the Regression-Discontinuity (RD) Analysis Model

$$y_i = \beta_0 + \beta_1 \tilde{x}_i + \beta_2 z_i + e_i$$

where:

y_i = Outcome score for the ith unit

β_0 = Coefficient for the intercept

β_1 = Pretest coefficient

β_2 = Mean difference for treatment

$\tilde{x}_i$ = Pretest − cutoff value

z_i = Dummy variable for treatment
     (0 = control, 1 = treatment)

e_i = Residual for the ith unit

FIGURE 12-17
The Regression Model for the Basic Regression-Discontinuity Design

$$y_i = \beta_0 + \beta_1 x_i + \beta_2 z_i + e_i$$

where:

y_i = Outcome score for the ith unit

β_0 = Coefficient for the intercept

β_1 = Pretest coefficient

β_2 = Mean difference for treatment

x_i = Covariate

z_i = Dummy variable for treatment
     (0 = control, 1 = treatment [$n = 1$])

e_i = Residual for the ith unit

FIGURE 12-18
The Regression Model for the RPD Design, Assuming a Linear Pre-Post Relationship

Once this adjustment is done, the adjusted pretest score is substituted for the original pretest in the same old ANCOVA model, as shown in Figure 12-17.

Okay, so that's the good news. The analysis of the simplest RD design is essentially a very basic variation of the same old ANCOVA regression model. The bad news? As with all of the quasi-experiments, things are seldom as simple in reality as they are in this simple model. For instance, in many situations, it will not be reasonable to assume that a straight line with the same slope is appropriate for both groups. In fact, if the data requires curved lines, the modeling can be considerably more complex. But however complex, it will almost certainly involve some variation of the general linear model. That's the key message that recurs throughout this chapter.

12-4c Regression Point Displacement Analysis

I come now to the last of the quasi-experimental designs I want to discuss in reference to analysis—the regression point displacement (RDP) design. At this point in the chapter, you should be able to anticipate the kind of analysis I'm going to suggest. You'll see that the principles are the same here as for all of the other analyses, especially in that this analysis also relies on the GLM and regression analysis.

The RPD design, like many of the others, involves a pretest, posttest, and a dummy variable to represent the treatment group (where 0 = comparison and 1 = program). These requirements are identical to the requirements for the ANCOVA model and should look very familiar by now. The only difference is that the RPD design has only a single treated group score. That is, only one pretest-posttest score pair reflects the treated group.

The analysis model for the RPD design is the now-familiar ANCOVA model, stated in regression model form (see Figure 12-18).

The only unusual feature is that for the dummy variable there will only be one treated pre-post unit. Of course, the usual warnings about reality apply here as well. If the pre-post distribution is not well described by a straight line, then we will need to adjust the model to allow for the appropriate curvilinearity. But these nuances are for more advanced texts. The important lesson is, once again, that a simple variation of the general linear model can be used for the RPD design, just as it is used for the all the others.

SUMMARY

Phew! I'm hoping for your sake that you weren't assigned to read this chapter in a single night. And I'm hoping you didn't put this off until the night before the exam. However, in case you did, let me summarize the salient points.

This chapter described data analysis for the basic research designs. The key to understanding such analyses, a branch of inferential statistics, is the general linear model (GLM). The GLM is a general formula and approach to modeling data, and every one of the designs discussed in this chapter can be analyzed using basic variation of the GLM. So, if you can learn about the GLM, you'll have a general tool that can be applied in almost any inferential analysis of a research design. There are several key concepts needed to understand the GLM. Especially critical are the ideas of a regression line and its formula, and the notion of a dummy variable and how it can be manipulated in a formula. If you can get the general sense of these ideas, you should be able to appreciate how the GLM can be applied and adapted to all of the designs.

To help make this point, and to summarize all of the models, I'll throw every one of the analysis models into a single table, Table 12-1.

Now, don't panic when you look at this just because there are a bunch of formulas there. Take a deep breath and look at the formulas. Scan down the column of formulas and look for similarities. Notice how each has the same symbol, y_i, to the left of the equal sign. That's because every one of

these designs has a posttest score, and y_i is the symbol we use to represent the posttest in the formula. Notice that each has a β_0 immediately to the right of the equals sign. In every model, that symbol is the intercept. If we drew graphs of the lines we were fitting to the data—and we could after analyzing the results draw such lines for each one—the β_0 symbol would always represent the intercept of those lines (that is, where the line is when $x = 0$). And notice that every formula has at least one z term. The z term represents different groups in the design. It is typically (but not always) the dummy variable where 1 represents the treated group and 0 represents the comparison or control. Notice also that many of the formulas have an x in them. The x represents a pretest value, sometimes called a *covariate*. And finally, notice that each formula ends with an e_i value that represents the presumably random component that remains in the data when we fit the rest of the model. That's it. In one sense, it's really not that hard. Even if you only have the beginning intuitive sense of how these models work, the table illustrates succinctly that all of the formulas are variations on a similar theme. They're all variations of the GLM, and for these designs, they're all variations of a specific subclass of the GLM known as *regression analysis*. So, when you take that statistics course down the road, you may want to keep this in mind when you cover regression analysis—that one statistical tool can provide you with a general way to do a lot of very useful specific things.

SUGGESTED WEBSITES

Note: These websites were functional when we went to press. Please access the Online Study Guide Edition for the most up-to-date URLs.

Web Interface for Statistics Education
http://wise.cgu.edu/
This website by Professor Dale Berger has much to offer you in statistics education. Try some of the tutorials and applets, and explore the glossary and links.

The American Statistical Association
http://www.amstat.org/
The American Statistical Association is the major professional organization in statistics in the United States. If you spend some time perusing this website, you can learn about the wide range of areas that statisticians are involved in and also explore resources that might enable you to further your statistical education.

TABLE 12-1 **Summary of the Statistical Models for the Experimental and Quasi-Experimental Research Designs**

Design	Analysis	Notes
Experimental Designs		
The two-group posttest-only randomized experiment	$y_i = \beta_0 + \beta_1 z_i + e_i$	No pretest term x_i needed. This is eqivalent to the t-test.
Factorial design (2 ← 2)	$y_i = \beta_0 + \beta_1 z_{1i} + \beta_2 z_{2i} + \beta_3 z_{1i} z_{2i} + e_i$	No pretest term x_i needed; the z terms are dummy variables for each of the two factors.
Factorial blocks	$y_i = \beta_0 + \beta_1 z_{1i} + \beta_2 z_{2i} + \beta_3 z_{3i} + \beta_4 z_{4i} + e_i$	No pretest term x_i needed; z_1 is dummy for treatment; z_{2-4} are dummies for blocks 2–4 of 4.
Analysis of covariance (ANCOVA)	$y_i = \beta_0 + \beta_1 x_i + \beta_2 z_i + e_i$	The analysis of covariance (ANCOVA) model
Quasi-Experimental Designs		
Nonequivalent groups design (NEGD)	$y_i = \beta_0 + \beta_1 x_{adj} + \beta_2 z_i + e_i$	$x_{adj} = \overline{x} + r(x - \overline{x})$ where $\overline{x}$ is the pretest average and r is the reliability estimate.
Regression discontinuity design (RD)	$y_i = \beta_0 + \beta_1 \tilde{x}_i + \beta_2 z_i + e_i$	$\tilde{x}_i = $ pretest (x_i) – cutoff value
Regression point displacement design (RPD)	$y_i = \beta_0 + \beta_1 x_i + \beta_2 z_i + e_i$	Identical to ANCOVA except that for dummy treatment variable, there is only one pre-post score pair where $z_i = 1$ (treated case).

KEY TERMS

REVIEW QUESTIONS

Note: You can find the correct answers to these questions by taking the quiz and then submitting your answers in the Online Study Guide Edition. The program will automatically score your submission. If you miss a question, the program will provide the correct answer, a rationale for the answer, and the section number in the chapter where the topic is discussed.

1. One of the key features of the general linear model that helps us look at differences between groups in research design is
   a. use of an experimental analysis.
   b. the existence of a linear relationship in variables.
   c. the existence and use of dummy variables.
   d. limited overlap in bell-shaped curves.

2. A dummy variable is one used in regression analysis to represent
   a. participants.
   b. subgroups of participants, such as different treatment groups.
   c. levels of measurement.
   d. sublevels of measurement, such as dependent variables.

3. Which of the following does *not* describe the function of a *t*-test?
   a. determination of whether the difference between two groups is important in practical terms
   b. measurement of the ratio of a program's signal to its noise
   c. determination of whether there is a statistically significant difference between the means of a treatment group and a control group
   d. analysis of the difference between group means divided by the standard error of the difference

4. In addition to an alpha level and a *t*-test value, what other information must a researcher have in order to look up a *t*-value in a standard table of significance?
   a. standard deviation
   b. standard error
   c. degrees of freedom
   d. dummy variables

5. Which distribution of scores between a control and a treatment group will most likely result in a statistically significant difference being discovered?
   a. similar means
   b. different means
   c. different means and significant overlap of scores
   d. different means and little overlap of scores

6. A straight line fitted to data in a statistical analysis is called
   a. the slope.
   b. the analysis of variance.
   c. a regression line.
   d. a linear model.

7. In general, the "error" in a general linear model is
   a. the squared sum of the distance of each score from the regression line.
   b. the vertical distance of each score from the regression line.
   c. the horizontal distance of each score from the regression line.
   d. the correlation value applied to the regression line.

8. The ratio used to find the *t*-value representing the difference between two groups is composed of
   a. the correlation of the groups over the standard deviation.
   b. the variance of the groups over the standard deviation.
   c. the difference between groups over the standard error of the difference.
   d. the sum of the groups over the sum of the differences between groups.

9. What are the three different ways to estimate a treatment effect for a researcher using the post-only two-group randomized experiment?
   a. independent *t*-test, one-way analysis of variance (ANOVA), and regression analysis
   b. independent *t*-test, two-way analysis of variance (ANOVA), and factorial design
   c. two-way analysis of variance (ANOVA), factorial design, and regression analysis
   d. two-way analysis of variance (ANOVA), randomized block analysis, and regression analysis

10. In a regression equation, the dummy variable
    a. represents the slope of the line.
    b. specifies the difference in group means.
    c. is treated statistically like an interval-level variable.
    d. is an error term.

11. The main difference between inferential and descriptive statistics is that inferential statistics are used to test a specific hypothesis.
    a. True
    b. False

12. The *t*-test, analysis of variance and covariance, and regression analysis are all very different kinds of analysis based on different underlying statistical models.
    a. True
    b. False

13. One reason that it is good to examine a plot of your data is to determine if the general picture is one of a relatively straight line, suggesting that the relationships observed are in fact linear and appropriate for one of the general linear model (GLM) analyses.
    a. True
    b. False

14. The slope of a regression line can be described as the change in the posttest given in pretest units.
    a. True
    b. False

15. It is possible to use regression analysis to study the results of an experiment in which you have a treatment and control group.
    a. True
    b. False

13

Write-Up

Chapter Outline

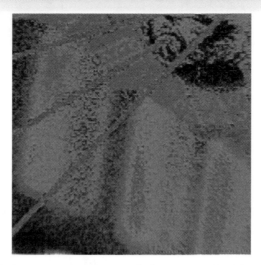

So, now that you've completed the research project, what do you do? I know you won't want to hear this, but your work is still far from done. In fact, this final stage—writing up your research—may be one of the most difficult. Developing a good, effective, and concise report is an art form in itself, and in many research projects, you will need to write multiple reports that present the results at different levels of detail for different audiences.

There are several general considerations to keep in mind when writing a report:

- *The audience*—Who is going to read the report? Reports will differ considerably depending on whether the audience will want or require technical detail, whether they are looking for a summary of results, or whether they are about to examine your research in a Ph.D. exam.

- *The story*—I believe that every research project has at least one major story in it. Sometimes, the story centers around a specific research finding. Sometimes, it is based on a methodological problem or challenge. When you write your report, you should attempt to tell the story to your reader. Even in formal journal articles where you will be required to be concise and detailed at the same time, a good story line can help make an otherwise dull report interesting to the reader.

     The hardest part of telling the story in your research is finding the story in the first place. Usually, when you come to writing up your research, you have been steeped in the details for weeks or months (and sometimes even for years). You've been worrying about sampling responses, struggling with operationalizing your measures, dealing with the details of design, and wrestling with the data analysis. You're a bit like the ostrich that has its head in the sand. To find the story in your research, you have to pull your head out of the sand and look at the big picture. You have to try to view your research from your audience's perspective. You may have to let go of some of the details that you obsessed so much about and leave them out of the write-up or bury them in technical appendices or tables.

- *Formatting considerations*—Are you writing a research report to submit for publication in a journal? If so, you should be aware that every journal requires that you follow specific formatting guidelines. Thinking of writing a book? Again, every publisher requires specific formatting. Writing a term paper? Most faculty members require you to follow specific guidelines. Doing your thesis or dissertation? Every university I know of has strict policies about formatting and style. There are legendary stories that circulate among graduate students about the dissertation that was rejected because the page margins were a quarter-inch off or the figures weren't labeled correctly.

To illustrate what a set of research report specifications might include, I present in this section general guidelines for the formatting of a research write-up for a class term paper. These guidelines are similar to the types of specifications you might be required to follow for a journal article. However, you need to check the specific formatting guidelines for the report you are writing; the ones presented here are likely to differ in some ways from any other guidelines that may be required in other contexts.

13-1 KEY ELEMENTS

This section describes the elements or criteria that you must typically address in a research write-up. The assumption here is that you are addressing a causal hypothesis in your paper.

I. Introduction

1. *Statement of the problem*—State the general problem area clearly and unambiguously. Discuss the importance and significance of the problem area.

2. *Literature review and citations*—Condense the literature in an intelligent fashion and include only the most relevant information. Cite literature only from reputable and appropriate sources (such as professional journals and books, and not *Time, Newsweek,* and so on). Ensure that all citations are in the correct format.

3. *Statement of constructs*—Explain each key construct in the research/evaluation project (for example, in a causal study, describe both the cause and effect). Ensure that explanations are readily understandable (that is, jargon-free) to an intelligent reader.

4. *The research questions or hypotheses*—Clearly state the major questions, objectives, or hypotheses for the research. For example, if you are studying a cause-effect relationship, describe the hypotheses and relate them sensibly to the statement of the problem. The relationship of the hypothesis to both the problem statement and literature review must be readily understood from reading the text.

II. Methods

Sample or Participants Section

1. *Sampling procedure specifications*—Describe the procedure for selecting units (such as subjects and records) for the study and ensure that it is appropriate. State which sampling method or approach you used and why. Describe the population and sampling frame where appropriate. Where the research participants are self-selected (volunteers), they should be described as such.

2. *Sample description*—Describe the sample accurately and ensure that it is appropriate. Describe problems in contacting and measuring the sample.

3. *External validity considerations*—Consider generalizability from the sample to the sampling frame and population.

Measurement Section

1. *Measures*—Describe each measurement construct briefly. For each construct, briefly describe the measure or measures and include an appropriate citation and reference (unless you created the measure). Describe how the measures that are used are relevant to the hypotheses or questions of the study.

2. *Construction of measures*—Clearly word questionnaires, tests, and interviews. They should be specific, appropriate for the population, and follow in a logical fashion. Follow the standards for good questions. For archival data, describe original data collection procedures and any indices (for example, combinations of individual measures) in sufficient detail. For scales, you must describe briefly the scaling procedure you used and how you implemented it. Describe the procedures you used for collecting any qualitative measures in detail.

3. *Reliability and validity*—You should address both the reliability and validity of *all* of your measures. For reliability, you should specify what estimation procedure(s) you used. For validity, you should explain how you assessed construct validity. Wherever possible, you should minimally address both convergent and discrim-

inant validity. The procedures used to examine reliability and validity should be appropriate for the measures and the type of research you are conducting.

Design and Procedures Section

1. *Design*—Clearly present the design in both notational and text form. Ensure that the design is appropriate for the problem and addresses the hypothesis.

2. *Internal validity*—Discuss threats to internal validity and how they are addressed by the design. Also consider any threats to internal validity that are not well controlled.

3. *Description of procedures*—Include a brief description of how the study was conducted. Describe the sequence of events and ensure that it is appropriate to the design. Include sufficient information so that the essential features of the study could be replicated by a reader.

III. Results

1. *Statement of results*—State the results concisely and relate them to the questions or hypotheses they address.

2. *Tables*—Format tables correctly.

3. *Figures*—Design figure(s) so that they clearly describe key results.

IV. Conclusions, Abstract, and Reference Sections

1. *Implications of the study*—Discuss the implications of the results. Briefly mention any remaining problems or limitations of the study.

2. *Abstract*—The abstract is typically 125 words or less and presents a concise picture of the proposed research. Include major constructs and hypotheses. The abstract is typically the first section of the write-up immediately following the title page.

3. *References*—Include all citations in the correct format and ensure that they are appropriate for the study described.

V. Stylistic Elements

1. *Professional writing*—Avoid first-person and sex-stereotyped forms. Present material in an unbiased and unemotional (for example, no feelings about things), but not necessarily uninteresting, fashion.

2. *Parallel construction*—Keep tense parallel within and between sentences (as appropriate).

3. *Sentence structure*—Use correct sentence structure and punctuation. Avoid incomplete and run-on sentences.

4. *Spelling and word usage*—Make sure that spelling and word usage are appropriate. Correctly capitalize and abbreviate words.

5. *General style*—Ensure that the document is neatly produced and reads well and that the format for the document has been correctly followed.

13-2 FORMATTING

In this section, I discuss formatting a research article or a research report. This discussion follows the formatting requirements stated in the *Publication Manual of the American Psychological Association* (American Psychological Association, 2001), often referred to as APA formatting. Although APA formatting is widely followed in the social sciences, it is not universally required. However, virtually every publisher adheres to some set of format guidelines. Please consult the specific guidelines that are required by the publisher for the type of document you are producing.

In APA format, for example, all sections of a research paper are typed, double-spaced on white 8 1/2-by-11-inch paper with 12-pitch typeface with all margins set to 1 inch. Every page has a header in the upper-right corner with the running header right-justified on the top line and the page number right-justified and double-spaced on the line below it. The paper must have all the following sections in the order given, using the specifications outlined for each section (all page numbers are my estimates of fairly typical proportions in a research article of about 15 to 25 typed pages in length; of course, you should adjust these as appropriate for your context):

- Title page
- Abstract (on a separate single page)
- Body (no page breaks between sections in the body)
  - Introduction (2 to 3 pages)
  - Methods (7 to 10 pages)
    - Sample (1 page)
    - Measures (2 to 3 pages)
    - Design (2 to 3 pages)
    - Procedures (2 to 3 pages)
  - Results (2 to 3 pages)
  - Conclusions (1 to 2 pages)
- References
- Tables (one to a page)
- Figures (one to a page)
- Appendices

13-2a Title Page

On separate lines and centered, the title page has the title of the study, the author's name, and the institutional affiliation. At the bottom of the title page, you should have the words (in caps) RUNNING HEADER: followed by a short identifying title (2 to 4 words) for the study. This running header should also appear on the top-right of every page of the paper.

13-2b Abstract

The abstract is limited to one page, double-spaced. At the top of the page, centered, you should have the word "Abstract." The abstract itself should be written in paragraph form and should be a concise summary of the entire paper, including the problem, major hypotheses, sample and population, a brief description of the measures, the name of the design or a short description (no design notation here), the major results, and the major conclusions. Obviously, to fit this all on one page, you have to be extremely concise.

13-2c Body

The first page of the body of the paper should have, centered, the complete title of the study.

13-2d Introduction

The first section in the body is the introduction. In APA format, you do not include a heading that says "Introduction." You simply begin the paper in paragraph form following the title. Every introduction will have the following (roughly in this order): a statement of the problem being addressed, a brief review of relevant literature (including citations), a description of the major constructs involved, and a statement of the research questions or hypotheses. The entire section should be in paragraph form with the possible exception of the questions or hypotheses, which may be indented.

13-2e Methods

The "Methods" section should begin immediately after the introduction (no page break) and should have the centered title, "Methods." In APA format, this section typically has four subsections: "Sample," "Measures," "Design," and "Procedures." Each of the four subsections should have an underlined, left-justified section heading.

Sample   This section should describe the population of interest, the sampling frame, the method for selecting the sample, and the sample itself. A brief discussion of external validity is appropriate here; that is, you should state the degree to which you believe results will be generalizable from your sample to the population. Sampling is covered in Chapter 2, "Sampling."

Measures   This section should include a brief description of your constructs and all measures used to operationalize them. You may present short instruments in their entirety in this section. If you have more lengthy instruments, you may present some typical questions to give the reader a sense of what you did (and depending on the context and the requirements of the publisher, include the full measure in an appendix). Appendices are typically labeled by letter (for example "Appendix A") and cited appropriately in the body of the text. For preexisting instruments, you should cite any relevant information about reliability and validity if it is available. For all instruments, you should briefly state how you determined reliability and validity, report the results, and discuss them. For reliability, you should describe the methods you used and report results. A brief discussion of how you have addressed construct validity is essential. In general, you should try to demonstrate both convergent and discriminant validity. You must discuss the evidence in support of the validity of your measures. Measurement is covered in Chapter 3, "The Theory of Measurement."

Design   Where appropriate, you should state the name of the design used and tell whether it is a true or quasi-experiment, nonequivalent-groups design, and so on. For nonstandard or tailored designs, you might also present the design structure (for instance, you might use the X and O notation used in this book). You should also include a discussion of internal validity that describes the major plausible threats in your study and how the design accounts for them, if at all. (Be your own study critic here and provide enough information to show that you understand the threats to validity and whether you've been able to account for them all in the design or not.)

Procedures   Generally, this section ties together the sampling, measurement, and research design. In this section, you should briefly describe the overall sequence of steps or events from beginning to end (including sampling, measurement, and use of groups in designs), any procedures followed to assure participants are protected and informed, and how their confidentiality was protected (where relevant). An essential part of this subsection in a causal study is the description of the program or independent variable that you are studying.

13-2f Results

The heading for this section is centered with upper- and lowercase letters. You should indicate concisely what results you found in this research. Your results don't have to confirm your hypotheses. In fact, the common experience in social research is the finding of no effect.

13-2g Conclusions

Here, you should describe the conclusions you reach (given the results described in the "Results" section). You should relate these conclusions back to the level of the construct and the general problem area that you described in the introduction. You should also discuss the overall strength of the research (for example, a general discussion of the strong and weak validity areas) and should present some suggestions for possible future research that would be sensible based on the results of this work.

13-2h References

There are really two parts to a reference citation. First, there is the way you cite the item in the text when you are discussing it. Second, there is the way you list the complete reference in the "Reference" section in the back of the report.

Reference Citations in the Text of Your Paper   Cited references appear in the text of your paper and are a way of giving credit to the source of the information you quoted or used in your paper. The rules for citing references in texts differ, sometimes dramatically, from one format to another. In APA format, they generally consist of the following bits of information:

- The author's last name, unless first initials are needed to distinguish between two authors with the same last name. If there are six or more authors, the first author is listed followed by the term *et al.*, and then the year of the publication is given in parentheses.
- Year of publication is shown in parentheses.
- Page numbers are given with a quotation or when only a specific part of a source was used.

   Example: "To be or not to be" (Shakespeare, 1660, p. 241)

For example, here is how you would cite a one-author or multiple-author reference:

One Work by One Author
Rogers (1994) compared reaction times . . .

One Work by Multiple Authors
If there are two authors, use both of their names every time you cite them. If there are three to five authors, cite as follows:

Wasserstein, Zappulla, Rosen, Gerstman, and Rock (1994) [first time you cite in text]

Wasserstein et al. (1994) found [subsequent times you cite in text]

   If there are six or more authors, use the "et al." citation approach every time you cite the article.

Reference List in Reference Section   There are a wide variety of reference citation formats. Before submitting any research report, you should check to see which type of format is considered acceptable for that context. If there is no official format requirement, the most sensible thing is for you to select one approach and implement it consistently. (There's nothing worse than a reference list with a variety of formats.) Here, I'll illustrate by example some of the major reference items and how they might be cited in the reference section.

   The references list includes all the articles, books, and other sources used in the research and preparation of the paper and cited with a parenthetical (textual) citation in the text. References are often listed in alphabetical order according to the authors' last names; if a source does not have an author, alphabetize according to the first word of the title, disregarding the articles *a*, *an*, and *the* if they are the first word in the title.

Examples

Book by One Author
Jones, T. (1940). *My life on the road.* New York: Doubleday.

Book by Two Authors
Williams, A., & Wilson, J. (1962). *New ways with chicken.* New York: Harcourt.

Book by Three or More Authors
Smith, J., Jones, J., & Williams, S. (1976). *Common names.* Chicago: University of Chicago Press.

Book with No Given Author or Editor
Handbook of Korea (4th ed.). (1982). Seoul: Korean Overseas Information, Ministry of Culture & Information: Author.

Two or More Books by the Same Author
Oates, J. C. (1990). *Because it is bitter, and because it is my heart.* New York: Dutton.

Oates, J. C. (1993). *Foxfire: Confessions of a girl gang.* New York: Dutton.

Note: Entries by the same author are arranged chronologically by the year of publication, with the earliest first. References with the same first author and different second and subsequent authors are listed alphabetically by the surname of the second author, and then by the surname of the third author. References with the same authors in the same order are entered chronologically by year of publication, with the earliest first. References by the same author (or by the same two or more authors in identical order) with the same publication date are listed alphabetically by the first word of the title following the date; lowercase letters (*a, b, c,* and so on) are included after the year, within the parentheses.

Book by a Group or Organizational Author
President's Commission on Higher Education. (1977). *Higher education for American democracy.* Washington, DC: U.S. Government Printing Office.

Book with an Editor
Bloom, H. (Ed.). (1988). *James Joyce's Dubliners.* New York: Chelsea House.

A Translation
Dostoevsky, F. (1964). *Crime and punishment* (J. Coulson, Trans.). New York: Norton. (Original work published 1866).

An Article or Reading in a Collection of Pieces by Several Authors (Anthology)
O'Connor, M. F. (1975). *Everything that rises must converge.* In J. R. Knott, Jr., & C. R. Raeske (Eds.), *Mirrors: An introduction to literature* (2nd ed., pp. 58–67). San Francisco: Canfield.

Edition of a Book
Tortora, G. J., Funke, B. R., & Case, C. L. (1989). *Microbiology: An introduction* (3rd ed.). Redwood City, CA: Benjamin/Cummings.

A Work in Several Volumes
Churchill, W. S. (1957). *A history of the English speaking peoples: Vol. 3. The age of revolution.* New York: Dodd, Mead.

Encyclopedia or Dictionary
Cockrell, D. (1980). Beatles. In *The new Grove dictionary of music and musicians* (6th ed., Vol. 2, pp. 321–322). London: Macmillan.

Article from a Weekly Magazine
Jones, W. (1970, August 14). Today's kids. *Newsweek, 76,* 10–15.

Article from a Monthly Magazine
Howe, I. (1968, September). James Baldwin: At ease in apocalypse. *Harper's, 237,* 92–100.

Article from a Newspaper

Brody, J. E. (1976, October 10). Multiple cancers termed on increase. *New York Times* (*national ed.*), p. A37.

Article from a Scholarly Academic or Professional Journal

Barber, B. K. (1994). Cultural, family, and personal contexts of parent-adolescent conflict. *Journal of Marriage and the Family, 56,* 375–386.

Government Publication

U.S. Department of Labor. Bureau of Labor Statistics. (1980). *Productivity.* Washington, DC: U.S. Government Printing Office.

Pamphlet or Brochure

Research and Training Center on Independent Living. (1993). *Guidelines for reporting and writing about people with disabilities* (4th ed.) [Brochure]. Lawrence, KS: Author.

There are several major software programs available that help you organize all of your literature references and automatically format them in the most commonly required formats. These programs, which are essentially literature database management systems, typically integrate with your word processing software and can be used to correctly insert citations and produce reference lists. Many of them even allow you to conduct literature searches over the web and download literature citations and abstracts. If you will be doing serious research (anything from an honors thesis to a large funded research grant), I highly recommend that you consider using a major bibliographic software program.

There are also increasingly good online and web-based sources for conducting literature searches. Many of these services will allow you to download formatted references into your bibliographic software, download the abstracts, and download or view the full text of research articles online. You should check with the reference librarians at your institution or local library to determine what electronic sources are available.

13-2i Tables

Any tables should have a heading with "Table #" (where # is the table number), followed by the title for the heading that describes concisely what is contained in the table. Tables and figures are typed on separate sheets at the end of the paper after the references and before the appendices. In the text, you should put a reference where each table or figure should be inserted using this form:

Insert Table 1 about here

13-2j Figures

Figures should be drawn on separate sheets at the end of the paper after the references and tables, and before the appendices. In the text, you should put a reference where each figure will be inserted using this form:

Insert Figure 1 about here

13-2k Appendices

Appendices should be used only when absolutely necessary. Generally, you will only use them for presentation of extensive measurement instruments, for detailed descriptions of the program or independent variable, and for any relevant supporting documents that you don't include in the body. Many publications severely restrict the number of pages you are allowed and will not accept appendices. Even if you include such appendices, you should briefly describe the relevant material in the body and give an accurate citation to the appropriate appendix (for example, "see Appendix A").

SUMMARY

This chapter discussed the last step in a typical research project—the write-up. I outlined the key elements that typically must be included somewhere in a standard research write-up—the introduction, methods, results, and conclusions—and described what should be included in each of these sections. I described the major style issues you should watch out for when writing the typical report. And I presented one way to format a research paper appropriately, including how to cite other research in your report. Even though formatting rules can vary widely from one field to another, once you see how a set of rules guides report writing, it's a simple matter to change the formatting for a different audience or editorial policy.

So, with the write-up, the formal part of the research process is complete. You've taken the journey down the research road, from the initial plan for your trip, through all of the challenges along the way, and now with the write-up, on to your final destination. Now what? If you're a researcher, you don't stay in one place for very long. The thrill of the journey is just too much to resist. You begin pulling out the road maps (formulating research questions and hypotheses) and thinking about how you'd like to get to your next destination. There's a certain restlessness, a bit of research-based wanderlust that sets in. And there are all the lessons you've learned from your previous research journeys. Now, if on this next trip you can only avoid the potholes!

I hope that when you set out on your own research journey, you'll take this book along. Consider it a brief guidebook, a companion that might help point the way when you're feeling lost. And be sure to watch out for those bumps in the road.

SUGGESTED WEBSITES

Note: These websites were functional when we went to press. Please access the Online Study Guide Edition for the most up-to-date URLs.

Tips for Scientific Writing
http://www.srh.noaa.gov/ssd/html/writetip.htm
The National Weather Service sponsors this site, which provides information on documenting the results of a scientific study with a quality paper. Note that even though meteorologists might be wrong about the weather once in a while, they try to be right when they write!

How to Write a Grant Application
http://www.niaid.nih.gov/ncn/grants/write/index.htm
At this website, you can learn the important characteristics of writing to obtain a grant to conduct a study. The National Institutes of Health, which sponsors this site, has additional resources for writing, so exploration is encouraged.

REVIEW QUESTIONS

Note: You can find the correct answers to these questions by taking the quiz and then submitting your answers in the Online Study Guide Edition. The program will automatically score your submission. If you miss a question, the program will provide the correct answer, a rationale for the answer, and the section number in the chapter where the topic is discussed.

1. What publication would be most appropriate to consult for further guidelines on writing research papers?
   a. *Publication Manual of the American Psychological Association*
   b. *Diagnostic and Statistical Manual-IV-R (DSM-IV-R)*
   c. *The American Psychologist Guide to Good Writing*
   d. *Webster's Encyclopedia of Writing*

2. In what context are write-up guidelines provided in Chapter 13?
   a. writing a paper for publication in a psychology journal
   b. formatting a research write-up for a class term paper
   c. submitting an article for print in a major newspaper
   d. writing a Ph.D. thesis

3. In which section of the research report should a statement of your hypothesis (or hypotheses) first appear?
   a. introduction
   b. methods
   c. results
   d. conclusions

4. Professional writing is generally considered
   a. unbiased and uninteresting.
   b. unbiased and unemotional.
   c. unemotional and uninteresting.
   d. unemotional and unrelenting.

5. In the introduction section of a research paper, which of the following should be presented?
   a. sample description
   b. brief description of major constructs
   c. description of procedures
   d. construction of measures

6. Name, in order, the sections of a typical research paper.
   a. title page, abstract, introduction, methods, results, conclusions, references
   b. title page, abstract, introduction, conclusions, methods, results, references
   c. title page, abstract, introduction, design, discussion
   d. title page, introduction, results, conclusions, references, abstract

7. Which of the following is *not* a guideline for formatting references by authors of books?
   a. Entries by the same author are arranged chronologically by the year of publication, with the most recent first.
   b. References with the same first author and different second and subsequent authors are listed alphabetically by the surname of the second author, and then by the surname of the third.

   c. References with the same authors in the same order are entered chronologically by year of publication, with the earliest first.
   d. References by the same author (or by the same two or more authors in identical order) with the same publication date are listed alphabetically by the first word of the title following the date; lowercase letters (*a, b, c,* etc.) are included after the year, within the parentheses.

8. In which part of the paper do you write about any controlled and/or uncontrolled threats to internal validity?
   a. appendices
   b. results
   c. design
   d. abstract

9. In your research project, you used a measure of achievement orientation that is one and a half pages in length. Where in your paper would it be most appropriate for you to present it?
   a. measures
   b. appendices
   c. results
   d. introduction

10. If you have six or more authors for a reference, do you need to list them all when citing the reference in the text?
    a. Yes. List all six each time you cite the article.
    b. Yes. List all six the first time you cite the article, and in subsequent references, list only the first author, followed by *et al.*
    c. No. List only the first author.
    d. No. List only the first author, followed by *et al.*

11. Formatting of a paper is consistent across disciplines and is also basically the same for term papers, theses, dissertations, and published studies.
    a. True
    b. False

12. If you are using previously published measures, you do not have to discuss reliability or validity.
    a. True
    b. False

13. An abstract typically just gives a summary of the results of a study.
    a. True
    b. False

14. A paper that begins with this sentence "I wanted to study this issue because it make me very upset" is a good example of professional scientific writing.
    a. True
    b. False

15. Material obtained from online sources does not need a reference citation.
    a. True
    b. False

Glossary

A

0.05 level of significance See *alpha level*.

alpha level The significance level. Specifically, alpha is the Type I error, or the probability of concluding that there is a treatment effect when, in reality, there is not.

alternative hypothesis A specific statement of prediction that usually states what you expect will happen in your study.

analysis of covariance (ANCOVA) An analysis that estimates the difference between the groups on the posttest after adjusting for differences on the pretest.

analysis of variance (ANOVA) An analysis that estimates the difference between groups on a posttest. The ANOVA could estimate the difference between a treatment and control group (thus being equivalent to the *t*-test) or can examine both main and interaction effects in a factorial design.

anonymity The assurance that no one, including the researchers, will be able to link data to a specific individual.

area random sampling (see *cluster random sampling*)

attribute A specific value of a variable. For instance, the variable *sex* or *gender* has two attributes: male and female.

B

bell curve Smoothed histogram or bar graph describing the expected frequency for each value of a variable. The name comes from the fact that such a distribution often has the shape of a bell.

C

case study An intensive study of a specific individual or specific context.

causal Pertaining to a cause-effect relationship.

causal relationship A cause-effect relationship. For example, when you evaluate whether your treatment or program causes an outcome to occur, you are examining a causal relationship.

cause construct Your abstract idea or theory of what the cause is in a cause-effect relationship you are investigating.

central tendency An estimate of the center of a distribution of values. The most usual measures of central tendency are the mean, median, and mode.

cluster random sampling A sampling method that involves dividing the population into groups called *clusters*, randomly selecting clusters, and then sampling each element in the selected clusters. This method is useful when sampling a population that is spread across a wide geographic area.

codebook A written description of the data that describes each variable and indicates where and how it can be accessed.

coding The process of categorizing qualitative data.

compensatory equalization of treatment A social threat to internal validity that occurs when the control group is given a program or treatment (usually by a well-meaning third party) designed to make up for or "compensate" for the treatment the program group gets.

compensatory rivalry A social threat to internal validity that occurs when one group knows the program another group is getting and, because of that, develops a competitive attitude with the other group.

conclusion validity The degree to which conclusions you reach about relationships in your data are reasonable.

concurrent validity An operationalization's ability to distinguish between groups that it should theoretically be able to distinguish between.

confidentiality An assurance made to study participants that identifying information about them acquired through the study will not be released to anyone outside of the study.

construct validity The degree to which inferences can legitimately be made from the operationalizations in your study to the theoretical constructs on which those operationalizations are based.

content analysis The analysis of text documents. The analysis can be quantitative, qualitative, or both. Typically, the major purpose of content analysis is to identify patterns in text.

content validity A check of the operationalization against the relevant content domain for the construct.

control group A group, comparable to the program group, that did not receive the program.

convergent validity The degree to which the operationalization is similar to (converges on) other operationalizations to which it should be theoretically similar.

correlation A single number that describes the degree of relationship between two variables.

correlation matrix A table of correlations showing all possible relationships among a set of variables. The diagonal of a correlation matrix (the numbers that go from the upper-left corner to the lower right) always consists of 1s because these are the correlations between each variable and itself (and a variable is always perfectly correlated with itself). Off-diagonal elements are the correlations of variables represented by the relevant row and column in the matrix.

covariates Variables you adjust for in your study.

covariation of the cause and effect A criterion for establishing a causal relationship that holds that the cause and effect must be related or co-vary.

criterion-related validity The validation of a measure based on its relationship to another independent measure as predicted by your theory of how the measures should behave.

Cronbach's alpha   One specific method of estimating the reliability of a measure. Although not calculated in this manner, Cronbach's alpha can be thought of as analogous to the average of all possible split-half correlations.

cross-sectional   A study that takes place at a single point in time.

D

data audit   A systematic assessment of data and data collection procedures conducted to establish and document the credibility of data collection processes and potential inaccuracies in the data.

deductive   Top-down reasoning that works from the more general to the more specific.

degrees of freedom (df)   A statistical term that is a function of the sample size. In the *t*-test formula, for instance, the df is the number of persons in both groups minus 2.

dependent variable   The variable affected by the independent variable; for example, the outcome.

descriptive statistics   Statistics used to describe the basic features of the data in a study.

dichotomous response format   A question with two possible responses.

dichotomous response scale   A question with two possible responses. The better term to use is dichotomous response *format*.

diffusion or imitation of treatment   A social threat to internal validity that occurs because a comparison group learns about the program either directly or indirectly from program group participants.

direct observation   The process of observing a phenomenon to gather information about it. This process is distinguished from participant observation in that a direct observer does not typically try to become a participant in the context and does strive to be as unobtrusive as possible so as not to bias the observations.

discriminant validity   The degree to which concepts that should not be related theoretically are, in fact, not interrelated in reality.

dispersion   The spread of the values around the central tendency. The two common measures of dispersion are the range and the standard deviation.

distribution   The manner in which a variable takes different values in your data.

double entry   An automated method for checking data-entry accuracy in which you enter data once and then enter it a second time, with the software automatically stopping each time a discrepancy is detected until the data enterer resolves the discrepancy. This procedure assures extremely high rates of data entry accuracy, although it requires twice as long for data entry.

double-pretest design   A design that includes two waves of measurement prior to the program.

dual-media survey   A survey that is distributed simultaneously in two ways. For instance, if you distribute a survey to participants as an attachment they can print, complete, and fax back or can complete directly on the web as a web form, you can describe this as a dual-media survey.

dummy variable   A variable that uses discrete numbers, usually 0 and 1, to represent different groups in your study. Dummy variables are often used in the equations.

E

ecological fallacy   Faulty reasoning that results from making conclusions about individuals based only on analyses of group data.

effect construct   Your abstract idea or theory of what the outcome is in a cause-effect relationship you are investigating.

electronic survey   Any survey that is administered to participants through an electronic medium, such as email or the web. An electronic survey is distinguishable from other forms of surveying in that the survey is never printed or completed by hand. Note that if you send a survey to participants via an email attachment but ask them to print it and fax back the results, this would not technically be an electronic survey.

email survey   Any survey that is distributed to respondents via email. Generally, the survey is either embedded in the email message and the respondent can reply to complete it, is transmitted as an email attachment that the respondent can complete and return via email, or is reached by providing a link in the email that directs the respondent to a website survey.

empirical   Based on direct observations and measurements of reality.

error term   A term in a regression equation that captures the degree to which the line is in error (that is, the residual) in describing each point.

ethnography   Study of a culture using qualitative field research.

exception dictionary   A dictionary that includes all nonessential words like *is*, *and*, and *of*, in a content analysis study.

exception fallacy   A faulty conclusion reached as a result of basing a conclusion on exceptional or unique cases.

exhaustive   The property of a variable that occurs when you include all possible answerable responses.

expert sampling   A sample of people with known or demonstrable experience and expertise in some area.

external validity   The degree to which the conclusions in your study would hold for other persons in other places and at other times.

F

face validity   A type of validity that assures that "on its face" the operationalization seems like a good translation of the construct.

factor   A major independent variable in an experimental design.

factorial designs   Designs that focus on the program or treatment, its components, and its major dimensions and enable you to determine whether the program has an effect, whether different subcomponents are effective, and whether there are interactions in the effects caused by subcomponents.

field research   A research method in which the researcher goes into the field to observe the phenomenon in its natural state.

filter or contingency question   A question you ask the respondents to determine whether they are qualified or experienced enough to answer a subsequent one.

fishing and the error rate problem   A problem that occurs as a result of conducting multiple analyses and treating each one as independent.

focus group   A qualitative measurement method where input on one or more focus topics is collected from participants in a small-group setting where the discussion is structured and guided by a facilitator.

frequency distribution   A summary of the frequency of individual values or ranges of values for a variable.

fully crossed factorial design   A design that includes the pairing of every combination of factor levels.

G

general linear model (GLM)   A system of equations that is used as the mathematical framework for most of the statistical analyses used in applied social research.

gradient of similarity   The dimension along which your study context can be related to other potential contexts to which you might wish to generalize. Contexts that are closer to yours along the gradient of similarity of place, time, people, and so on can be generalized to with more confidence than ones that are further away.

grounded theory   An iterative qualitative approach that includes initial generative questions, gathering qualitative data, identifying theoretical concepts, verifying emerging concepts in data, reconsidering theoretical concepts, and so on, until a detailed theory that is grounded in observation is achieved.

group-administered questionnaire   A survey that is administered to respondents in a group setting. For instance, if a survey is administered to all students in a classroom, we would describe that as a group-administered questionnaire.

group interview   An interview that is administered to respondents in a group setting. For instance, if a survey is administered to all students in a classroom, we would describe that as a group-administered questionnaire. A focus group is a structured form of group interview.

Guttman scaling   The process of developing a scale in which the items are assigned scale values that allow them to be placed in a cumulative ordering with respect to the construct being scaled.

H

heterogeneity sampling   Sampling for diversity or variety.

hierarchical modeling   The incorporation of multiple units of analysis at different levels of a hierarchy within a single analytic model. For instance, in an educational study, you might want to compare student performance with teacher expectations. To examine this relationship would require averaging student performance for each class because each teacher has multiple students and you are collecting data at both the teacher and student level.

history threat   A threat to internal validity that occurs when some historical event affects the study outcome.

household drop-off survey   A paper-and-pencil survey that is administered by dropping it off at the respondent's household and either picking it up at a later time or having the respondent return it directly. The household drop-off method assures a direct personal contact with the respondent, while also allowing the respondent the time and privacy to respond to the survey on his or her own.

hypothesis   A specific statement of prediction.

hypothetico-deductive model   A model in which two mutually exclusive hypotheses that together exhaust all possible outcomes are tested, such that if one hypothesis is accepted, the second must therefore be rejected.

I

incomplete factorial design   A design in which some cells or combinations in a fully crossed factorial design are intentionally left empty.

independent variable   The variable that you manipulate. For instance, a program or treatment is typically an independent variable.

index   A quantitative score that measures a construct of interest by applying a formula or a set of rules that combines relevant data.

indirect measure   An unobtrusive measure that occurs naturally in a research context.

inductive   Bottom-up reasoning that begins with specific observations and measures and ends up as general conclusion or theory.

inferential statistics   Statistical analyses used to reach conclusions that extend beyond the immediate data alone.

informed consent   A policy of informing study participants about the procedures and risks involved in research that ensures that all participants must give their consent to participate.

institutional review board (IRB)   A panel of people who review research proposals with respect to ethical implications and decide whether additional actions need to be taken to assure the safety and rights of participants.

instrumentation threat   A threat to internal validity that arises when the instruments (or observers) used on the posttest and the pretest differ.

interaction effect   An effect that occurs when differences on one factor depend on which level you are on another factor.

internal validity   The approximate truth of inferences regarding cause-effect or causal relationships.

interval response scale A response measured on an interval level, where the size of the interval between potential response values is meaningful. Most 1-to-5 rating responses can be considered interval level. The better term to use is interval response *format*.

interval-level response format A response measured on an interval level, where the size of the interval between potential response values is meaningful. Most 1-to-5 rating responses can be considered interval level.

L

level In an experimental design, a subdivision of a factor into components or features.

Likert response format An interval-level response format that uses a 5-point integer scale. For instance, a 1-to-5 rating would be considered a Likert response format.

Likert scaling The process of developing a scale in which the ratings of the items are summed to get the final scale score. Ratings are usually done using a 1-to-5 Disagree-to-Agree response format. Likert scales are also sometimes called summated scales.

linear model Any statistical model that uses equations to estimate lines.

longitudinal A study that takes place over time.

M

mail survey A paper-and-pencil survey that is sent to respondents through the mail.

main effect An outcome that shows consistent differences between all levels of a factor.

maturation threat A threat to validity that is a result of natural maturation that occurs between pre- and postmeasurement.

mean A description of the central tendency in which you add all the values and divide by the number of values.

measurement error Any influence on an observed score not related to what you are attempting to measure.

median The middle number in a series of numbers or the score found at the exact middle or fiftieth percentile of the set of values. One way to compute the median is to list all scores in numerical order and then locate the score in the center of the sample.

mixed methods research Any research that uses multiple research methods to take advantage of the unique advantages that each method offers. For instance, a study that combines case study interviews with an experimental design can be considered mixed methods.

modal instance sampling Sampling for the most typical case.

mode The most frequently occurring value in the set of scores.

model specification The process of stating the equation that you believe best summarizes the data for a study.

mono-method bias A threat to construct validity that occurs because you use only a single method of measurement.

mono-operation bias A threat to construct validity that occurs when you rely on only a single implementation of your independent variable, cause, program, or treatment in your study.

mortality threat A threat to validity that occurs because a significant number of participants drop out.

multioption variable A question format in which the respondent can pick multiple variables from a list.

multiple-group threat An internal validity threat that occurs in studies that use multiple groups—for instance, a program and a comparison group.

multistage sampling The combining of several sampling techniques to create a more efficient or effective sample than the use of any one sampling type can achieve on its own.

mutually exclusive The property of a variable that ensures that the respondent is not able to assign two attributes simultaneously. For example, gender is a variable with mutually exclusive options if it is impossible for the respondents to simultaneously claim to be both male and female.

N

negative relationship A relationship between variables in which high values for one variable are associated with low values on another variable.

nominal response format A response format that has a number beside each choice where the number has no meaning except as a placeholder for that response.

nonequivalent dependent variables (NEDV) design A single-group pre-post quasi-experimental design with two outcome measures, where only one measure is theoretically predicted to be affected by the treatment and the other is not.

nonequivalent-groups design (NEGD) A pre-post two-group quasi-experimental design structured like a pretest-posttest randomized experiment, but lacking random assignment to group.

nonprobability sampling Sampling that does not involve random selection.

nonproportional quota sampling A sampling method in which you sample until you achieve a specific number of sampled units for each subgroup of a population, where the proportions in each group are not the same.

null case A situation in which the treatment has no effect.

null hypothesis The hypothesis that describes the possible outcomes other than the alternative hypothesis. Usually, the null hypothesis predicts there will be no effect of a program or treatment you are studying.

O

one-tailed hypothesis A hypothesis that specifies a direction; for example, when your hypothesis predicts that your program will increase the outcome.

operationalization The act of translating a construct into its manifestation—for example, translating the idea of your treatment or program into the actual program, or translating the idea of what you want to measure into the real measure. The result is also referred to as an *operationalization;* that is, you might describe your actual program as an *operationalized program.*

ordinal response format A response format in which respondents are asked to rank the possible answers in order of preference.

P

participant observation A method of qualitative observation in which the researcher becomes a participant in the culture or context being observed.

pattern-matching The degree of correspondence between two data items. For instance, you might look at a pattern match of a theoretical expectation pattern with an observed pattern to see if you are getting the outcomes you expect.

pattern-matching NEDV design A single-group pre-post quasi-experimental design with multiple outcome measures where there is a theoretically specified pattern of expected effects across the measures. To assess the treatment effect, the theoretical pattern of expected outcomes is correlated or matched with the observed pattern of outcomes as measured.

Pearson product moment correlation A particular type of correlation used when both variables can be assumed to be measured at an interval level of measurement.

personal interview A one-on-one interview between an interviewer and respondent. The interviewer typically uses an interview guide that provides a script for asking questions and follow-up prompts.

phenomenology A philosophical perspective as well as an approach to qualitative methodology that focuses on people's subjective experiences and interpretations of the world.

plausible alternative explanation Any other cause that can bring about an effect that is different from your hypothesized or manipulated cause.

population The group you want to generalize to and the group you sample from in a study.

population parameter The mean or average you would obtain if you were able to sample the entire population.

positive relationship A relationship between variables in which high values for one variable are associated with high values on another variable, and low values are associated with low values.

posttest-only nonexperimental design A research design in which only a posttest is given. It is referred to as *nonexperimental* because no control group exists.

posttest-only randomized experiment An experiment in which the groups are randomly assigned and receive only a posttest.

predictive validity A type of construct validity based on the idea that your measure is able to predict what it theoretically should be able to predict.

pre-post nonequivalent groups quasi-experiment A research design in which groups receive both a pre- and posttest, and group assignment is not randomized, and therefore, the groups may be nonequivalent, making it a quasi-experiment.

probabilistic Based on probabilities.

probabilistic equivalence The notion that two groups, if measured infinitely, would on average perform identically. Note that two groups that are probabilistically equivalent would seldom obtain the exact same average score in a real setting.

probability sampling Method of sampling that utilizes some form of *random selection.*

proportional quota sampling A sampling method in which you sample until you achieve a specific number of sampled units for each subgroup of a population, where the proportions in each group are the same.

proximal similarity model A model for generalizing from your study to another context based upon the degree to which the other context is similar to your study context.

proxy-pretest design A post-only design in which, after the fact, a pretest measure is constructed from preexisting data. This is usually done to make up for the fact that the research did not include a true pretest.

Q

qualitative The descriptive nonnumerical characteristic of some object. A qualitative variable is a descriptive nonnumerical observation.

qualitative data Data in which the variables are not in a numerical form, but are in the form of text, photographs, sound bytes, and so on.

qualitative measures Data not recorded in numerical form.

quantitative The numerical representation of some object. A quantitative variable is any variable that is measured using numbers.

quantitative data Data that appears in numerical form.

quasi-experimental designs Research designs that have several of the key features of randomized experimental designs, such as pre-post measurement and treatment-control group comparisons, but lack random assignment to a treatment group.

quota sampling Any sampling method in which you sample until you achieve a specific number of sampled units for each subgroup of a population.

R

random assignment Process of assigning your sample into two or more subgroups by chance. Procedures for random assignment can vary from flipping a coin to using a table of random numbers to using the random number capability built into a computer.

random selection Process or procedure that assures that the different units in your population are selected by chance.

randomized block design Experimental designs in which the sample is grouped into relatively homogeneous subgroups or blocks within which your experiment is replicated. This procedure reduces noise or variance in the data.

range The highest value minus the lowest value.

regression analysis A general statistical analysis that enables us to model relationships in data and test for treatment effects. In regression analysis, we model relationships that can be depicted in graphic form with lines that are called *regression lines*.

regression artifact See *regression threat*.

regression line A line that describes the relationship between two or more variables.

regression point displacement (RPD) design A pre-post quasi-experimental research design where the treatment is given to only one unit in the sample, with all remaining units acting as controls. This design is particularly useful to study the effects of community-level interventions, where outcome data is routinely collected at the community level.

regression threat A statistical phenomenon that causes a group's average performance on one measure to regress toward or appear closer to the mean of that measure than anticipated or predicted. Regression occurs whenever you have a nonrandom sample from a population and two measures that are imperfectly correlated. A regression threat will bias your estimate of the group's posttest performance and can lead to incorrect causal inferences.

regression to the mean See *regression threat*.

regression-discontinuity (RD) design A pretest-posttest program-comparison group quasi-experimental design in which a cut-off criterion on the preprogram measure is the method of assignment to group.

relationship Refers to the correspondence between two variables.

reliability The degree to which a measure is consistent or dependable; the degree to which it would give you the same result over and over again, assuming the underlying phenomenon is not changing.

repeated measures Two or more waves of measurement over time.

requests for proposals (RFPs) RFPs, published by government agencies and some companies, describe some problem that the agency would like researchers to address. Typically, the RFP describes the problem that needs addressing, the contexts in which it operates, the approach the agency would like you to take to investigate the problem, and the amount the agency would be willing to pay for such research.

research question The central issue being addressed in the study, which is typically phrased in the language of theory.

resentful demoralization A social threat to internal validity that occurs when the comparison group knows what the program group is getting and becomes discouraged or angry and gives up.

response A specific measurement value that a sampling unit supplies.

response brackets A question response type that includes groups of answers, such as between 30 and 40 years old, or between $50,000 and $100,000 annual income.

response format The format you use to collect the answer from the respondent.

response scale A sequential numerical response format, such as a 1-to-5 rating format.

right to service The ethical issue involved when participants do not receive a service that they would be eligible for if they were not in your study. For example, members of a control group might not receive a drug because they are in a study.

S

sample The actual units you select to participate in your study.

sampling The process of drawing a subset of objects from a population so that results with the subset may be generalized to the population.

sampling distribution The theoretical distribution of an infinite number of samples of the population of interest in your study.

sampling error The error in measurement associated with sampling.

sampling frame The list from which you draw your sample. In some cases, there is no list; you draw your sample based upon an explicit rule. For instance, when doing quota sampling of passersby at the local mall, you do not have a list per se, and the sampling frame consists of both the population of people who pass by within the time frame of your study and the rule(s) you use to decide whom to select.

sampling model A model for generalizing in which you identify your population, draw a fair sample, conduct your research, and finally, generalize your results to other population groups.

scaling The branch of measurement that involves the construction of an instrument that associates qualitative constructs with quantitative metric units.

secondary analysis Analysis that makes use of already existing data sources.

selection bias Any factor other than the program that leads to posttest differences between groups.

selection threat See *selection bias*.

selection-history threat A threat to internal validity that results from any other event that occurs between pretest and posttest that the groups experience differently.

selection-instrumentation threat A threat to internal validity that results from differential changes in the test used for each group from pretest to posttest.

selection-maturation threat A threat to internal validity that arises from any differential rates of normal growth between pretest and posttest for the groups.

selection-mortality threat A threat to internal validity that arises when there is differential nonrandom dropout between groups during the test.

selection-regression threat A threat to internal validity that occurs when there are different rates of regression to the mean in the two groups.

selection-testing threat A threat to internal validity that occurs when a differential effect of taking the pretest exists between groups on the posttest.

semantic differential A scaling method in which the respondent assesses an object on a set of bipolar adjective pairs.

separate pre-post samples A design in which the people who receive the pretest are not the same as the people who take the posttest.

simple random sampling A method of sampling that involves drawing a sample from a population so that every possible sample has an equal probability of being selected.

single-group threat A threat to internal validity that occurs in a study that uses only a single program or treatment group and no comparison or control.

single-option variable A question response list from which the respondent can check only one response.

slope The change in y for a change in x of one unit.

snowball sampling A sampling method in which you sample participants based upon referral from prior participants.

social interaction threats Threats to internal validity that arise because social research is conducted in real-world human contexts where people react to not only what affects them, but also to what is happening to others around them.

standard deviation The spread or variability of the scores around their average in a *single sample*. The standard deviation, often abbreviated SD, is mathematically the square root of the variance. The standard deviation and variance both measure dispersion, but because the standard deviation is measured in the same units as the original measure and the variance is measured in squared units, the standard deviation is usually more directly interpretable and meaningful.

standard error The spread of the averages around the average of averages in a sampling distribution.

standard error of the difference A statistical estimate of the standard deviation one would obtain from the distribution of an infinite number of estimates of the difference between the means of two groups.

statistic A specific value that is estimated from data.

statistical power The probability of correctly concluding that there is a treatment or program effect in your data.

statistics A branch of mathematics dealing with the collection, analysis, interpretation, and presentation of quantitative data.

stratified random sampling A method of sampling that involves dividing your population into homogeneous subgroups and then taking a simple random sample in each subgroup.

structured response formats A response format that is determined prior to administration.

switching replications design A two-group design in two phases defined by three waves of measurement. The implementation of the treatment is repeated in both phases. In the repetition of the treatment, the two groups *switch* roles: The original control group in phase 1 becomes the treatment group in phase 2, whereas the original treatment acts as the control. By the end of the study, all participants have received the treatment.

symmetric matrix A square (as many rows as columns) table of numbers that describes the relationships among a set of variables, where each variable represents a row or column. Each value in the table represents the relationship between the row and column variable for that cell of the table. The table is "symmetric" when the relationship between a specific row and column variable is identical to the relationship between the same column and row. A correlation matrix is a symmetric matrix.

systematic random sampling A sampling method in which you determine randomly where you want to start selecting in the sampling frame and then follow a rule to select every xth element in the sampling frame list (where the ordering of the list is assumed to be random).

T

t-test A statistical test of the difference between the means of two groups, often a program and comparison group. The t-test is the simplest variation of the one-way analysis of variance (ANOVA).

t-value The estimate of the difference between the groups relative to the variability of the scores in the groups.

telephone interview A personal interview that is conducted over the telephone.

temporal precedence One criterion for establishing a causal relationship that holds that the cause must occur before the effect.

testing threat A threat to internal validity that occurs when taking the pretest affects how participants do on the posttest.

theoretical Pertaining to theory. Social research is theoretical, meaning that much of it is concerned with developing, exploring, or testing the theories or ideas that social researchers have about how the world operates.

third-variable problem An unobserved variable that accounts for a correlation between two variables.

threat to conclusion validity Any factor that can lead you to reach an incorrect conclusion about a relationship in your observations.

threat to construct validity Any factor that causes you to make an incorrect conclusion about whether your operationalized variables (for example, your program or outcome) reflect well the construct they are intended to represent.

threat to external validity Any factor that can lead you to make an incorrect generalization from the results of your study to other persons, places, times, or settings.

threat to internal validity Any factor that can lead you to reach an incorrect conclusion about whether there is a causal relationship in your study.

threats to validity Reasons your conclusion or inference might be wrong.

Thurstone scaling The process of developing a scale in which the scale items have interval-level numerical values where the final score is the average scale value of all items with which the respondent agreed.

time series Many waves of measurement over time.

translation validity A type of construct validity related to how well you translated the idea of your measure into its operationalization.

true score theory A theory that maintains that every measurement is an additive composite of two components: the true ability of the respondent and random error.

two-group posttest-only randomized experiment A research design in which two randomly assigned groups participate. Only one group receives the program, and both groups receive a posttest.

two-tailed hypothesis A hypothesis that does not specify a direction. For example, if your hypothesis is that your program or intervention will have an effect on an outcome, but you are unwilling to specify whether that effect will be positive or negative, you are using a two-tailed hypothesis.

U

unit of analysis The entity that you are analyzing in your analysis; for example, individuals, groups, or social interactions.

unitizing In content analysis, the process of breaking continuous text into separate units that can subsequently be coded.

unobtrusive measures Methods used to collect data without interfering in the lives of the respondents.

unstructured interviewing An interviewing method that uses no predetermined interview protocol or survey and in which the interview questions emerge and evolve as the interview proceeds.

unstructured response formats A response format that is not predetermined and where the response is determined by the respondent. An open-ended question is a type of unstructured response format.

V

validity The best available approximation of the truth of a given proposition, inference, or conclusion.

variability The extent to which the values measured or observed for a variable differ.

variable Any entity that can take on different values. For instance, age can be considered a variable because age can take on different values for different people at different times.

variance A statistic that describes the variability in the data for a variable. The variance is the spread of the scores around the mean of a distribution. Specifically, the variance is the sum of the squared deviations from the mean divided by the number of observations minus 1.

voluntary participation For ethical reasons, researchers must ensure that study participants are taking part in a study voluntarily and are not coerced.

W

web survey A survey that is administered over a website (either intranet or Internet). Respondents use their web browser to reach the website and complete the survey.

weighted index A quantitative score that measures a construct of interest by applying a formula or a set of rules that combines relevant data where the data components are weighted differently.

References

A

Adams, J. L. (1980). *Conceptual blockbusting: A guide to better ideas* (2nd ed.). New York: Norton.

American Psychological Association. (2001). *Publication manual of the American Psychological Association* (5th ed.). Washington, DC: American Psychological Association.

Annas, G. J., & Grodin, M. A. (Eds.). (1995). *The Nazi doctors and the Nuremberg code: Human rights in human experimentation.* Tucson, AZ: Galen Press.

B

Beveridge, W. I. B. (1950). *The art of scientific investigation.* New York: Vintage Books.

Box, G. E. P., & Jenkins, G. M. (1976). *Time series analysis: Forecasting and control.* San Francisco, CA: Holden-Day.

Bridgman, P. W. (1927). *The logic of modern physics.* New York: Macmillan.

Brown, S. R., & Melamed, L. E. (1990). *Experimental design and analysis* (Vol. 74). Beverly Hills, CA: Sage.

C

Campbell, D. T. (1986). Relabeling internal and external validity for applied social scientists. In W. Trochim (Ed.), *Advances in quasi-experimental design and analysis* (Vol. 31, pp. 67–77). San Francisco: Jossey-Bass.

Campbell, D. T. (1988). The experimenting society. In E. S. Overman (Ed.), *Methodology and epistemology for social science: Selected papers* (pp. 290–314). Chicago: University of Chicago Press.

Campbell, D. T., & Fiske, D. W. (1959). Convergent and discriminant validation by the multitrait-multimethod matrix. *Psychological Bulletin, 56,* 81–105.

Campbell, D. T., & Kenny, D. A. (1999). *A primer on regression artifacts.* New York: Guilford Press.

Cohen, J. (1988). *Statistical power analysis for the behavioral sciences* (2nd ed.). Mahwah, NJ: Lawrence Erlbaum Associates.

Cook, T. D., & Campbell, D. T. (1979). *Quasi-experimentation: Design and analysis for field settings.* Boston: Houghton Mifflin.

Cronbach, L. J., & Meehl, P. E. (1955). Construct validity in psychological tests. *Psychological Bulletin, 52,* 281–302.

D

Dillman, D. A. (1999). *Mail and Internet surveys.* New York: Wiley.

Duncan, O. D. (1981). A socioeconomic index for all occupations. In A. J. Reiss, Jr. (Ed.), *Occupations and social status* (pp. 139–161). New York: Free Press.

F

Fisher, R. A. (1925). *Statistical methods for research workers.* Edinburgh: Oliver & Boyd.

Fowler, F. (2001). *Survey research methods* (Vol. 1). Beverly Hills, CA: Sage.

G

Glaser, B., & Strauss, A. (1967). *The discovery of grounded theory: Strategies for qualitative research.* Chicago, IL: Aldine De Gruyther.

Guba, E. G., & Lincoln, Y. S. (1981). *Effective evaluation: Improving the usefulness of evaluation results through responsive and naturalistic approaches.* San Francisco: Jossey-Bass.

Guttman, L. (1950). The basis for scalogram analysis. In S. A. Stouffer (Ed.), *Measurement and prediction* (Vol. IV of *Studies in Social Psychology in World War II*). Princeton, NJ: Princeton University Press.

H

Hauser, R. M., & Warren, J. R. (1996). *Socioeconomic indexes for occupations: A review, update, and critique.* Madison, WI: Center for Demography and Ecology.

Heckathorn, D. (1997). Respondent-driven sampling: A new approach to the study of hidden populations. *Social Problems, 44* (2), 174–199.

Hempel, C. G. (1966). *Philosophy of natural science.* Englewood Cliffs, NJ: Prentice Hall.

Henry, G. (1990). *Practical sampling.* Beverly Hills, CA: Sage.

I

Iversen, G. R., & Norpoth, H. (1976). *Analysis of variance* (Vol. 1). Beverly Hills, CA: Sage.

J

Jones, J. H. (1993). *Bad blood: The Tuskegee syphilis experiment.* New York: Free Press.

K

Kalton, G. (1983). *Introduction to survey sampling* (Vol. 07-001). Beverly Hills, CA: Sage.

Keppel, G. (1991). *Design and analysis: A researcher's handbook.* Englewood Cliffs, NJ: Prentice Hall.

Kish, L. (1995). *Survey sampling.* New York: Wiley Interscience.

Krippendorff, K. (2004). *Content analysis: An introduction to its methodology* (2d ed.). Thousand Oaks, CA: Sage.

L

Leong, F. T. L., & Pfaltzgraff, R. E. (1996). Finding a research topic. In F. T. Leong & J. T. Austin (Eds.), *The psychology research handbook*. Thousand Oaks, CA: Sage.

Lord, F. M., & Novick, M. R. (1968). *Statistical theories of mental test scores*. Reading, MA: Addison-Wesley.

M

Marriott, F. H. (1990). *A dictionary of statistical terms*. New York: Longman Scientific and Technical.

McCracken, G. (1988). *The long interview* (Vol. 13). Beverly Hills, CA: Sage.

Miles, M. B., & Huberman, M. (1994). *Qualitative data analysis*. Thousand Oaks, CA: Sage.

Miller, M. B. (1995). Coefficient alpha: A basic introduction from the perspectives of classical test theory and structural equation modeling. *Structural Equation Modeling, 2*, 255–273.

Murphy, G., & Likert, R. (1938). *Public opinion and the individual: A psychological study of student attitudes on public questions with a re-test five years later*. New York: Harper.

N

Nagel, E. (1979). *The structure of science: Problems in the logic of scientific explanation* (2nd ed.). Indianapolis, IN: Hackett Publishing.

P

Popper, K. R. (1959). *The logic of scientific discovery*. New York: Basic Books.

R

Resnik, D. (1998). *The ethics of science: An introduction (philosophical issues in science)*. New York: Routledge.

Robinson, W. S. (1950). Ecological correlations and the behavior of individuals. *American Sociological Review, 15*, 351–357.

Rosenberg, M. (1965). *Society and the adolescent self image*. Princeton, NJ: Princeton University Press.

Rosenthal, R. (1966). *Experimenter effects in behavioral research*. New York: Appleton-Century-Crofts.

S

Sales, B. D., & Folkman, S. (Eds.). (2000). *Ethics in research with human participants*. Washington, DC: American Psychological Association.

Shadish, W. R., Cook, T. D., & Campbell, D. T. (2002). *Experimental and quasi-experimental designs for generalized causal research*. Boston: Houghton Mifflin.

Spector, P. E. (1981). *Research designs* (Vol. 23). Beverly Hills, CA: Sage.

Stevens, G., & Cho, J. H. (1985). Socioeconomic indices and the new 1980 census occupational classification scheme. *Social Science Research, 14*, 142–168.

Stevens, S. S. (1946). On the theory of scales of measurement. *Science, 103*, 677–680.

Sudman, S. (1976). *Applied sampling*. New York: Academic Press.

T

Thurstone, L. L. (1925). A method of scaling psychological and educational tests. *Journal of Educational Psychology, 16*, 433–451.

Trochim, W. (1984). Research design for program evaluation: The regression-discontinuity approach. Newbury Park, CA: Sage. Available at: http://www.socialresearchmethods.net/research/rd.htm.

Trochim, W., and Land, D. (1982). Designing designs for research. *The Researcher, 1*, 1, 1–6.

U

U.S. Department of Labor. (2004). Consumer Price Index, 2004, from www.bls.gov/cpi/home.htm.

W

Webb, E. J., Campbell, D. T., Schwartz, R. D., Sechrest, L., & Grove, J. B. (1981). *Nonreactive measures in the social sciences* (2nd ed.). Boston: Houghton Mifflin.

Williams, B. (1978). *A sampler on sampling*. New York: Wiley.